P9-CRI-137

INSTANT ENTERPRISE JAVABEANS

Instant Enterprise JavaBeans

Paul Tremblett

CARROLL COLLEGE LIBRARY
WAUKESHA, WI 53186

QA
76
.73
.J38
T74
2001

McGraw-Hill

New York   Chicago   San Francisco
Lisbon   London   Madrid   Mexico City
Milan   New Delhi   San Juan   Seoul
Singapore   Sydney   Toronto

McGraw-Hill

A Division of The McGraw·Hill Companies

Copyright © 2001 by The McGraw-Hill Companies, Inc. All rights reserved. Printed in the United States of America. Except as permitted under the United States Copyright Act of 1976, no part of this publication may be reproduced or distributed in any form or by any means, or stored in a data base or retrieval system, without the prior written permission of the publisher.

1 2 3 4 5 6 7 8 9 0   AGM/AGM   0 5 4 3 2 1

P/N 0-07-212942-5
PART OF ISBN 0-07-212943-3

The sponsoring editor for this book was Rebekah Young, the editing supervisor was Penny Linskey, and the production supervisor was Clare Stanley. It was set in Century Schoolbook by North Market Street Graphics.

Printed and bound by Quebecor/Martinsburg.

Throughout this book, trademarked names are used. Rather than put a trademark symbol after every occurrence of a trademarked name, we used the names in an editorial fashion only, and to the benefit of the trademark owner, with no intention of infringement of the trademark. Where such designations appear in this book, they have been printed with initial caps.

Information contained in this work has been obtained by The McGraw-Hill Companies, Inc. ("McGraw-Hill") from sources believed to be reliable. However, neither McGraw-Hill nor its authors guarantees the accuracy or completeness of any information published herein and neither McGraw-Hill nor its authors shall be responsible for any errors, omissions, or damages arising out of use of this information. This work is published with the understanding that McGraw-Hill and its authors are supplying information but are not attempting to render engineering or other professional services. If such services are required, the assistance of an appropriate professional should be sought.

This book is printed on recycled, acid-free paper containing a minimum of 50% recycled, de-inked fiber.

To my wife, Eleanor, who cheered me on when things were going well, encouraged me when they weren't, and who understood and supported me all the way

CONTENTS

Contents

Contents

Contents

                 Helper Class   481

                 A Multiline Order   482
                 The Helper Class   485
                 Using the Helper Class   486
                     The Remote Interface   486
                     The Home Interface   487
                     The Enterprise Bean   487
                 The Client   489
                     The HTML   489
                     The JSP   490
                     The Intermediate JavaBean   491
                     Packaging and Deploying   493
                     Running the Client   493
                 MultiLineOrderBean.java   493
                 Summary   500

                 Appendix A   501
                 Index   541

PREFACE

The contribution Java 2 Enterprise Edition is making to the world of distributed computing is every bit as important as the contribution the Structured Query Language (SQL) made to the world of relational databases. Developers who don't want to be left behind know the importance of learning to develop applications that can be deployed on J2EE-compliant servers. J2EE is made up of many components. This book is devoted to one of these components—Enterprise JavaBeans.

Who Should Read This Book

This book was written for software developers who program in Java but who have not yet tackled Enterprise JavaBeans. It is aimed at those programmers who learn best by studying working examples. It uses complete examples rather than code snippets.

Book Organization

Each chapter contains the full source code for one or more examples designed to illustrate the topic being covered in the chapter. In the early chapters, the procedure for packaging and deploying the application is presented in detail. In later chapters, as the reader becomes familiar with the procedure, the level of detail is decreased.

Most readers will want to examine the source code, compile it, deploy the application and run the client designed to use the beans the application contains. For these readers, soft copy of all source code, batch files, and data files can be found on the CD. For those readers who only want to study the source code and run the examples, a *.ear* file that can be deployed in a few easy steps is supplied for each application. Compiled versions of each client are also supplied.

Technical Notes

All of the examples in the book were developed and tested using Version 1.2.1 of the Reference Implementation of the Java 2 SDK Enterprise Edition from Sun Microsystems running on Microsoft's Windows NT 4.0 (Build 1381 Service Pack 5). Each of the *.ear* files was deployed and tested using the Linux port of the J2SDKEE running on Red hat Version 6.2.

The Reference Implementation does have some minor quirks. The most bothersome of these is the difficulty one encounters when trying to replace an application that has already been deployed. You will occasionally find it necessary to stop and restart the server. I found the following procedure, which I developed empirically, to be helpful when all else failed:

1. Undeploy the application using the Undeploy button in the Application Development Tool.

2. Remove the server on which the application was deployed.

3. Shut down the server.

4. Invoke the cleanup script.

5. Restart the server.

6. Add the server back in the Application Deployment Tool.

7. Re-deploy the application.

NOTE: *The cleanup script behaves differently under Linux than it does under NT. If you are unaware of this, as I was at first, you can lose your source files.*

If you only want to deploy and run the examples, the procedure is:

1. Select the "Open Application…" option from the "File" menu in the Application Deployment Tool.

2. Navigate to the directory containing the appropriate *.ear* file.

3. Load the *.ear* file

4. Deploy the application using the "Deploy Application…" option from the "Tools" menu.

5. Run the appropriate client.

ACKNOWLEDGMENTS

My first words of thanks are to my wife. Many of the hours I spent on the book, Ellie, were taken from time that belonged to both of us. Your generosity was enormous. I would also like to thank Adrian Colyer for his sharp mind, keen eye, depth of knowledge, and intense desire to improve things whenever and however possible. Thanks also to Rebekah, whose picture should surely be placed next to facilitator in the dictionary. Finally, I want to thank my friends at YOURWAP.com who answered my request for permission to include screen shots of a WAP emulator with instant cooperation when others answered me with bureaucracy or indifference.

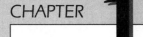

An Overview of Java 2 Platform Enterprise Edition

In this chapter:

- Two-Tier and *n*-Tier Architectures
- The J2EE Server
- Enterprise JavaBeans
- The EJB Container
- Session Beans
- Stateless and Stateful Session Beans
- Entity Beans
- Container-Managed and Bean-Managed Persistence
- Roles in Developing and Deploying EJBs

Enterprise JavaBeans (EJBs) are best understood when one understands the environment in which they are used—namely, the Java 2 Platform Enterprise Edition (J2EE); so, this chapter begins with a high-level look at J2EE.

One of the main goals of J2EE is to provide an environment in which application developers are free to concentrate on what should be their prime concern—business logic. It does this by rendering system plumbing invisible to the developer. Such invisibility can be achieved only when management of system services such as client access, security, database access, and transaction management is hidden as much as possible from the application programmer. This type of management is provided by the J2EE platform.

The power of J2EE can be largely attributed to its use of an *n*-tier architecture, where $n \geqq 3$. The benefits derived from using an *n*-tier architecture are perhaps best appreciated by examining the older architecture it replaces—the two-tier architecture.

The Two-Tier Architecture

For years, users thought of corporate data in terms of the boxes of reports printed on fanfold paper and delivered to them on a weekly or monthly basis. This changed forever with the introduction of the personal computer. Users quickly discovered that this inexpensive device provided them with a means whereby they could release corporate data from the confines of the big glass room. They no longer had to wait for weekly or monthly reports or battle a bureaucracy to obtain nonscheduled reports. They simply obtained a copy of that portion of corporate data they needed and analyzed and manipulated it as they saw fit. All at once, life was wonderful—or was it?

It was not long before the frustrations of dealing with the big glass room were replaced by a new set of frustrations. These included trying to manage isolated islands of data, figuring out what and where data were, whether they had been altered, by whom had they been altered, and how current they were. Users had learned the hard way the truth of the old admonition "Be careful of what you ask for—you just might get it." The result of the experiment was that they were forced to concede custody of corporate data to the keepers of the glass house. The experiment, however, was not a total failure. Once users had experienced the benefits of using corporate data when and how it best suited them, they demanded that the IS department deliver a solution that provided access to the data. One such solution took the form of the client-server architecture, in which enterprise computers served data to client software installed on personal computers. The two major roles in this architecture were mapped to two tiers, as shown in Figure 1-1.

Limitations of the Two-Tier Architecture

The two-tier architecture had to accommodate three components: the software required to deliver the data from the server, the business logic required to manipulate the data, and the software that enabled interaction with the user. The arithmetic here was simple— three components divided by two tiers leaves a remainder. The user

Figure 1-1
Simple Representation
of Client-Server

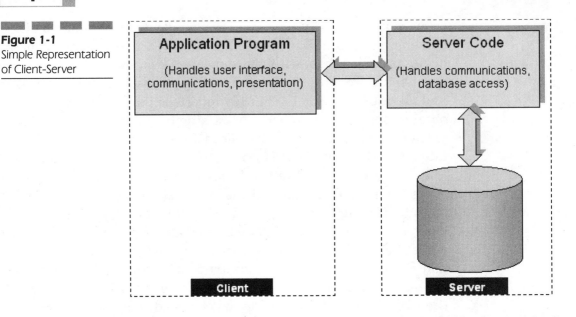

interface code obviously belonged in the client tier and the code that delivered data from the server belonged in the server tier. The question was what to do with the business logic. Earlier architectures placed the business logic in the client tier, resulting in the "fat client" shown in Figure 1-2.

Figure 1-2
The Fat Client—
A Simple View

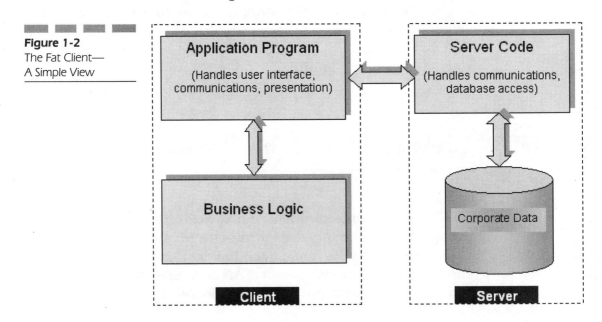

The fat client was problematic. Each application required installation and configuration of application-specific software on the client. It is quite easy to imagine the problems associated with distributing and maintaining such software when hundreds of clients were involved. The problem multiplied when the number of applications on each client grew as shown in Figure 1-3. This proliferation of applications, coupled with the fact that applications were becoming increasingly complex, set in motion an ever-increasing demand for more memory on faster computers with larger hard drives. Cost of ownership—which included the cost of the equip-

Figure 1-3
The Fat Client Growing Fatter

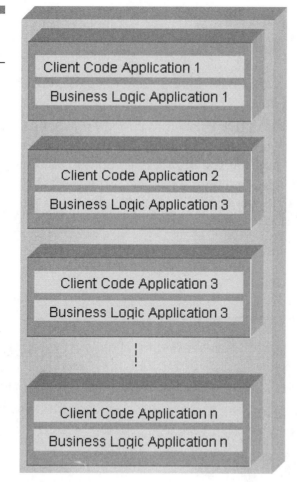

ment, the salaries of the programmers who developed the applications, and the salaries of the staff required to install and maintain the hardware and software—skyrocketed.

The solution to the "fat client," as you might suspect, was to remove the fat. Removing the business logic from the client tier resulted in the "skinny client" shown in Figure 1-4. While moving the business logic to the server does solve the client replication and management issues, it introduces new problems. It places a heavy load on the server and makes the server hard to maintain when many different applications want to work with the same data. This architecture did not scale well to support large numbers of clients.

The Three-Tier Architecture

The answer to the "three-into-two" dilemma was deceptively simple. It finally occurred to some architects that there was no hard-and-fast rule limiting the number of tiers to two. Placing business logic in a tier of its own resulted in the three-tier architecture as shown in Figure 1-5. This architecture naturally led to the multitier architectures that are common today.

Figure 1-4
The Skinny Client in a Two-Tier Architecture

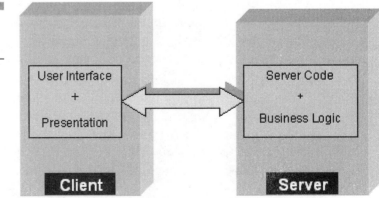

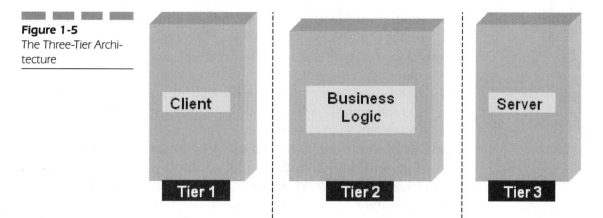

Figure 1-5
The Three-Tier Architecture

The Middle Tier—The J2EE Server

Placing business in a separate middle tier represented a significant architectural improvement but did not completely solve all of the problems that plagued client–server solutions. The most troublesome of these problems was that application programmers were spending far too much time dealing with infrastructure. To put it in perspective, imagine that, if each time you wanted a new automobile, you had to start by building an engine, a transmission, suspension, and so forth. As ridiculous as that might sound, it is exactly what programmers did for years. Stop for a minute and think about how many socket interfaces you have written, how many login procedures you have written—and the list could go on. Although it is true that creating infrastructure is challenging and fun for "bits-and-bytes" programmers, it diminishes the productivity of applications developers. To use the automobile analogy, if you wanted to go to the supermarket to get groceries, your involvement with the car would consist of placing the key in the ignition, starting the motor, and steering toward your destination. Thousands of properly functioning parts are involved. These were challenging and fun for those who engineered and built the car but they are all invisible to you.

The Common Request Broker Architecture (CORBA), with the introduction of object services, saved programmers from having to rewrite many basic services by making transaction services, persistence, and naming services all well defined and available. The problem was that the programmer had to make explicit use of them. The learning curve was steep and the resultant code clouded the business logic.

The Java 2 Platform Enterprise Edition enables applications programmers to approach the task of constructing an application with little awareness of the underlying services by taking a different approach. Rather than providing the programmer with a definition of the underlying services, it provides a middle tier that implements the services and makes them implicit via deployment descriptors. The programmer simply uses a tool to provide declarative statements that form these descriptors. We will see such descriptors in subsequent chapters. Some of the services provided by J2EE are shown in Figure 1-6. We will discuss only a few of them.

JNDI

When computing was younger, the number of resources used was small. Managing them required nothing more than simple documentation that instructed the user concerning which program to

Figure 1-6
Some of the Services Provided by J2EE Middle Tier

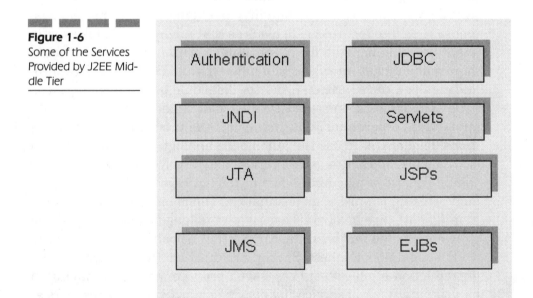

execute, which files to make available for input, and the name of the files that would contain the output. The number of resources involved in today's enterprise-class applications is much greater and these resources are not always located in a single place. Some programs are started once and run for months; others are executed on demand as the result of requests made by remote users. There is little, if any, human intervention. Programs must be able to easily identify the resources they need and accurately locate them. This task is facilitated by naming and directory services. You are undoubtedly familiar with many of these services such as Lightweight Directory Access Protocol (LDAP), Domain Name Service (DNS), and Novell Directory Services (NDS).

The Java Naming and Directory Interface (JNDI) is a standard Java extension that provides a uniform API for accessing a variety of naming and directory services. JNDI is shown in Figure 1-7.

Figure 1-7
The Java Naming and Directory Interface (JNDI)

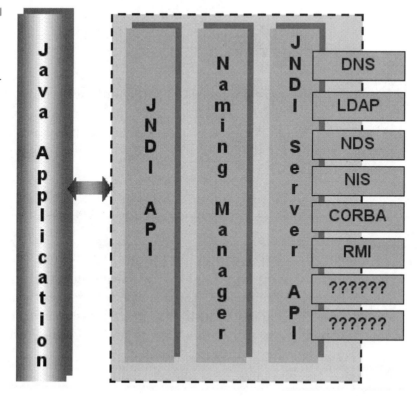

Authentication

Some enterprise applications such as browsing a product catalog are intended for an unrestricted audience. Other applications access sensitive corporate data, so it is imperative that persons who use such applications prove their identity. This process of proving one's identity is *authentication*. The J2EE middle tier provides authentication services using the concepts of users, realms, and groups. We discuss this in detail later in the book.

JDBC

Java Database Connectivity (JDBC) is an API that enables Java programs to interact with SQL-compliant databases by executing SQL statements.

Servlets

Servlets are server-side components written in Java that provide a general framework for implementing the request-response paradigm. Servlets are a platform-independent, high-performance replacement for CGI. Like CGI, servlets can dynamically generate HTML.

JSPs

The JavaServer Pages (JSP) technology is an extension of the Servlet technology that simplifies generation of dynamic Web pages. It uses XML-like tags and Java *scriptlets* to encapsulate the logic required to generate pages. Unlike other scripting tools, it is platform-independent.

JMS

The Java Messaging Service (JMS) is a framework and API that enables developers to build enterprise applications that use messaging to pass data.

JTA

The Java Transaction API (JTA) specification defines JTA as standard Java interfaces between a transaction manager and the parties involved in a transaction: the application, the resource manager, and the application server. It defines the JTA package as consisting of three parts:

1. A high-level application interface that allows a transactional application to demarcate transaction boundaries.
2. A Java mapping of the industry standard X/Open XA protocol that allows a transactional resource manager to participate in a global transaction controlled by an external transaction manager.
3. A high-level transaction manager interface that allows an application server to control transaction boundary demarcation for an application being managed by the application server.

EJBs

Another service provided by a J2EE server—and the one that is the focus of this book—is support for Enterprise JavaBeans (EJBs). We will develop a full understanding of what EJBs are when we work with them in later chapters. For now, let us state that they are simple, portable, scalable, reusable, deployable software components that can be assembled to create enterprise-class applications. Desirable as all these attributes are, they are not the reason EJBs are attractive to developers of enterprise applications. The power of EJBs comes from their ability to hide system plumbing. They do not accomplish this task by themselves but by relying on the container in which they run.

The EJB Container

EJB instances run in an EJB container, which is a runtime environment that manages enterprise beans and provides them with system-level services. The services provided by the EJB container are shown in Figure 1-8. What the container does is strictly defined by the EJB specification; how it does so is left up to the vendor who implements the container.

A client never accesses a bean directly but does so via the *Home* interface and the *Remote* interface as shown in Figure 1-9. We will see more of these interfaces later. For now, we will just say that the *Home* interface defines the bean's life cycle by defining methods for

Figure 1-8
The EJB Container

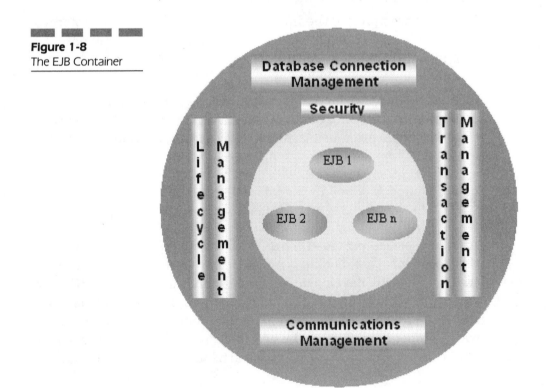

creating, removing, and finding beans and the *Remote* interface defines the methods a bean presents to the outside world to do its work.

Enterprise JavaBeans

We have seen that the J2EE server provides support for Enterprise JavaBeans. There are two types of Enterprise JavaBeans. Session beans model business processes and entity beans model business data. Another way of stating this is that session beans are the verbs of an enterprise application and entity beans are the nouns.

Session Beans

A session bean is scoped to a single client and performs work on behalf of that client, and is created in response to a request from a client and is dedicated to that client. The client communicates with the session bean by invoking its methods. A session bean is not guaranteed to recover from a server failure.

Figure 1-9
The EJB Architecture

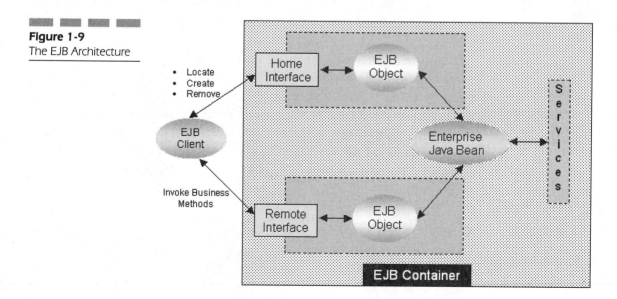

There are two types of session beans, stateless and stateful.

Stateless

A stateless session bean, as its name implies, does not maintain a conversational state. It may indeed have a state that can be changed by invoking its methods but it has no *client-specific* state.

A stateless session bean has a well-defined life cycle, during which it can be in one of two states: the *Does Not Exist* state and the *Ready* state. As the name implies, when a stateless session bean is in the *Does Not Exist* state, it has not yet been instantiated. As you can see from Figure 1-10, a series of three method invocations—all of which are container-initiated—results in the bean transitioning from the *Does Not Exist* state to the *Ready* state. The three methods are as follows:

1. `newInstance()`, which instantiates the bean
2. `setSessionContext()`, which gives the bean a session context
3. `ejbCreate()`, which provides the bean with an opportunity to perform any initialization tasks it might require

The client has a simple point of view. It obtains access to a stateless bean by invoking the `create()` method, invokes the business method(s) it needs, and then relinquishes access to the bean by invoking the `remove()` method.

When the container decides that it no longer needs a stateless session bean, it invokes the bean's `ejbRemove()` method and then transitions it back to the *Does Not Exist* state by destroying it.

Typically, what actually happens is that the container creates a pool of bean instances. Since a stateless session bean has no permanent association with a client, the size of the pool can grow or shrink to a size deemed appropriate by the container.

NOTE: *Do not be concerned if much of what is covered here does not seem to make sense or fit together. When we start to actually write and deploy some enterprise beans, things will become clearer.*

Figure 1-10
Life Cycle of a State-
less Session Bean

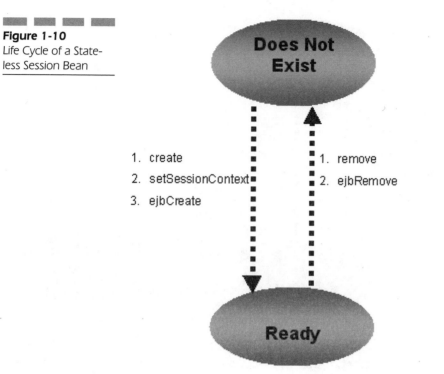

1. create
2. setSessionContext
3. ejbCreate

1. remove
2. ejbRemove

Stateful

A stateful session bean is dedicated to one client for the life of the
bean instance and maintains a conversational state. Instance data
that are set by one method invocation can be retrieved during a
subsequent method invocation. Every method invocation from a
client is against the same instance. The life cycle of a stateful session bean, which is more complex than the simple two-state cycle of
its stateless counterpart, is shown in Figure 1-11.

NOTE: *Depending on the implementation of the container, different*
method invocations from a client may actually be handled by different
instances; however, the client can conceptually assume that the same state-
ful bean instance services all requests.

Like a stateless session bean, a stateful session beans starts life in
the *Does Not Exist* state. It has not been instantiated. Its transition

Figure 1-11
Life Cycle of a Stateful
Session Bean

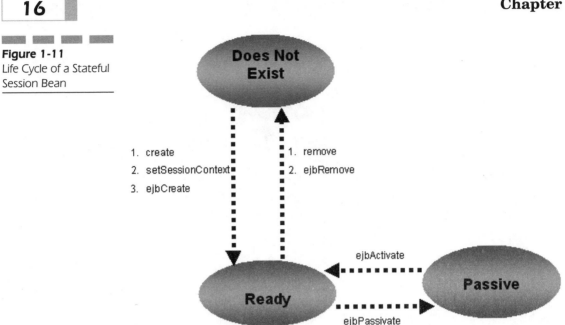

to the *Ready* state proceeds in the same manner as that of its stateless counterpart. Once in the *Ready* state, however, life is different for a stateful session bean. The container cannot discard it to shrink the size of a pool of beans; that would destroy its relationship with the client. The container can, however, remove from memory any stateful bean that is not actively servicing a method call. This process of migrating a bean to an auxiliary store is called *passivation*. Before the bean enters the passive state, the container calls its ejbPassivate() method. This provides the bean with an opportunity to release any resources it holds and to prepare itself for serialization by setting all transient and nonserializable fields to null. When the container later determines that the passivated bean must be made available, it reactivates the bean by restoring its state from the serialized copy that had been saved and then invokes its ejbActivate() method, allowing it to once again obtain the resources it had released in the ejbPassivate() method and to initialize transient fields. The process is called *activation*. At this point, the bean transitions back into the *Ready* state. When the container determines that a stateless bean can be safely destroyed, it invokes its ejbRemove() method and transitions it to the *Does Not Exist* state.

Entity Beans

An entity bean, as its name implies, represent an entity. The entity can be something real such as a customer, a billing statement, or an inventory item; it can also be something abstract such as a hotel reservation. The most important characteristic of an entity bean is that it is persistent. The state of the bean exists on some external media—typically a record in a database—and is available for subsequent use, even after the application that created it terminates.

Like session beans, an entity bean has a clearly defined life cycle. This life cycle is shown in Figure 1-12.

Like stateless and stateful session beans, an entity bean begins life in the *Does Not Exist* state. When an entity bean leaves the *Does Not Exist* state, it transitions into the *Pooled* state. While it is in the *Pooled* state, an entity bean is available to the container to service a request from a client. The bean can transition from the

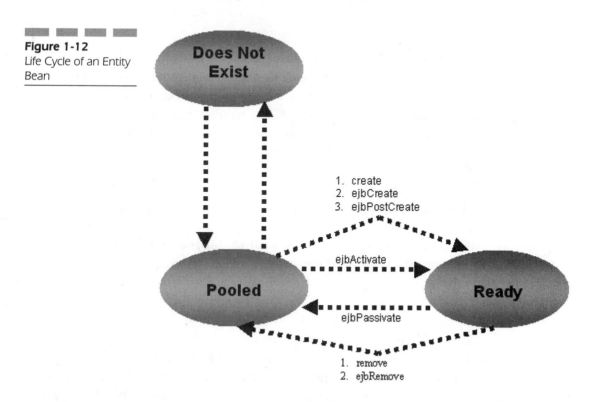

Figure 1-12
Life Cycle of an Entity Bean

Pooled state to the *Ready* state as the result of a *create* request from a client, execution of a *find* method, or by *activation*. The activation process is similar to what we already saw when we mentioned stateful session beans, except that entity beans are not normally concerned with serialization. Once the bean is in the *Ready* state, it can handle requests from clients. When the container decides to decrease the number of instances of entity beans in the pool, quite often in response to a demand for memory from some other part of the system, it releases the bean. The bean then transitions back to the *Does Not Exist* state.

Persistence

Persistence of entity beans can be managed in two ways: by the container or by the bean.

Container-Managed Persistence

When the container manages persistence, it generates all of the necessary database calls. The actual mechanism depends on the implementation. Most typically, if the underlying persistent store is a relational database, when the client creates the entity bean the container generates an SQL INSERT statement to create a new row in the database. When instance variables that correspond to database columns are modified, the container generates the SQL UPDATE statement(s) required to keep the database synchronized with the bean.

Since entity beans that use container-managed persistence contain no SQL statements written by the bean developer, they are simpler to write.

Bean-Managed Persistence

When persistence is managed by the bean, all database calls are the responsibility of the person writing the bean. The issue of synchronization between the data in the bean and the data in the database is the responsibility of the bean developer. The container assists in the process via a series of well-defined callbacks.

When we work with EJBs in later chapters, we will develop an understanding as to when it is appropriate to use session beans and when we should use entity beans. For now, a simple comparison is sufficient. Table 1-1 shows this comparison.

Roles in Developing and Deploying Enterprise JavaBeans

The application programmer does not assume full responsibility for deployment of an enterprise application that uses EJBs. This task involves many roles, which are discussed next.

EJB Server Provider

As the name implies, the EJB server provider provides an EJB server. An EJB server contains EJB containers and provides these containers with all of the services they need to do their job.

EJB Container Provider

The EJB container, whose responsibilities include providing services to the bean and isolating and protecting it from the world

TABLE 1-1

A Comparison of Session Beans and Entity Beans

	Role	Persistence	Relationship to Client
Session Bean	· Offers a service to a client.	No long-term persistence.	May have only one client.
Entity Bean	Represents a business entity object.	Persistent. Has primary key.	May be shared by multiple clients.

around it, is written by the container provider. Typically, you will find that the container provider and the server provider are one and the same.

Enterprise Bean Provider

The EJB provider is the person who provides the package containing the bean and the classes required to support it. The bean provider should have a strong knowledge of the business logic that the bean implements, should know enough Java to write acceptable code, and should understand EJBs. The actual packaging is usually done with the aid of a graphical tool. The role of the EJB provider is the only one that is covered in this book.

Application Assembler

The application assembler is the consumer of what the bean provider produces and builds applications using beans that were obtained commercially or written internally by a programming group.

Deployer

The deployer is the consumer of the output from the application assembler. The deployer typically maps resource references used by beans to resources existing in the target system. This role is often assumed by the system administrator.

System Administrator

The system administrator of an EJB server has the same responsibilities as the system administrator of any other computer. These responsibilities include monitoring performance of the system and performing backups. Additionally, the EJB system administrator keeps security information current.

Summary

In this chapter, we have superficially covered some of the terms and concepts you will encounter as you work with EJBs. The only way to become proficient at developing EJBs is by doing. The reminder of the book is devoted to exactly that.

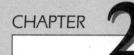

Our First Enterprise JavaBean

In this chapter:

- Remote Interface
- Home Interface
- The Enterprise Bean
- Creating a J2EE Application
- Packaging the Bean
- Deploying the Bean
- Client Code
- Maintaining an EJB

In keeping with what has become a tradition, we start our study of Enterprise JavaBeans with the famous *HelloWorld* program. Since your very first Java program was probably *HelloWorld,* using this program as a starting point will afford you the opportunity to compare your first standalone Java application with its counterpart, written as an enterprise bean suitable for deployment in the J2EE environment. As you make the comparison, keep an open mind. Your first impression will undoubtedly be that the difference between the two is like that between fixing a sandwich and preparing a seven-course meal. Admittedly, developing and deploying an EJB is not a trivial process; however, as you will see, much of the work is done with the aid of a graphical tool that simplifies things considerably.

NOTE: *If you want to run all of the examples yourself, you will need a J2EE-compliant environment. The examples in this book were all developed using Sun's Java 2 SDK, Enterprise Edition. Version 1.2.1 of this Reference Implementation is freely available from* java.sun.com. *All of the examples in the book were developed and tested using Microsoft's Windows NT for Workstations Version 4.0 and so the scripts used to compile and run the code are* .bat *files. If you are using another platform, you must supply equivalent script files for your platform.*

■■ ■■   Writing the Code

All enterprise beans are comprised of up to four units of code:

1. The Remote Interface
2. The Home Interface
3. The Bean
4. A primary key class for entity beans (which we discuss in a
   later chapter)

The Remote Interface

The remote interface defines all of the business methods a client can
invoke to interact with an EJB on the server. The kinds of business
methods a client can call should reflect the fact that the client views
an EJB as a component that implements *business* logic. Appropriate
methods might include `calculateYearlyInterest()`, `isCus-`
`tomerCreditOk()`, and `minimumReorderThresholdReached()`.
The remote interface should *not* contain a definition of a method
that reflects awareness of infrastructure.

The code for our remote interface looks like this:

■■ ■ ■■ ■■ ■ ■ ■ ■ ■ ■ ■ ■ ■ ■ ■ ■ ■

***Chapter2\\code\\HelloWorld.java*

```
import javax.ejb.EJBObject;
import java.rmi.RemoteException;
public interface HelloWorld extends EJBObject {
public String sayHello() throws RemoteException;
}
```

The first thing you should observe is that the remote interface
extends the `javax.ejb.EJBObject` interface. This is true for all
remote interfaces. If you examine the definition for `EJBObject`,
you will see that is reads as follows:

```
public interface EJBObject
```

You will see that `EJBObject` extends `java.rmi.Remote`. The `sayHello()` method is the interface that the client invokes. Although it is declared here in the remote interface, it is actually implemented in the enterprise bean; so we will see this method again later when we examine the code for the enterprise bean. The remote interface defines the entire set of business methods a client can invoke.

You will notice that the `sayHello()` method throws `java.rmi.RemoteException`. Each method of an interface that extends `java.rmi.Remote` *must* list this exception in its throws clause. RemoteException is the common superclass for a number of communication-related exceptions that may occur during the execution of a remote method call.

The Home Interface

The home interface defines those methods the client can invoke to *create* or *find* an EJB object and to *remove* it. Session beans are created; entity beans are found or created. We see more about this in later chapters.

Our home interface looks like this:

\Chapter2\code\HelloWorldHome.java

```
import java.io.Serializable;
import java.rmi.RemoteException;
import javax.ejb.CreateException;
import javax.ejb.EJBHome;
public interface HelloWorldHome extends EJBHome {
    HelloWorld create() throws RemoteException, CreateException;
}
```

The home interface extends the `javax.ejb.EJBHome` interface, which extends `java.rmi.Remote`. As we previously stated when we discussed the code for the remote interface, each method of an interface that extends `java.rmi.Remote` *must* list `java.rmi.RemoteException` in its throws clause and the `create()` method does exactly that.

When a client wishes to use a bean, it uses JNDI to obtain a reference to an object that is an instance of the home interface and then invokes the `create()` method. Note that the `create()` method returns an object of type *HelloWorld* which, as we saw in the previous section, is the type of our remote interface. The client uses this instance of the remote interface to invoke the enterprise bean's business methods.

The Enterprise Bean

We have taken care of the interfaces, so the only remaining code we must write is that which actually implements the business methods we defined in the remote interface. We defined only the single business method `sayHello()`. Here is the code that implements it:

 \Chapter2\code\HelloWorldBean.java

```
import java.rmi.RemoteException;
import javax.ejb.SessionBean;
import javax.ejb.SessionContext;
public class HelloWorldBean implements SessionBean {
    public String sayHello() {
        return "Hello World!";
    }
    public HelloWorldBean() {}
    public void ejbCreate() {}
    public void ejbRemove() {}
    public void ejbActivate() {}
    public void ejbPassivate() {}
    public void setSessionContext(SessionContext sc) {}
}
```

Our enterprise bean implements the `SessionBean` interface and so we see the following methods defined:

- `ejbActivate()`
- `ejbPassivate()`
- `ejbRemove()`
- `setSessionContext()`

These methods are callback methods that are invoked by the container to notify the bean that a life-cycle event has occurred.

The `setSessionContext()` method is invoked immediately after the bean instance is created by the container. It receives a single argument of type *SessionContext,* which it should save in an instance variable and use to access container-provided security and transaction management services.

After the container calls the `setSessionContext()` method, it calls the `ejbCreate()` method. For each `create()` method defined in its home interface, a bean must implement a corresponding `ejbCreate()` method that has a *void* return type and contains the same number and type of arguments as the corresponding `create()` method. A stateless session bean can have only a single `ejbCreate()` method that takes no arguments.

Compiling the Code

The code we have written is compiled in exactly the same manner as any other Java code you have previously written, simply by running the Java compiler. The way in which you invoke the compiler will vary, depending on the environment in which you are working. In our case, we will use the following script, which you would save as `compileHelloWorld.bat`.

\Chapter2\code\compileHelloWorld.bat

```
set J2EE_HOME=c:\j2sdkee1.2.1
set CPATH=.;%J2EE_HOME%\lib\j2ee.jar
javac -classpath %CPATH% HelloWorldBean.java HelloWorldHome.java
HelloWorld.java
```

When the `.bat` file has completed, you should have three `.class` files that contain the remote interface, the home interface, and the enterprise bean.

Creating a J2EE Application

Deployment of an enterprise bean is not carried out directly. The process involves first adding the bean to a J2EE application and deploying that application. The J2EE server and support tools we will be using are those delivered as part of the J2EE Reference Implementation made available by Sun Microsystems. If you wish to follow along as we develop our enterprise beans in this and succeeding chapters, you should first download and install the Reference Implementation from `java.sun.com`.

Before doing anything else, we must first start the J2EE server by typing the command:

```
j2ee -verbose
```

As it is starting, the server will display informational messages as shown in Figure 2-1. If you omit the `-verbose` option, the server will simply display a message containing the names of the files to which it is redirecting the output and error streams. You can refer to these log files to monitor server activity. Regardless of which startup method you choose, the final message should indicate successful startup.

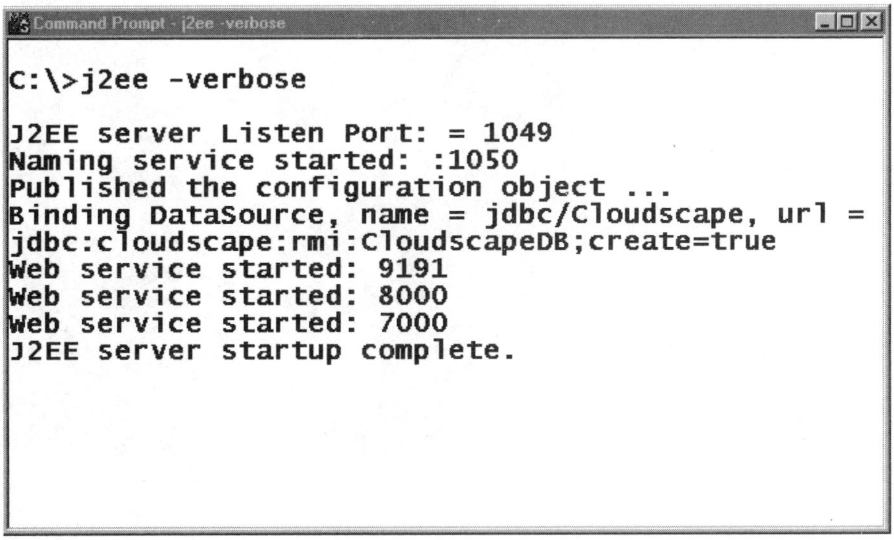

Figure 2-1
Starting the J2EE Server

```
C:\>j2ee -verbose

J2EE server Listen Port: = 1049
Naming service started: :1050
Published the configuration object ...
Binding DataSource, name = jdbc/Cloudscape, url =
jdbc:cloudscape:rmi:CloudscapeDB;create=true
Web service started: 9191
Web service started: 8000
Web service started: 7000
J2EE server startup complete.
```

Once the J2EE server has been started, we start the Application Deployment Tool by simply typing the command:

```
deploytool
```

As the Deployment Tool starts, it displays a splash screen like that shown in Figure 2-2; when the startup process is complete, you should see a screen like the one shown in Figure 2-3.

We are now ready to create a J2EE application. We start by selecting the "New Application . . ." option from the "File" menu as shown in Figure 2-4. When we do so, we see the dialog box shown in Figure 2-5.

When we click on the BROWSE button in the dialog box shown in Figure 2-5, we see the navigational dialog shown in Figure 2-6. Using the tree-view of the local file system that is presented when we click on the selection arrow of the drop-down list labeled "Look in:", we navigate to the directory in which we wish to cre-

Figure 2-2
Deployment Tool
Startup Screen

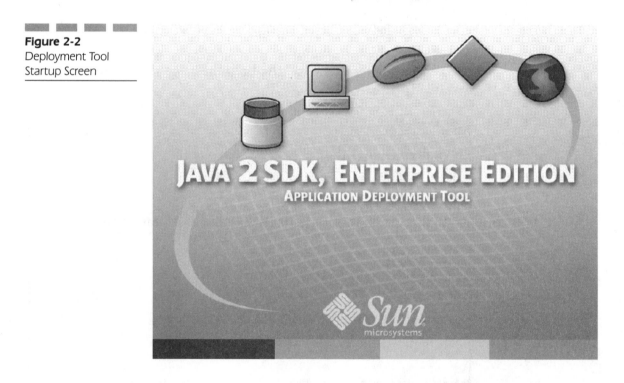

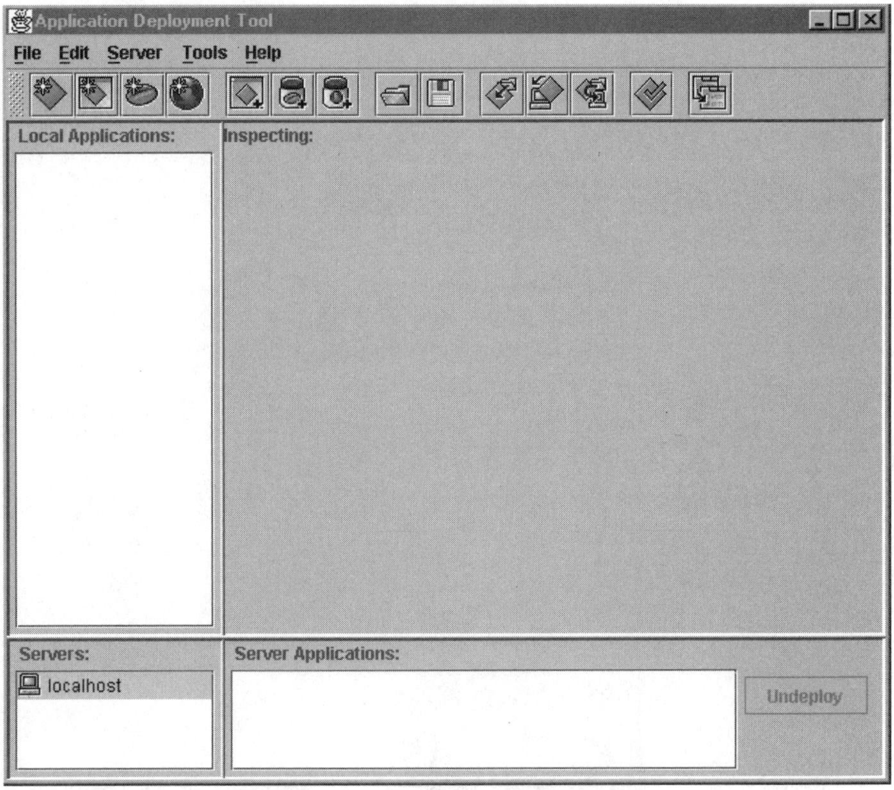

Figure 2-3
The Deployment Tool
Initial Screen

ate the new J2EE application and select that directory. For the example shown, it is d:\instant_ejb\Chapter2\code. If you are following along and developing the examples yourself, it would be the directory in which you saved your files. After the directory has been selected, we type into the entry field labeled "File Name:", the name of the .ear file that contains the J2EE application. We will use *HelloWorldApp.ear*. When the name has been specified, clicking on the NEW APPLICATION button returns us to the "New Application" dialog shown in Figure 2-5, although now we see that both entry fields labeled "Application File Name" and "Application Display Name" are populated. We complete the process by clicking on the OK button and see the screen shown in Figure 2-7.

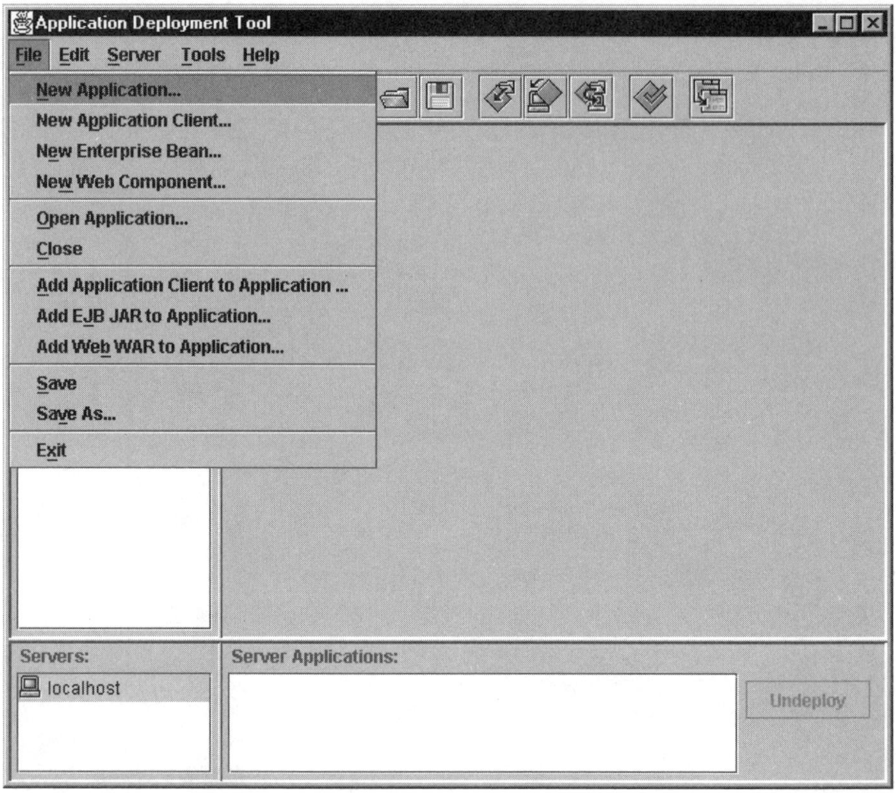

Figure 2-4
Creating a New J2EE
Application

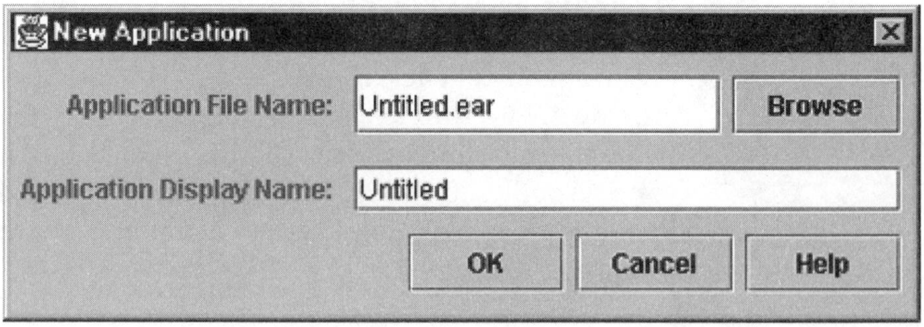

Figure 2-5
The "New Application"
Dialog Box

Figure 2-6
Specifying the `.ear`
File Name

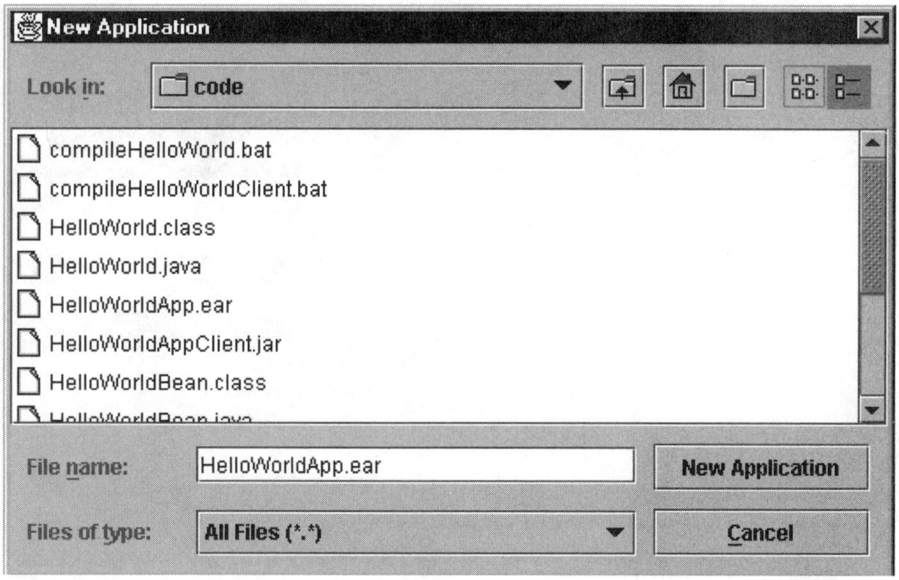

NOTE: *The material presented in the remainder of this section is not required to develop and deploy the bean. Its purpose is to provide a more in-depth look for those who might be interested. If you are impatient to move on, you can skip ahead to the section entitled "Packaging Hello-World."*

Figure 2-7 shows that we have created a file named *HelloWorld-App.ear* and lists the contents of the file. Any `.ear` file can be processed by the jar utility that is distributed with the Java Developer's Kit. Let's take a look at our new `.ear` file by typing the command:

```
D:\instant_ejb\CHAPTER2\code>jar -tvf helloworldapp.ear
```

The output from running the jar utility, which agrees with what is listed in Figure 2-7, is as follows:

```
  2 Sat Jun 10 22:50:18 EDT 2000 META-INF/MANIFEST.MF
319 Sat Jun 10 22:50:18 EDT 2000 META-INF/application.xml
160 Sat Jun 10 22:50:18 EDT 2000 META-INF/sun-j2ee-ri.xml
```

Figure 2-7
The New J2EE
Application

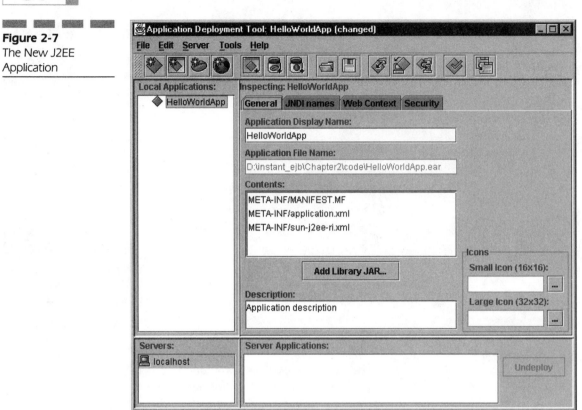

Now it's time to show what the Application Deployment Tool has done for us and to get some idea of how much work we would have had to perform without such a tool. To do this, we will take a little side tour and explore the contents of the .ear file.

We start by copying the .ear file to a separate directory; we choose \instant_ejb\explore.

NOTE: *Do not extract the contents of the* HelloWorldApp.ear *file into the directory in which the* .ear *file was created. Move it to a separate directory.*

We extract the contents of the .ear file by running the jar utility specifying the options -xvf as follows:

```
D:\instant_ejb\explore>jar -xvf HelloWorldApp.ear
```

Here is the result of running the jar utility:

```
extracted: META-INF/MANIFEST.MF
extracted: META-INF/application.xml
extracted: META-INF/sun-j2ee-ri.xml
```

Using `dir/s`, we can see that we now have a directory named META-INF that contains the two `.xml` files listed in Figure 2-7. We will not discuss the contents of these `.xml` files but will simply list them. This should partially satisfy the curiosity of those developers who hate to use graphical tools blindly.

Here is the listing of *application.xml:*

```
<?xml version="1.0" encoding="Cp1252"?>
<!DOCTYPE application PUBLIC '-//Sun Microsystems, Inc.//DTD J2EE
Application 1.2//EN' 'http://java.sun.com/j2ee/dtds/application_1_2
.dtd'>
<application>
  <display-name>HelloWorldApp</display-name>
  <description>Application description</description>
</application>
```

The second file, `sun-j2ee-ri.xml`, looks like this:

```
<?xml version="1.0" encoding="Cp1252"?>
<j2ee-ri-specific-information>
  <server-name></server-name>
  <rolemapping />
</j2ee-ri-specific-information>
```

Packaging HelloWorld

Packaging a bean involves using the New Enterprise Bean Wizard of the Application Deployment Tool to perform three activities:

1. Creating the bean's deployment descriptor

2. Packaging the deployment descriptor and the bean's classes in an EJB `.jar` file

3. Inserting the EJB `.jar` file into the `.ear` file we created earlier

We start the wizard by selecting the "New Enterprise Bean . . ." option from the "File" menu as shown in Figure 2-8. This results in the appearance of the introductory screen shown in Figure 2-9.

After you read the instructions and click on the button labeled NEXT>, you see the screen shown in Figure 2-10, which we will use to add a JAR to our application and add our .class files to the new JAR.

If the drop-down list labeled "Enterprise Bean Will Go In:" does not already show *HelloWorldApp,* select it from the list. In the entry field labeled "JAR Display Name:" type *HelloWorldJAR.*

To add the .class files representing the remote interface, the home interface, and the bean to the JAR, click on the ADD button to the right of the box labeled CONTENTS. When the dialog shown in Figure 2-11 appears, select *HelloWorld.class* and click on ADD.

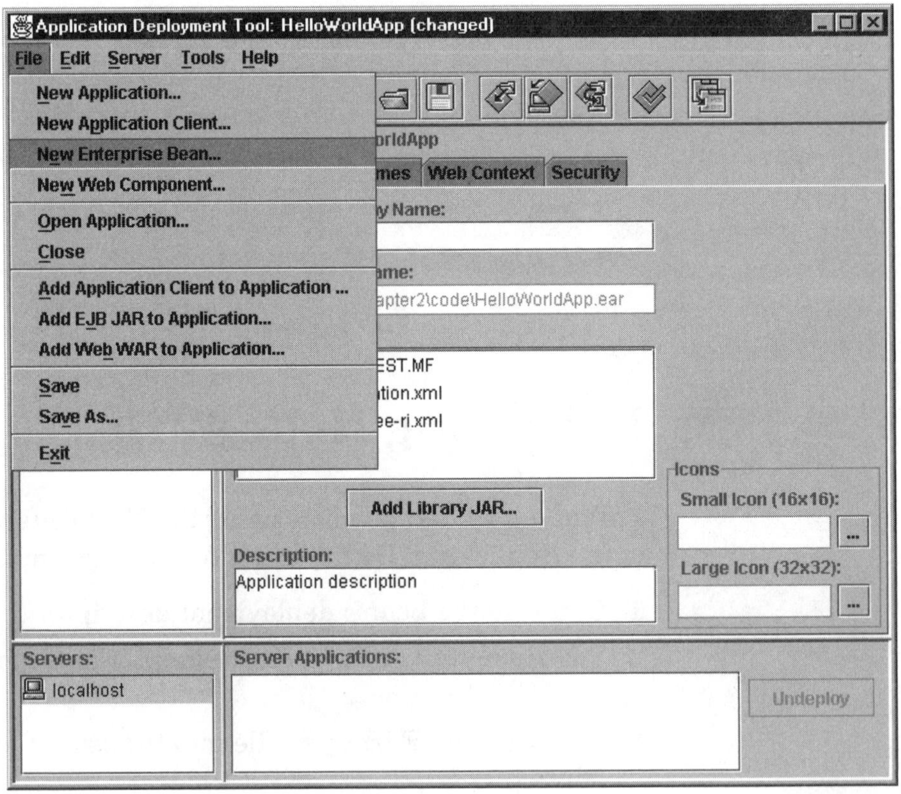

Figure 2-8
Starting the New
Enterprise Bean
Wizard

Figure 2-9
New Enterprise Bean
Wizard Intro

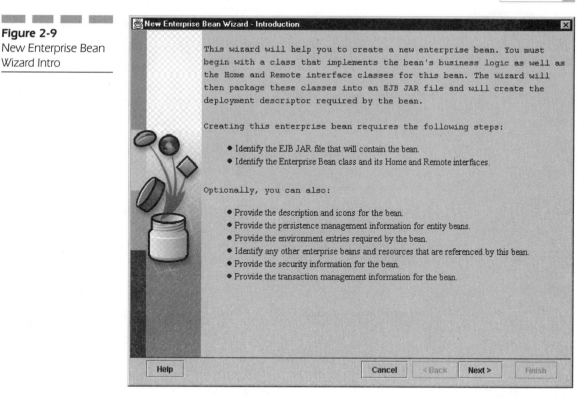

This wizard will help you to create a new enterprise bean. You must begin with a class that implements the bean's business logic as well as the Home and Remote interface classes for this bean. The wizard will then package these classes into an EJB JAR file and will create the deployment descriptor required by the bean.

Creating this enterprise bean requires the following steps:

- Identify the EJB JAR file that will contain the bean.
- Identify the Enterprise Bean class and its Home and Remote interfaces.

Optionally, you can also:

- Provide the description and icons for the bean.
- Provide the persistence management information for entity beans.
- Provide the environment entries required by the bean.
- Identify any other enterprise beans and resources that are referenced by this bean.
- Provide the security information for the bean.
- Provide the transaction management information for the bean.

Next, select *HelloWorldHome.class* and click on ADD and do the same for *HelloWorldBean.class.* The three classes you added should appear in the bottom box labeled FILES TO BE ADDED: as shown in Figure 2-12.

After we verify that the three files have been added and click on the OK button, we should see the screen shown in Figure 2-13. We continue the process by clicking on NEXT>.

From the drop-down list labeled "Enterprise Bean Class:" we select *HelloWorldBean.* (See Figure 2-14.) From the two drop-downs labeled "Home Interface:" and "Remote Interface:" we select *HelloWorldHome* and *HelloWorld,* respectively. We then click on the radio buttons that specify this is to be a session bean and is to be stateless. Finally, in the entry field labeled "Enterprise Bean Display Name:" we type *HelloWorldBean.* The General Dialog should now look like Figure 2-15.

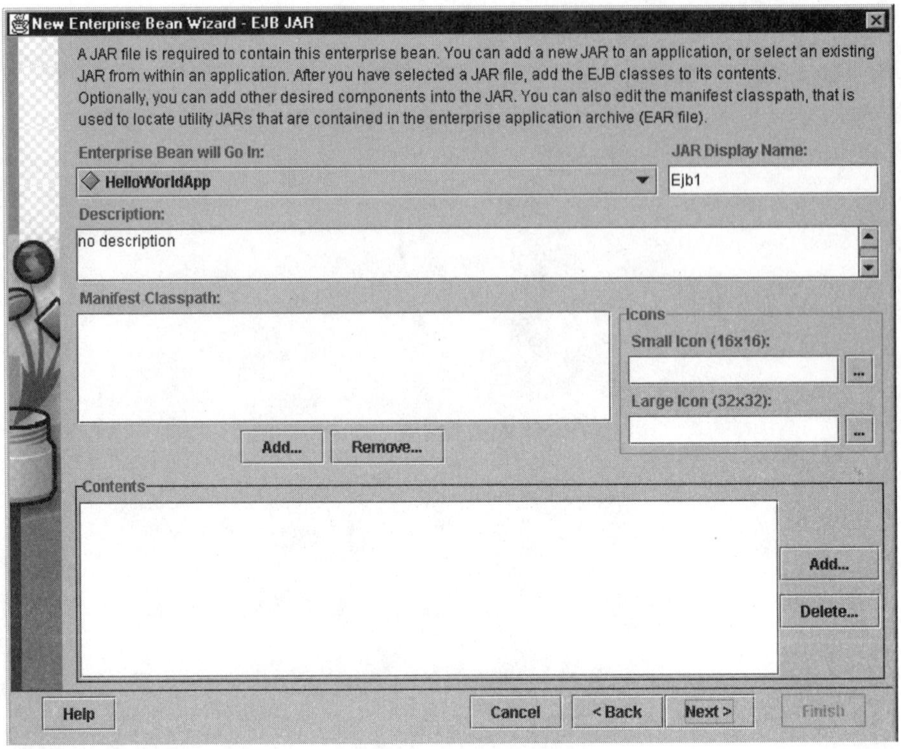

Figure 2-10
Adding a New JAR to
the Application

For this application, we will not specify any environment entries and so we simply click on NEXT> and then click on FINISH> in the dialog that appears. When we do, we see a screen like the one shown in Figure 2-16.

NOTE: *The remaining material in this section is not an essential part of packaging our bean. It is presented to provide a look at a deployment descriptor. You may safely skip ahead to the section entitled "Deploying HelloWorld."*

When we have finished packaging our bean, if we look at *HelloWorldApp.ear,* we notice that a file named *ejb-jar-ic.jar* has been added to it. If we extract the contents of *HelloWorldApp.ear* into a separate directory as we did before and then extract the contents of

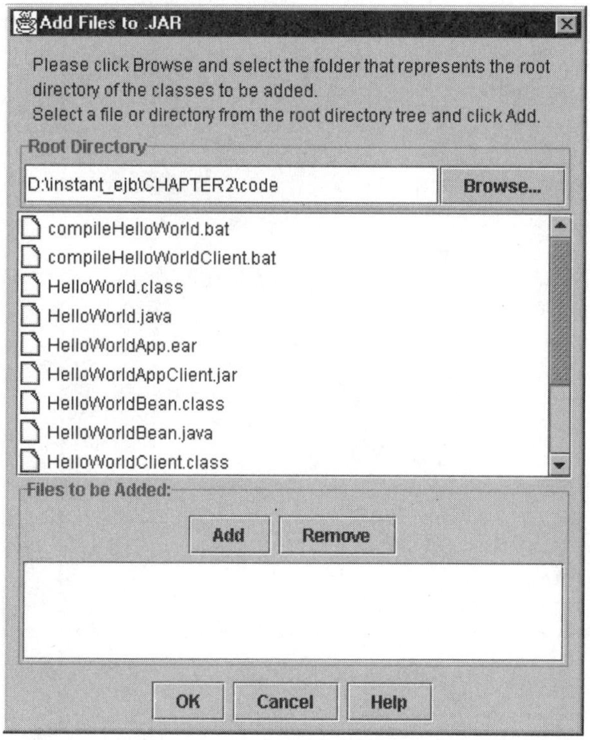

Figure 2-11
Add Files to .JAR
Dialog

ejb-jar-ic.jar, we see a file named *ejb-jar.xml*. This is the deployment descriptor, which looks like this:

```xml
<?xml version="1.0" encoding="Cp1252"?>
<!DOCTYPE ejb-jar PUBLIC '-//Sun Microsystems, Inc.//DTD Enterprise
JavaBeans
1.1//EN' 'http://java.sun.com/j2ee/dtds/ejb-jar_1_1.dtd'>
<ejb-jar>
  <description>Chapter 2 Hello Example</description>
  <display-name>HelloWorldJAR</display-name>
  <enterprise-beans>
    <session>
      <display-name>HelloWorldBean</display-name>
      <ejb-name>HelloWorldBean</ejb-name>
      <home>HelloWorldHome</home>
      <remote>HelloWorld</remote>
      <ejb-class>HelloWorldBean</ejb-class>
      <session-type>Stateless</session-type>
      <transaction-type>Bean</transaction-type>
    </session>
  </enterprise-beans>
</ejb-jar>
```

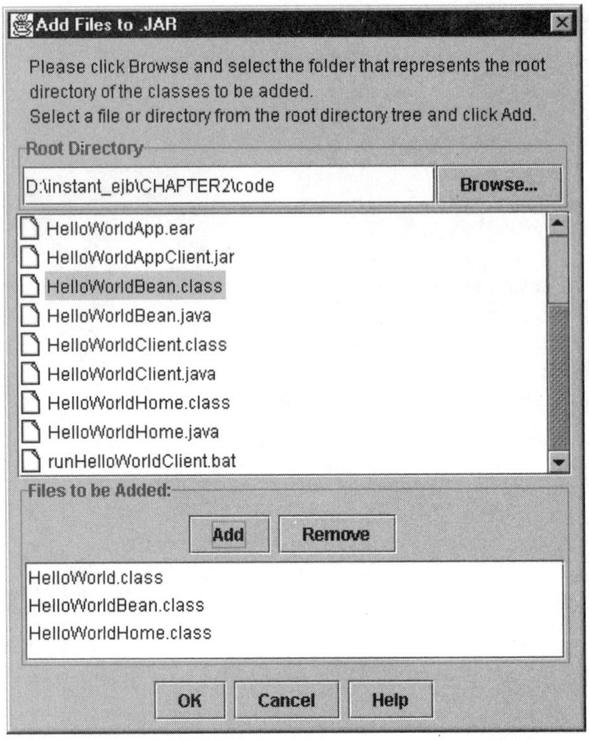

Figure 2-12
New Files Added
to .JAR

The EJB specification states that the role of the deployment descriptor is to capture the declarative information (i.e., information that is not included directly in the enterprise beans' code) that is intended for the consumer of the *ejb-jar* file. Since the names of the tags in the file are clearly indicative of the type of data they describe, you can see how the information we specified during packaging is represented in the *.xml* file.

Deploying HelloWorld

Our newly created application now contains a bean and is ready to be deployed. We start the deployment process by selecting the

Figure 2-13
The New JAR File
and Its Contents

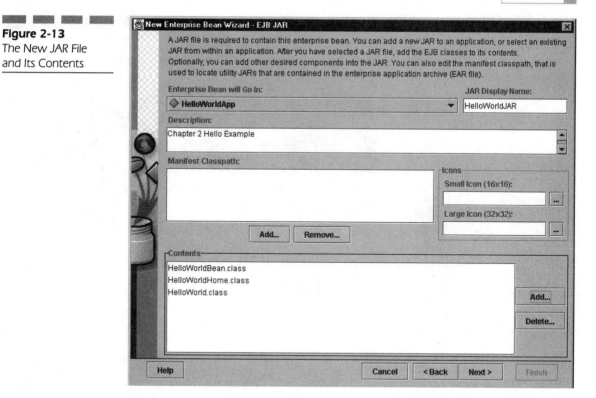

JNDI NAMES tab in the screen shown in Figure 2-16. This results in the screen shown in Figure 2-17 being displayed. In the rightmost column with the header "JNDI" name, we enter *MyHello-World*. This is the name that will be used by clients to locate our enterprise bean.

Finally, we choose the "Deploy Application . . ." option from the "Tools" menu item as shown in Figure 2-18. When the deployment dialog shown in Figure 2-19 is displayed, we click to select the checkbox labeled RETURN CLIENT JAR and then click on NEXT>. This results in the appearance of a screen like that in Figure 2-20.

After we verify that the JNDI name in the rightmost column is *MyHelloWorld,* we click on the NEXT> button and see the screen shown in Figure 2-21. We start the deployment by clicking on FINISH>. As the deployment process takes place, a progress screen

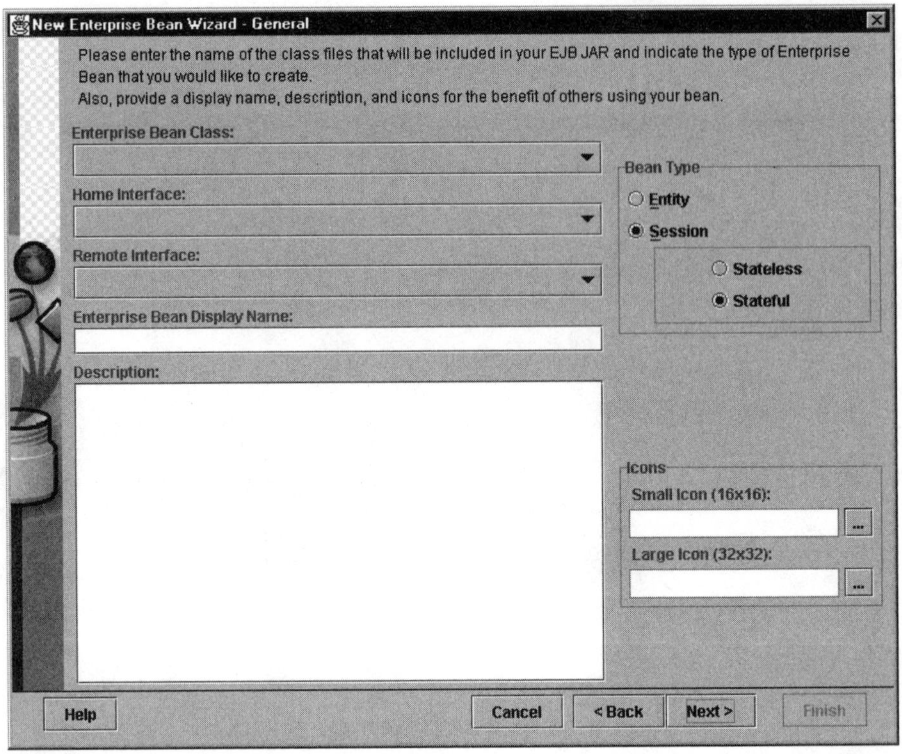

Figure 2-14
The New Enterprise
Bean Wizard—
General Dialog Box

like that shown in Figure 2-22 is displayed. When the operation is complete, the CANCEL button is replaced by an OK button as shown in Figure 2-23. After we click on the OK button, our job is done.

If you look at the window in which we started the J2EE server and the window in which we started the Application Deployment Tool, we see a report of the operations that were performed. Figures 2-24 and 2-25 show the windows.

Writing a Client for HelloWorld

Here is the source for a standalone client:

Figure 2-15
General Dialog After
Specifying Values

New Enterprise Bean Wizard - General

Please enter the name of the class files that will be included in your EJB JAR and indicate the type of Enterprise Bean that you would like to create.
Also, provide a display name, description, and icons for the benefit of others using your bean.

Enterprise Bean Class:
HelloWorldBean

Home Interface:
HelloWorldHome

Remote Interface:
HelloWorld

Enterprise Bean Display Name:
HelloWorldBean

Description:

Bean Type
○ Entity
● Session
　　● Stateless
　　○ Stateful

Icons
Small Icon (16x16):

Large Icon (32x32):

Help　　　　Cancel　　< Back　　Next >　　Finish

On the CD

\Chapter2\code\HelloWorldClient.java

```java
import javax.naming.Context;
import javax.naming.InitialContext;
import javax.rmi.PortableRemoteObject;
import HelloWorldBean;
import HelloWorldHome;
public class HelloWorldClient {
   public static void main(String[] args) {
       try {
           Context initial = new InitialContext();
           Object objref = initial.lookup("MyHelloWorld");
           HelloWorldHome home =
               (HelloWorldHome)PortableRemoteObject.narrow(objref,
                                               HelloWorldHome.class);
           HelloWorld helloBean = home.create();
           String msg = helloBean.sayHello();
           System.out.println();
           System.out.println(msg);
       } catch (Exception ex) {
           System.err.println("Caught an unexpected exception!");
```

Figure 2-16
Packaging Complete

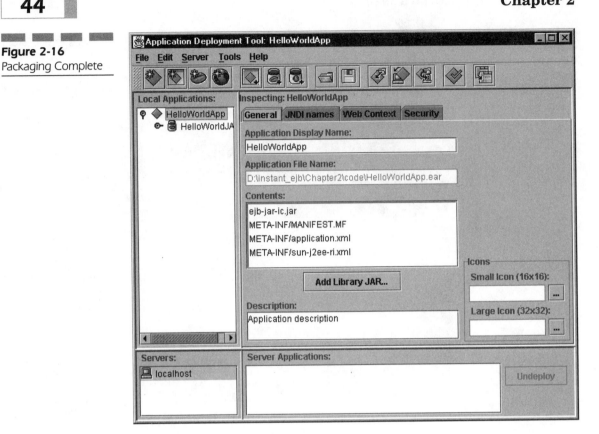

```
            ex.printStackTrace();
        }
    }
}
```

Examining the Client Code

Successful execution of the client requires that three tasks be performed. These are:

1. Finding the Home Interface
2. Creating a HelloWord instance
3. Invoking the business method

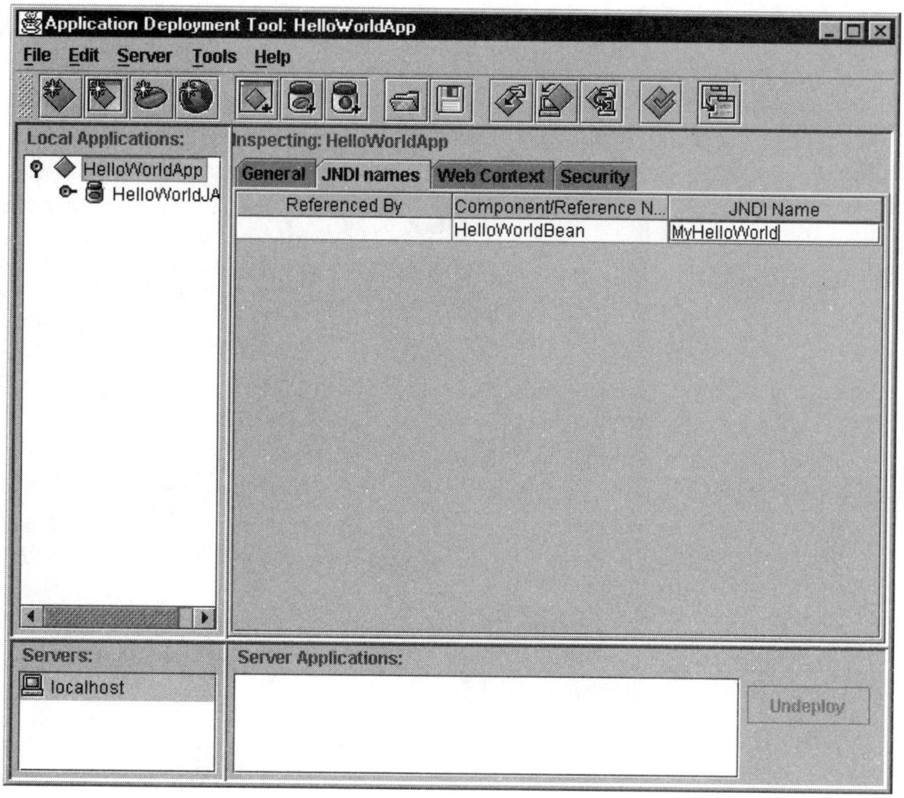

Figure 2-17
Specifying the JNDI
Name of the Bean

We now examine each of these tasks.

Finding the Home Interface

At this point, the *HelloWorldBean* is in the *Does Not Exist* state. Before the client can effect the transition to the *Ready* state, it must first locate the home interface by executing the following statements:

```
Context initial = new InitialContext();
```

This creates a JNDI naming context. A *context* consists of a set of name-to-object bindings and contains methods for examining and updating these bindings.

Figure 2-18
Preparing to Deploy
the Application

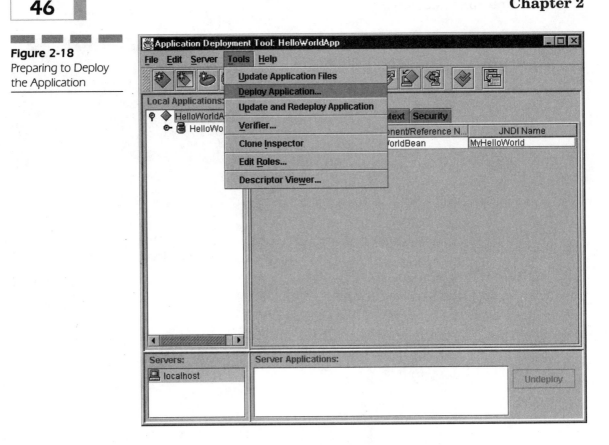

```
Object objref = initial.lookup("MyHelloWorld");
```

Using the name we specified in Figure 2-17, this line of code retrieves the object bound to that name.

```
HelloWorldHome home =
    (HelloWorldHome)PortableRemoteObject.narrow(objref,
                                        HelloWorldHome.class);
```

This line narrows the reference to a HelloWorldHome object. The `narrow()` method checks to ensure that an object of a remote or abstract interface type can be cast to a desired type.

Creating the Enterprise Bean Instance

```
HelloWorld helloBean = home.create();
```

Figure 2-19
The Deployment
Dialog

Figure 2-19
The Deployment
Dialog

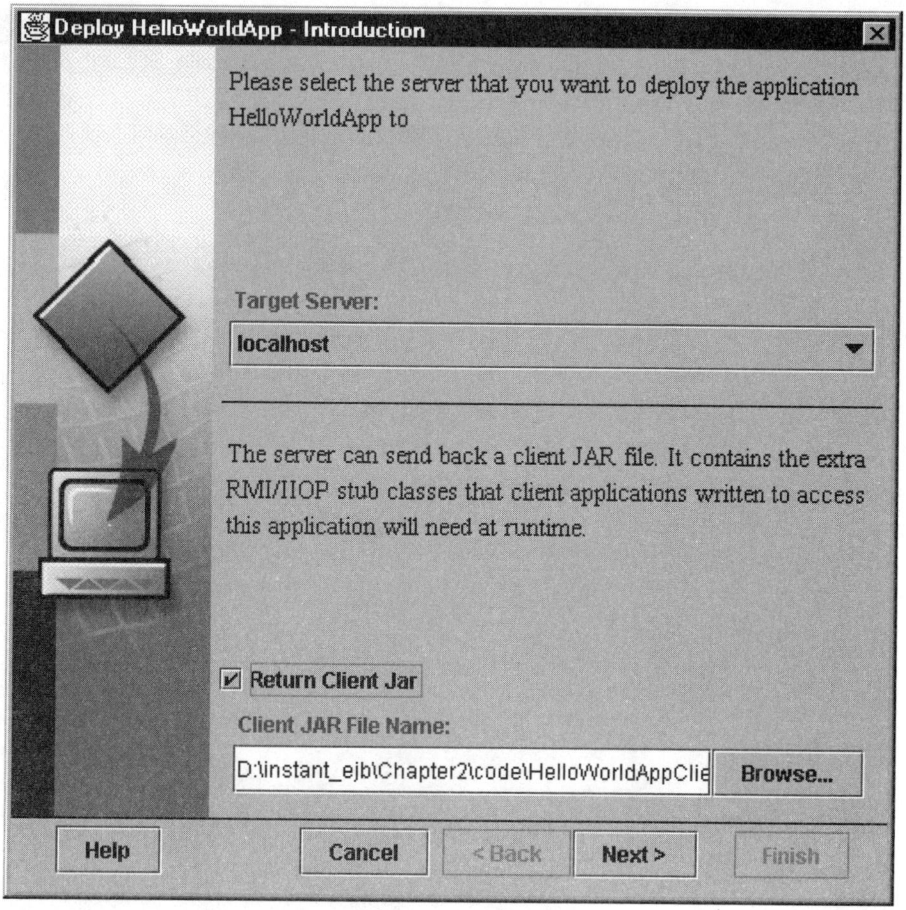

The `create()` method returns an object whose type is *Hello-World*—the type of the remote interface. The bean is now in the *Ready* state, so its methods can be invoked.

Invoking the Bean's Method

```
String msg = helloBean.sayHello();
System.out.println(msg);
```

The client invokes the `sayHello()` method of the remote interface. The EJB container invokes the corresponding method on the instance of HelloWorldBean that is running on the server.

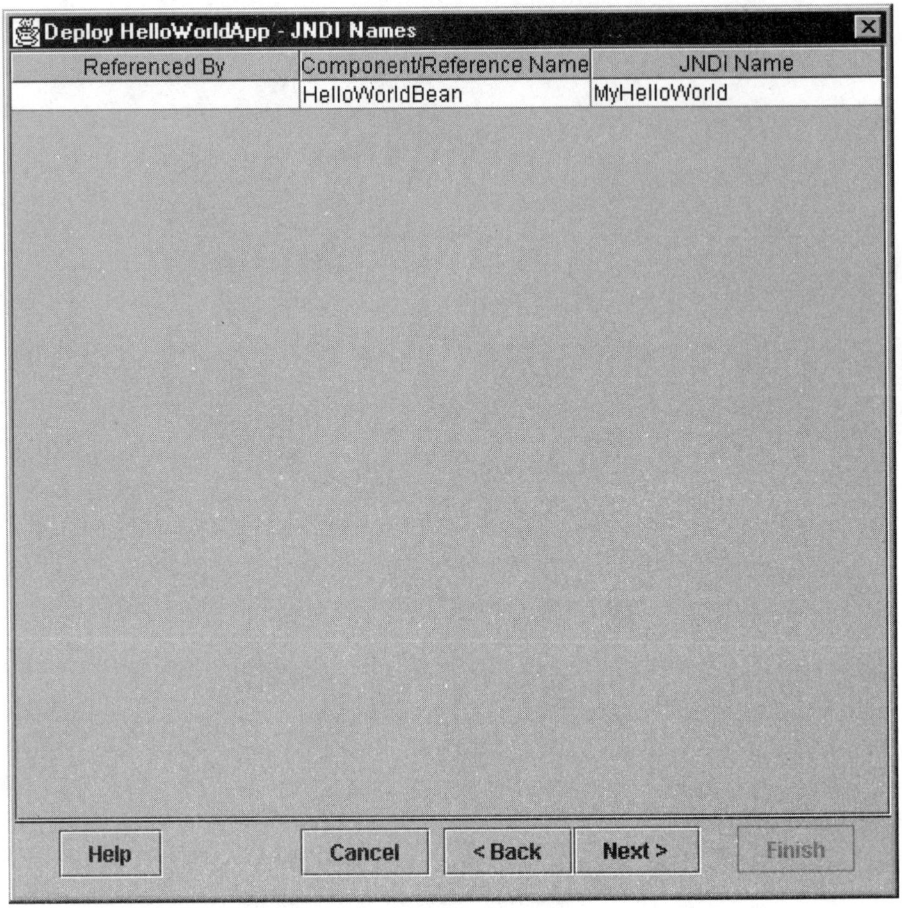

Figure 2-20
Verifying the
JNDI Name

Deploy HelloWorldApp - JNDI Names		✕
Referenced By	Component/Reference Name	JNDI Name
	HelloWorldBean	MyHelloWorld

Help   Cancel   < Back   Next >   Finish

Compiling the Client

We compile the client code using `javac`, the Java compiler. The following script can be used in an NT environment:

```
set J2EE_HOME=c:\j2sdkee1.2.1
set CPATH=.;%J2EE_HOME%\lib\j2ee.jar
javac  -classpath %CPATH% HelloWorldClient.java
```

\Chapter2\code\compileHelloWorldClient.bat

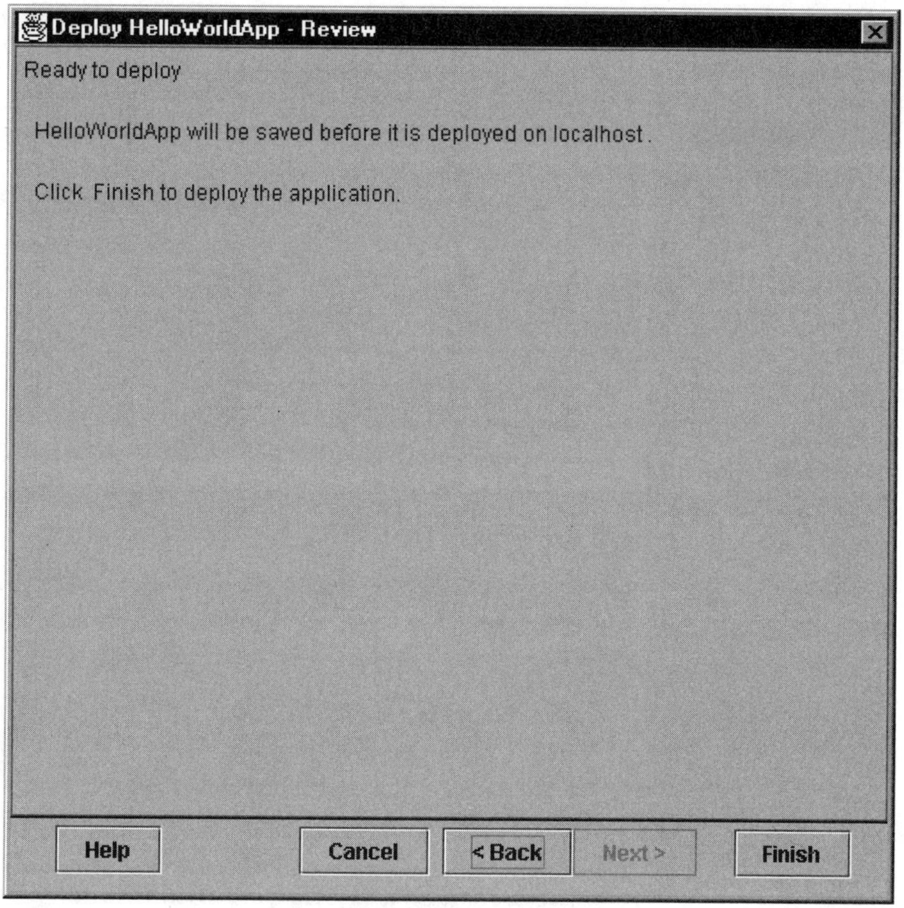

Figure 2-21
Ready for Deployment

The Fruit of Our Labor

At this point, we have written, compiled, packaged, and deployed our enterprise bean and have written and compiled a client that can use it. The only thing left is to execute the client. To communicate with the enterprise bean instance that is running in the EJB container, the client needs to access the *HelloAppClient.jar* file that we created in Figure 2-19 when we checked RETURN CLIENT JAR as we deployed the J2EE application. To enable the client to access the *.jar* file, we add it to the CLASSPATH environment variable. The following script modifies CLASSPATH and runs our client code:

Figure 2-22
Deployment in
Progress

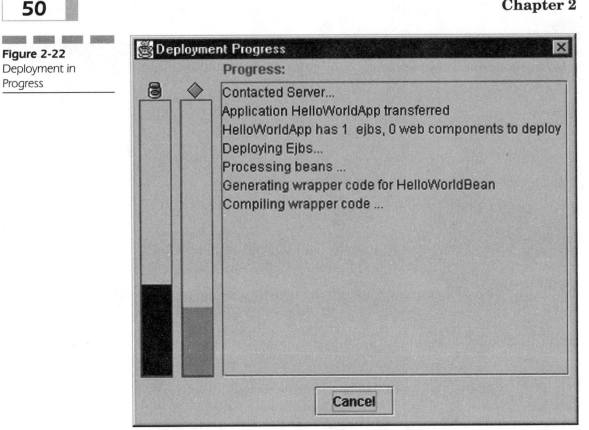

 On The CD

\\\Chapter2\\code\\runHelloWorldClient.bat

```
set J2EE_HOME=c\j2sdkee1.2.1
set CPATH=.;%J2EE_HOME%\lib\j2ee.jar;HelloAppClient.jar
java -classpath "%CPATH%" HelloClient
```

The output from running the .*bat* file is shown in Figure 2-26.

Maintaining an EJB

Now let's see how making a change to an enterprise bean differs
from making a change to the simpler, traditional programs we

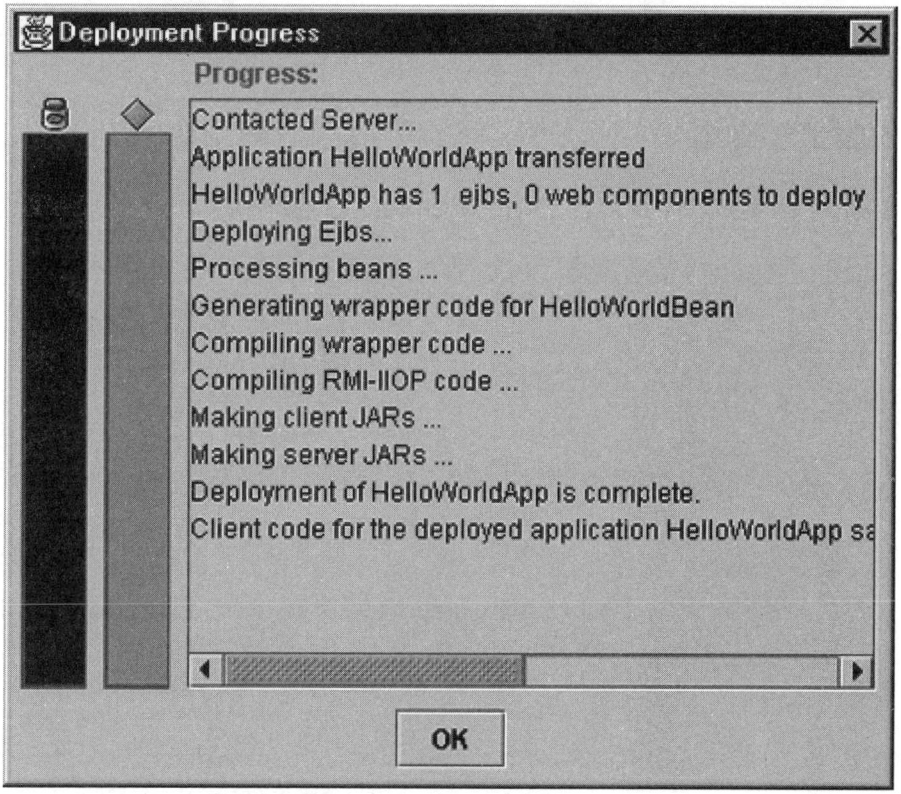

Figure 2-23
Deployment
Complete

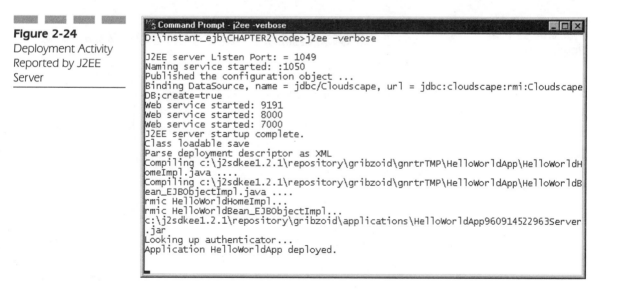

Figure 2-24
Deployment Activity
Reported by J2EE
Server

Figure 2-25
Deployment Activity
Reported by Application Deployment Tool

```
Command Prompt - deploytool                                    _ □ ×

D:\instant_ejb\CHAPTER2\code>deploytool

Deployment tool version 1.2.1. Type deploytool -help for command line options. S
tarting...
Deploy the application in D:\instant_ejb\Chapter2\code\HelloWorldApp.ear on the
server localhost saving the client jar as D:\instant_ejb\Chapter2\code\HelloWorl
dAppClient.jar
Sender object Deploy Tool : Deploy HelloWorldApp on localhost
Remote message: Contacted Server....
Remote message: Application HelloWorldApp transferred.
Remote message: HelloWorldApp has 1 ejbs, 0 web components to deploy.
Remote message: Deploying Ejbs....
Remote message: Processing beans ....
Remote message: Generating wrapper code for HelloWorldBean.
Remote message: Compiling wrapper code ....
Remote message: Compiling RMI-IIOP code ....
Remote message: Making client JARs ....
Remote message: Making server JARs ....
Remote message: Deployment of HelloWorldApp is complete..
Sender object Deploy Tool : client code at http://127.0.0.1:9191/HelloWorldAppCl
ient.jar
Remote message: Client code for the deployed application HelloWorldApp saved to
D:\instant_ejb\Chapter2\code\HelloWorldAppClient.jar.
```

have maintained before. If we were requested to change the message displayed by a simple *HelloWorld* program from "Hello World!" to "Hi there, world!", we would simply edit the source code, recompile the program, and perform a quick test run. Making a similar change to our *HelloWorldBean* starts out the same—modifying the source code and recompiling it.

Figure 2-26
Output from
HelloWorldClient

```
Command Prompt                                                 _ □ ×

D:\instant_ejb\CHAPTER2\code>runHelloWorldClient

D:\instant_ejb\CHAPTER2\code>set J2EE_HOME=c:\j2sdkee1.2.1

D:\instant_ejb\CHAPTER2\code>set CPATH=.;c:\j2sdkee1.2.1\lib\j2ee.jar;
HelloWorldAppClient.jar

D:\instant_ejb\CHAPTER2\code>java -classpath ".;c:\j2sdkee1.2.1\lib\j2
ee.jar;HelloWorldAppClient.jar" HelloWorldClient

Hello World!

D:\instant_ejb\CHAPTER2\code>_
```

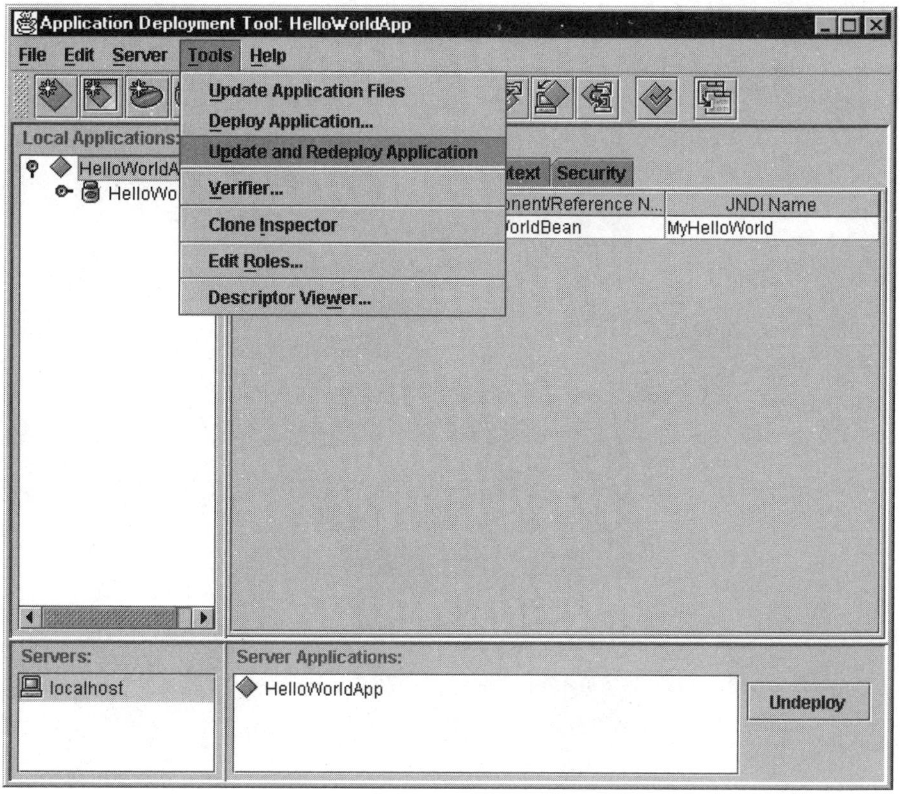

Figure 2-27
Preparing to Update
and Redeploy
Application

Figure 2-27
Preparing to Update
and Redeploy
Application

```java
import java.rmi.RemoteException;
import javax.ejb.SessionBean;
import javax.ejb.SessionContext;
public class HelloWorldBean implements SessionBean {
    public String sayHello() {
       return "Hi there, World!";
    }
    public HelloWorldBean() {}
    public void ejbCreate() {}
    public void ejbRemove() {}
    public void ejbActivate() {}
    public void ejbPassivate() {}
    public void setSessionContext(SessionContext sc) {}
}
```

The change we made is reflected in the line:

```
return "Hi there, World!";
```

We recompile our code using the same .bat file as we did before
by typing the command:

Figure 2-28
Redeployment
Complete

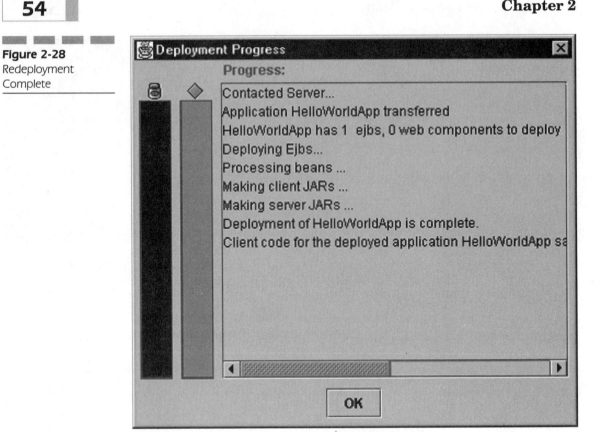

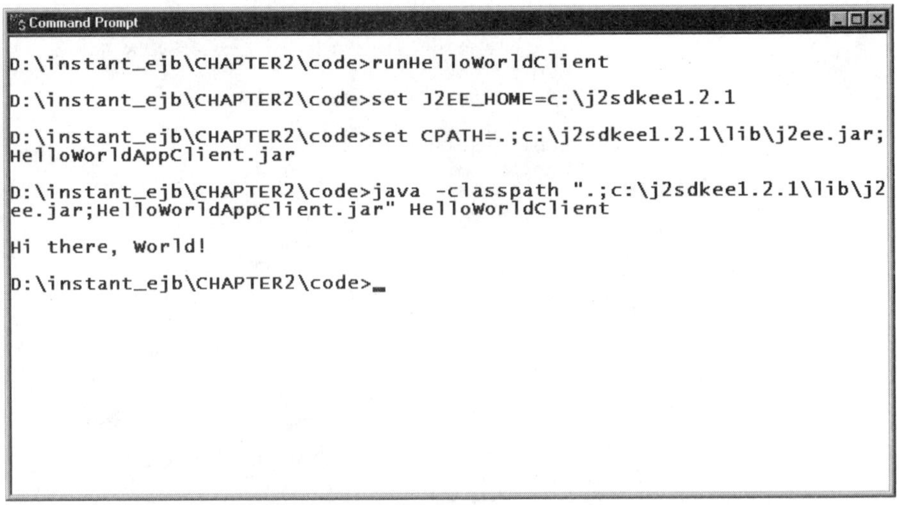

Figure 2-29
Output from the
Modified Bean

`compileHelloWorld`

To complete the process, we must use the Application Deployment Tool. We select the "Update and Redeploy Application" option from the "Tools" menu item as shown in Figure 2-27. When we do so, a "Deployment Progress" dialog like the one we saw when we initially deployed the application is displayed. When deployment is complete, the dialog will look like Figure 2-28.

When the CANCEL button in the "Deployment Progress" dialog changes to OK, the redeployment process is complete. We can now click on OK and run our client. We see from Figure 2-29 that the output reflects the change we made.

NOTE: *This version of the server does not detect the change until the server is stopped and restarted.*

Summary

In this chapter we have made the point that developing and deploying an enterprise bean is somewhat complex; however, we are shielded from most of the complexity by a graphical tool, which in our case, was the Deployment Tool that is included as part of the Reference Implementation. The J2EE-compliant environment you use might be different but you will recognize the principles presented in this chapter.

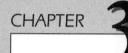

A Few Simple Stateless Session Beans

In this chapter:

- Temperature conversion
- State/province abbreviation validation
- Zip code/postal code verifier
- DES encoder/decoder
- Base64 encoder/decoder

In the last chapter, we saw how to write the Java code for a simple enterprise bean, how to use the Application Deployment Tool to package and deploy it, and how to write a simple client to test our bean. In this chapter, we examine several additional examples of stateless session beans. These are only slightly more complex than *HelloWorld;* however, they serve to demonstrate some situations in which session beans are an appropriate solution. By the end of this chapter, you should be comfortable writing a bean's code and should think of it as a trivial task.

Temperature Conversion

This bean performs simple conversions between temperatures on the Celsius, Fahrenheit, and Kelvin scales. Such conversions are perfect candidates for stateless session beans.

- The only variable data required for any of the bean's methods to accomplish its task are passed to it by the client as arguments.
- The result of a temperature conversion by one of the bean's methods has no effect on subsequent invocations of that method or any other method.
- After it performs a temperature conversion for one client, the bean can be assigned to perform work on behalf of another client.

The Remote Interface

The code for the remote interface is shown below. This is the client's view of the bean. The only methods the client can invoke are those that are declared in the remote interface.

 \Chapter3\code\Temperature.java

```
import javax.ejb.EJBObject;
import java.rmi.RemoteException;

public interface Temperature extends EJBObject {

  public double celsiusToFahrenheit(double celsius)
    throws RemoteException;

  public double celsiusToKelvin(double celsius)
    throws RemoteException;

  public double fahrenheitToCelsius(double fahrenheit)
    throws RemoteException;

  public double fahrenheitToKelvin(double fahrenheit)
    throws RemoteException;

  public double kelvinToFahrenheit(double kelvin)
    throws RemoteException;

  public double kelvinToCelsius(double kelvin)
    throws RemoteException;
}
```

The Home Interface

This is the client's initial point of contact with the bean. When a client wishes to uses a bean, it uses the Java Naming and Directory Interface (JNDI) to locate the bean. JNDI returns a remote reference to the bean's EJB home, which implements the home interface. As we will see shortly when we examine the client code, the client invokes the create() method on the home interface to obtain a reference to the bean's remote interface. Here is the code:

\Chapter3\code\TemperatureHome.java

```
import java.io.Serializable;
import java.rmi.RemoteException;
import javax.ejb.CreateException;
import javax.ejb.EJBHome;

public interface TemperatureHome
        extends EJBHome {
    Temperature create()
        throws RemoteException, CreateException;
}
```

The Enterprise Bean

This code implements those business methods declared in the remote interface. When the client invokes a method on the remote interface (which is actually a remote reference to an EJB object), the EJB object delegates that method call to the bean class.

\Chapter3\code\TemperatureBean.java

```
import java.rmi.RemoteException;
import javax.ejb.SessionBean;
import javax.ejb.SessionContext;

public class TemperatureBean
  implements SessionBean {

  private static final double ABSOLUTE_ZERO = -273.16;

  public double celsiusToFahrenheit(double celsius) {
    return celsius * 9.0/ 5.0 + 32.0;
  }
```

```
public double celsiusToKelvin(double celsius) {
  return celsius + ABSOLUTE_ZERO;
}

public double fahrenheitToCelsius(double fahrenheit) {
  return (fahrenheit - 32.0) * 5.0 /9.0;
}

public double fahrenheitToKelvin(double fahrenheit) {
  return celsiusToKelvin(fahrenheitToCelsius(fahrenheit));
}

public double kelvinToFahrenheit(double kelvin) {
  return celsiusToFahrenheit(kelvinToCelsius(kelvin));
}

public double kelvinToCelsius(double kelvin) {
  return ABSOLUTE_ZERO - kelvin;
}

public void ejbCreate() {}
public void ejbRemove() {}
public void ejbActivate() {}
public void ejbPassivate() {}
public void setSessionContext(SessionContext sc) {}
}
```

Packaging and Deploying the Bean

 \Chapter3\code\compileTemperature.bat

In the interest of conserving space, we will not present a step-by-step description of how to package and deploy the bean. The procedure begins with compilation of the remote interface, home interface, and bean code using *compileTemperature.bat* and after that is the same as that which we followed to package and deploy *HelloWorld*. The parameters you will need are shown in Table 3-1.

When you have packaged and deployed the application containing the *Temperature* bean, the Application Deployment Tool should look like Figure 3-1.

TABLE 3-1

Parameters Required
to Package and
Deploy Temperature
EJB

Parameter	Value
Application File Name	TemperatureApp.ear
Application Display Name	TemperatureApp
JAR DisplayName	TemperatureJAR
Enterprise Bean Class	TemperatureBean
Home Interface	TemperatureHome
Remote Interface	Temperature
Enterprise Bean Display Name	TemperatureBean
JNDI Name	MyTemperature

Figure 3-1
TemperatureApp
Packaged and
Deployed

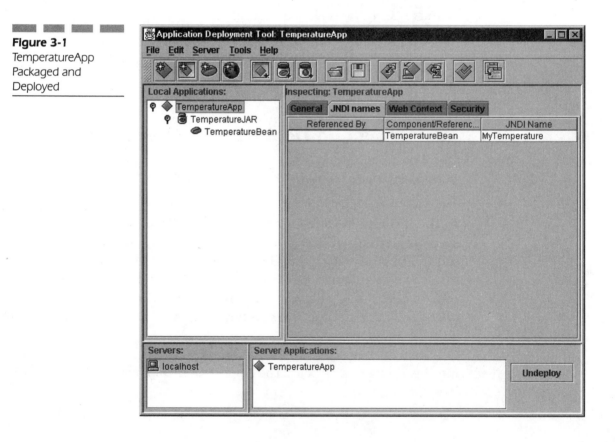

NOTE: *To avoid clutter and distractions in the book, before each application was deployed, all prior applications were undeployed and their components were removed. If you have done the exercise from Chapter 2 and the contents of your Application Deployment Tool does not look like Figure 3-1 but contains your HelloWorld, this is OK.*

The Client

The client code we will use to test the *Temperature* bean, shown below, performs the following actions:

- locates the home interface
- creates a bean instance
- invokes the bean's methods

***Chapter3\\code\\TemperatureClient.java*

```java
import javax.naming.Context;
import javax.naming.InitialContext;
import javax.rmi.PortableRemoteObject;

import TemperatureBean;

import TemperatureHome;

public class TemperatureClient {

  public static void main(String[] args) {

    try {
      Context initial = new InitialContext();
      Object objref = initial.lookup("MyTemperature");

      TemperatureHome home =
        (TemperatureHome)PortableRemoteObject.narrow(objref,
          TemperatureHome.class);

      Temperature converter = home.create();

      double bpH2OCelsius = 100;
      double bpH2OFahrenheit =
        converter.celsiusToFahrenheit(bpH2OCelsius);
```

```
        double bpH2OKelvin =
          converter.celsiusToKelvin(bpH2OCelsius);

        System.out.println();
        System.out.println("Boiling point of water:");
        System.out.println(bpH2OCelsius + "C");
        System.out.println(bpH2OFahrenheit + "F");
        System.out.println(bpH2OKelvin + "K");

        double bodyTemperatureFahrenheit = 98.6;
        double bodyTemperatureCelsius =
          converter.fahrenheitToCelsius(bodyTemperatureFahrenheit);
        double bodyTemperatureKelvin =
          converter.fahrenheitToKelvin(bodyTemperatureFahrenheit);

        System.out.println();
        System.out.println("Human body temperature:");
        System.out.println(bodyTemperatureFahrenheit + "F");
        System.out.println(bodyTemperatureCelsius + "C");
        System.out.println(bodyTemperatureKelvin + "K");

        double absZeroCelsius =
          converter.kelvinToCelsius(0.0);
        double absZeroFahrenheit =
          converter.kelvinToFahrenheit(0.0);

        System.out.println();
        System.out.println("Absolute Zero:");
        System.out.println(absZeroCelsius + "C");
        System.out.println(absZeroFahrenheit + "F");
      }
      catch (Exception ex) {
        System.err.println("Caught an unexpected exception!");
        ex.printStackTrace();
      }
    }
  }
```

\Chapter3\code\TemperatureClient.bat

We use *compileTemperatureClient.bat* to compile the client code. When we use *runTemperatureClient.bat* to execute our client code, we see output like that shown in Figure 3-2.

\Chapter3\code\compileTemperatureClient.bat
\Chapter3\code\runTemperatureClient.bat

Figure 3-2
Output from
Temperature-
Client

```
Command Prompt                                                        _□×
D:\instant_ejb\CHAPTER3\code>runTemperatureClient

D:\instant_ejb\CHAPTER3\code>set J2EE_HOME=c:\j2sdkee1.2.1

D:\instant_ejb\CHAPTER3\code>set CPATH=.;c:\j2sdkee1.2.1\lib\j2ee.jar;Temperatur
eAppClient.jar

D:\instant_ejb\CHAPTER3\code>java -classpath ".;c:\j2sdkee1.2.1\lib\j2ee.jar;Tem
peratureAppClient.jar" TemperatureClient
Boiling point of water:
100.0C
212.0F
-173.16000000000003K

Human body temperature:
98.6F
37.0C
-236.16000000000003K

Absolute Zero:
-273.16C
-459.688F

D:\instant_ejb\CHAPTER3\code>_
```

Packaging and Deploying Groups of Beans

Up to this point, the applications we have seen have contained a single `.jar` file that contained a single bean. Real-world solutions usually require a variety of beans with beans that implement the business logic for related activities being stored in the same `.jar` file. Let us see how that is accomplished.

Let us suppose we were implementing a system that mails invoices. To ensure that the postal service could deliver our mailings, we should validate the addresses our customers provide. Let's examine two beans that we would use in the validation process.

State/Province Abbreviation Validation

The first bean is used to check whether a two-character abbreviation represents a U.S. state or a Canadian province. Since this involves nothing more than a simple table lookup, we can use a stateless session bean.

The Remote Interface

The remote interface is shown below. It advertises two methods that a client can invoke: isValidAbbreviation() and getStateProvinceName().

\Chapter3\code\StateProvince.java

```
import javax.ejb.EJBObject;
import java.rmi.RemoteException;

public interface StateProvince
  extends EJBObject {

  public boolean isValidAbbreviation(String abbr)
    throws RemoteException;

  public String getStateProvinceName(String abbr)
    throws RemoteException;
}
```

The Home Interface

Here is the code for the home interface:

\Chapter3\code\StateProvinceHome.java

```
import java.io.Serializable;
import java.rmi.RemoteException;
import javax.ejb.CreateException;
import javax.ejb.EJBHome;

public interface StateProvinceHome
      extends EJBHome {
    StateProvince create()
      throws RemoteException, CreateException;
}
```

The Enterprise Bean

The bean's code is shown below. This is the first bean we have seen whose `ejbCreate()` method is not empty. Each time the EJB container creates an instance, the `ejbCreate()` method is invoked. The code in this method creates and populates a hashtable, which is saved in the instance variable `spTable`.

You may be wondering why a stateless session bean contains an instance variable. After all, isn't an object's state at any point in time defined by the contents of its instance variables? The answer is that stateless session beans can indeed have instance variables but these variables cannot contain data that define a *conversational* state. You should keep in mind that a client must never assume that the same bean instance will service it every time. Since the instance variable `spTable` contains identical data for every instance, it makes no difference what instance is used to satisfy a client request. If, however, you decided you could speed things up by performing the lookup only if the value passed as an argument by the client was different from the contents of an instance variable named `lastAbbrev`, you would encounter problems. The `lastAbbrev` you check might not belong to the same object as the one that processed the last client call.

 On the CD

\Chapter3\code\StateProvinceBean.java

```java
import java.rmi.RemoteException;
import javax.ejb.SessionBean;
import javax.ejb.SessionContext;

import java.util.Hashtable;

public class StateProvinceBean

  implements SessionBean {

  private Hashtable spTable;

  public boolean isValidAbbreviation(String abbr) {
    return spTable.containsKey(abbr);
  }
```

```
public String getStateProvinceName(String abbr) {
  return (String)spTable.get(abbr);
}

public void ejbCreate() {
  String[][] spData =
    {{"AL","Alabama"},
     {"AK","Alaska"},
     {"AS","American Samoa"},

                 .
                 .
                 .

     {"QC","Quebec"},
     {"SK","Saskatchewan"},
     {"YT","Yukon"}};

  spTable = new Hashtable();
  for (int i = 0; i < spData.length; ++i) {
    spTable.put(spData[i][0], spData[i][1]);
  }
}

public void ejbRemove() {}
public void ejbActivate() {}
public void ejbPassivate() {}
public void setSessionContext(SessionContext sc) {}
}
```

NOTE: *In the interest of conserving space, only a portion of the two-dimensional array* spData *is shown. The complete code is contained on the CD.*

Zip Code/Postal Code Verifier

The next component in our small validation suite is one that determines whether a string contains a valid U.S. ZIP code or Canadian postal code.

The Remote Interface

The remote interface defines two business methods: isValid-PostalCode() and isValidZipCode(). Here is the code:

\Chapter3\code\PostalCode.java

```java
import javax.ejb.EJBObject;
import java.rmi.RemoteException;

public interface PostalCode extends EJBObject {

  public boolean isValidPostalCode(String code)
    throws RemoteException;

  public boolean isValidZipCode(String code)
    throws RemoteException;
}
```

The Home Interface

The home interface looks like this:

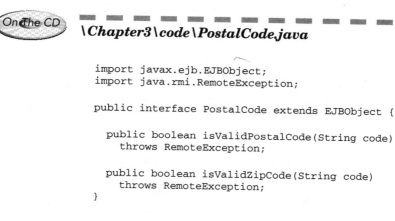 **\Chapter3\code\PostalCodeHome.java**

```java
import java.io.Serializable;
import java.rmi.RemoteException;
import javax.ejb.CreateException;
import javax.ejb.EJBHome;

public interface PostalCodeHome
      extends EJBHome {
    PostalCode create()
       throws RemoteException, CreateException;
}
```

The Enterprise Bean

The final piece of code is the bean:

 \Chapter3\code\PostalCodeBean.java

```java
import java.rmi.RemoteException;
import javax.ejb.SessionBean;
import javax.ejb.SessionContext;
```

```
public class PostalCodeBean
  implements SessionBean {

  public boolean isValidPostalCode(String code) {
    int len;
    char c;

    if ((len = code.length()) != 7) {
      return false;
    }
    if ((!Character.isDigit(code.charAt(1))) ||
        (!Character.isDigit(code.charAt(4))) ||
        (!Character.isDigit(code.charAt(6))) ||
        (!Character.isSpaceChar(code.charAt(3))))
      return false;

    String ucs = code.toUpperCase();
    if ((!Character.isLetter(ucs.charAt(0))) ||
        (!Character.isLetter(ucs.charAt(2))) ||
        (!Character.isLetter(ucs.charAt(5))))
      return false;
    return true;
  }

  public boolean isValidZipCode(String code) {
    boolean tf;
    switch (code.length()) {
      case 5:
        tf = isNumericString(code);
        break;
      case 10:
        if (code.charAt(5) != '-')
          return false;
        tf = isNumericString(code.substring(0,5)) &
          isNumericString(code.substring(6));
        break;
      default:
        tf = false;
    }
    return tf;
  }

  private boolean isNumericString(String str) {
    for (int i = 0; i < str.length(); ++i) {
      if (!Character.isDigit(str.charAt(i))) {
        return false;
      }
    }
    return true;
  }

  public void ejbCreate() {}
  public void ejbRemove() {}
  public void ejbActivate() {}
```

```
        public void ejbPassivate() {}
        public void setSessionContext(SessionContext sc) {}
    }
```

Packaging and Deploying PostalApp

We are now ready to package and deploy an application containing a JAR with two beans. The process begins with compilation of the two beans using *compileStateProvince.bat* and *compilePostalCode.bat*.

Chapter3\\code\\compileStateProvince.bat
Chapter3\\code\\compilePostalCode.bat

If you package the *StateProvinceBean* first using the parameters shown in Table 3-2, you should end up with the Application Deployment Tool looking like Figure 3-3.

We are now ready to add another bean to the JAR. We start by clicking on PostalJAR to select it from the box labeled Local Applications: as shown in Figure 3-4. We then select "New Enterprise Bean . . ." from the "File" menu item. This results in the

TABLE 3-2	Parameter	Value
Parameters Required to Package *StateProvince* EJB	Application File Name	PostalApp.ear
	Application Display Name	PostalApp
	JAR DisplayName	PostalJAR
	Enterprise Bean Class	StateProvinceBean
	Home Interface	StateProvinceHome
	Remote Interface	StateProvince
	Enterprise Bean Display Name	StateProvinceBean
	JNDI Name	MyStateProvince

Figure 3-3
PostalApp After
Addition of First Bean

appearance of the "Bean Wizard—Introduction" dialog. When we click on NEXT> in this dialog, we see the screen shown in Figure 3-5. Notice that the entry field labeled "JAR Display Name:" is already populated with the value "PostalJAR" and is grayed out, indicating that it cannot be modified. Notice also that the box labeled CONTENTS contains the class files that comprise the *StateProvince* bean that we just finished inserting into the JAR.

From this point forward, the procedure is identical to that which we have already followed (i.e., clicking on the ADD . . . button to the right of the box labeled CONTENTS, selecting and adding the *.class* files, etc.). The information you need to complete the process is shown in Table 3-3.

Figure 3-4
Selecting JAR to Add
a New Bean

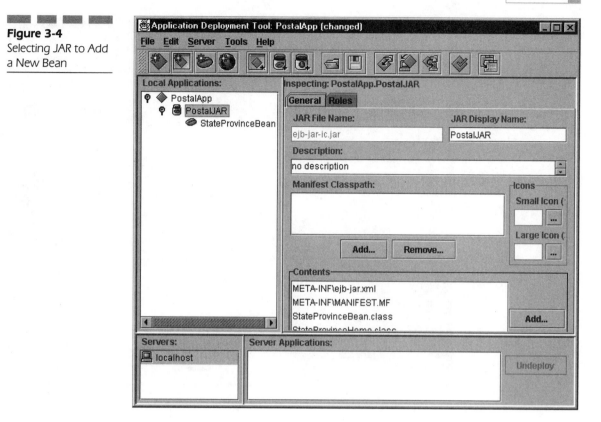

Figure 3-4
Selecting JAR to Add
a New Bean

After we have finished adding the second bean, we select "PostalApp" from the box labeled LOCAL APPLICATIONS: and enter *MyPostalCode* as a JNDI name. We should now be looking at a screen like that shown in Figure 3-6.

The final stage is deployment, which is carried out according to the same procedure as we have already seen.

The Client

The client code we will use to test our new beans can be found in the file named *PostalClient.java*. We compile it using *compilePostalClient.bat* and run it using *runPostalClient.bat*. Here it is:

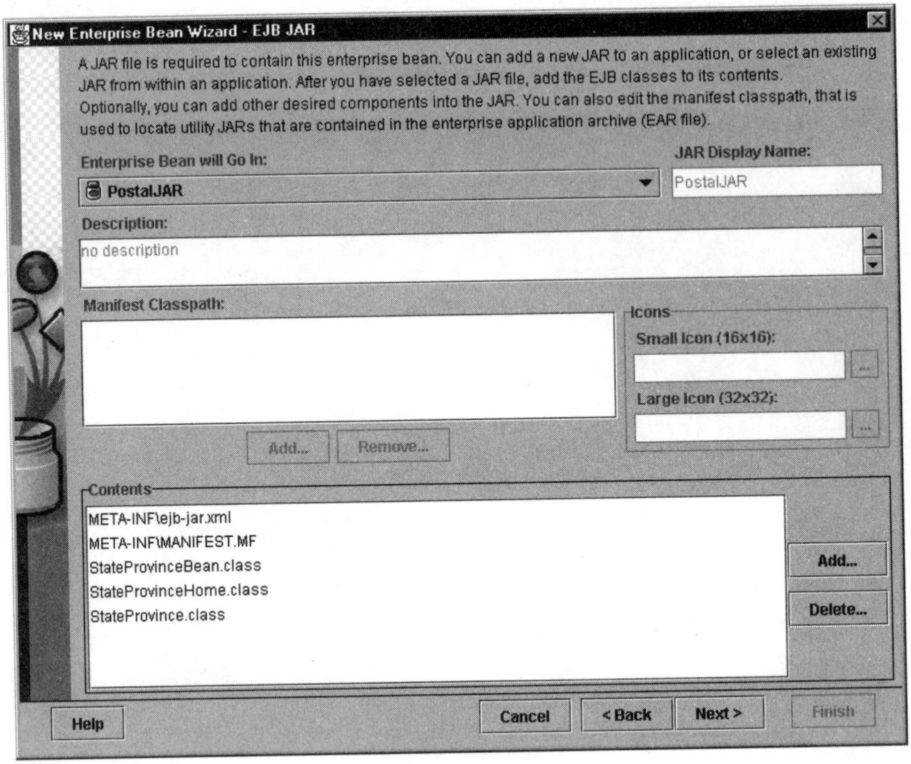

Figure 3-5
Adding Another Bean
to the JAR

New Enterprise Bean Wizard - EJB JAR

A JAR file is required to contain this enterprise bean. You can add a new JAR to an application, or select an existing JAR from within an application. After you have selected a JAR file, add the EJB classes to its contents. Optionally, you can add other desired components into the JAR. You can also edit the manifest classpath, that is used to locate utility JARs that are contained in the enterprise application archive (EAR file).

Enterprise Bean will Go In:

JAR Display Name:

PostalJAR

PostalJAR

Description:

no description

Manifest Classpath:

Icons

Small Icon (16x16):

Large Icon (32x32):

Add... | Remove...

Contents

META-INF\ejb-jar.xml
META-INF\MANIFEST.MF
StateProvinceBean.class
StateProvinceHome.class
StateProvince.class

Add...

Delete...

Help | Cancel | < Back | Next > | Finish

TABLE 3-3

Parameters Required
to Package
PostalCode EJB

Parameter	Value
Enterprise Bean Class	StateProvinceBean
Home Interface	StateProvinceHome
Remote Interface	StateProvince
Enterprise Bean Display Name	StateProvinceBean
JNDI Name	MyStateProvince

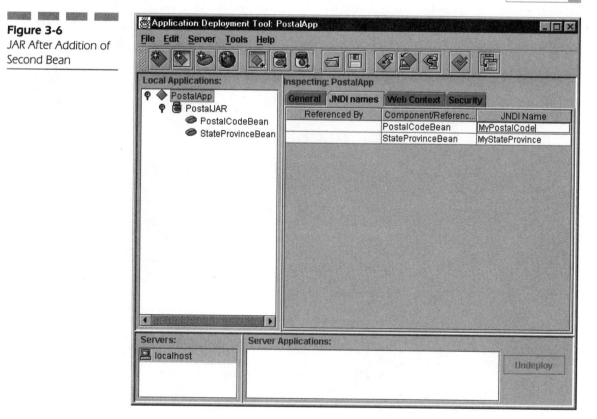

Figure 3-6
JAR After Addition of
Second Bean

 On the CD

\Chapter3\code\PostalClient.java
\Chapter3\code\compilePostalClient.bat
\Chapter3\code\runPostalClient.bat

```java
import javax.naming.Context;
import javax.naming.InitialContext;
import javax.rmi.PortableRemoteObject;

import StateProvinceBean;
import StateProvinceHome;

import PostalCodeBean;
import PostalCodeHome;
```

```
public class PostalClient {

public static void main(String[] args) {

    String[] testAbbrevs = {"AL","AX","NF","GU"};
    String[] testCodes = {"A2A 1M7","999","07871-1341","10801"};

    try {
      Context initial = new InitialContext();
      Object objref = initial.lookup("MyStateProvince");
      StateProvinceHome spHome =
        (StateProvinceHome)PortableRemoteObject.narrow(objref,
          StateProvinceHome.class);

      StateProvince sp = spHome.create();

      objref = initial.lookup("MyPostalCode");

      PostalCodeHome pcHome =
        (PostalCodeHome)PortableRemoteObject.narrow(objref,
          PostalCodeHome.class);

      PostalCode pc = pcHome.create();

      for (int i = 0; i < testAbbrevs.length; ++i) {
        System.out.print(testAbbrevs[i]);
        if (sp.isValidAbbreviation(testAbbrevs[i])) {
          System.out.println(" is the abbreviation for " +
            sp.getStateProvinceName(testAbbrevs[i]));
        }
        else {
          System.out.println(" is not an valid abbreviation " +
            "for a state or province");
        }
      }

        for (int i = 0; i < testCodes.length; ++i) {
          System.out.print(testCodes[i]);
          if (pc.isValidPostalCode(testCodes[i])) {
            System.out.println(" is a valid Canadian postal code");
          }
          else
            if (pc.isValidZipCode(testCodes[i])) {
              System.out.println(" is a valid US ZIP code");
            }
            else {
              System.out.println(" is not a valid code");
            }
        }
      }
    catch (Exception ex) {
```

```
        System.err.println("Caught an unexpected exception!");
        ex.printStackTrace();
    }
  }
}
```

The client starts by executing the following code:

```
Context initial = new InitialContext();
```

This creates a JNDI naming context. This same instance of *Context* can be used to locate both beans we will be using. We get a remote reference to the first bean's remote interface using the following code:

```
Object objref = initial.lookup("MyStateProvince");
StateProvinceHome spHome =
  (StateProvinceHome)PortableRemoteObject.narrow(objref,
    StateProvinceHome.class);
StateProvince sp = spHome.create();
```

Since the object objref is used only as an intermediary, we can reuse it to obtain a remote reference to the next bean's remote interface as follows:

```
objref = initial.lookup("MyPostalCode");

    PostalCodeHome pcHome =
      (PostalCodeHome)PortableRemoteObject.narrow(objref,
        PostalCodeHome.class);

    PostalCode pc = pcHome.create();
```

The remainder of the client code simply invokes the business methods of our two beans and prints the result as shown in Figure 3-7.

DES Encoder/Decoder

The last application we will deploy also contains a JAR with two beans. The first of these is a bean that uses the Digital Encryption

Figure 3-7
Result ot Running
PostalClient

```
Command Prompt                                                    _ □ ×
D:\instant_ejb\CHAPTER3\code>runPostalClient

D:\instant_ejb\CHAPTER3\code>set J2EE_HOME=c:\j2sdkee1.2.1

D:\instant_ejb\CHAPTER3\code>set CPATH=.;c:\j2sdkee1.2.1\lib\j2ee.jar;PostalAppC
lient.jar

D:\instant_ejb\CHAPTER3\code>java -classpath ".;c:\j2sdkee1.2.1\lib\j2ee.jar;Pos
talAppClient.jar" PostalClient
AL is the abbreviation for Alabama
AX is not an valid abbreviation for a state or province
NF is the abbreviation for Newfoundland
GU is the abbreviation for Guam
A2A 1M7 is a valid Canadian postal code
999 is not a valid code
07871-1341 is a valid US ZIP code
10801 is a valid US ZIP code

D:\instant_ejb\CHAPTER3\code>_
```

Standard (DES) algorithm to encrypt cleartext or decrypt ciphertext, using a key that is passed as a parameter. Since we already
know the roles of the remote interface, home interface, and bean
code, we will simply present the code without discussion.

The Remote Interface

The code for the remote interface is as follows:

On the CD **\Chapter3\code\SimpleDES.java**

```java
import javax.ejb.EJBObject;
import java.rmi.RemoteException;

public interface SimpleDES
  extends EJBObject {
  public byte[] encode(byte[] clearText, byte[] rawKey)
    throws RemoteException;

  public byte[] decode(byte[] cipherText, byte[] rawKey)
    throws RemoteException;
}
```

The Home Interface

Here is the home interface:

\Chapter3\code\SimpleDESHome.java

```java
import java.security.NoSuchAlgorithmException;

import javax.crypto.NoSuchPaddingException;

import java.io.Serializable;
import java.rmi.RemoteException;
import javax.ejb.CreateException;
import javax.ejb.EJBHome;

public interface SimpleDESHome
    extends EJBHome {
  SimpleDES create()
    throws RemoteException, CreateException;
}
```

The Enterprise Bean

The bean code listing follows:

\Chapter3\code\SimpleDESBean.java

```java
import java.security.InvalidKeyException;
import java.security.NoSuchAlgorithmException;

import javax.crypto.Cipher;
import javax.crypto.BadPaddingException;
import javax.crypto.IllegalBlockSizeException;
import javax.crypto.NoSuchPaddingException;
import javax.crypto.spec.SecretKeySpec;

import java.rmi.RemoteException;
import javax.ejb.SessionBean;
import javax.ejb.SessionContext;
public class SimpleDESBean
  implements SessionBean {

  public byte[] encode(byte[] clearText, byte[] rawKey)
      throws RemoteException {
```

```
SecretKeySpec skeySpec = new SecretKeySpec(rawKey, "DES");

try {
  Cipher desCipher = Cipher.getInstance("DES");

  desCipher.init(Cipher.ENCRYPT_MODE, skeySpec);

  return desCipher.doFinal(clearText);
}

catch (NoSuchAlgorithmException e) {
  throw new RemoteException("NoSuchAlgorithm");
}
catch (NoSuchPaddingException e) {
  throw new RemoteException("NoSuchPaddingException");
}
catch (BadPaddingException e) {
  throw new RemoteException("BadPaddingException");
}
catch (InvalidKeyException e) {
  throw new RemoteException("InvalidKeyException");
}

catch (IllegalBlockSizeException e) {
  throw new RemoteException("IllegalBlockSizeException");
}
}

public byte[] decode(byte[] cipherText, byte[] rawKey)
    throws RemoteException {

  SecretKeySpec skeySpec = new SecretKeySpec(rawKey, "DES");

  try {
    Cipher desCipher = Cipher.getInstance("DES");
    desCipher.init(Cipher.DECRYPT_MODE, skeySpec);
    return desCipher.doFinal(cipherText);
  }
  catch (NoSuchAlgorithmException e) {
    throw new RemoteException("NoSuchAlgorithm");
  }
  catch (NoSuchPaddingException e) {
    throw new RemoteException("NoSuchPaddingException");
  }
  catch (InvalidKeyException e) {
    throw new RemoteException("InvalidKeyException");
  }
  catch (IllegalBlockSizeException e) {
    throw new RemoteException("IllegalBlockSizeException");
  }
  catch (BadPaddingException e) {
    throw new RemoteException("BadPaddingException");
  }
}
```

```
public void ejbCreate() {
}

public void ejbRemove() {}
public void ejbActivate() {}
public void ejbPassivate() {}
public void setSessionContext(SessionContext sc) {}
}
```

> **NOTE:** *Compilation of the bean code requires the Java Cryptography Extension (JCE), which can be downloaded from* `java.sun.com`. *The latest version is exportable. Developers from the United States and Canada can download the domestic distribution bundle; others can download the global distribution bundle. Be careful to follow the installation instructions. It is easiest to install all the JAR files as "installed" extensions by placing them in the directory* `JAVA_HOME\lib\ext`. *The file* `JAVA_HOME\jre\lib\security\java.security` *must also be modified to include the JCE provider.*

Packaging the Bean

The bean code can be compiled using *compileSimpleDES.bat* and packaged in the same manner as we packaged the *StateProvince* bean.

Chapter3\\code\\compileSimpleDES.bat

The required parameters are shown in Table 3-4.

Base64 Encoder/Decoder

Ciphertext can contain characters that make transmission of such text using email unreliable. For this reason, ciphertext is usually encoded as base64 by a sender and decoded by the recipient. Our

TABLE 3-4

Parameters Required
to Package the
DESBean

Parameter	Value
Application File Name	CryptoApp.ear
Application Display Name	CryptoApp
JAR DisplayName	CryptoJAR
Enterprise Bean Class	SimpleDESBean
Home Interface	SimpleDESHome
Remote Interface	SimpleDES
Enterprise Bean Display Name	SimpleDESBean
JNDI Name	MySimpleDES

last bean in this chapter is a Base64 encoder/decoder. As was the case with the *SimpleDESBean,* we will simply present the code without discussion.

The Remote Interface

This is the code for the remote interface:

On the CD **\Chapter3\code\Base64.java**

```java
import javax.ejb.EJBObject;
import java.rmi.RemoteException;

public interface Base64
  extends EJBObject {

  public String encode(byte[] ba)
    throws RemoteException;

  public byte[] decode(String s)
    throws RemoteException;
}
```

The Home Interface

This is the home interface:

\Chapter3\code\Base64Home.java

```java
import java.io.Serializable;
import java.rmi.RemoteException;
import javax.ejb.CreateException;
import javax.ejb.EJBHome;

public interface Base64Home
      extends EJBHome {
   Base64 create()
      throws RemoteException, CreateException;
}
```

The Enterprise Bean

Here is the listing of the bean code:

\Chapter3\code\Base64Bean.java

```java
import java.rmi.RemoteException;
import javax.ejb.SessionBean;
import javax.ejb.SessionContext;

public class Base64Bean
   implements SessionBean {

   private final static char[] map = {
      'A', 'B', 'C', 'D', 'E', 'F', 'G', 'H',
      'I', 'J', 'K', 'L', 'M', 'N', 'O', 'P',
      'Q', 'R', 'S', 'T', 'U', 'V', 'W', 'X',
      'Y', 'Z', 'a', 'b', 'c', 'd', 'e', 'f',
      'g', 'h', 'i', 'j', 'k', 'l', 'm', 'n',
      'o', 'p', 'q', 'r', 's', 't', 'u', 'v',
      'w', 'x', 'y', 'z', '0', '1', '2', '3',
      '4', '5', '6', '7', '8', '9', '+', '/'
   };

   public String encode(byte[] ba) {
      int sz = ba.length;
```

```java
      StringBuffer sb = new StringBuffer();
      int j;
      int i;
      for (i = 0, j = 0; i < (sz -2); i += 3) {
        sb.append(map[(ba[i] >>> 2) & 0x3F]);
        sb.append(map[((ba[i] << 4) & 0x30) + ((ba[i+1] >>> 4) &
          0xf)]);
        sb.append(map[((ba[i+1] << 2) & 0x3c) + ((ba[i+2] >>> 6) &
          0x3)]);
        sb.append(map[ba[i+2] & 0X3F]);
      }
      switch (sz - i) {
        case 0:
          break;
        case 1:
          sb.append(map[(ba[i] >>> 2) & 0x3F]);
          sb.append(map[((ba[i] << 4) & 0x30)]);
          sb.append('=');
          sb.append('=');
          break;
        case 2:
          sb.append(map[(ba[i] >>> 2) & 0x3F]);
          sb.append(map[((ba[i] << 4) & 0x30) + ((ba[+1] >>> 4) &
            0xf)]);
          sb.append(map[((ba[i+1] << 2) & 0x3c)]);
          sb.append('=');
          break;
      }
      return sb.toString();
    }

  public byte[] decode(String s)
      throws RemoteException {
      int nb;
      byte[] bo = new byte[s.length()];
      int boi = 0;
      byte [] b = s.getBytes();
      byte b1 = (byte)-1, b2 = (byte)-1, b3 = (byte)-1, b4 = (byte)-1;
      for (int i = 0; i < s.length(); i += 4) {
        for (int j = 0; j < 64; ++j) {
          if (b[i] == map[j])
            b1 = (byte)j;
          if (b[i+1] == map[j])
            b2 = (byte)j;
          if (b[i+2] == map[j])
            b3 = (byte)j;
          if (b[i+3] == map[j])
            b4 = (byte)j;
      }
      if ((b1 <0) || (b2 < 0) )
        throw new RemoteException("decode invalid character");
      nb = 3;
      if (b[i+3] == '=')
        nb = 2;
      if (b[i+2] == '=')
        nb = 1;
      switch (nb) {
```

```
            case 1:
              bo[boi++] = (byte)((b1 << 2) | (b2 >>> 4));
              break;
            case 2:
              bo[boi++] = (byte)((b1 << 2) | (b2 >>> 4));
              bo[boi++] = (byte)((b2 << 4) | (b3 >>> 2));
              break;
            case 3:
              bo[boi++] = (byte)((b1 << 2) | (b2 >>> 4));
              bo[boi++] = (byte)((b2 << 4) | (b3 >>> 2));
              bo[boi++] = (byte)((b3 << 6) | b4);
              break;
            }
        }
        byte[] br = new byte[boi];
        for (int i = 0; i < boi; ++i)
          br[i] = bo[i];
        return br;
      }

    public void ejbCreate() {}
    public void ejbRemove() {}
    public void ejbActivate() {}
    public void ejbPassivate() {}
    public void setSessionContext(SessionContext sc) {}
}
```

Packaging and Deploying

We will place the second bean, which we compile using *compile-Base64.bat,* in *CryptoJAR* following the same procedure as we did when we packaged *PostalCode.* The necessary parameters are shown in Table 3-5.

TABLE 3-5	Parameter	Value
Parameters Required to Package Base64Bean	Enterprise Bean Class	Base64Bean
	Home Interface	Base64Home
	Remote Interface	Base64
	Enterprise Bean Display Name	Base64Bean
	JNDI Name	MyBase64

\Chapter3\code\compileBase64.bat

First Crypto Client—Encrypting Data

We will now compile and run two pieces of client code. The first will encrypt data, base64 encode it, and save it in a file. The second will read the file, decrypt the ciphertext, and display the recovered cleartext.

Before we begin, we will need a key suitable for use with the DES algorithm. The code to generate such a key and save it in a file named *myKey* looks like this:

\Chapter3\code\GenerateDESKey.java

```java
import java.io.*;
import java.security.*;
import javax.crypto.*;
import javax.crypto.spec.*;

public class GenerateDESKey {

  public static void main(String[] args) throws Exception {

    KeyGenerator kgen = KeyGenerator.getInstance("DES");
    SecretKey skey = kgen.generateKey();
    byte[] rkey = skey.getEncoded();
    BufferedOutputStream bos = new BufferedOutputStream(
      new FileOutputStream("myKey"));
    bos.write(rkey,0,rkey.length);
    bos.close();
  }
}
```

We compile this code using the command:

```
javac GenerateDESKey.java
```

Before we run our client code, we first generate a DES key by running *GenerateDESKey* using the command:

```
java GenerateDESKey
```

Here is the code for the first of our two clients:

On The CD

\Chapter3\code\CryptoClient1.java

```java
import java.io.*;

import javax.naming.Context;
import javax.naming.InitialContext;
import javax.rmi.PortableRemoteObject;

import SimpleDESBean;
import SimpleDESHome;

public class CryptoClient1 {

  public static void main(String[] args) {

    String clearText =
      "Ah, But I was so much older then. I'm younger than that
now";

    byte[] rawKey = null;

    try {
      File f = new File("myKey");
      int fl = (int)f.length();
      rawKey = new byte[fl];
      BufferedInputStream bis = new BufferedInputStream(
        new FileInputStream(f));
      bis.read(rawKey,0,fl);
      bis.close();
    }
    catch (FileNotFoundException e) {
      System.out.println(e.getMessage());
    }
    catch (IOException e) {
      System.out.println(e.getMessage());
    }

    try {
      Context initial = new InitialContext();
      Object objref = initial.lookup("MySimpleDES");

      SimpleDESHome dh =
        (SimpleDESHome)PortableRemoteObject.narrow(objref,
          SimpleDESHome.class);

      SimpleDES cipher = dh.create();

      byte[] encodedText =
        cipher.encode(clearText.getBytes(), rawKey);
```

```
    System.out.println("encoded text contains " +
encodedText.length + " bytes");
        objref = initial.lookup("MyBase64");

      Base64Home h64 =
        (Base64Home)PortableRemoteObject.narrow(objref,
          Base64Home.class);

      Base64 base64Encoder = h64.create();
      String s64 = base64Encoder.encode(encodedText);

    boolean more = true;
    int sp = 0;
    int len = s64.length();
    if (len <= 8)
      more = false;
    while (more) {
      System.out.println(s64.substring(sp,sp + 8));
      sp += 8;
      if ((sp + 8) >= len)
        more = false;
    }
    if (sp < len)
      System.out.println(s64.substring(sp));

      BufferedWriter bw = new BufferedWriter(
        new FileWriter("EncryptedData"));
      bw.write(s64,0,s64.length());
      bw.close();
    }
    catch (FileNotFoundException e) {
      System.out.println(e.getMessage());
    }
    catch (IOException e) {
      System.out.println(e.getMessage());
    }
    catch (Exception ex) {
      System.err.println("Caught an unexpected exception!");
      ex.printStackTrace();
    }
  }
}
```

When we compile this client code using *compileCrypto-Client1.bat* and run it using *runCryptoClient1.bat*, we create a file called *EncryptedData*. The contents of this file are shown in Figure 3-8.

\Chapter3\code\compileCryptoClient1.bat
\Chapter3\code\runCryptoClient1.bat

Figure 3-8
Contents of File
EncryptedData
(base64)

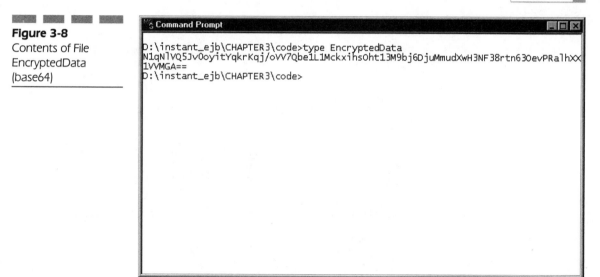

```
Command Prompt                                                    _ □ ×
D:\instant_ejb\CHAPTER3\code>type EncryptedData
N1qNlVQ5Jv0oyitYqkrKqj/oVV7Qbe1L1MckxihsOht13M9bj6DjuMmudXwH3NF38rtn630evPRalhXX
1VVMGA==
D:\instant_ejb\CHAPTER3\code>
```

NOTE: *Successful execution of the client code requires that the policy file be modified to grant permission for* java.lang.Runtime. createSecurityManager.

Second Crypto Client—Recovering Data

The code for our second client is as follows:

On the CD

\Chapter3\code\CryptoClient2.java

```java
import java.io.*;

import javax.naming.Context;
import javax.naming.InitialContext;
import javax.rmi.PortableRemoteObject;

import SimpleDESBean;
import SimpleDESHome;
```

```
public class CryptoClient2 {

  public static void main(String[] args) {

    byte[] rawKey = null;

    byte[] b64 = null;
    try {
      File f = new File("myKey");
      int fl = (int)f.length();
      rawKey = new byte[fl];
      BufferedInputStream bis = new BufferedInputStream(
        new FileInputStream(f));
      bis.read(rawKey,0,fl);
      bis.close();
    }
    catch (FileNotFoundException e) {
      System.out.println(e.getMessage());
    }
    catch (IOException e) {
      System.out.println(e.getMessage());
    }


    try {
      File f = new File("EncryptedData");
      int fl = (int)f.length();
      b64 = new byte [fl];
      BufferedInputStream bis = new BufferedInputStream(
        new FileInputStream(f));
      bis.read(b64,0,fl);
      bis.close();
    }
    catch (FileNotFoundException e) {
      System.out.println(e.getMessage());
    }
    catch (IOException e) {
      System.out.println(e.getMessage());
    }


    String s64 = new String(b64);
    try {
      Context initial = new InitialContext();
      Object objref = initial.lookup("MyBase64");

      Base64Home h64 =
        (Base64Home)PortableRemoteObject.narrow(objref,
          Base64Home.class);

      Base64 base64Encoder = h64.create();
      b64 = base64Encoder.decode(s64);

      objref = initial.lookup("MySimpleDES");
```

```
            SimpleDESHome dh =
              (SimpleDESHome)PortableRemoteObject.narrow(objref,
                SimpleDESHome.class);

            SimpleDES cipher = dh.create();

            byte[] clearText =
              cipher.decode(b64, rawKey);

            System.out.println(new String(clearText));
          }

          catch (IOException e) {
            System.out.println(e.getMessage());
          }

          catch (Exception ex) {
            System.err.println("Caught an unexpected exception!");
            ex.printStackTrace();
          }
        }
      }
```

When we compile *CryptoClient2.java* using *compileCryptoClient2.bat* and run it using *runCryptoClient2.bat*, we get the results shown in Figure 3-9.

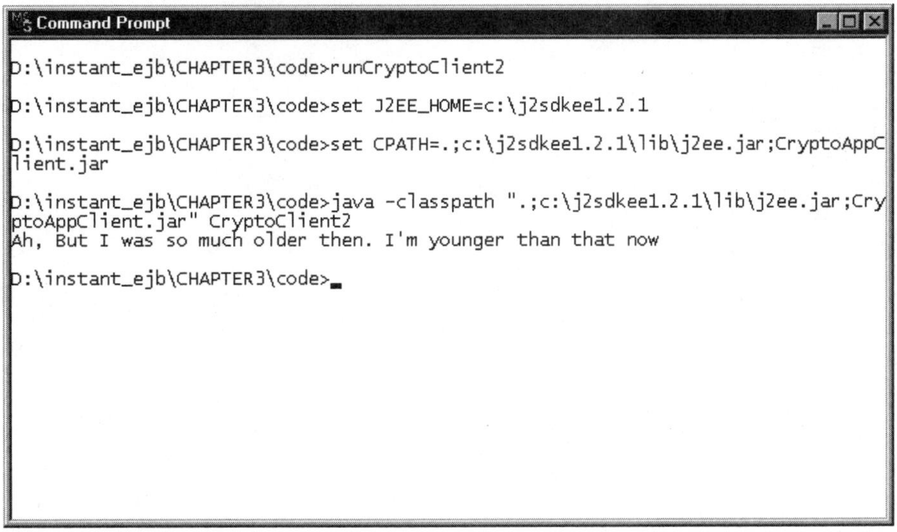

Figure 3-9
Output from
CryptoClient2

```
Command Prompt                                                        _ □ ✕

D:\instant_ejb\CHAPTER3\code>runCryptoClient2

D:\instant_ejb\CHAPTER3\code>set J2EE_HOME=c:\j2sdkee1.2.1

D:\instant_ejb\CHAPTER3\code>set CPATH=.;c:\j2sdkee1.2.1\lib\j2ee.jar;CryptoAppC
lient.jar

D:\instant_ejb\CHAPTER3\code>java -classpath ".;c:\j2sdkee1.2.1\lib\j2ee.jar;Cry
ptoAppClient.jar" CryptoClient2
Ah, But I was so much older then. I'm younger than that now

D:\instant_ejb\CHAPTER3\code>_
```

\Chapter3\code\compileCryptoClient2.bat
\Chapter3\code\runCryptoClient2.bat

Summary

In this chapter, we have seen real examples of several stateless session beans. Such beans are assigned to a client for the duration of a single-method invocation. They maintain no conversational state. They can be assigned to a different client whenever they are not actively executing code in one of their business methods.

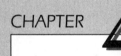

Some Simple Stateful Session Beans

In this chapter:

- Fibonacci Numbers
- A J2EE Client
- Min/Max Temperatures
- Stateful Bean Life Cycle

In the last chapter, we wrote and compiled a few stateless session beans and used the Application Deployment Tool to package and deploy them. We also wrote standalone client code to test each of the beans we wrote. In this chapter, we do the same for stateful session beans. We introduce another kind of client—the J2EE application client—and present code that can be used to demonstrate the life cycle of a stateful session bean.

Fibonacci Numbers

Our first stateful bean is one that returns the next number in the Fibonacci series each time its next() method is invoked. The Fibonacci series, named for the 13th-century Italian mathematician Leonardo Fibonacci, consists of the integers 1, 1, 2, 3, 5, 8, . . . Each number in the series is the sum of the two preceding numbers.

The Remote Interface

The code for the remote interface is shown below. It has all of the characteristics of the remote interfaces we have already examined for stateless session beans:

- It extends the `javax.ejb.EJBObject` interface.
- It contains a method signature for each method a client can invoke—in this case, the single method `next()`.
- Each of its methods throws `java.rmi.RemoteException`.

\Chapter4\code\Fibonacci.java

```
import javax.ejb.EJBObject;
import java.rmi.RemoteException;

public interface Fibonacci extends EJBObject {

  public String next ()
    throws RemoteException;
}
```

The Home Interface

Just as we saw with the remote interface, the home interface looks exactly like the home interface of each of the stateless session beans we have seen. The code is as follows:

\Chapter4\code\FibonacciHome.java

```
import java.io.Serializable;
import java.rmi.RemoteException;
import javax.ejb.CreateException;
import javax.ejb.EJBHome;

public interface FibonacciHome
     extends EJBHome {
   Fibonacci create()
     throws RemoteException, CreateException;
}
```

The Enterprise Bean

Here is the code for the enterprise bean. It implements the `next()` method that was declared in the remote interface. Like other bean code that we saw for stateless session beans, this code implements the *SessionBean* interface and so we see the following methods defined:

- ejbActivate()
- ejbPassivate()
- ejbRemove()
- setSessionContext()

These methods are callback methods that are invoked by the container to notify the bean that a life-cycle event has occurred.

 \Chapter4\code\FibonacciBean.java

```java
import java.math.BigInteger;

import java.rmi.RemoteException;
import javax.ejb.CreateException;
import javax.ejb.SessionBean;
import javax.ejb.SessionContext;

public class FibonacciBean
    implements SessionBean {

  BigInteger current;
  BigInteger prev;

  public String next() {
    BigInteger next = current.add(prev);
    prev = current;
    current = next;
    return next.toString();
  }

  public void ejbCreate() throws CreateException {
    current = BigInteger.ZERO;
    prev = BigInteger.ONE;
  }
  public void ejbRemove() {}
  public void ejbActivate() {}
  public void ejbPassivate() {}
  public void setSessionContext(SessionContext sc) {}
}
```

Notice the presence of the two instance variables current and next. These are used to maintain the state of the bean. The following code in the next() method calculates the value of the instance variable next, which is ultimately returned as a string to the client.

```
BigInteger next = current.add(prev);
```

We have finally encountered something about a stateful session bean that is different. It maintains a state of which the client can become aware by calling the `next()` method. For this to work, the reference the client is given to the bean must remain constant from the time the bean is created on behalf of the client to the time the client requests its removal. Stateful session beans cannot be arbitrarily reassigned to different clients.

So how does the container know that a session bean should be treated as stateful? The answer, as we see in the next section, does not lie in the code but rather in a declarative statement that is contained in the deployment descriptor and acted upon at runtime by the container.

Packaging and Deploying the Bean

The procedure for packaging and deploying our Fibonacci bean is exactly the same as that which we followed to package and deploy *HelloWorld* in Chapter 2, with one exception. In the General Dialog of the New Enterprise Bean Wizard, we must make sure that the radio buttons labeled SESSION and STATEFUL are clicked, as shown in Figure 4-1. In the interest of conserving space, we will not present a step-by-step description of the packaging and deployment process. The file *compileFibonacci.bat* can be used to compile the remote interface, home interface, and bean code.

 ▬
\Chapter4\code\compileFibonacci.bat

The information we will need for the packaging and deployment is shown in Table 4-1.

We mentioned in the preceding section that the *stateful* property of the bean, which we declared in Figure 4-1, appears in the deployment descriptor. In Chapter 2, we examined the contents of a descriptor by copying the `Jar` file to a separate directory and using

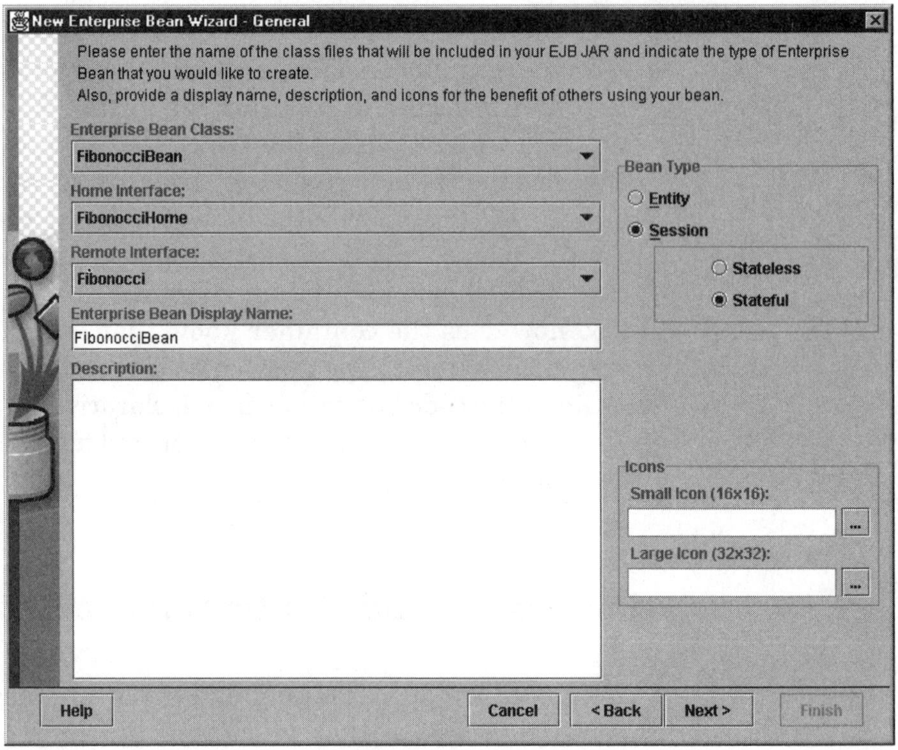

Figure 4-1
Creating a Stateful
Session Bean

TABLE 4-1

Parameters Required
to Package and
Deploy Fibonacci
EJB

Parameter	Value
Application File Name	FibonacciApp.ear
Application Display Name	FibonacciApp
JAR DisplayName	FibonacciJAR
Enterprise Bean Class	FibonacciBean
Home Interface	FibonacciHome
Remote Interface	Fibonacci
Enterprise Bean Display Name	FibonacciBean
JNDI Name	MyFibonacci

the *jar* utility. We recursively extracted the contents of the .jar files until we had extracted the XML files that contained the descriptors. We took this approach so you could see and appreciate how the Application Deployment Tool had transformed information we specified in dialog boxes into an XML document. Preparing such a document manually would have been tedious and prone to errors. We now see that there is a much easier way to examine the descriptor files.

In the Application Deployment Tool in the box labeled LOCAL APPLICATIONS:, select *FibonacciApp* by clicking on it. Then select "Descriptor Viewer . . ." from the "Tools" drop-down menu as shown in Figure 4-2. The dialog shown in Figure 4-3 appears. The contents are easily recognized as XML. This is the deployment descriptor for the *FibonacciApp* component.

Figure 4-2
Starting the
Descriptor Viewer for
FibonacciApp
Component

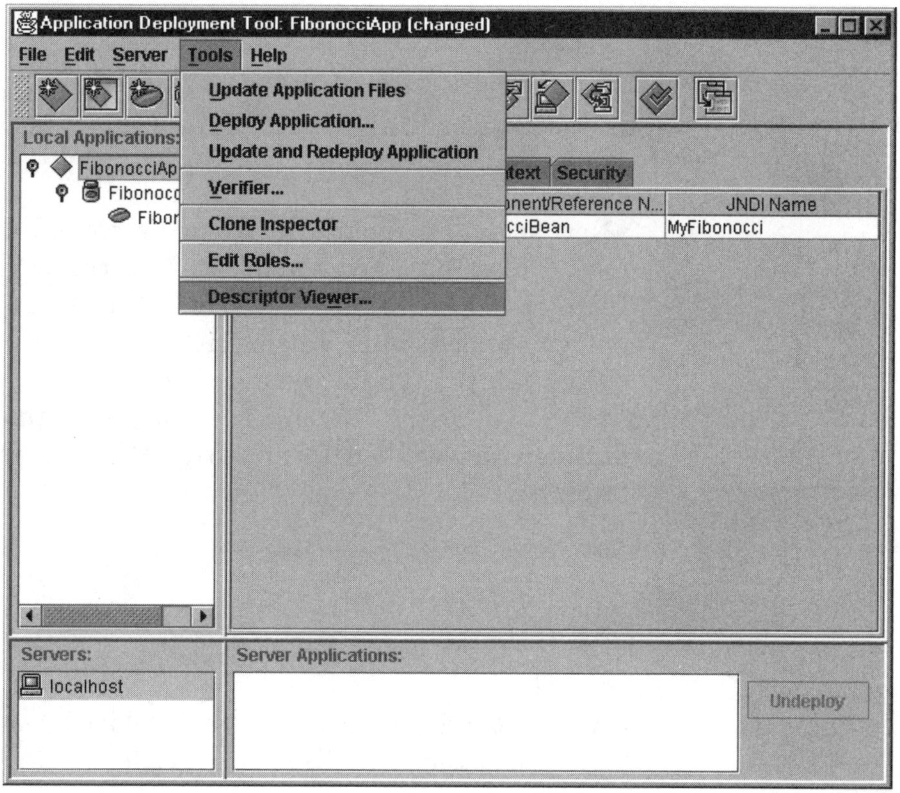

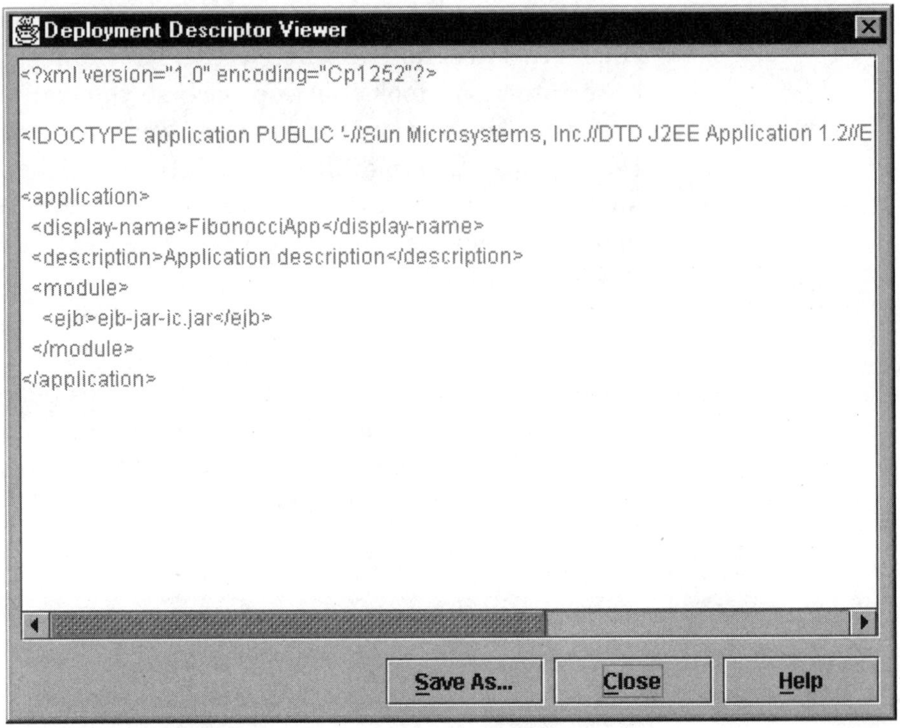

Figure 4-3
Deployment Descriptor for FibonacciApp
Component

```
Deployment Descriptor Viewer                                    ⊠

<?xml version="1.0" encoding="Cp1252"?>

<!DOCTYPE application PUBLIC '-//Sun Microsystems, Inc.//DTD J2EE Application 1.2//E

<application>
 <display-name>FibonacciApp</display-name>
 <description>Application description</description>
 <module>
  <ejb>ejb-jar-ic.jar</ejb>
 </module>
</application>



                              Save As...      Close       Help
```

Now select *FibonacciJAR* from the box labeled LOCAL APPLICA-
TIONS:. This time, when you select "Descriptor Viewer . . ." from the
"Tools" menu, the dialog shown in Figure 4-4 is displayed. It is the
deployment descriptor FibonacciJar.

The value Stateful bounded by the tag pair <session-
type>...</session-type> is the value that is parsed out at
runtime and used to determine that the bean should be treated as
stateful.

The Client

As we did for the other beans we developed, we write a standalone
client to test the bean. Here is the code:

Figure 4-4
Deployment
Descriptor for
FibonacciJAR

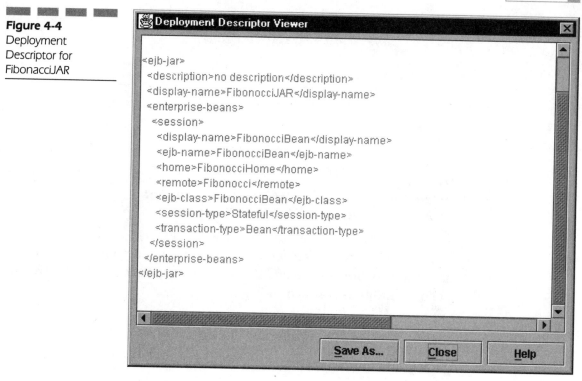

```
<ejb-jar>
 <description>no description</description>
 <display-name>FibonocciJAR</display-name>
 <enterprise-beans>
  <session>
   <display-name>FibonocciBean</display-name>
   <ejb-name>FibonocciBean</ejb-name>
   <home>FibonocciHome</home>
   <remote>Fibonocci</remote>
   <ejb-class>FibonocciBean</ejb-class>
   <session-type>Stateful</session-type>
   <transaction-type>Bean</transaction-type>
  </session>
 </enterprise-beans>
</ejb-jar>
```

 On the CD

\Chapter4\code\FibonacciClient.java

```java
import javax.naming.Context;
import javax.naming.InitialContext;
import javax.rmi.PortableRemoteObject;

import Fibonacci;
import FibonacciHome;

public class FibonacciClient {

  public static void main(String[] args) {
    try {
      Context initial = new InitialContext();
      Object objref = initial.lookup("MyFibonacci");

      FibonacciHome home =
        (FibonacciHome)PortableRemoteObject.narrow(objref,
          FibonacciHome.class);
```

```
        Fibonacci fib = home.create();
        for (int i = 0; i < 25; ++i) {
          System.out.println(fib.next());
        }
      }
      catch (Exception ex) {
        System.err.println("Caught an unexpected exception!");
        ex.printStackTrace();
      }
    }
  }
```

Chapter4\code\compileFibonacciClient.bat
Chapter4\code\runFibonacciClient.bat

After using *compileFibonacciClient.bat* to compile the client, we use the file *runFibonacciClient.bat* to run the client code. We see results like those shown in Figure 4-5.

Chapter4\code\compileFibonacciClient.bat
Chapter4\code\runFibonacciClient.bat

Figure 4-5
Output from
FibonacciClient

```
Command Prompt                                                        _ □ X
D:\instant_ejb\CHAPTER4\code>runFibonocciClient
1
1
2
3
5
8
13
21
34
55
89
144
233
377
610
987
1597
2584
4181
6765
10946
17711
28657
46368
75025

D:\instant_ejb\CHAPTER4\code>_
```

A J2EE Application Client

Up to this point, all of the clients we wrote were standalone. A bean can have a number of other kinds of clients. We see some of them in subsequent chapters but right now we examine a J2EE application client.

A J2EE application client differs from a standalone client because it is a J2EE component and, as such, it can access J2EE services. The most useful service our client will take advantage of, and the one that will be most obvious when we execute the client, is security authentication. We will also see how our J2EE application client uses JNDI services.

Here is the code for our first J2EE application client:

\Chapter4\code\FibonacciClientJ2EE.java

```java
import javax.naming.Context;
import javax.naming.InitialContext;
import javax.rmi.PortableRemoteObject;

import Fibonacci;
import FibonacciHome;

public class FibonacciClientJ2EE {

  public static void main(String[] args) {
    try {
      Context initial = new InitialContext();
      Object objref =
        initial.lookup("java:comp/env/ejb/FibonacciSequence");

      FibonacciHome home =
        (FibonacciHome)PortableRemoteObject.narrow(objref,
          FibonacciHome.class);

      Fibonacci fib = home.create();
      for (int i = 0; i < 25; ++i) {
        System.out.println(fib.next());
      }

    }
    catch (Exception ex) {
      System.err.println("Caught an unexpected exception!");
      ex.printStackTrace();
    }
  }
}
```

If you compare this code to the standalone application, the only difference you detect is this single line of code:

```
Object objref =
    initial.lookup("java:comp/env/ejb/FibonacciSequence");
```

We discuss the significance of this line of code shortly but first we will compile the code and create the client. We compile the code using `compileFibonacciClientJ2EE.bat`.

\Chapter4\code\compileFibonacciClientJ2EE.bat

Because the J2EE application client is a J2EE component, we use the Application Deployment Tool to create it. We start the process by selecting "New Application Client . . ." from the "File" menu drop-down list as shown in Figure 4-6. When we do, the introduction to the New Application Client Wizard shown in Figure 4-7 is displayed.

After we read the instructions and click on NEXT>, the General Dialog shown in Figure 4-8 appears. Clicking on the ADD button to the right of the box labeled CONTENTS: results in the appearance of the "Add Files to .JAR" dialog. When we select *Fibonacci-ClientJ2EE.class* from the top box and click on the ADD button, the selected component appears in the bottom box and the dialog looks like Figure 4-9.

After we have clicked on OK in Figure 4-9, we return to the General Dialog and notice that the drop-down list labeled "Main Class" now displays *FibonacciClientJ2EE*. We then type *FibonacciClient* into the text entry field labeled "Display Name:" so that the General Dialog looks like Figure 4-10.

When we click on NEXT>, the "Environment Entries" dialog appears. We will not be creating any environment entries so we bypass this dialog by clicking on NEXT>, causing the dialog shown in Figure 4-11 to appear. When we click on the ADD button in Figure 4-11, the text entry fields shown in Figure 4-12 appear.

In the text entry field under the column header "Coded Name", we enter *ejb/FibonacciSequence*. In the text entry field under the

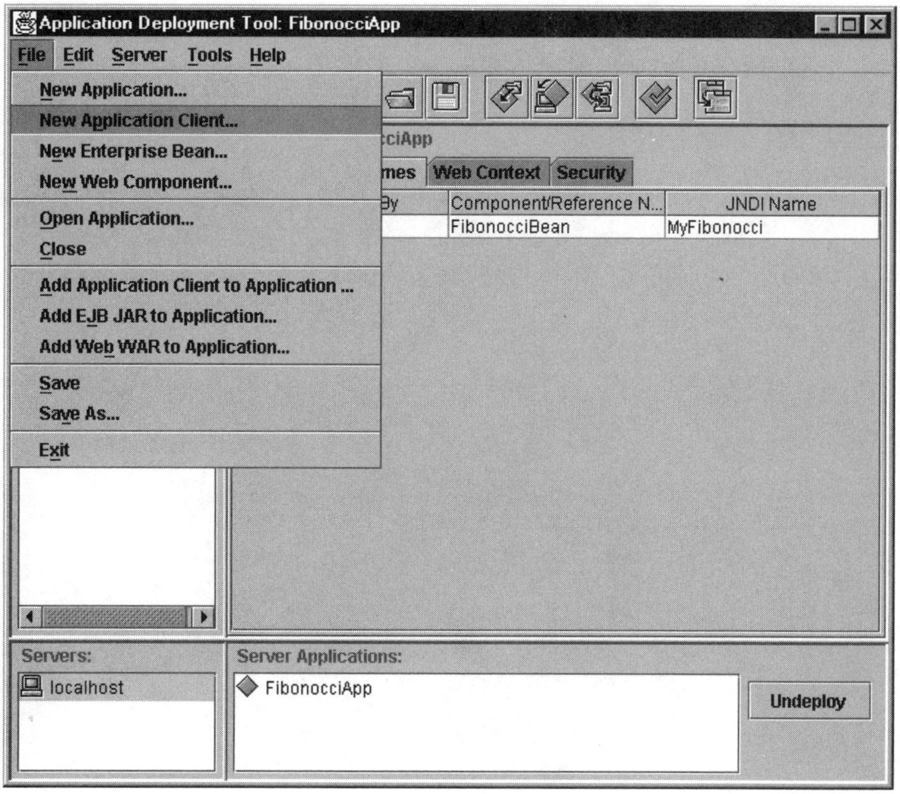

Figure 4-6
Starting New
Application
Client Wizard

column header "Home", we enter *FibonacciHome*. The drop-down list under the column header "Type" should already display *Session;* if it does not, we select *Session*. In the text entry field under the column header "Remote", we enter *Fibonacci*. The dialog should now look like Figure 4-13.

Clicking on FINISH> in Figure 4-13 completes the process and returns us to the Application Deployment Tool's main window. We now click on the tab labeled JNDI NAMES so that the main window looks like Figure 4-14.

Our objective here is to map the coded name "ejb/Fibonacci-Sequence" we saw in Figure 4-13 to the JNDI name "MyFibonacci" we specified when we packaged and deployed the bean. To do this, we enter *MyFibonacci* under the column header "JNDI Name" on the line containing the coded name so that the Application Deployment Tool main window looks like Figure 4-15.

Figure 4-7
New Application
Client Wizard—
Introduction

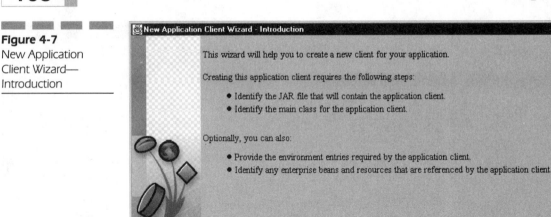

Figure 4-7
New Application
Client Wizard—
Introduction

Now that the addition of the J2EE application client is complete, we deploy the *FibonacciApp* application. We start the process by selecting "Deploy Application . . ." from the "Tools" drop-down menu as shown in Figure 4-16. In the dialog that appears, we click on the checkbox labeled RETURN CLIENT JAR so that the dialog looks like Figure 4-17.

Clicking on the button labeled NEXT> results in the appearance of the next dialog shown in Figure 4-18. This dialog is presented to provide us an opportunity to verify the JNDI names before continuing with the deployment process.

After we have reviewed the JNDI names, we click on NEXT> and one final dialog informs us that the deployment procedure is about to start. This dialog is shown in Figure 4-19.

Clicking on FINISH> starts the deployment. The progress of the process is reported in a dialog like the one shown in Figure 4-20. If

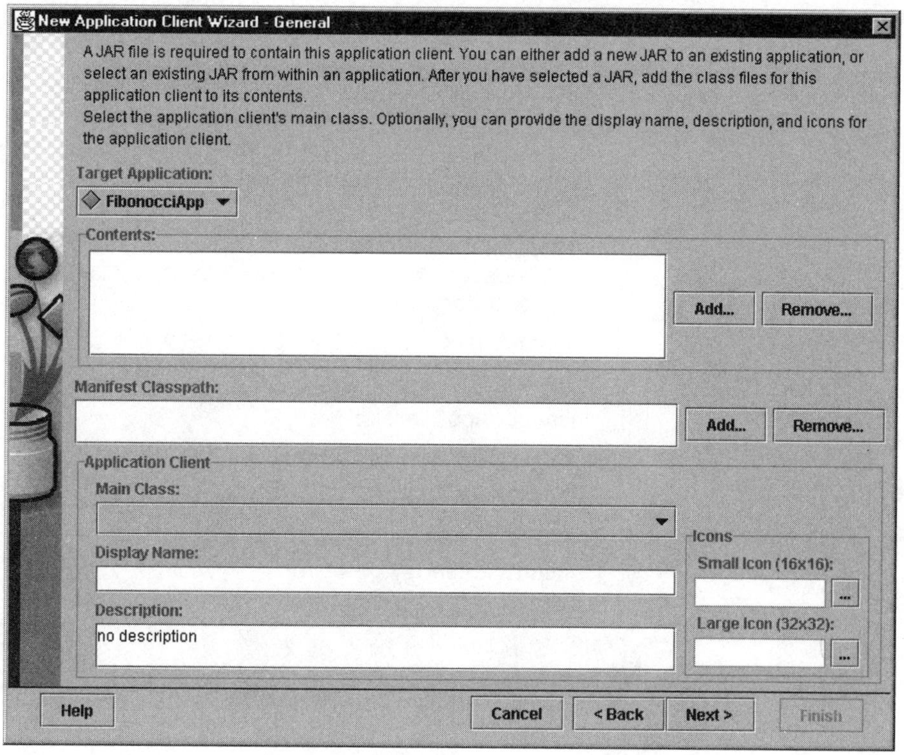

Figure 4-8
New Application
Client Wizard—
General Dialog

no errors are encountered, the final appearance of the dialog box looks like Figure 4-21.

Running the J2EE Application Client

A J2EE application client is executed using the `runclient` script, which has the following syntax:

```
runclient -client <appjar> [-name <name>] [<app-args>]
```

The options are as follows:

appjar   The J2EE application `.ear` file

name   The display name of the J2EE application client component

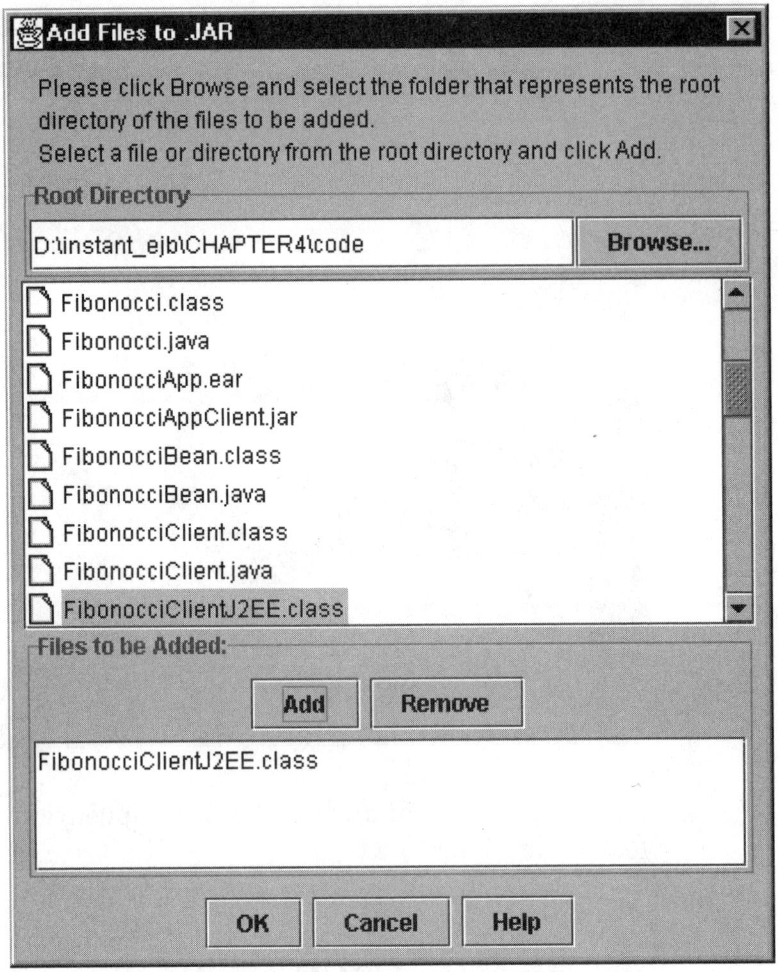

Figure 4-9
Adding File to JAR

Add Files to JAR

Please click Browse and select the folder that represents the root directory of the files to be added.
Select a file or directory from the root directory and click Add.

Root Directory

D:\instant_ejb\CHAPTER4\code   **Browse...**

- Fibonocci.class
- Fibonocci.java
- FibonocciApp.ear
- FibonocciAppClient.jar
- FibonocciBean.class
- FibonocciBean.java
- FibonocciClient.class
- FibonocciClient.java
- FibonocciClientJ2EE.class

Files to be Added:

Add   **Remove**

FibonocciClientJ2EE.class

OK   **Cancel**   **Help**

<app-args> Arguments defined by the application

So, we type:

```
runclient -client FibonacciApp.ear -name FibonacciClient
```

When we start the *runclient* script, the window in which we started it looks like Figure 4-22. After the message "Initiating login . . ." is displayed, a dialog like the one shown in Figure 4-23 pops up. We now see one of the advantages of using a J2EE application instead of a standalone client. Without writing a single line

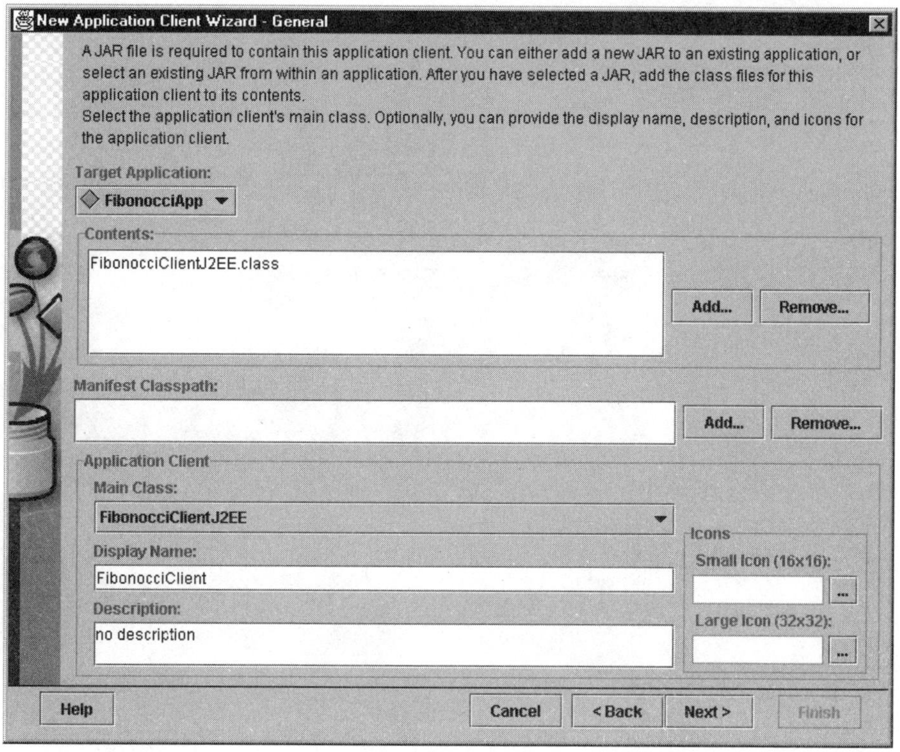

■■■ ■■■ ■■■ ■■

Figure 4-10
New Application
Client Wizard with
All Required Fields
Populated

of code, we have added authentication. Only persons who can prove their identity by supplying a username and password can execute the client.

We enter a username of *guest* and a password of *guest123*. User names and passwords are administered using the *realmtool* utility, which we discuss in greater detail in Chapter 12. If we enter an incorrect username or password, the application will throw a `com.sun.enterprise.security.LoginException` and terminate. When we enter a correct username and password and click on OK, the dialog is dismissed and the application starts executing and produces the output shown in Figure 4-24.

When we first introduced the J2EE application, we said that it could access two J2EE services. The first of these, authentication, made itself obvious when the Login dialog popped up. Now it is time to discuss the second, the JNDI service, which brings us to the

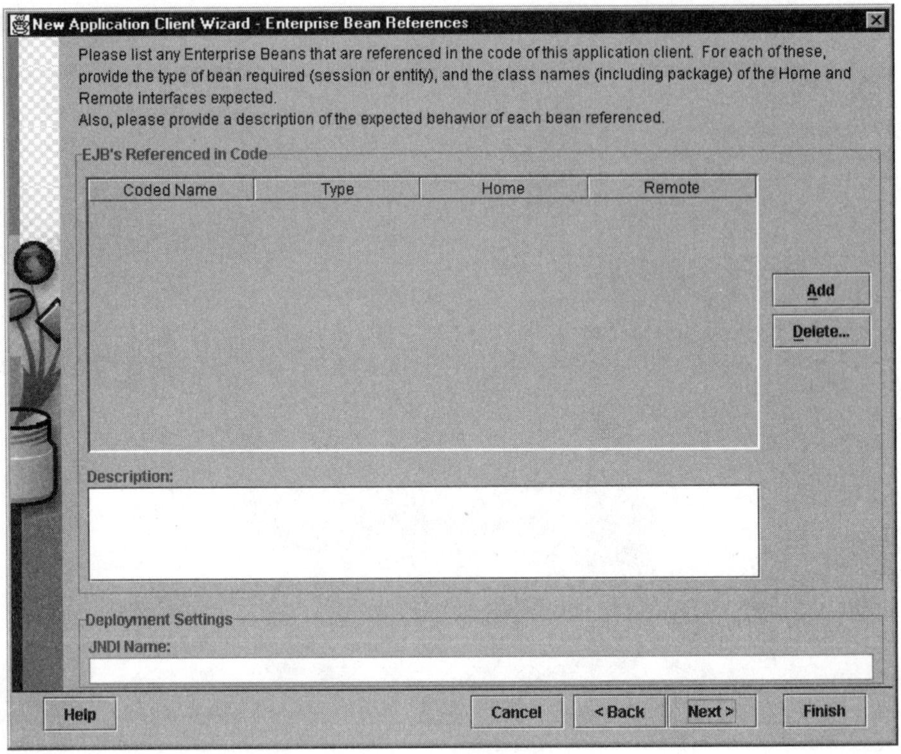

Figure 4-11
Enterprise Bean
References Dialog

Figure 4-11
Enterprise Bean
References Dialog

line of code we singled out earlier as differentiating the J2EE application client code from standalone client code. Again, this line of code reads:

```
Object objref =
initial.lookup("java:comp/env/ejb/FibonacciSequence");
```

When the lookup() method of InitialContext receives a String as an argument, it performs a name lookup in one of two ways, depending on the characteristics of the string. When the string is a simple string such as *MyFibonacci* like we used in the standalone client, the string is treated as a name relative to the initial context. If the string contains the colon character, the lookup() method interprets it as a URL string, which has the syntax:

scheme:scheme-specific-parts

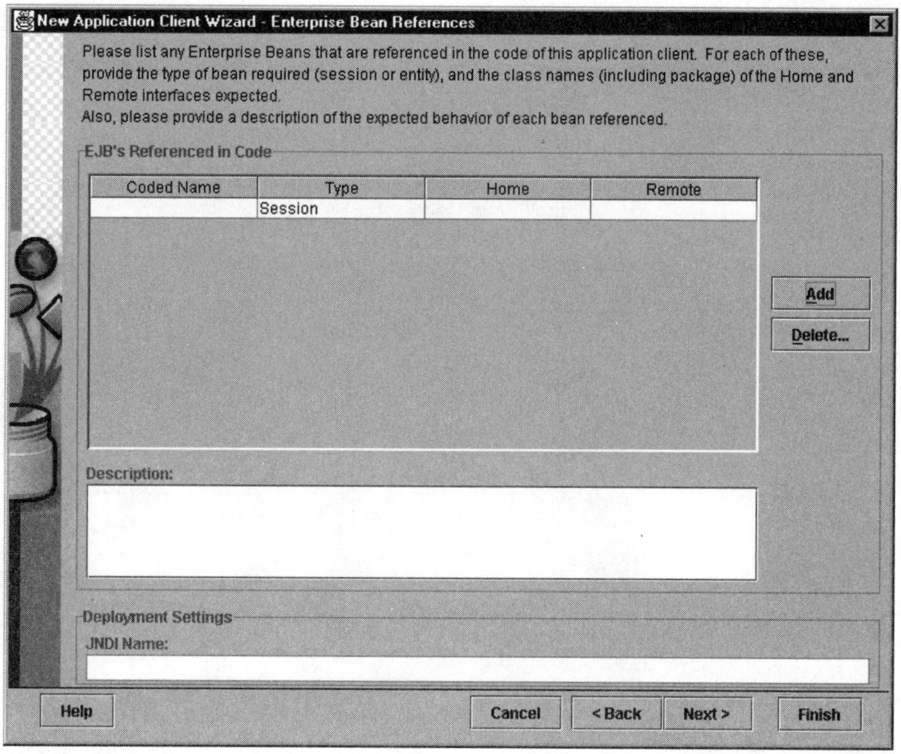

Figure 4-12
New Application
Client Wizard—
Preparing to Add a
Bean Reference

Some examples of URL strings with which we are already familiar are:

- `http://myhost.com`
- `https://mysecurehost.com`
- `ftp://myftpsite.com`

If you have used JNDI before, you might have seen code that looks like:

```
Object obj = new InitialContext.lookup(
  ""ldap://localhost:389/cn=Paul Tremblett,ou=People,o=tutorial");
```

After determining the scheme by extracting the portion of the string to the left of the colon, JNDI attempts to find a URL context

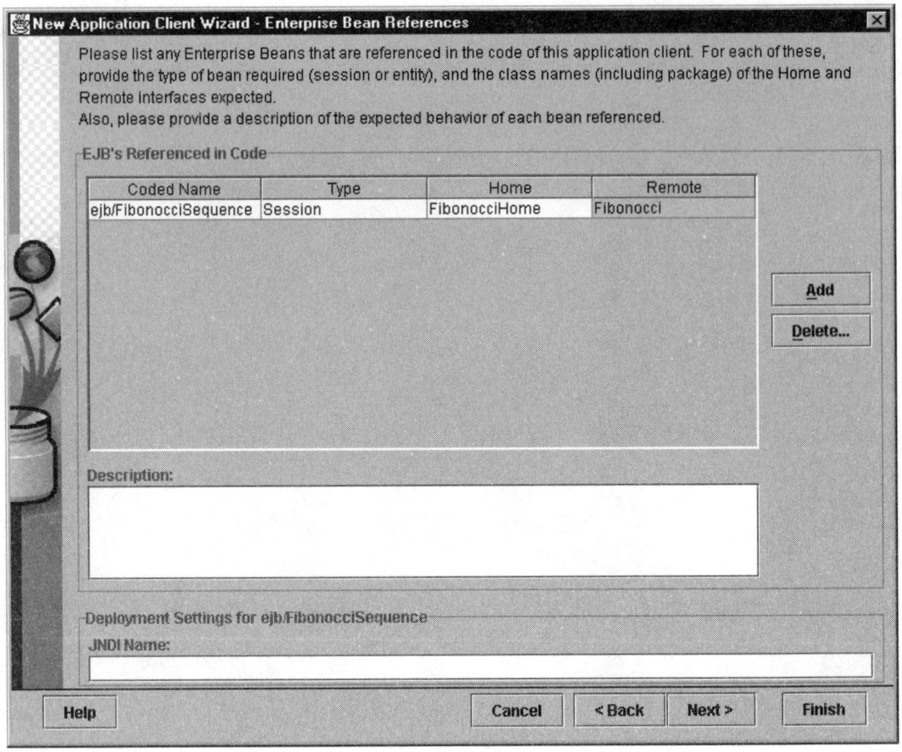

Figure 4-13

New Application
Client Wizard with
Reference Information
All Supplied

implementation for that scheme (in this case, ldap). It uses that implementation to find the name in its namespace.

J2EE defines a logical namespace and the URL in which it is rooted. The URL scheme is "java:". The scheme-specific part of the URL defines a hierarchical namespace. The scheme-specific component "comp", short for component, is bound to a subtree of the "java:" scheme that is dedicated to component-related bindings. This subtree splits into two subtrees, one of which is "env". The subtree bound to "env", short for environment, is dedicated to a component's environment-related bindings. Such environment-related bindings are found in the deployment descriptor. Beneath the "env" subtree, the structure is not formally defined; however, it is recommended that EJBs be placed in a subtree bound to the name "ejb".

Figure 4-14
Application
Deployment Tool—
JNDI Names Dialog

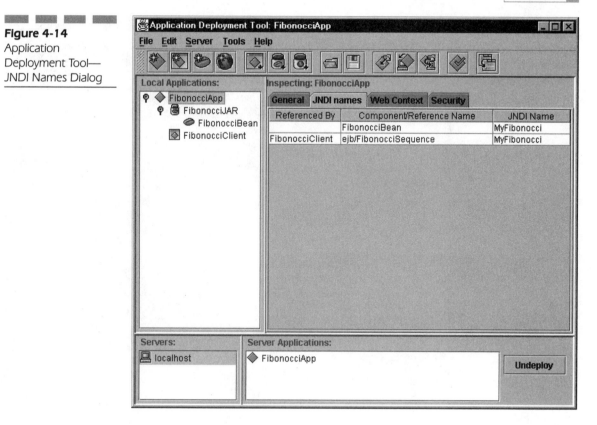

When we prepared our J2EE application component for deployment, we mapped the coded name *ejb/FibonacciSequence,* which is referenced by *FibonacciClient,* to the JNDI name *MyFibonacci,* which is mapped to FibonacciBean. When the `lookup()` method processes the string *java:comp/env/ejb/FibonacciSequence,* it finds *FibonacciBean.*

What does this extra level of indirection add other than overhead? The answer is flexibility, which is so important in distributed computing. If you change a JNDI name, you must modify the code for every standalone client that uses that JNDI name. If the clients are J2EE application clients, you simply change the mapping of the coded name so that it references the new JNDI name.

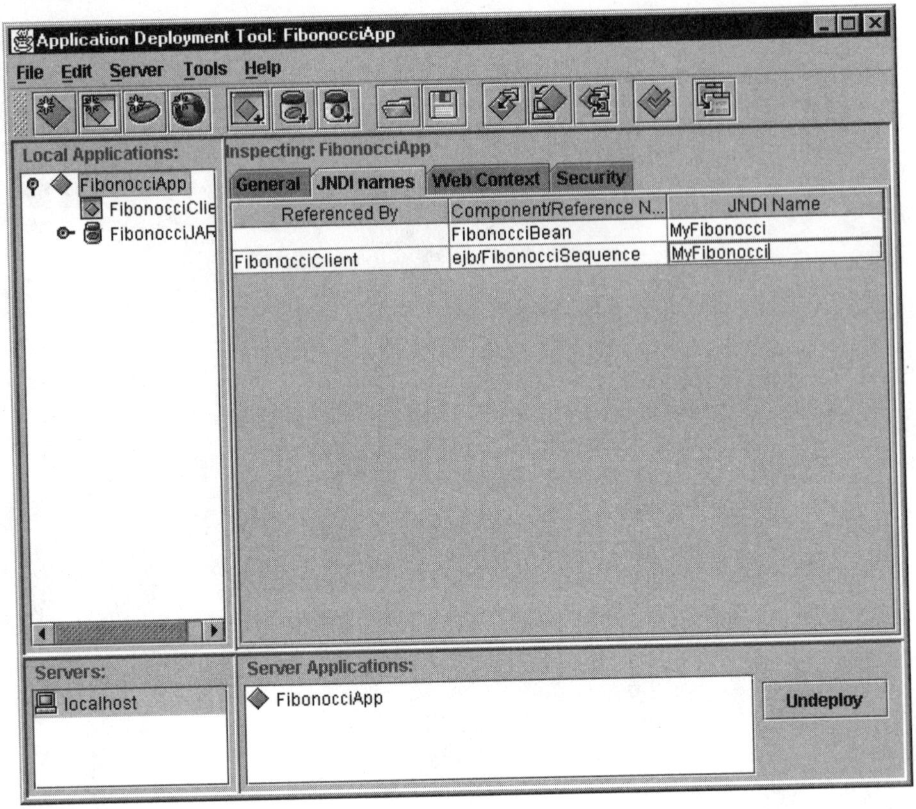

Figure 4-15
Application
Deployment Tool
with JNDI Names
Supplied

This is far less time consuming, less prone to errors, and requires less testing.

Min/Max Temperature Monitor

To further illustrate stateful beans, we will create a bean that takes temperature readings as input. A client of this bean can invoke methods to adjust the temperature and request the current temperature, the minimum temperature, and the maximum temperature.

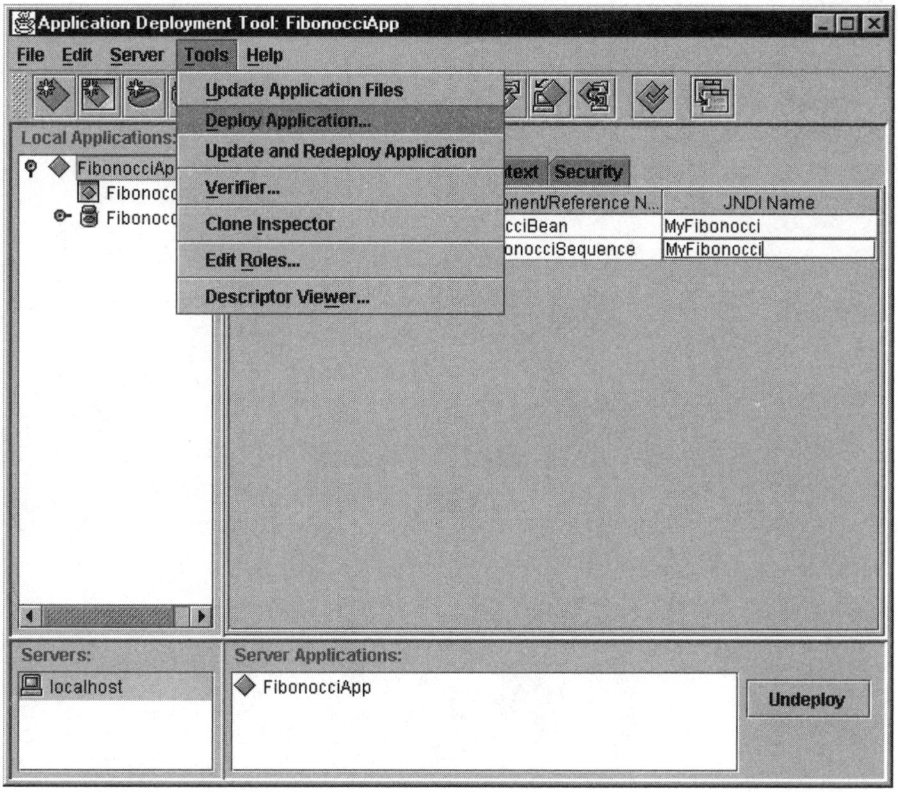

Figure 4-16 Preparing to Deploy the Application

The code for the remote interface, the home interface, and the enterprise bean are simply presented without further discussion.

The Remote Interface

On The CD

\Chapter4\code\MinMaxTemp.java

```
import javax.ejb.EJBObject;
import java.rmi.RemoteException;
```

Figure 4-17
Deployment Dialog—
Specifying "Return
Client Jar"

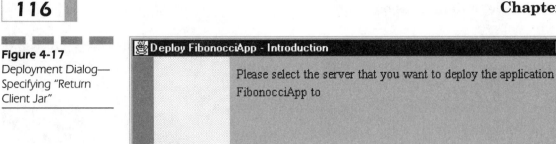

```
public interface MinMaxTemp extends EJBObject {

  public void adjustTemperature(double delta)
    throws RemoteException;

  public double getCurrentTemperature()
    throws RemoteException;

  public double getMinTemperature()
    throws RemoteException;

  public double getMaxTemperature()
    throws RemoteException;
}
```

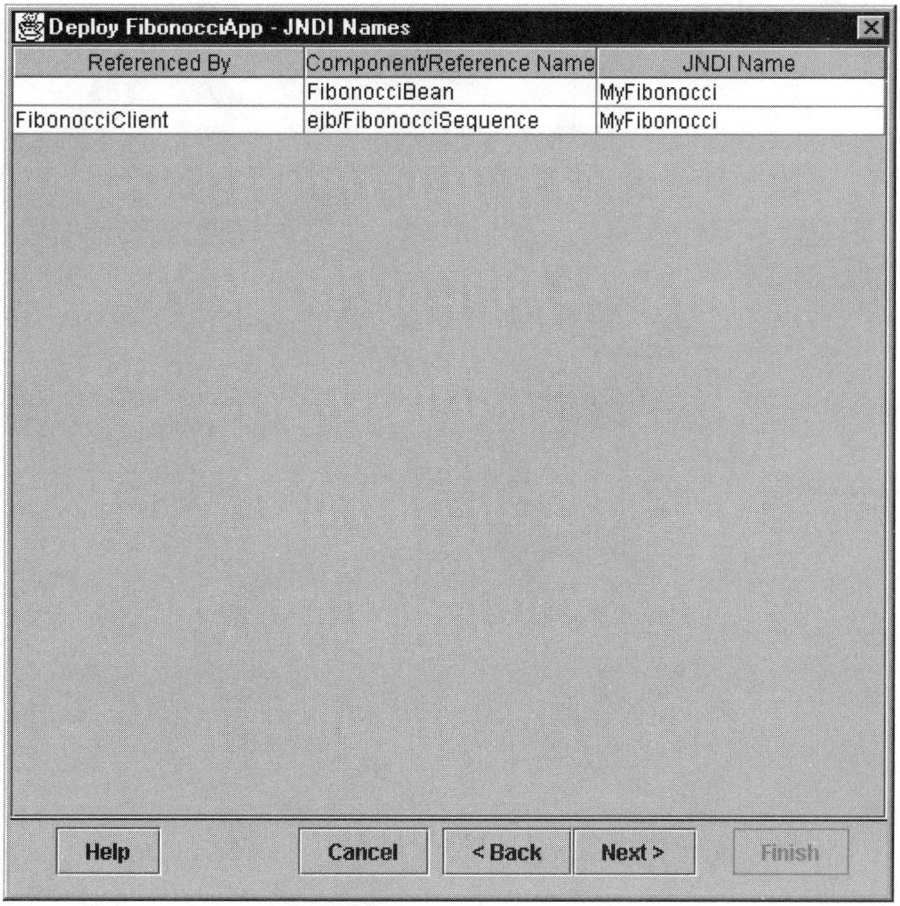

Figure 4-18
Verifying JNDI Names
Before Deployment

Referenced By	Component/Reference Name	JNDI Name
	FibonocciBean	MyFibonocci
FibonocciClient	ejb/FibonocciSequence	MyFibonocci

Deploy FibonocciApp - JNDI Names

| Help | Cancel | < Back | Next > | Finish |

The Home Interface

\Chapter4\code\MinMaxTempHome.java

```java
import java.io.Serializable;
import java.rmi.RemoteException;
import javax.ejb.CreateException;
import javax.ejb.EJBHome;

public interface MinMaxTempHome
    extends EJBHome {
  MinMaxTemp create(double t)
```

Figure 4-19
Ready to Deploy
Application

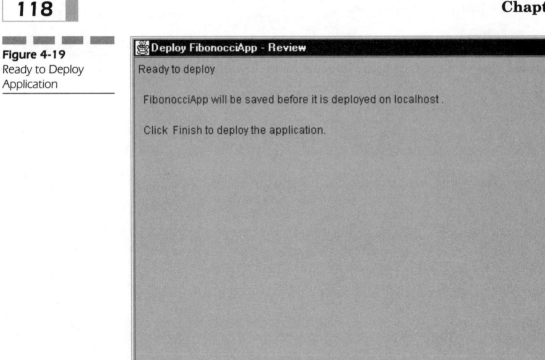

```
            throws RemoteException, CreateException;
    }
```

The Enterprise Bean

 \Chapter4\code\MinMaxTempBean.java

```java
import java.rmi.RemoteException;
import javax.ejb.CreateException;
import javax.ejb.SessionBean;
import javax.ejb.SessionContext;
```

Figure 4-20
Deployment Progress
Dialog

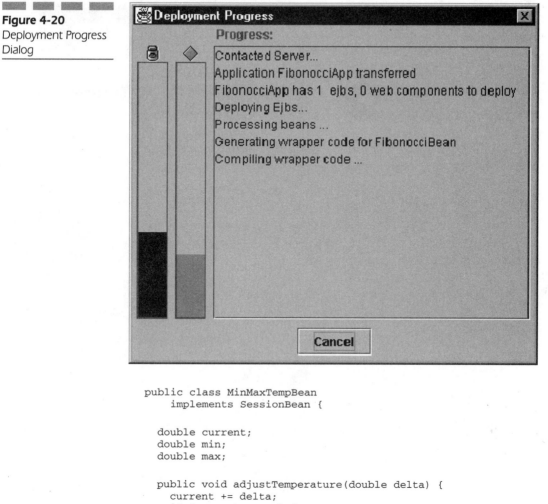

```
public class MinMaxTempBean
    implements SessionBean {

  double current;
  double min;
  double max;

  public void adjustTemperature(double delta) {
    current += delta;
    if (current > max) {
      max = current;
    }
    else if (current < min) {
      min = current;
    }
  }

  public double getCurrentTemperature() {
    return current;
  }

  public double getMinTemperature() {
    return min;
  }
```

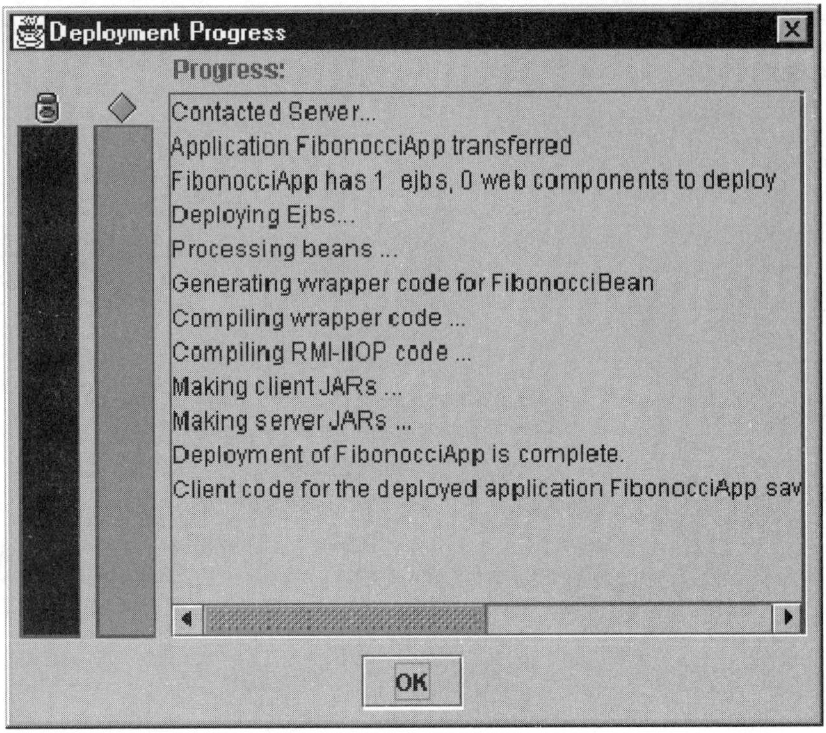

Figure 4-21
Deployment
Complete

```
public double getMaxTemperature() {
  return max;
}

public void ejbCreate(double temp)
    throws CreateException {
  min = max = current = temp;
}

public void ejbRemove() {}
public void ejbActivate() {}
public void ejbPassivate() {}
public void setSessionContext(SessionContext sc) {}
}
```

Packaging and Deploying

The remote interface, home interface, and enterprise bean can be compiled using *compileMinMaxTemp.bat*.

Figure 4-22
Starting the J2EE
Client

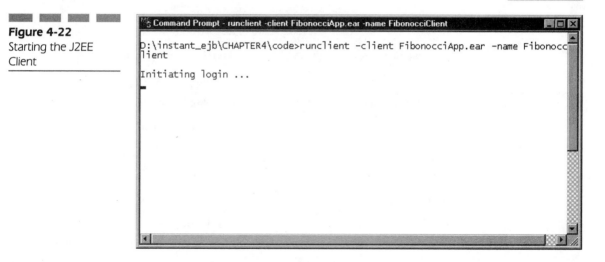

```
Command Prompt - runclient -client FibonocciApp.ear -name FibonocciClient

D:\instant_ejb\CHAPTER4\code>runclient -client FibonocciApp.ear -name Fibonocc
ient

Initiating login ...
```

On the CD

\Chapter4\code\compileMinMaxTemp.bat

The parameters we need to package and deploy the bean are shown in Table 4-2.

A J2EE Client

Here is the code for a J2EE application client that we can use to test our bean:

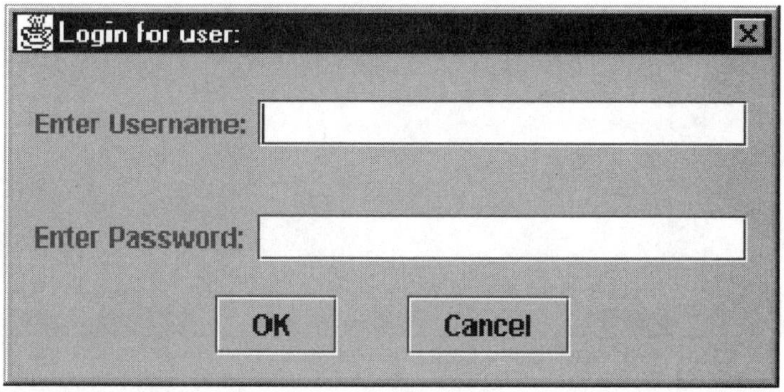

Figure 4-23
Login Dialog

Login for user:

Enter Username:

Enter Password:

OK   Cancel

TABLE 4-2

Parameters Required
to Package
and Deploy
MinMaxTemp EJB

Parameter	Value
Application File Name	MinMaxTempApp.ear
Application Display Name	MinMaxTempApp
JAR DisplayName	MinMaxTempJAR
Enterprise Bean Class	MinMaxTempBean
Home Interface	MinMaxTempHome
Remote Interface	MinMaxTemp
Enterprise Bean Display Name	MinMaxTempBean
JNDI Name	MyMinMaxTemp

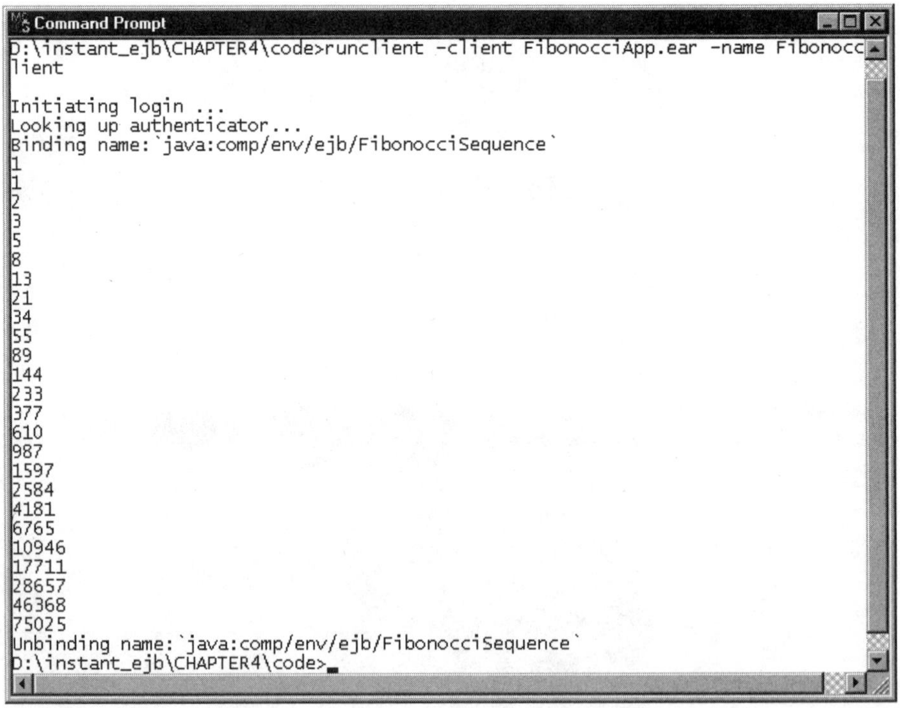

Figure 4-24
Output from
Fibonacci J2EE Client

```
Command Prompt                                                        _ □ ×
D:\instant_ejb\CHAPTER4\code>runclient -client FibonocciApp.ear -name Fibonocc
lient

Initiating login ...
Looking up authenticator...
Binding name:`java:comp/env/ejb/FibonocciSequence`
1
1
2
3
5
8
13
21
34
55
89
144
233
377
610
987
1597
2584
4181
6765
10946
17711
28657
46368
75025
Unbinding name:`java:comp/env/ejb/FibonocciSequence`
D:\instant_ejb\CHAPTER4\code>
```

On The CD *\Chapter4\code\MinMaxTempClientJ2EE.java*

```java
import javax.naming.Context;
import javax.naming.InitialContext;
import javax.rmi.PortableRemoteObject;

import MinMaxTemp;
import MinMaxTempHome;

public class MinMaxTempClientJ2EE {

  public static void main(String[] args) {

    double[] deltas = { -1.5, 4.2, -2.6, -4.7, +6.8, -1.1};

    try {
      Context initial = new InitialContext();
      Object objref =
        initial.lookup("java:comp/env/ejb/MinMaxTemp");
      MinMaxTempHome home =
        (MinMaxTempHome)PortableRemoteObject.narrow(objref,
          MinMaxTempHome.class);

      MinMaxTemp minmax = home.create(20.0);
      System.out.println("current temp = " +
        minmax.currentTemperature());

      for (int i = 0; i < deltas.length; ++i) {
        minmax.adjustTemperature(deltas[i]);
        System.out.println("applying delta " + deltas[i]);
        System.out.println("current temp = " +
          minmax.getCurrentTemperature());
      }
      System.out.println("minimum temperature was " +
        minmax.getMinTemperature());
      System.out.println("maximum temperature was " +
        minmax.getMaxTemperature());
    }
    catch (Exception ex) {
      System.err.println("Caught an unexpected exception!");
      ex.printStackTrace();
    }
  }
}
```

This code finds the enterprise bean mapped to the coded name *ejb/MixMaxTemp*. It creates a bean instance with an initial temperature of 20.0 degrees. This is the first time we have seen a create method taking an argument. Notice the method signatures of the `create()` method in the home interface and the `ejbCreate()` method in the bean code. Every `create()` method must be matched by an `ejbCreate()` method with the same signature.

The client applies deltas to the temperature by passing these deltas to the `adjustTemperature()` method. After each delta is applied, the current temperature is obtained by invoking the `getCurrentTemperature()` method. When all deltas have been applied, the minimum and maximum temperatures are determined by invoking the `getMinTemperature()` and `getMaxTemperature()` methods, respectively.

Creating J2EEApplication Client

We compile the client using *compileMinMaxTempClientJ2EE. bat:*

***Chapter4\\code\\compileMinMaxTempClientJ2EE.bat*

We have already discussed the procedure that should be followed to create a J2EE application client. The parameters required to create *MinMaxTempClientJ2EE* are shown in Table 4-3.

Running the J2EE client application produces the output shown in Figure 4-25.

TABLE 4-3

Parameters Required to Create MinMax-TempClientJ2EE

Parameter	Value
Application File Name	MinMaxTempApp.ear
DisplayName	MinMaxTempClient
Component/Reference Name	ejb/MinMaxTemp

Figure 4-25
Output from
MinMaxTemp-
ClientJ2EE

```
Command Prompt                                                    _ □ ×

D:\instant_ejb\CHAPTER4\code>runclient -client MinMaxTempApp.ear  -name MinMaxTem
pClient

Initiating login ...
Looking up authenticator...
Binding name:`java:comp/env/ejb/MinMaxTemp`
current temp = 20.0
applying delta -1.5
current temp = 18.5
applying delta 4.2
current temp = 22.7
applying delta -2.6
current temp = 20.099999999999998
applying delta -4.7
current temp = 15.399999999999999
applying delta 6.8
current temp = 22.2
applying delta -1.1
current temp = 21.099999999999998
minimum temperature was 15.399999999999999
maximum temperature was 22.7
Unbinding name:`java:comp/env/ejb/MinMaxTemp`
D:\instant_ejb\CHAPTER4\code>
```

The Stateful Session Bean Life Cycle

The code presented in this section is designed to demonstrate the life cycle of a stateful session bean. If your interest consists only of learning how to write and deploy EJBs, you can safely skip over this section.

Stateful session beans cannot be shared among clients. This presents a problem when the number of clients becomes large. The number of session beans required to service a large number of clients can result in a demand for more memory than is available to the container. The solution to this problem is a process called *passivation*. When it becomes necessary to temporarily reclaim memory occupied by an instance of a stateless session bean, the container serializes the bean instance and writes it out to external storage. Before it does so, it invokes the `ejbPassivate()` method of the bean instance. This provides the bean with an opportunity to perform the processing required to release resources that should not or cannot participate in the serialization process. When a client subsequently invokes a method on a bean that has been passivated, the container creates an instance of the bean using the serialized representation it has written to external storage. It then associates the instance with the handle by which the client knows the bean. This process is called *activation*. Before invoking the method that triggered the activation process, the container invokes the `ejbActivate()` method of the bean instance. This provides the bean with an opportunity to reacquire those resources it released in the `ejbPassivate()` method.

The code in this section does nothing useful; it simply reports *creation, passivation, activation,* and *removal* life-cycle events as they occur. The remote interface and home interface are simply presented without discussion.

The Remote Interface

This is the code for the remote interface:

\Chapter4\code\StatefulLifeDemo.java

```
import javax.ejb.EJBObject;
import java.rmi.RemoteException;

public interface StatefulLifeDemo extends EJBObject {

   public void doSomeWork()
      throws RemoteException;
```

The Home Interface

This is the code for the home interface:

\Chapter4\code\StatefulLifeDemoHome.java

```
import java.io.Serializable;
import java.rmi.RemoteException;
```

```
import javax.ejb.CreateException;
import javax.ejb.EJBHome;

public interface StatefulLifeDemoHome
      extends EJBHome {
   StatefulLifeDemo create(String id)
      throws RemoteException, CreateException;
}
```

The Enterprise Bean

Here is the code for the enterprise bean:

 ━ ━ ━ ━ ━ ━ ━ ━ ━ ━ ━ ━ ━ ━ ━

\Chapter4\code\StatefulLifeDemoBean.java

```
import java.rmi.RemoteException;
import javax.ejb.CreateException;
import javax.ejb.EJBObject;
import javax.ejb.SessionBean;
import javax.ejb.SessionContext;

public class StatefulLifeDemoBean
    implements SessionBean {

  SessionContext context;
  String display_id;
  int blobSize = 1024 * 1024;
  byte[] storageBlob;

  public void doSomeWork() {
    System.out.println(display_id + " doSomeWork");
    for (int i = 0; i < blobSize; ++i) {
      storageBlob[i] = (byte)0xff;
    }
  }

  public void ejbCreate(String id) throws CreateException {
    storageBlob = new byte[blobSize];
    EJBObject ejbo = context.getEJBObject();
    try {
      display_id =
        id + " " + ejbo.getEJBHome().getHomeHandle().toString();
      System.out.println(display_id + " ejbCreate");
    }
    catch (RemoteException e) {
      throw new CreateException();
    }
  }
```

```
public void ejbRemove() {
   System.out.println(display_id + " ejbRemove");
}

public void ejbActivate() {
   System.out.println(display_id + " ejbActivate");
}

public void ejbPassivate() {
   System.out.println(display_id + " ejbPassivate");
}

public void setSessionContext(SessionContext sc) {
   System.out.println("setSessionContext");
   context = sc;
}
}
```

At the very beginning of the bean's life cycle, the container passes a SessionContext to the bean's `setSessionContext()` method. The bean displays a message on `System.out` and saves the context it receives as an argument in the instance variable `context`.

The container then invokes the bean's `ejbCreate()` method, which receives as an argument a string containing a process identifier (we will see just what this is when we run our client code). The code in the `ejbCreate()` method creates a 1 MB byte array. It does this for no reason other than to consume memory at such a rate that it triggers the conditions under which the container will passivate one or more beans. The method's code then invokes the `getEJBObject()` method of the SessionContext in the instance variable `context`. It continues by invoking the `getEJBHome()` method on the object returned by `getEJBObject()` and finally invoking the `getHomeHandle()` method on the object returned by `getEJBHome()`. The result is converted to a string and concatenated to the process identifier received by `ejbCreate()` as an argument. The resultant string, which serves to identify the bean and the process that created it, is saved in the instance variable `internal_id`. This identifier is displayed on `System.out` as each of the bean's life-cycle methods is invoked by the container.

The bean contains a single business method `doSomeWork()`, which displays the identifier mentioned earlier and assigns a value of 0xff to each element of the byte array. If the bean had been passivated prior to invocation of this method, the container would invoke the bean's ejbActivate() method before invoking doSome-Work().

The remaining life-cycle methods are `ejbActivate()`, `ejb-Passivate()`, and `ejbRemove()`. Our implementation of these methods does nothing more than display the bean identifier and the name of the method.

Packaging and Deploying

The file *compileStatefulLifeDemo.bat* can be used to compile the remote interface, home interface, and enterprise bean code.

\Chapter4\code\compileStatefulLifeDemo.bat

The parameters required to package and deploy the bean are shown in Table 4-4.

TABLE 4-4	Parameter	Value
Parameters Required to Package and Deploy Stateful-LifeDemo	Application File Name	StatefulLifeDemoApp.ear
	Application Display Name	StatefulLifeDemoApp
	JAR DisplayName	StatefulLifeDemoJAR
	Enterprise Bean Class	StatefulLifeDemoBeanBean
	Home Interface	StatefulLifeDemoHome
	Remote Interface	StatefulLifeDemo
	Enterprise Bean Display Name	StatefulLifeDemoBean
	JNDI Name	MyStatefulLifeDemo

Standalone Client

We will be running multiple, simultaneous instances of our client code. Since we do not want one instance to run to completion before another instance completes its startup, the startup process should be short. For this reason, we will use a standalone process, which does not require security authentication at startup.

Here is the code for the client:

\Chapter4\code\StatefulLifeDemoClient.java

```java
import javax.naming.Context;
import javax.naming.InitialContext;
import javax.rmi.PortableRemoteObject;

import StatefulLifeDemo;
import StatefulLifeDemoHome;

public class StatefulLifeDemoClient {

  public static void main(String[] args) {

    String id = null;

    if (args.length != 1) {
      abort("You must specify a job identifier");
    }

    try {
      int i = Integer.parseInt(args[0]);
    }
    catch (NumberFormatException e) {
      abort("The job identifier must be numeric");
    }

    try {
      Context initial = new InitialContext();
      Object objref = initial.lookup("MyStatefulLifeDemo");

      StatefulLifeDemoHome home =
        (StatefulLifeDemoHome)PortableRemoteObject.narrow(objref,
          StatefulLifeDemoHome.class);

      StatefulLifeDemo demo[] = new StatefulLifeDemo[10];

      for (int i = 0; i < 10; ++i) {
        Thread.sleep(1000L);
```

```
        demo[i] = home.create(args[0]);
      }

      for (int i = 0; i < 10; ++i) {
        for (int j = 1; j < 10; ++j) {
          demo[i].doSomeWork();
          Thread.sleep(5000L);
        }
      }

      for (int i = 0; i < 10; ++i) {
        demo[i].remove();
      }
    }
    catch (Exception ex) {
      System.err.println("Caught an unexpected exception!");
      ex.printStackTrace();
    }
  }

  static void abort(String message) {
    System.out.println(message);
    System.out.println("aborting");
    System.exit(0);
  }
}
```

Running the Client

Before running the client, we should take a look at the *default.properties* file, which is located in the `config` subdirectory under the directory in which the J2SDKEE was installed. We are interested in the line that reads:

```
passivation.threshold.memory=128000000
```

As its name implies, this tag/value pair indicates that passivation will be triggered when the demand for memory exceeds 128,000,000 bytes. We can adjust this value downward to force passivation to occur sooner before we run our client code.

NOTE: *It is always a wise idea to adopt a "belts-and-suspenders" approach when modifying any configuration file. Before making any modifications, you should copy the file to* `default.properties.dist`*. The* *name is a reminder that this is the distributed version of the file that can be used for recovery if a mistake is made. Additionally, it is recommended that a line never be modified directly. If the configuration file being modified supports comments, you should make a copy of the original line, comment out the original, and modify the copy. That way, restoration consists of uncommenting the original line and either commenting out or deleting the modified line.*

We run the client using the command:

```
start runStatefulLifeDemoClient 1
```

This executes `runStatefulLifeDemoClient.bat` as a separate process and returns to the command prompt.

\Chapter4\code\runStatefulLifeDemoClient.bat

The argument 1, a process identifier, is passed to our client code that the `.bat` file executes. We then recall the last command, change the argument (process identifier) to 2, and immediately start another process. The number of copies of the client we need to run to guarantee that we see all of the life-cycle methods invoked depends on the speed of the processor we are using, the amount of memory it has, and the value we supplied in the *default.properties* file. You are encouraged to experiment.

The messages displayed by the `System.out.println()` calls in our bean code that will be displayed in the window in which we started the J2EE server if we specified the -verbose flag; otherwise, they are written to the log file reported by the J2EE server as it starts. In our case we choose to omit the -verbose flag. A portion of the `system.out` log resulting from running multiple, simultaneous instances of the client is shown in Figure 4-26.

Only selected portions of the system.out log are shown. Notice the first call to `ejbActivate()` for the bean from process 1, whose identifier is 1cd75a. You can see in an earlier log entry where it had been passivated. The call to `ejbActivate()` is in response to a

Figure 4-26

Selected Entries from
`system.out` Log

```
setSessionContext
setSessionContext
2 com.sun.ejb.containers.HomeHandleImpl@5acccc ejbCreate
1 com.sun.ejb.containers.HomeHandleImpl@122f46 ejbCreate
setSessionContext
setSessionContext
1 com.sun.ejb.containers.HomeHandleImpl@691dee ejbPassivate
1 com.sun.ejb.containers.HomeHandleImpl@5ada24 ejbCreate
2 com.sun.ejb.containers.HomeHandleImpl@578aab ejbPassivate
1 com.sun.ejb.containers.HomeHandleImpl@1cd75a ejbPassivate
setSessionContext
1 com.sun.ejb.containers.HomeHandleImpl@5428dd ejbCreate
2 com.sun.ejb.containers.HomeHandleImpl@678c96 ejbPassivate
2 com.sun.ejb.containers.HomeHandleImpl@35bb0f ejbCreate
.

1 com.sun.ejb.containers.HomeHandleImpl@1cd75a ejbActivate
1 com.sun.ejb.containers.HomeHandleImpl@52c6b4 ejbPassivate
1 com.sun.ejb.containers.HomeHandleImpl@1cd75a doSomeWork
.

2 com.sun.ejb.containers.HomeHandleImpl@678c96 ejbActivate
2 com.sun.ejb.containers.HomeHandleImpl@678c96 doSomeWork
1 com.sun.ejb.containers.HomeHandleImpl@1cd75a doSomeWork
```

client call to `doSomeWork()`. You can see that, to activate bean
1cd75a, the container had to passivate the bean from process 1,
whose identifier is 52c6b4. After the `ejbActivate()` method completes, you then see the call to `doSomeWork()`.

Summary

In this chapter we have seen how to write, package, and deploy
stateful session beans. We also introduced another kind of client,
the J2EE application client. Finally, we examined the life cycle of
a stateful session bean.

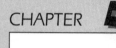

The Center
of Business—
The Customer

In this chapter:

- Entity Beans
- Customer Record
- Customer Account
- Servlet as Client

In the last two chapters, we concentrated on session beans. In this chapter, we shift our focus to entity beans, developing two of the most common entity beans encountered in the business world—a customer record and an account record. We also show how a servlet can be a client of a bean.

Before we start writing code, we should discuss entity beans in some detail. The three characteristics of entity beans that differentiate them from session beans are:

- Persistence
- Shared access
- Primary keys

Persistence

We have seen that session beans are transient in nature. Even a stateful session bean, which exists for an entire session, is destroyed when the session ends. If the server experiences a failure, the state of a session bean at the time of failure is lost. Entity beans, on the other hand, are persistent. Their state is preserved on some external storage medium, usually a database. The bean exists after the application using it terminates and even after the J2EE server is stopped. The bean survives failure of the application or the J2EE server.

There are two types of persistence: bean-managed and container-managed. A bean's persistence type, like other bean properties, is determined by a declarative statement recorded in the bean's deployment descriptor by the Application Deployment Tool.

With bean-managed persistence, all calls that access the database are contained in the entity bean code. The `ejbCreate()` method issues the SQL `insert` call that creates the database record. The `ejbRemove()` method issues the SQL `delete` call that deletes the database record. The author of the bean code is responsible for synchronizing the bean's instance variables with the data in the underlying database using SQL `update` calls in the `ejbLoad()` and `ejbStore()` methods.

With container-managed persistence, the bean's code contains no SQL calls; the calls are generated by the container. The container also assumes responsibility for synchronization. The declarative approach that by now is becoming so familiar to us is used to identify those fields that are to be container-managed and the Application Deployment Tool creates a list of these fields in the bean's deployment descriptor.

NOTE: *The statement that the code for a bean whose persistence is container-managed contains no SQL calls should be qualified. The bean can indeed issue SQL calls; however, these calls do not directly maintain the bean's state. By way of example, an entity bean could contain code that issues an* SQL SELECT *against some database table(s) and use the results of the query to modify one or more of the bean's instance variables. It would not, however, issue the* SQL UPDATE *that synchronizes the modified data with the database containing the bean.*

Although the choice of which type of persistence to use is yours to make, you should consider the following:

- Container-managed persistence requires less code and less code usually means fewer problems.
- Container-managed persistence provides greater portability. If the underlying data store is changed from a relational database to an object database, no changes to the bean's code are necessary.
- Some vendors' implementations might contain restrictions that limit portability.

■ The calls generated by container-managed persistence to maintain synchronization can possibly carry a performance penalty that could be lessened by using bean-managed persistence.

Shared Access

Many clients can share an entity bean. If, for example, the entity bean represents an item in a store's inventory, a clerk could be checking the quantity on hand before selling one of the items to a customer. At the same time, a stockroom employee who is processing a recently received shipment of parts might be updating the quantity on hand by scanning each item in the shipment using a barcode scanner. As you might expect, whenever multiple, simultaneous access is a possibility, transaction management is involved. The transaction boundaries are marked by the container and not coded by the author of the bean. The transaction attributes are specified using the declarative approach and are written into the bean's deployment descriptor by the Application Deployment Tool. We learn more about transactions in a later chapter.

Primary Keys

Because entity beans exist on a storage medium, a mechanism must be provided for finding them. This mechanism is a unique identifier called a *primary key*. The primary key is an object whose class is specified with the Application Deployment Tool. In most cases, the primary key class is *java.lang.String*. There are cases in which unique identification of an entity bean involves multiple fields. In such cases, you would define your own primary key class.

Whether the primary key class is a class that belongs to the *java* package or one that you define yourself, it must meet the following requirements:

- The access control modifier must be public.
- All fields must be public.
- If the persistence type is container-managed, field names must correspond to container-managed fields in the entity bean class.
- A public default (null argument) constructor must be provided.
- The `hashCode()` and `equals()` methods must be implemented.
- The class must be serializable.

The Customer Record

Now that we have discussed some of the characteristics of entity beans, it is time to create one. Our first example will be a light-weight version of what is undoubtedly the most common entity bean in the business world—the customer record. Since the record we are creating is for learning purposes only, we will limit the number of fields to three: social security number, first name, and last name. If we were developing a real-world application, the record might contain such fields as mailing address, telephone number, credit liability, and possibly demographic information such as sex and age. After you have seen how we develop our simple version, you might want to tackle a heavyweight version.

The first entity bean we are developing uses bean-managed persistence.

The Remote Interface

The entity bean we are creating has two business methods: `getFirstName()` and `getLastName()`. By now, we know that these must be declared in the remote interface; an examination of the code reveals that they are. Here is the code:

On the CD

\Chapter5\code\Customer.java

```
import javax.ejb.EJBObject;
import java.rmi.RemoteException;
public interface Customer extends EJBObject {

    public String getFirstName()
        throws RemoteException;

    public String getLastName()
        throws RemoteException;
}
```

The Home Interface

Our entity bean's home interface bears close examination. The home interface for each of the session beans we have examined so far defined one or more methods that allowed a client to create the bean. Because of the persistent nature of entity beans, in addition to creating a bean instance, a client can get an instance by finding a bean that had been previously created. Therefore, in addition to methods that allow a client to create a bean, the home interface of an entity bean contains one or more methods that allow a client to find a bean. The home interface also defines *finder* methods, which are the methods you see below, whose names begin with *find*. We discuss these methods shortly.

Here is the code for the home interface:

On the CD

\Chapter5\code\CustomerHome.java

```
import java.util.Collection;
import java.rmi.RemoteException;
import javax.ejb.*;

public interface CustomerHome extends EJBHome {

    public Customer create(String ssn, String firstName,
        String lastName)
            throws RemoteException, CreateException;
```

```
public Customer findByPrimaryKey(String ssn)
    throws FinderException, RemoteException;

public Collection findByFirstName(String firstName)
    throws FinderException, RemoteException;

public Collection findByLastName(String lastName)
    throws FinderException, RemoteException;
}
```

The Enterprise Bean Code

The code for the enterprise bean is rather lengthy. We discuss portions of the code here. The complete listing can be found at the end of the chapter.

Take a look at the definition of the *CustomerBean* class.

```
public class CustomerBean implements EntityBean
```

Every entity enterprise bean class *must* implement the *EntityBean* interface. In addition to the `ejbActivate()` and `ejb-Passivate()` methods we have already discussed in the *SessionBean* interface, the *EntityBean* interface declares the following methods:

- `ejbLoad()`
- `ejbStore()`
- `setEntityContext()`
- `unsetEntityContext()`

These methods are invoked by the container to notify the enterprise bean instance of life-cycle events. Now, let's look at each of the life-cycle methods in our bean.

ejbCreate()

Each enterprise bean must implement an `ejbCreate()` method that matches the signature of a corresponding `create()` method in the home interface. When the client invokes a `create()`

method, the container finds an `ejbCreate()` method with the identical signature and invokes that method on behalf of the client.

Here is the `ejbCreate()` method:

```
public String ejbCreate(String ssn, String firstName,
    String lastName)
        throws CreateException {

    String insertStatement =
      "INSERT INTO customer VALUES ( ? , ? , ? )";

    try {
      PreparedStatement ps =
        con.prepareStatement(insertStatement);
      ps.setString(1, ssn);
      ps.setString(2, firstName);
      ps.setString(3, lastName);
      ps.executeUpdate();
      ps.close();
    }
    catch (SQLException e) {
      throw new CreateException("Error inserting ssn: "
        + ssn + ". " + e.getMessage());
    }

    this.ssn = ssn;
    this.firstName = firstName;
    this.lastName = lastName;

    return ssn;
  }
```

The method constructs a *PreparedStatement* using the method's three arguments. It then invokes the `executeUpdate()` method to execute an SQL `INSERT` call in the *PreparedStatement*. If the `INSERT` call fails, the resulting *SQLException* is caught and a *CreateException* containing the text returned by the *SQLException*'s `getMessage()` method is thrown; otherwise, the method initializes the bean's instance variables and returns the primary key.

ejbPostCreate()

In addition to `ejbCreate()`, entity beans have an `ejbPostCreate()` method. The `ejbPostCreate()` method is invoked by the container immediately upon return from the `ejbCreate()` method.

Just as there must be an `ejbCreate()` method corresponding to each `create()` method in the home interface, there must be an `ejbPostCreate()` method that corresponds to each `ejbCreate()` method.

The characteristics of an `ejbPostCreate()` method are as follows:

- The number and types of its arguments must match the number and types of the arguments of an `ejbCreate()` method.
- The access control modifier must be `public`.
- The method modifier may not be `static` or `final`.
- The method must return `void`.

In our case, and indeed in most cases, the `ejbPostCreate()` method is empty; however, if we know that at some later point we will be passing a reference to our bean to another bean, the `ejbPostCreate()` method gives us a chance to obtain our entity bean's object reference by invoking the `getEJBObject()` method of the *EntityContext* interface and save it.

NOTE: *You cannot pass* `this` *to another bean as a reference to the current entity bean. Instead, you must pass the entity bean's object reference.*

setEntityContext

The container invokes the `setEntityContext()` method on an instance after the instance has been created. Our implementation of the `setEntityMethod()` looks like this:

```
public void setEntityContext(EntityContext context) {

    this.context = context;

    try {
      InitialContext ic = new InitialContext();
      DataSource ds = (DataSource) ic.lookup(dbName);
      con = ds.getConnection();
    }
    catch (Exception e) {
```

```
      throw new EJBException("Unable to connect to database. " +
        e.getMessage());
    }
  }
```

The method first saves the *EntityContext* it receives as an argument. The bean can use this *EntityContext* to make requests of the container. An example of such a request is using the getPrimary-Key() method to obtain the bean's primary key whenever the bean's ejbActivate() method is invoked.

Since setEntityContext() is invoked once after the bean instance is created, this method is the perfect place to establish a database connection and our code does exactly that.

ejbLoad()

Whenever the container determines that it is necessary to synchronize the bean's instance variables with the values in the underlying database, it invokes the ejbLoad() method. Only the container may invoke this method. The client is not permitted to do so.

NOTE: *ejbLoad() and ejbStore() can only be relied on for synchronizing the state of an entity bean when the business method is associated with a transaction. We learn more about transactions later in the book; but for now, always make sure you mark your business methods with the Required or RequiresNew transaction attribute.*

Here is the code for our ejbLoad() method:

```
public void ejbLoad() {
    String selectStatement =
      "SELECT firstname, lastname " +
      "FROM customer WHERE ssn = ? ";

    try {
      PreparedStatement ps =
        con.prepareStatement(selectStatement);
      ps.setString(1, this.ssn);
      ResultSet rs = ps.executeQuery();
      if (rs.next()) {
```

```
            this.firstName = rs.getString(1);
            this.lastName = rs.getString(2);
            ps.close();
        }
        else {
            ps.close();
            throw new NoSuchEntityException("Row for ssn " + ssn +
              " not found in database.");
        }
    }
    catch (SQLException ex) {
        throw new EJBException("ejbLoad: " +
          ex.getMessage());
    }
}
```

This code first creates a *PreparedStatement* and uses the `exe-cuteQuery()` method of the *PreparedStatement* to execute an SQL SELECT call to retrieve from the row identified by the primary key (`ssn`) those columns that correspond to `firstName` and `last-Name`. It refreshes the instance variables using the values loaded from the database.

The code tests whether the result set returned by the SQL QUERY is empty. If it is, the method throws a *NoSuchEntityException*. The container wraps this exception in a *RemoteException* and throws the *RemoteException* to the client.

Notice that the method definition does not include a `throws` clause. It does not have to because the *NoSuchEntityException* is a subclass of *EJBException*, which in turn is a subclass of *Runtime-Exception*.

ejbStore

Whenever the container determines that it is necessary to update the database to reflect changes in the bean's instance variables, it invokes the `ejbStore()` method. As was the case with `ejbLoad()`, only the container may invoke this method. The client is not permitted to do so. Whenever a business method is associated with a transaction, the container determines when to invoke the `ejbStore()` method upon return from the business method.

Since `ejbStore()` is the counterpart of `ejbLoad()`, with the main difference being execution of an SQL UPDATE instead of an

SQL QUERY, we will not present or discuss the code here. Instead, you can examine method's code in the full listing at the end of the chapter.

The Finder Methods

An examination of the bean code reveals the presence of three methods whose names begin with ejbFind.... These methods, called *finder* methods, are used to find instances of the bean. They are:

- ejbFindByPrimaryKey()
- ejbFindByFirstName()
- ejbFindByLastName()

When we examine the home interface code, you will notice the presence of the following three methods corresponding to the methods implemented by the bean:

- findByPrimaryName()
- findByFirstName()
- findByLastName()

The pattern should be familiar by now since it is the same as the one we have seen for create() methods. The container finds the ejbFind... method in the bean that has an identical signature to a find... method invoked by a client and invokes that method on behalf of the client.

The first method, ejbFindByPrimaryKey(), *must* be implemented by every entity bean. As its name implies, this method takes the primary key as an argument and uses this key to locate a single instance of the entity bean in the database.

The other finder methods are optional and are specific to your application. The rules for finder methods when bean-managed persistence is used are:

- The method name must start with ejbFind.
- The access control modifier must be public.

- The method modifier may not be `static` or `final`.
- The arguments and return types must be legal for RMI.
- The return type must be either the type of the primary key class as defined in the deployment descriptor or a collection of such types.
- When the finder method is expected to return a single primary key, if no entity bean containing that primary key is found, the method should throw the *ObjectNotFound* exception.
- When the finder method can return a collection of primary keys, if the collection is empty, the method should throw the *FinderException*.
- Every `find...()` method in the home interface needs a matching `ejbFind...()` method.

ejbRemove

The `ejbRemove()` method is the counterpart of `ejbCreate()` and works in the same way (i.e., the client invokes the `remove()` method and the container invokes `ejbRemove()` on behalf of the client).

The code for our `ejbRemove()` method is as follows:

```
String deleteStatement =
    "DELETE FROM customer WHERE ssn = ? ";

    try {
      PreparedStatement ps =
        con.prepareStatement(deleteStatement);
      ps.setString(1, ssn);
      ps.executeUpdate();
      ps.close();
    }
    catch (SQLException e) {
      throw new EJBException("ejbRemove: " +
        e.getMessage());
    }
```

The code uses the primary key it receives as an argument to construct a *PreparedStatement* and invokes the `executeUpdate()` method of the *PreparedStatement* to execute the SQL `DELETE` call that removes the record from the database.

unsetEntityContext

Before the container removes an instance of an entity bean, it invokes the bean's `unsetEntityContext()` method. Here is the code for our bean's `unsetEntityContext()` method:

```java
public void unsetEntityContext() {

    try {
      con.close();
    }
    catch (SQLException ex) {
      throw new EJBException("unsetEntityContext: " +
ex.getMessage());
    }
  }
```

The method attempts to close the database connection that was opened in the `setEntityContext()` method.

Business Methods

The only methods we have not discussed are the business methods. As you write business methods, keep in mind that such methods should *only* contain business logic. Remember when we discussed `ejbLoad()` and `ejbStore()` we mentioned that, if you want to guarantee that the instance variables used by a business method are in synch with the underlying database, you should associate the business method with a transaction.

The two business methods in our example, `getFirstName()` and `getLastName()`, are declared in the remote interface.

Packaging and Deploying

The file *compileCustomer.bat* can be used to compile the remote interface, home interface, and enterprise bean code.

\Chapter5\code\compileCustomer.bat

We use the Application Deployment Tool to package and deploy the entity bean. We start exactly as we did when we packaged and deployed session beans (i.e., we create an application called *CustomerApp* and then select the "New Enterprise Bean . . ." option from the "File" menu to start the New Enterprise Bean Wizard).

After we have created a Jar file called *CustomerJAR,* we add the files *Customer.class, CustomerHome.class,* and *CustomerBean .class* to it and click on NEXT>. When the General dialog appears, we select *CustomerBean, CustomerHome,* and *Customer* from the drop-down lists labeled "Enterprise Bean Class:", "Home Interface:", and "Remote Interface:", respectively. We then type *CustomerBean* in the entry field labeled "Enterprise Bean Display Name:".

From this point on, the procedure is different from that which we followed for session beans. We click on the radio button labeled ENTITY in the group box labeled BEAN TYPE. Since this indicates that the bean is to be an entity bean, the buttons labeled STATE-LESS and STATEFUL become grayed out, indicating that they are not selectable as options. This makes sense since they apply only to session beans. The General dialog should now look like Figure 5-1.

When we click on NEXT>, the Entity Settings dialog shown in Figure 5-2 appears. Our bean contains code that issues the SQL calls that access the database, indicating that we will be using bean-managed persistence. We indicate this by clicking on the radio button labeled BEAN-MANAGED PERSISTENCE. We also change the Primary Key Type from *java.lang.Object* to *java.lang.String*.

Clicking on NEXT> in the Entity setting dialog results in the appearance of the Environment Entries dialog. We will not be defining any environment entries and so we skip this dialog by clicking on NEXT>. We can also skip the Enterprise Bean References dialog so that we are looking at the Resource References dialog shown in Figure 5-3.

When we click on the ADD button, the dialog changes to look like Figure 5-4. Under the column labeled "Coded Name", we enter *jdbc/CustomerDB*. The drop-down lists in the columns labeled "Type" and "Authentication" should have *javax.sql.DataSource* and

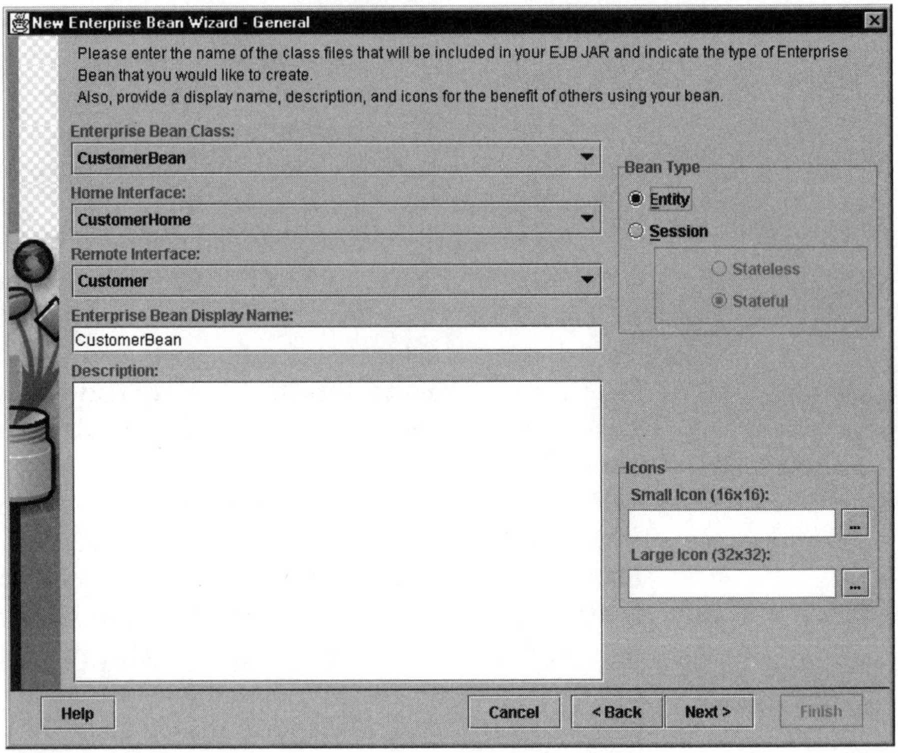

Figure 5-1
General Dialog for an
Entity Bean

Container selected. Before we continue, the dialog should look like Figure 5-5.

Clicking NEXT> takes us to the Security dialog, which we can skip by clicking NEXT> again. This takes us to the Transaction Management dialog shown in Figure 5-6.

Because we are creating an entity bean, we *must* choose container-managed transactions and so the radio buttons labeled BEAN-MANAGED TRANSACTIONS and CONTAINER-MANAGED TRANSACTIONS are grayed out. We specify a type of *Required* for each of our business methods. We do this by clicking on the value listed in the column labeled "Transaction Type". This causes a list like that shown in Figure 5-7 to appear. We select *Required* from that list. After this process has been completed for each of the business methods, the Transaction Management dialog should look like Figure 5-8.

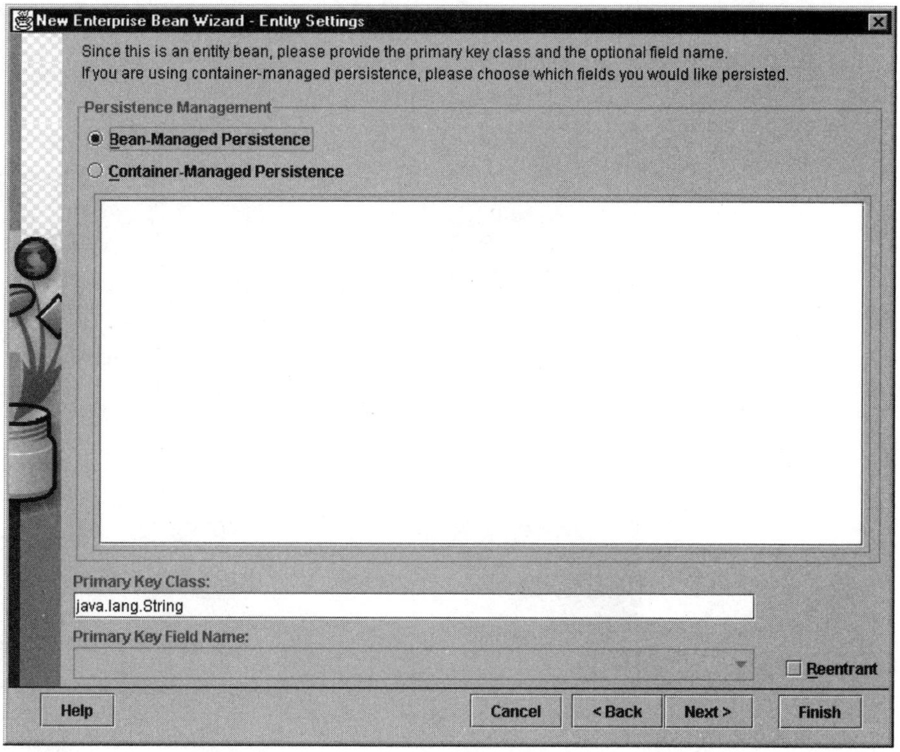

Figure 5-2
Specifying Bean-
Managed Persistence

When we click on NEXT> in the Transaction Management dialog, the Review Settings dialog shown in Figure 5-9 is displayed. You will recognize the text displayed as XML. It is the deployment descriptor. After reviewing the settings in the descriptor, we click on FINISH. The main window of the Application Deployment Tool now looks like Figure 5-10.

We are now ready to deploy the application. We start the process by selecting "Deploy Application . . ." from the "Tools" drop-down menu. After clicking on the checkbox labeled RETURN CLIENT JAR in the Introduction dialog and clicking on NEXT>, the JNDI Names dialog shown in Figure 5-11 appears.

In the column labeled "JNDI Name" in the row containing the CustomerBean component, we enter *MyCustomer*. In the same JNDI Name column, we enter *jdbc/Cloudscape* in the row containing the reference *jdbc/CustomerDB*. This provides the mapping

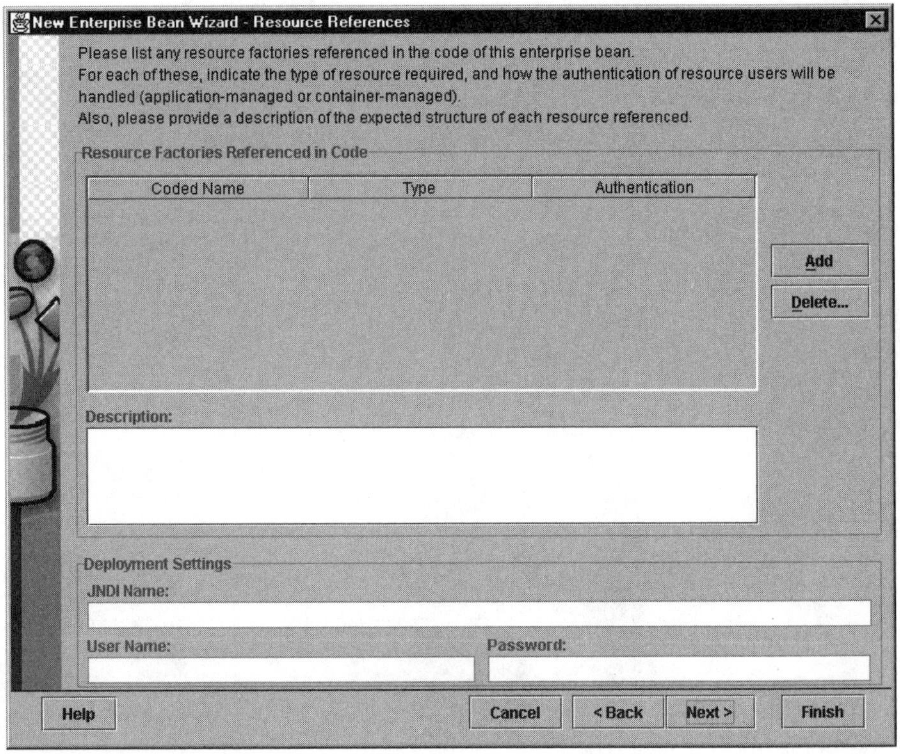

Figure 5-3
The Resources
References Dialog

necessary for the container to find the bean and the database table at runtime. When all data are entered, the JNDI Names dialog should look like Figure 5-12.

After the data have been entered, we click on NEXT>, and then click on FINISH in the Review dialog. A Deployment Progress dialog appears that is similar to the kind we saw when we deployed session beans. When the deployment process has completed, we click on OK in the dialog. This returns us to the Application Deployment Tool main window.

The Client

We are now ready to test our entity bean. Since we have introduced a significant amount of new material, we will stick to a simple

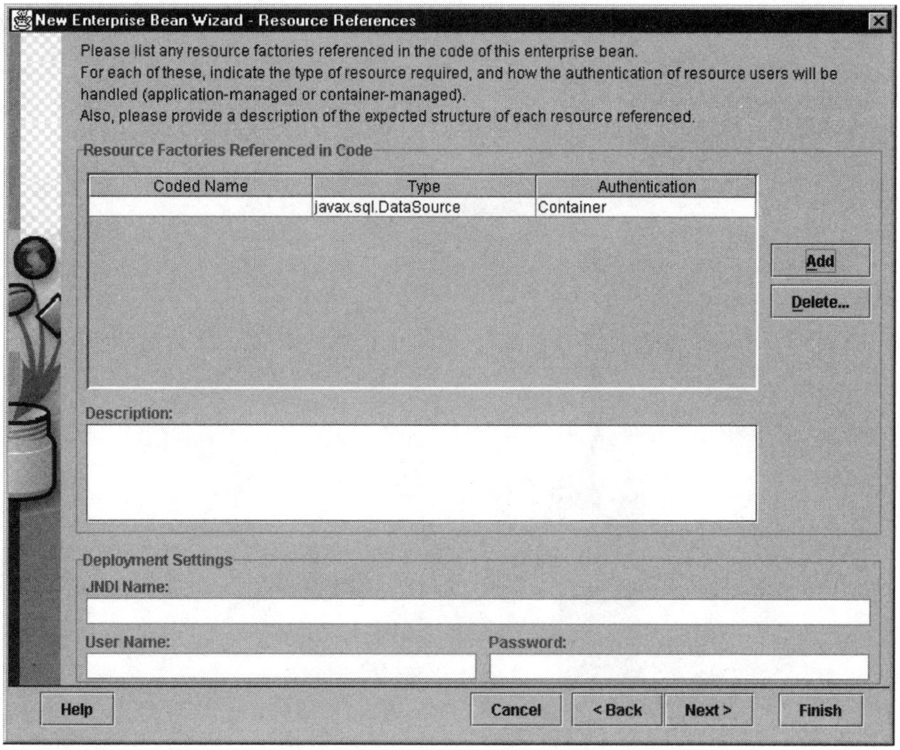

Figure 5-4

Preparing to Add a
Resource Reference

standalone client. We discuss selected portions of the code, shown in its entirety, at the end of this chapter.

The client starts by executing the same code as our other stand-alone clients did. It obtains an *InitialContext*, uses the `lookup()` method to obtain a reference to the bean's home interface, and saves the reference in the variable `home`.

The code now executes the following for loop:

```
for (int i = 0; i < custRecs.length; ++i) {
    try {
      home.create(custRecs[i][0],custRecs[i][1],custRecs[i] [2]);
      System.out.println("record created for ssn: " +
        custRecs[i] [0]);
    }
    catch (RemoteException e) {
      System.err.println("RemoteException");
    }
    catch (CreateException e) {
```

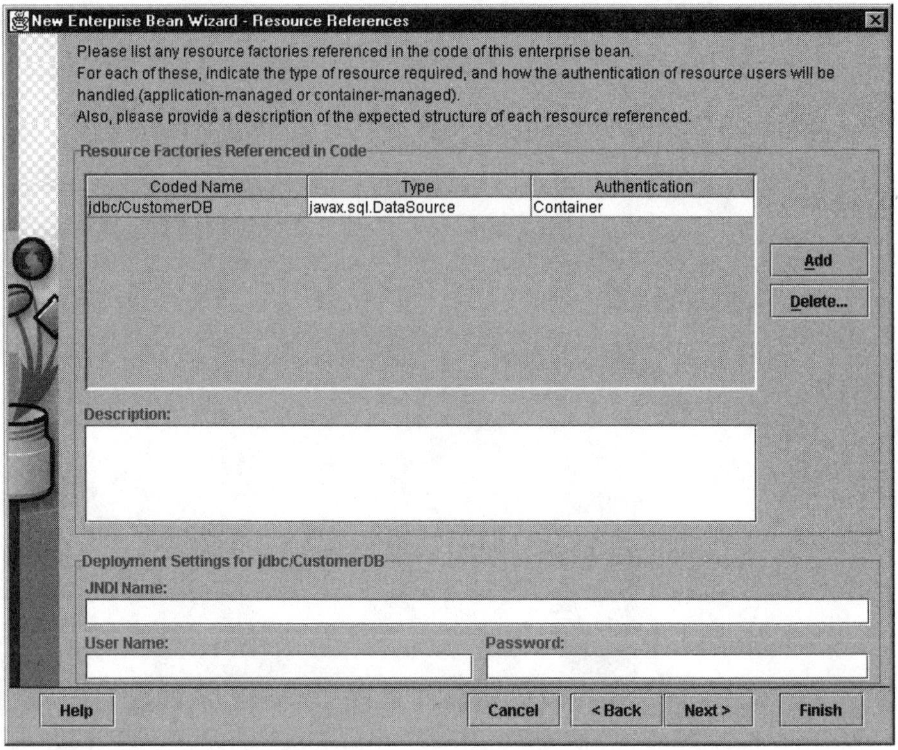

Figure 5-5
Resource References
Dialog After Adding
Reference

```
        System.out.println("create failed for ssn: " +
          custRecs[i][0]);
      }
    }
```

For each iteration, strings containing a social security number, a first name, and a last name are passed as arguments to the create() method of the bean's home interface. The container invokes the corresponding ejbCreate() method in the bean code and that method executes the SQL INSERT that creates a new record in the database. If a record containing the specified primary key already exists in the database, a *CreateException* is thrown containing the text from the *SQLException*.

The code then executes two more for loops that exercise the finder methods and business methods.

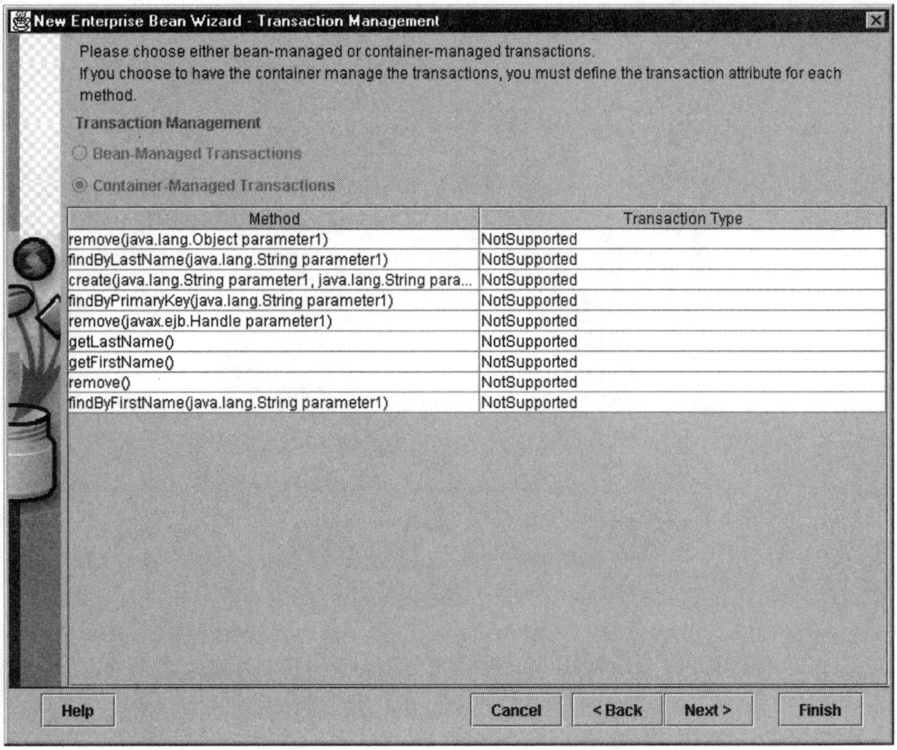

Figure 5-6
The Transaction
Management Dialog

The Transaction Management Dialog showing the New Enterprise Bean Wizard:

Please choose either bean-managed or container-managed transactions.
If you choose to have the container manage the transactions, you must define the transaction attribute for each method.

Transaction Management

○ Bean-Managed Transactions
◉ Container-Managed Transactions

Method	Transaction Type
remove(java.lang.Object parameter1)	NotSupported
findByLastName(java.lang.String parameter1)	NotSupported
create(java.lang.String parameter1, java.lang.String para...	NotSupported
findByPrimaryKey(java.lang.String parameter1)	NotSupported
remove(javax.ejb.Handle parameter1)	NotSupported
getLastName()	NotSupported
getFirstName()	NotSupported
remove()	NotSupported
findByFirstName(java.lang.String parameter1)	NotSupported

Help   Cancel   < Back   Next >   Finish

The Database

The Java 2 SDK Enterprise Edition includes the Cloudscape
DBMS. This product is designed to be used by enterprise beans
and is the database we will use to run all of our sample code.

Starting the Database Server

Before any application can access a Cloudscape database, the
Cloudscape Server must be started. This can be done from the command line by typing:

```
cloudscape -start
```

Figure 5-7
Selecting a
Transaction Type

New Enterprise Bean Wizard - Transaction Management

Please choose either bean-managed or container-managed transactions.
If you choose to have the container manage the transactions, you must define the transaction attribute for each method.

Transaction Management

○ Bean-Managed Transactions

◉ Container-Managed Transactions

Method	Transaction Type
remove(java.lang.Object parameter1)	NotSupported
findByLastName(java.lang.String parameter1)	NotSupported
create(java.lang.String parameter1, java.lang.String para...	NotSupported
findByPrimaryKey(java.lang.String parameter1)	NotSupported
remove(javax.ejb.Handle parameter1)	NotSupported
getLastName()	NotSupported ▼
getFirstName()	Mandatory
remove()	Never
findByFirstName(java.lang.String parameter1)	NotSupported
	Required
	RequiresNew
	Supports

| Help | | Cancel | < Back | Next > | Finish |

As the server starts up, it displays messages like those shown in Figure 5-13.

Creating the Customer Table

Instances of the entity bean we wrote correspond to rows in a table in the database and the instance variables correspond to columns. We have coded all the required SQL calls and we need to create a database table on which these calls can act. The file *createCustomerTable.bat* creates the table by passing the name of the file *createCustomer.sql* to the *ij* utility.

Here is the .bat file:

\Chapter5\code\createCustomerTable.bat

Figure 5-8
Final Appearance of
the Transaction
Management Dialog

New Enterprise Bean Wizard - Transaction Management

Please choose either bean-managed or container-managed transactions.
If you choose to have the container manage the transactions, you must define the transaction attribute for each method.

Transaction Management

○ Bean-Managed Transactions

◉ Container-Managed Transactions

Method	Transaction Type
remove(java.lang.Object parameter1)	NotSupported
findByLastName(java.lang.String parameter1)	NotSupported
create(java.lang.String parameter1, java.lang.String para...	NotSupported
findByPrimaryKey(java.lang.String parameter1)	NotSupported
remove(javax.ejb.Handle parameter1)	NotSupported
getLastName()	Required
getFirstName()	Required
remove()	NotSupported
findByFirstName(java.lang.String parameter1)	NotSupported

| Help | Cancel | < Back | Next > | Finish |

```
java -
Dij.connection.CloudscapeDB=jdbc:rmi://localhost:1099/jdbc:cloud
scape:CloudscapeDB\create=true -Dcloudscape.system.home=%J2EE_HOME%\
cloudscape -classpath %J2EE_HOME%\lib\cloudscape\client.jar;%J2EE_
HOME%\lib\cloudscape\tools.jar;%J2EE_HOME%\lib\cloudscape\cloud
scape.jar;%J2EE_HOME%\lib\cloudscape\RmiJdbc.jar;%J2EE_HOME%\lib\
cloudscape\license.jar;%CLASSPATH% -ms16m - mx32mCOM.cloudscape.
tools.ij createCustomer.sql
```

We can see that the *ij* utility—a utility for running scripts against a Cloudscape database—uses *createCustomer.sql*, which looks like this:

\Chapter5\code\createCustomer.sql

```
drop table customer;
create table customer
(ssn char(9) constraint pk_customer primary key,
firstname varchar(24),
lastname varchar(24));

exit;
```

Figure 5-9
The Review Settings
Dialog

When we execute *createCustomerTable.bat,* it runs the *ij* utility,
which displays messages like those shown in Figure 5-14.

NOTE: *The ij utility can be used to perform a wide variety of database
administration and maintenance functions. The Java 2 SDK Enterprise
Edition contains a Cloudscape Documentation Bundle in which an entire
section is devoted to the ij utility.*

Running the Client

We are finally ready to run the client. We do so by executing *run-
Customerclient.bat.*

\Chapter5\code\runCustomerClient.bat

Figure 5-10
CustomerApp

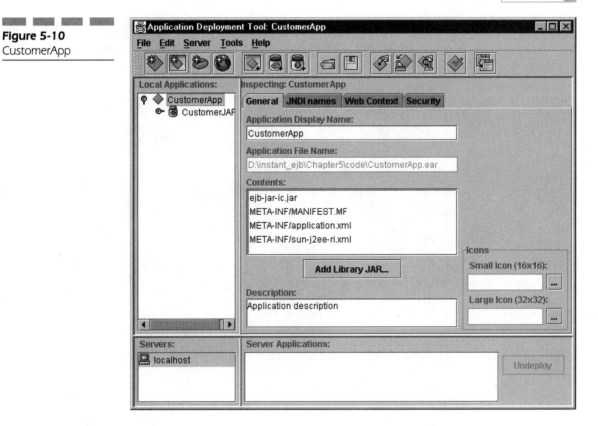

As the client code executes, it generates the messages shown in Figure 5-15. Notice that the second attempt to insert a record with a primary key of '123456789' fails. The ejbCreate() method catches the *SQLException* and uses its message text to create and throw a *CreateException*. As an experiment, you might want to modify *CustomerClient.java* so that the catch block displays the *CreateException's* message. The code would look like:

```
catch (CreateException e) {
  System.out.println(e.getMessage());
  System.out.println("create failed for ssn: " +
    custRecs[i][0]);
}
```

As yet another experiment, you might want to add code similar to that which was used in Chapter 4 in *StatefulLifeDemo* and run

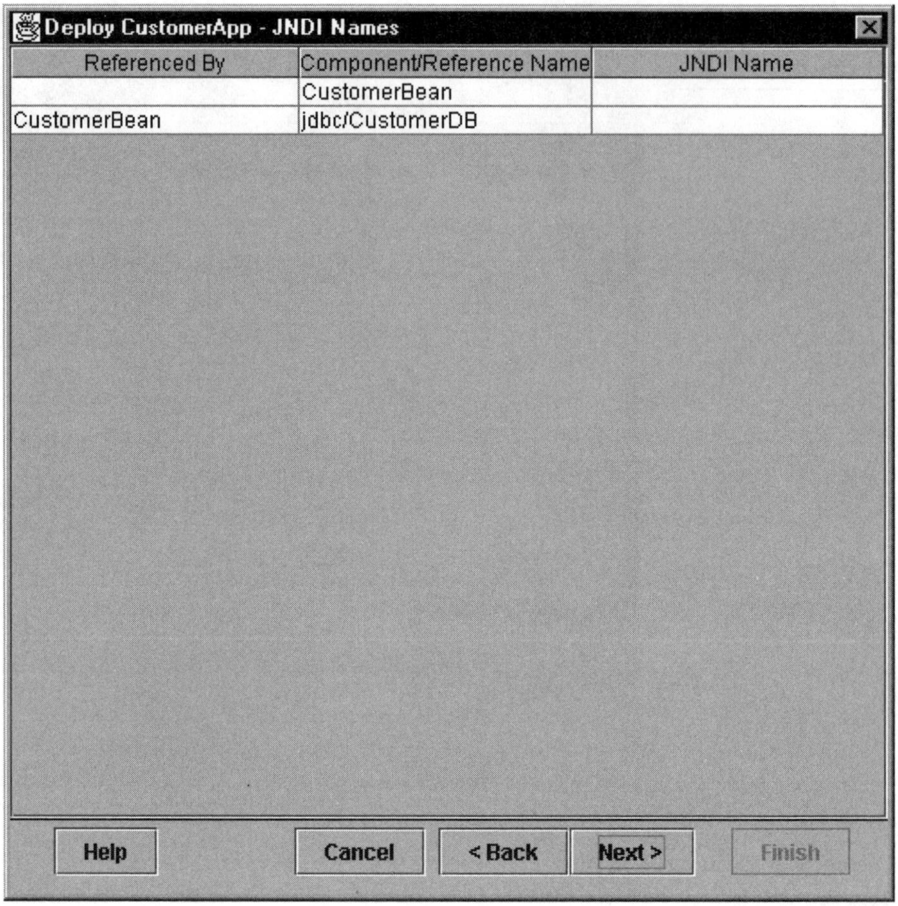

Figure 5-11
The JNDI Names
Dialog

Referenced By	Component/Reference Name	JNDI Name
	CustomerBean	
CustomerBean	jdbc/CustomerDB	

multiple, simultaneous instances of *CustomerClient*. The output of such a program would provide visual feedback from the life cycle of an entity bean.

The Account Record

The customer record we just saw is often used in conjunction with a record that represents that customer's account. We will

Figure 5-12
JNDI Names Dialog
After Mapping Is
Complete

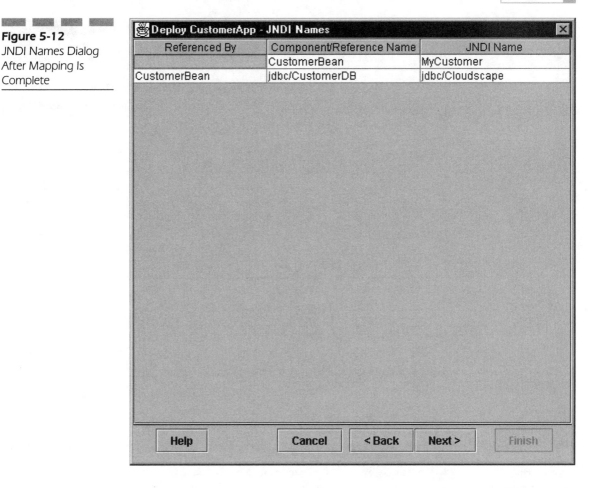

now implement an account record. Like the customer record, our account record will be minimal and contain only a sufficient number of fields to be functional. The primary reason for developing the *Account* bean is to provide a bean to use with a new type of client we will be introducing. The coding for the remote interface, home interface, and bean code is similar to coding for the *Customer* entity bean and so will simply be listed without discussion.

As was the case with the customer record, you might want to consider implementing a more complete and robust version.

Figure 5-13
Starting the
Cloudscape Server

Figure 5-13
Starting the
Cloudscape Server

```
Command Prompt - cloudscape -start                                    _ □ X

D:\instant_ejb\CHAPTER5\code>cloudscape -start
Mon Jul 10 10:12:21 EDT 2000: [RmiJdbc] COM.cloudscape.core.JDBCDriver registere
d in DriverManager
Mon Jul 10 10:12:21 EDT 2000: [RmiJdbc] Binding RmiJdbcServer...
Mon Jul 10 10:12:21 EDT 2000: [RmiJdbc] No installation of RMI Security Manager.
..
Mon Jul 10 10:12:23 EDT 2000: [RmiJdbc] RmiJdbcServer bound in rmi registry
```

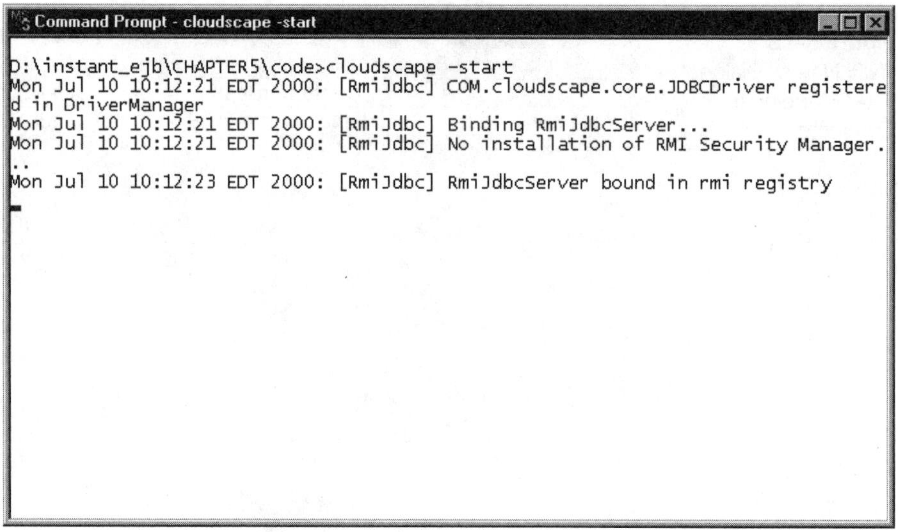

Figure 5-14
Creating the
Customer Database
Table

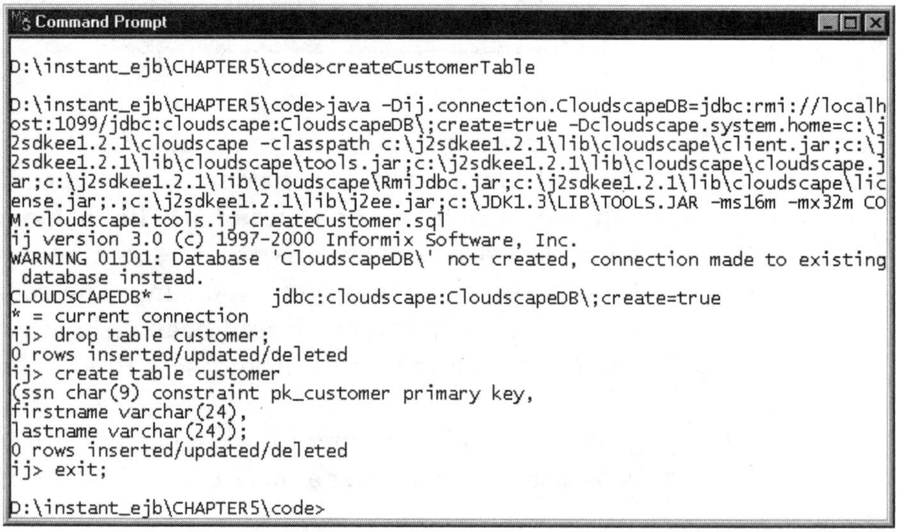

```
Command Prompt                                                        _ □ X

D:\instant_ejb\CHAPTER5\code>createCustomerTable

D:\instant_ejb\CHAPTER5\code>java -Dij.connection.CloudscapeDB=jdbc:rmi://localh
ost:1099/jdbc:cloudscape:CloudscapeDB\;create=true -Dcloudscape.system.home=c:\j
2sdkee1.2.1\cloudscape -classpath c:\j2sdkee1.2.1\lib\cloudscape\client.jar;c:\j
2sdkee1.2.1\lib\cloudscape\tools.jar;c:\j2sdkee1.2.1\lib\cloudscape\cloudscape.j
ar;c:\j2sdkee1.2.1\lib\cloudscape\RmiJdbc.jar;c:\j2sdkee1.2.1\lib\cloudscape\lic
ense.jar;.;c:\j2sdkee1.2.1\lib\j2ee.jar;c:\JDK1.3\LIB\TOOLS.JAR -ms16m -mx32m CO
M.cloudscape.tools.ij createCustomer.sql
ij version 3.0 (c) 1997-2000 Informix Software, Inc.
WARNING 01J01: Database 'CloudscapeDB\' not created, connection made to existing
 database instead.
CLOUDSCAPEDB* -          jdbc:cloudscape:CloudscapeDB\;create=true
* = current connection
ij> drop table customer;
0 rows inserted/updated/deleted
ij> create table customer
(ssn char(9) constraint pk_customer primary key,
firstname varchar(24),
lastname varchar(24));
0 rows inserted/updated/deleted
ij> exit;

D:\instant_ejb\CHAPTER5\code>
```

Figure 5-15
Output from
CustomerClient

```
Command Prompt

D:\instant_ejb\CHAPTER5\code>runCustomerClient
--- CREATING RECORDS ---
record created for ssn: 123456789
record created for ssn: 456789123
record created for ssn: 234567891
record created for ssn: 567891234
record created for ssn: 345678912
record created for ssn: 678912345
create failed for ssn: 123456789
record created for ssn: 789123456
record created for ssn: 891234567
record created for ssn: 912345678
--- RECORDS CREATED ---
Customers with last name = Jones
789123456: George Jones
891234567: John Jones
Customers with last name = Smith
** NONE **
Customers with first name = Barbara:
456789123: Barbara Hickey
912345678: Barbara Feldon

D:\instant_ejb\CHAPTER5\code>
```

The Remote Interface

The remote interface looks like this:

 On the CD

\Chapter5\code\Account.java

```java
import javax.ejb.EJBObject;
import java.rmi.RemoteException;

public interface Account extends EJBObject {

    public void debit(double amount)
        throws RemoteException;

    public void credit(double amount)
        throws RemoteException;

    public double getBalance()
        throws RemoteException;

    public void activateAccount()
        throws RemoteException;

    public void suspendAccount()
        throws RemoteException;
}
```

The Home Interface

Here is the home interface:

 \Chapter5\code\AccountHome.java

```java
import java.util.Collection;
import java.rmi.RemoteException;
import javax.ejb.*;

public interface AccountHome extends EJBHome {

    public Account create(String ssn)
        throws RemoteException, CreateException;

    public Account findByPrimaryKey(String ssn)
        throws FinderException, RemoteException;
}
```

The Enterprise Bean

Here is the enterprise bean:

 \Chapter5\code\AccountBean.java

```java
import java.sql.*;
import javax.ejb.*;
import javax.naming.*;
import javax.sql.*;

public class AccountBean implements EntityBean {

  private String ssn;
  private int status;
  private double balance;
  private EntityContext context;
  private Connection con;
  private String dbName = "java:comp/env/jdbc/AccountDB";

  private static final int ACCOUNT_ACTIVE = 1;
  private static final int ACCOUNT_SUSPENDED = 2;
```

```java
private static final double zeroBalance = 0.0;
private static final String connectionFailure =
  "Unable to connect to database ";

public void credit(double amt) {
  balance += amt;
}

public void debit(double amt) {

  balance -= amt;

}

public void activateAccount() {
  status = ACCOUNT_ACTIVE;
}

public void suspendAccount() {
  status = ACCOUNT_SUSPENDED;
}
public double getBalance() {
  return balance;
}

public String ejbCreate(String ssn) throws CreateException {

  String insertStatement =
    "INSERT INTO account VALUES ( ? , ?, ? )";

  try
    PreparedStatement ps =
      con.prepareStatement(insertStatement);

    ps.setString(1, ssn);
    ps.setInt(2,ACCOUNT_ACTIVE);
    ps.setDouble(3, zeroBalance);

    ps.executeUpdate();
    ps.close();
  }
  catch (SQLException e) {
    throw new CreateException("Error inserting ssn: "
      + ssn + ". " + e.getMessage());
  }

  this.ssn = ssn;
  status = ACCOUNT_ACTIVE;
  balance = zeroBalance;

  return ssn;
}
```

```java
public String ejbFindByPrimaryKey(String primaryKey)
    throws FinderException {

  boolean found;

  String selectStatement =
    "SELECT ssn " +
    "FROM account WHERE ssn = ? ";

  try {
    PreparedStatement ps =
      con.prepareStatement(selectStatement);
    ps.setString(1, primaryKey);

    ResultSet rs = ps.executeQuery();
    found = rs.next();
    ps.close();
    if (found) {
      return primaryKey;
     }
    else {
      throw new ObjectNotFoundException
        ("no row found for ssn " + primaryKey);
    }
  }
  catch (SQLException e) {
    throw new FinderException(e.getMessage());
  }
}


public void ejbRemove() {
  String deleteStatement =
    "DELETE FROM account WHERE ssn = ? ";
  try {
    PreparedStatement ps =
      con.prepareStatement(deleteStatement);

    ps.setString(1, ssn);
    ps.executeUpdate();
    ps.close();
  }
  catch (SQLException e) {
    throw new EJBException("ejbRemove: " +
      e.getMessage());
  }
}


public void setEntityContext (EntityContext context) {

  this.context = context;
  try {
    InitialContext ic = new InitialContext();
```

```java
      DataSource ds = (DataSource) ic.lookup(dbName);
      con = ds.getConnection();
    }
    catch (NamingException e) {
      throw new EJBException(connectionFailure + e.getMessage());
    }
    catch (SQLException e) {
      throw new EJBException(connectionFailure + e.getMessage());
    }
  }


  public void unsetEntityContext() {

    try {
      con.close();
    }
    catch (SQLException ex) {
      throw new EJBException("unsetEntityContext: " +
        ex.getMessage());
    }
  }


  public void ejbActivate() {
    ssn = (String)context.getPrimaryKey();
  }


  public void ejbPassivate() {

    ssn = null;
  }


  public void ejbLoad() {

    String selectStatement =
      "SELECT status, balance " +
      "FROM account WHERE ssn = ? ";

    try {
      PreparedStatement ps =
        con.prepareStatement(selectStatement);

      ps.setString(1, this.ssn);

      ResultSet rs = ps.executeQuery();

      if (rs.next()) {
        this.status = rs.getInt(1);
        this.balance = rs.getDouble(2);
        ps.close();
      }
```

```
      else {
        ps.close();
        throw new NoSuchEntityException("Row for ssn " + ssn +
          " not found in database.");
      }
    }
    catch (SQLException e) {
      throw new EJBException("ejbLoad: " + e.getMessage());
    }
  }

  public void ejbStore() {

    String updateStatement =
      "UPDATE account SET status = ? ," +
      "balance = ? " +
      "WHERE ssn = ?";

    try {
      PreparedStatement ps =
        con.prepareStatement(updateStatement);

      ps.setInt(1,status);
      ps.setDouble(2, balance);
      ps.setString(3,ssn);
      int rowCount = ps.executeUpdate();
      ps.close();

      if (rowCount == 0) {
        throw new EJBException("Storing row for ssn " +
          ssn + " failed.");
      }
    }
    catch (SQLException e) {
      throw new EJBException("ejbLoad: " + e.getMessage());
    }
  }

  public void ejbPostCreate(String ssn) {
  }
}
```

Packaging the Bean

The parameters required to package the *Account* entity bean are shown in Table 5-1.

The required mappings are shown in Table 5-2.

We must also make sure that we set the Transaction Type of each of our business methods to *Required*.

TABLE 5-1

Parameters Required to Package the Account Bean

Parameter	Value
Application File Name	AccountApp.ear
Application Display Name	AccountApp
JAR DisplayName	AccountJAR
Enterprise Bean Class	AccountBean
Home Interface	AccountHome
Remote Interface	Account
Enterprise Bean Display Name	AccountBean
JNDI Name	MyAccount

A Servlet as a Client of the Bean

In the previous chapter, we introduced the J2EE application client and saw the benefits derived from its use. Now it's time to introduce yet another kind of client—a servlet.

Since a browser is a client of a servlet, making the servlet a client of an enterprise bean allows the browser to indirectly interact with that bean.

The Servlet Code

The servlet code is listed in its entirety at the end of the chapter. We discuss some of its methods in this section.

The `init()` method of a servlet is invoked once. It is a good place to obtain resources or open connections that will be used throughout the life of the servlet. Here is the `init()` method from

TABLE 5-2

Mappings for Account Bean

Referenced By	Component/Reference Name	JNDI Name
	AccountBean	MyAccount
AccountBean	jdbc/AccountDB	jdbc/Cloudscape

AccountServlet:

```
public void init() throws ServletException {
    try {
      InitialContext ic = new InitialContext();
      Object objref = ic.lookup("java:comp/env/ejb/Account");
      home = (AccountHome) PortableRemoteObject.narrow(objref,
              AccountHome.class);
    }
    catch(Exception e) {
      e.printStackTrace();
        throw new ServletException(e.getMessage());
    }
  }
```

The `init()` method creates an *InitialContext* and uses the `lookup()` method to find the *Account* bean. It gets a reference to the home interface and saves it in the instance variable `home`. We see later how other methods use this reference.

The `doPost()` method uses the `getParameter()` and `getParameterValues()` methods to obtain the values of the request parameters named `ssn`, `transaction`, and `amount`. The first parameter is the social security number and is the primary key that will be used to find an instance of the *Account* bean, if one exists in the database. The second parameter is the value of a radio button that is used to indicate whether the account should be credited or debited. The final parameter is the amount by which the account is to be adjusted.

After it obtains these values, the `doPost()` method sets the content type to "text/html" and then invokes the response object's `getPrintWriter()` method to get the *PrintWriter* object that can be used to send character text to the client.

The code now uses the reference to the bean's home interface that was saved in the `init()` method. It invokes the `findByPrimaryKey()` method to find the entity bean whose primary key is the social security number it passes as an argument to the finder method. It saves the object that is returned in the variable `account`. The type of the variable `account` is *Account* (the remote interface). If no exception is thrown, the `doPost()` method uses a `switch` statement to invoke either the `credit()` or `debit()` method on the remote interface. Finally, it obtains the updated balance by invoking the business method `getBalance()` and passes the new balance and the response object's *PrintWriter* to the gen-eratePage() method, which emits HTML that presents the updated balance to the browser.

If the doPost() method catches a *FinderException,* it invokes the generateErrorPage() method. This method emits an HTML page that informs the user that no record exists for the specified social security number and provides the user with a way to retry the request.

The HTML Code

The servlet we just saw is the target of the action parameter of the <form> tag in an HTML page. Here is the code for that page:

\Chapter5\code\UpdateAccount.html

```html
<html>
<head>
    <title>Update Customer Account</title>
</head>
<body>
 
<center>
<b>
<font face="Arial,Helvetica"><font size=+1>
Enter customer ID and amount
<br>
Click on OK when done
</font></font>
</b>
<form method="post" action="AccountAlias">
<table border width="60%" BGCOLOR="#e6e6e6">
  <tr>
    <td>
<table BORDER=0 COLS=2 WIDTH="100%" >
<tr>
  <td ALIGN=LEFT VALIGN=BOTTOM WIDTH="10%">
    SSN:
    <input name="ssn" type="text">
  </td>

</tr>
</table>

<br>
<br>
```

```
<br>
<br>

<table BORDER=0 COLS=2 WIDTH="100%" >
<tr>
  <td ALIGN=LEFT VALIGN=CENTER WIDTH="20%" HEIGHT="50%">
    <table BORDER=0 COLS=1 WIDTH="100%" >
      <tr>
        <td ALIGN=LEFT VALIGN=CENTER>
          <input type="radio" name="transaction" value="1" checked>
          credit
        </td>
      </tr>

      <tr>
        <td ALIGN=LEFT VALIGN=CENTER>
          <input type="radio" name="transaction" value="2">
          debit
        </td>
      </tr>
    </table>
  </td>

    <td ALIGN=LEFT VALIGN=CENTER>
      Amount:
      <input type=text name="amount">
    </td>
    <td ALIGN=LEFT VALIGN=CENTER>
    </td>
</tr>
</table>
</td>
</tr>
</table>
<br>
<input type="submit" value="OK">
</form>
</center>

</body>
</html>
```

Packaging and Deploying the Servlet

We have already seen that deployment of J2EE components
involves adding components to an application and deploying that
application. We used wizards to package and deploy beans and
J2EE application clients. We also deploy our servlet using the New
Web Component Wizard, which we start by selecting "New Web

Component . . ." from the "File" drop-down menu as shown in Figure 5-16. The wizard starts by displaying the Introduction dialog in Figure 5-17.

Clicking on NEXT> takes us to the WAR File General Properties dialog. We enter *AccountWAR* in the entry field labeled "WAR Display Name:". At this point, the dialog should look like Figure 5-18.

Next, we click on the ADD . . . button in the group box labeled CONTENTS:. This results in the appearance of the "Add Content Files Dialog". We select *UpdateAccount.html* by clicking on it so that the dialog looks like Figure 5-19.

The next sequence we follow is:

■ Click on ADD

■ Click on NEXT>

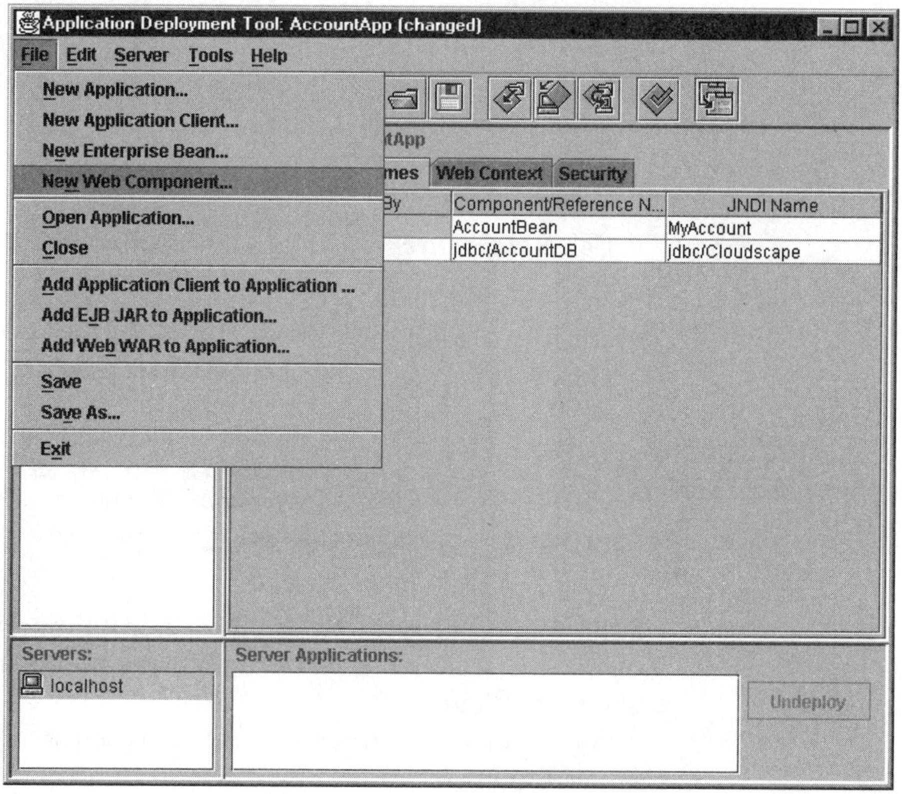

Figure 5-16
Starting the New Web
Application Wizard

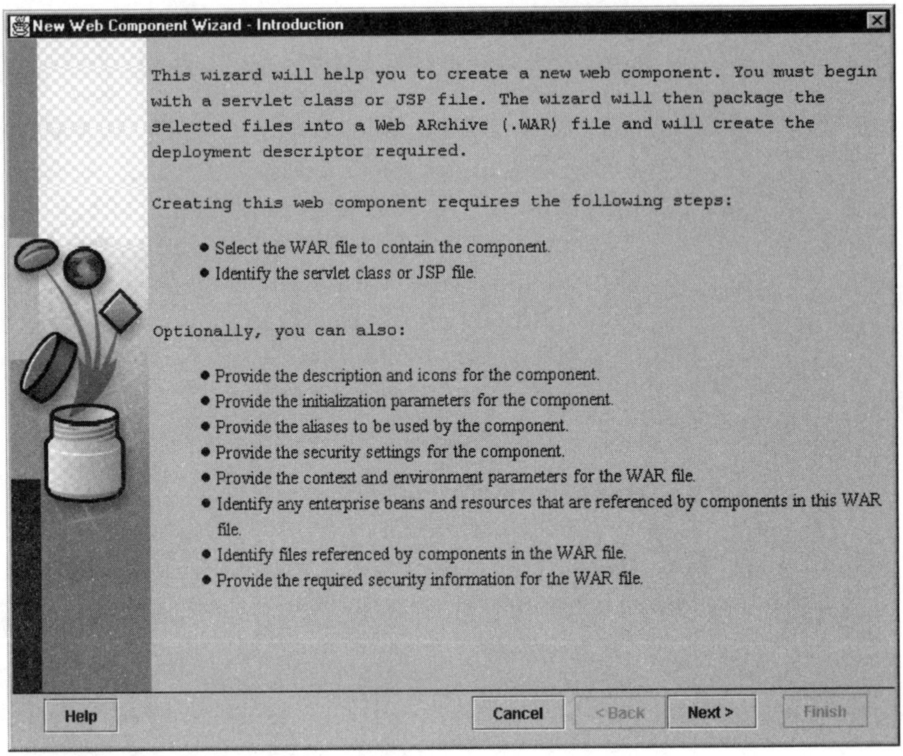
New Web Component Wizard - Introduction
This wizard will help you to create a new web component. You must begin with a servlet class or JSP file. The wizard will then package the selected files into a Web ARchive (.WAR) file and will create the deployment descriptor required.
Creating this web component requires the following steps:
• Select the WAR file to contain the component.
• Identify the servlet class or JSP file.
Optionally, you can also:
• Provide the description and icons for the component.
• Provide the initialization parameters for the component.
• Provide the aliases to be used by the component.
• Provide the security settings for the component.
• Provide the context and environment parameters for the WAR file.
• Identify any enterprise beans and resources that are referenced by components in this WAR file.
• Identify files referenced by components in the WAR file.
• Provide the required security information for the WAR file.
Help
Cancel
< Back
Next >
Finish

Figure 5-17 The New Web Application Wizard Introduction

- Select *AccountServlet.class* by clicking on it
- Click on ADD
- Click on FINISH then finish. When the dialog box reappears, click NEXT> to get Figure 5-20.

NOTE: *The preceding steps must be followed exactly as presented. If you try repeated select/add sequences, it will not work.*

After we return to the WAR File General Properties dialog, we click on NEXT>. This takes us to the Choose Component Type dialog as shown in Figure 5-20.

Since we are adding a servlet, we click on the radio button labeled SERVLET and click on NEXT> to proceed to the Component

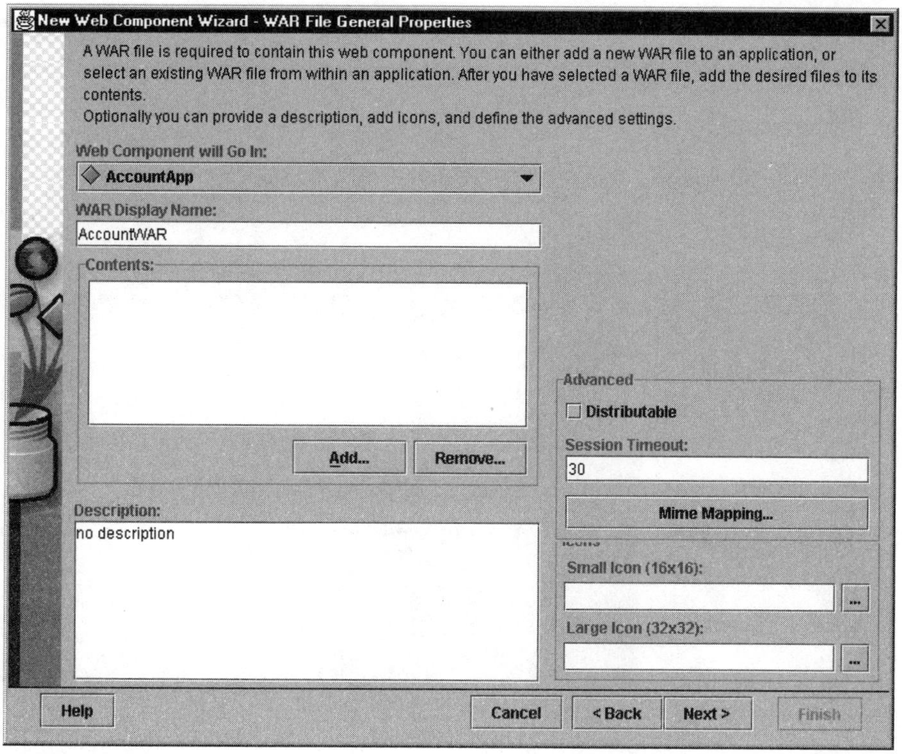

Figure 5-18
WAR File General
Properties Dialog

General Properties dialog. We select *AccountServlet* in the drop-down list labeled "ServletClass" and enter *AccountWebComponent* in the entry field labeled "Web Component Display Name:". The Component General Properties dialog should now look like Figure 5-21.

We can skip over the "Component Initialization Parameters Dialog," which we see when we click on NEXT>. This brings us to the "Component Aliases Dialog". We click on ADD and type *Account-Alias* into the field that appears. The "Component Aliases Dialog" now looks like Figure 5-22.

Skipping over the "Component Security Dialog" and the "Environment Entries Dialog" takes us to the "Enterprise Bean References Dialog". Clicking on ADD causes a table row to appear into which we type *ejb/Account* under the column labeled "Coded Name". From the drop-down list underneath the column header labeled "Type", we

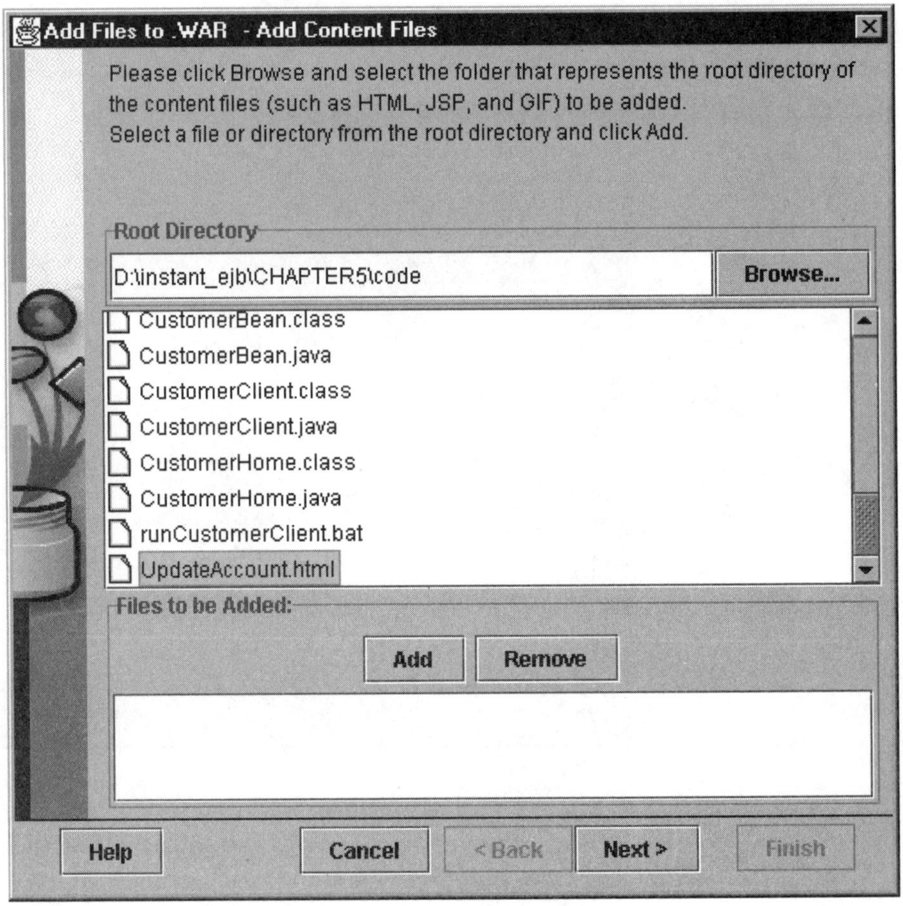

Figure 5-19
The Add Content Files
Dialog

select *Entity*. In the column labeled "Home" and "Remote", we type *AccountHome* and *Account*, respectively. The "Enterprise Bean References Dialog" should now look like Figure 5-23.

When we click on *Finish*, we notice that the box in the Application Deployment Tool labeled "Local Applications:" now contains a WAR component. (See Figure 5-24.)

We must now provide the mappings required by JNDI. To do this, we click on the tab labeled JNDI NAMES. Under the column header labeled "JNDI Name", we enter *MyAccount* next to *AccountBean* and *ejb/Account;* next, we enter *jdbc/Cloudscape* next to *jdbc/AccountDB*. The Application Deployment Tool main window should now look like Figure 5-25.

Figure 5-20
Choose Component
Type Dialog

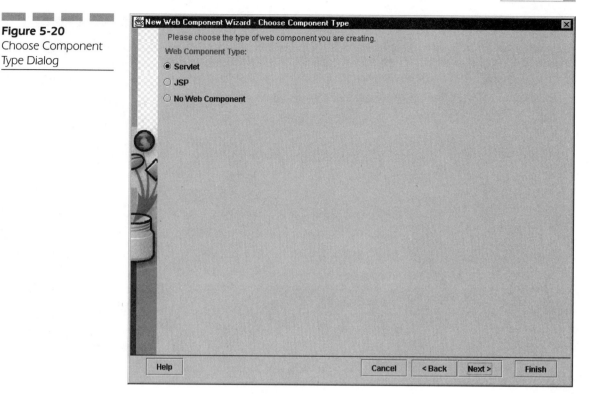

We are now ready for deployment, which we start by selecting "Deploy Application . . ." from the "Tools" drop-down menu. When the "Deployment Dialog" appears, we do *not* check the box labeled RETURN CLIENT JAR but simply click on NEXT>. After we review the JNDI names in the ensuing dialog, we again click on NEXT> and see the WAR Context Root dialog. After we type *AccountContextRoot* into the entry field in the column labeled "Context Root", the WAR Context Root dialog looks like Figure 5-26.

We now click on NEXT> and when the Review dialog appears, we click on FINISH. A Progress dialog like the one shown in Figure 5-27. The Progress dialogs we saw before displayed progress for the deployment of two components, the bean Jar and the application. The present dialog includes a third component, the WAR component.

When the Deployment Progress dialog indicates that deployment is complete, our servlet is ready to run.

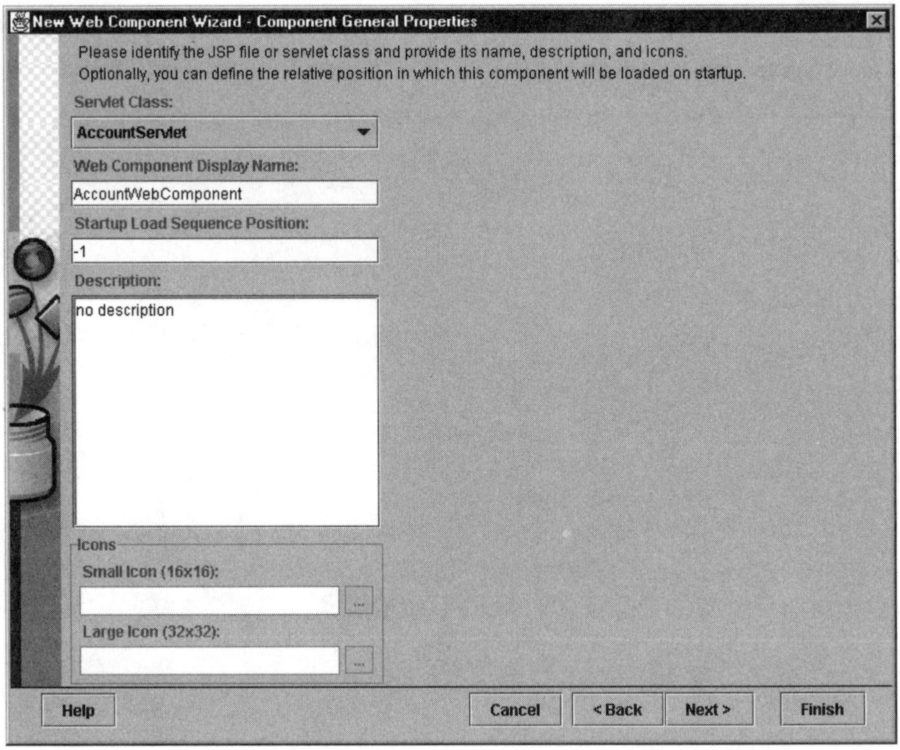

Figure 5-21
Component General
Properties Dialog

This deployment process represents a big improvement over the traditional way of installing servlets and HTML pages. Stop and think how many times you had to find out whether the servlet code went in the /bin or /cgi-bin directory; or maybe it should be /classes or perhaps there might even be some local naming convention. The same was true for HTML pages—was the document root /htdocs or /public_html? The deployment tool that is provided with whichever J2EE server you decide to use hides such details.

Testing the Servlet

After we make sure the Cloudscape Server is running, we run *createAccountTable.bat* to create a database table named *account* and

Figure 5-22
Component Aliases
Dialog

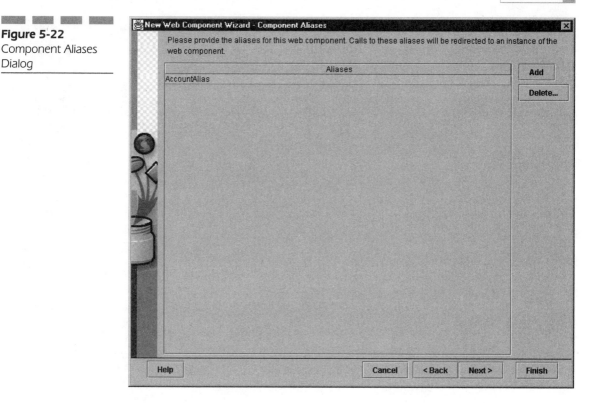

insert a single record into it. Here is the listing of *createAccount-Table.bat:*

Chapter5\\code\\createAccountTable.bat

```
java -
Dij.connection.CloudscapeDB=jdbc:rmi://localhost:1099/jdbc:cloudsca
pe:CloudscapeDB\create=true -Dcloudscape.system.home=%J2EE_HOME%\
cloudscape -classpath %J2EE_HOME%\lib\cloudscape\client.jar;%J2EE_
HOME%\lib\cloudscape\tools.jar;%J2EE_HOME%\lib\cloudscape\cloud
scape.jar;%J2EE_HOME%\lib\cloudscape\RmiJdbc.jar;%J2EE_HOME%\lib\
cloudscape\license.jar;%CLASSPATH% -ms16m -mx32mCOM.cloudscape.
tools.ij createAccount.sql
```

This .bat file uses *createAccount.sql,* which looks like this:

Chapter5\\code\\createAccount.sql

```
drop table account;
```

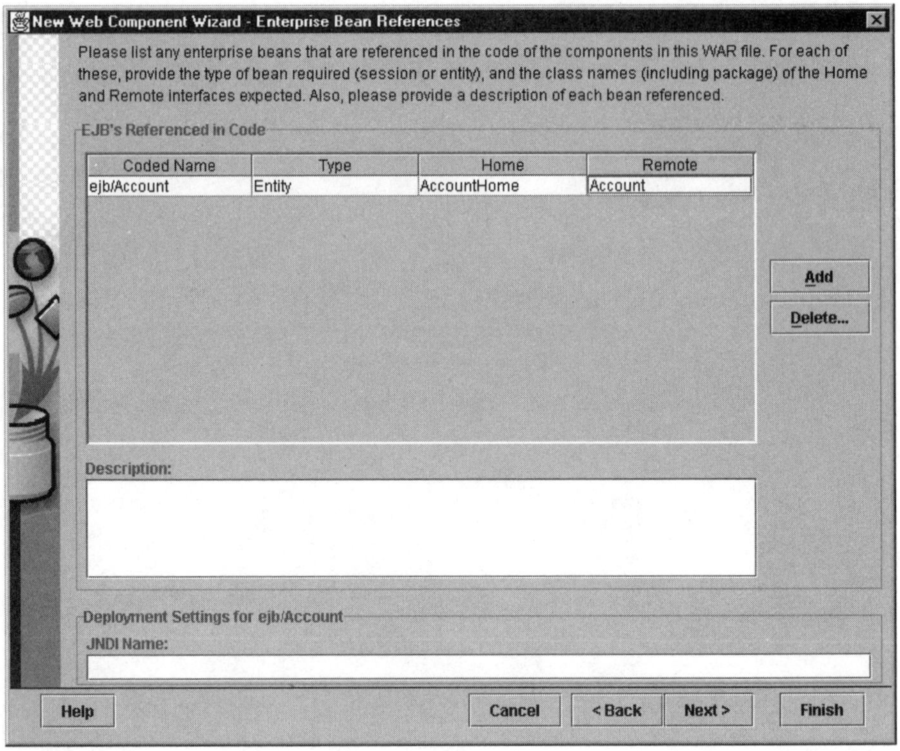

Figure 5-23
The Enterprise Bean
References Dialog

```
create table account
(ssn char(9) constraint pk_account primary key,
status integer,
balance double precision);

insert into account values
('123456789',1,0.0);

exit;
```

We test our servlet by first accessing the URL `http://local-host:8000/AccountContextRoot/UpdateAccount.html` from a browser. After we have entered data into the appropriate fields, the browser should look like Figure 5-28.

When we click on the OK button, a request is sent to the server. This request is delivered to the servlet, which is running in the Web container. The `doPost()` method we discussed earlier executes and delivers HTML back to the browser, which now looks like Figure 5-29. If we enter a social security number for which no record exists, the page shown in Figure 5-30 is displayed.

Figure 5-24
After Addition
of WAR File

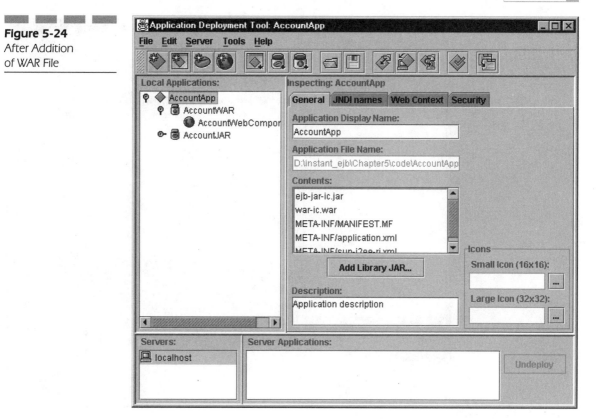

The Customer Enterprise Bean

 \Chapter5\code\CustomerBean.java

```java
import java.sql.*;
import java.util.*;
import javax.ejb.*;
import javax.naming.*;


public class CustomerBean implements EntityBean {

    private String ssn;
    private String firstName;
    private String lastName;
    private EntityContext context;
    private Connection con;
    private String dbName = "java:comp/env/jdbc/CustomerDB";
```

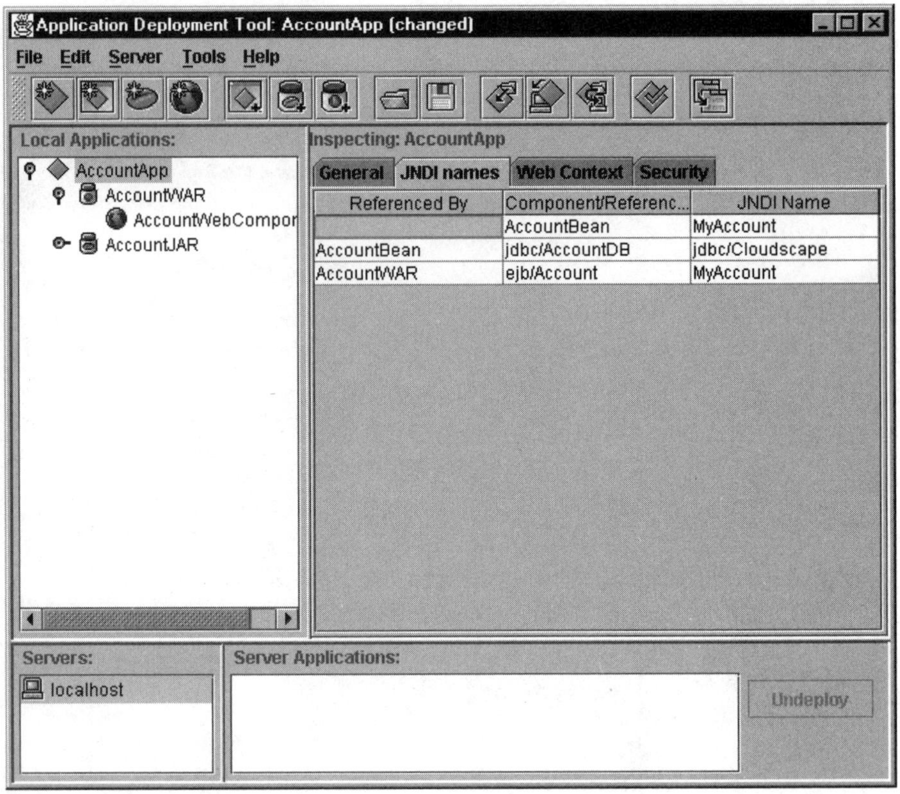

Figure 5-25
JNDI Names

```
public String getFirstName() {
  return firstName;
}
public String getLastName() {
  return lastName;
}


public String ejbCreate(String ssn, String firstName,
  String lastName)
      throws CreateException {

  String insertStatement =
    "INSERT INTO customer VALUES ( ? , ? , ? )";

  try {
    Preparedstatement ps =
      con.prepareStatement(insertStatement);
    ps.setString(1, ssn);
    ps.setString(2, firstName);
    ps.setString(3, lastName);
    ps.executeUpdate();
```

Figure 5-26
The WAR Context
Dialog

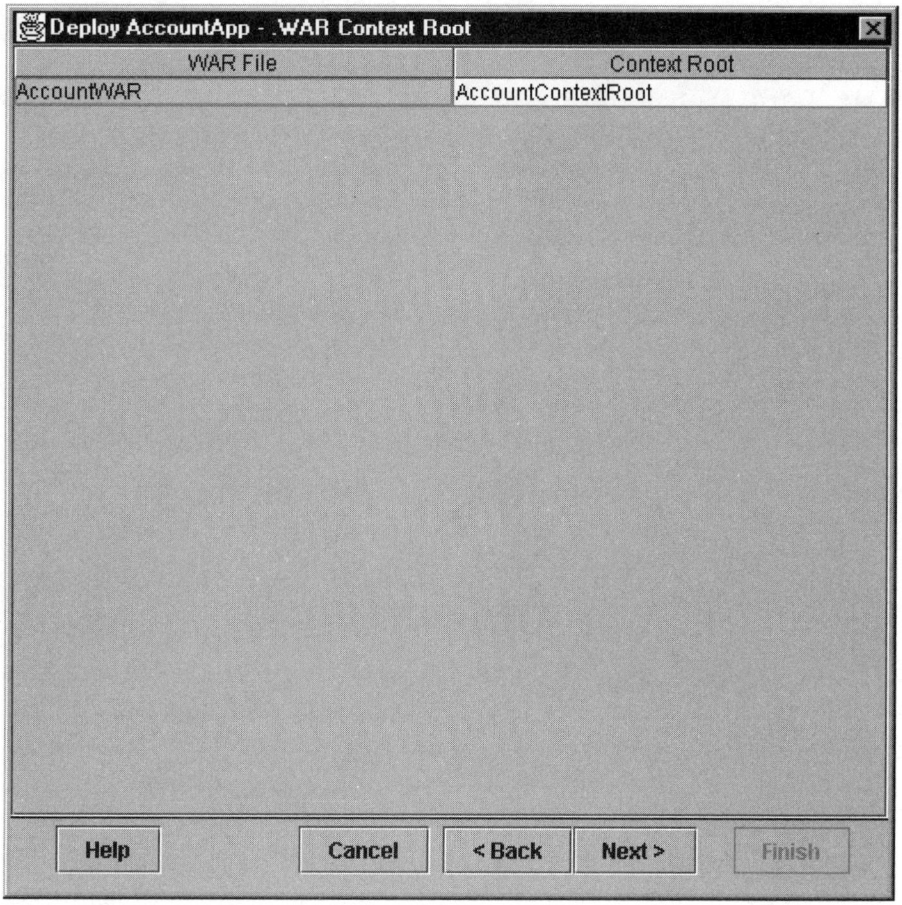

```
    ps.close();
  }
  catch (SQLException e) {
    throw new CreateException("Error inserting ssn: "
      + ssn + ". " + e.getMessage());
  }

  this.ssn = ssn;
  this.firstName = firstName;
  this.lastName = lastName;

  return ssn;
}

public void ejbPostCreate(String ssn, String firstName,
  String lastName) {
}
```

Figure 5-27
The Deployment
Progress Dialog

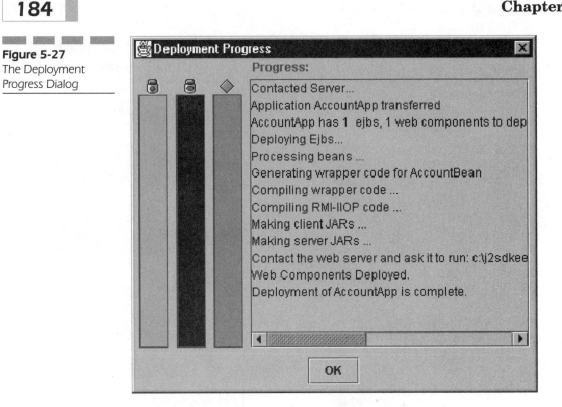

```java
public String ejbFindByPrimaryKey(String primaryKey)
    throws FinderException {

  boolean found;

  String selectStatement =
    "SELECT ssn " +
    "FROM customer WHERE ssn = ? ";

  try {
    PreparedStatement ps =
      con.prepareStatement(selectStatement);
    ps.setString(1, primaryKey);
    ResultSet rs = ps.executeQuery();
    found = rs.next();
    ps.close();
    if (found) {
      return primaryKey;
    }
    else {
      throw new ObjectNotFoundException
        ("no row found for ssn " + primaryKey);
    }
  }
  catch (SQLException e) {
```

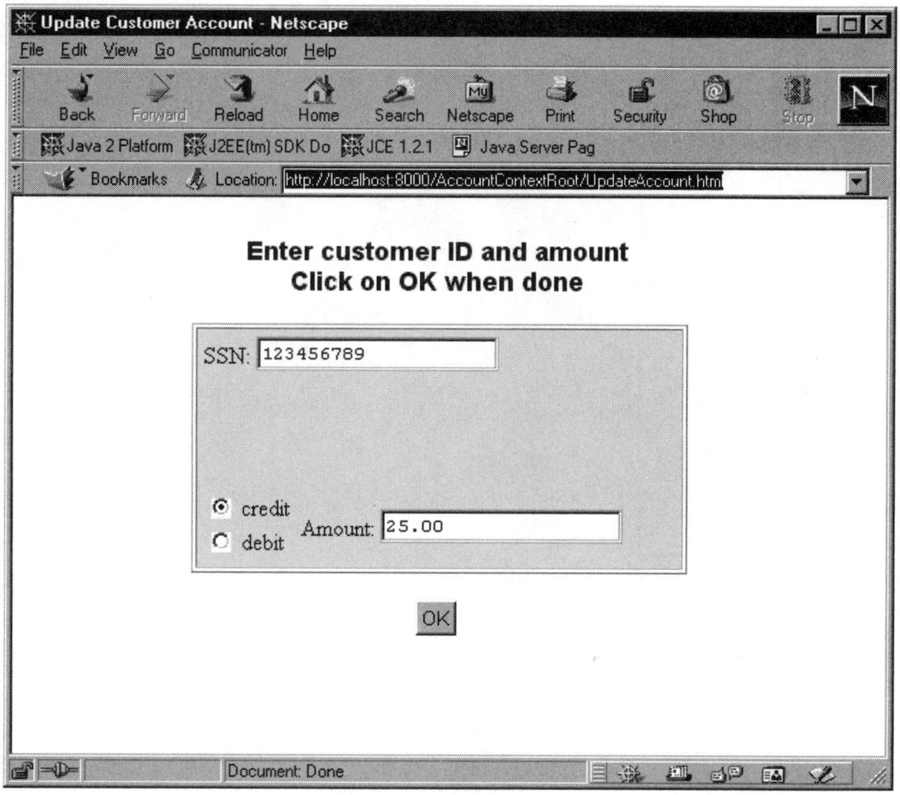

Figure 5-28

Request for Account Update Info

```
        throw new FinderException(e.getMessage());
    }
}

public Collection ejbFindByFirstName(String firstName)
    throws FinderException {

  String selectStatement =
    "SELECT ssn " +
    "FROM customer WHERE firstname = ? ";

  ResultSet rs = null;
  ArrayList a;

  try {
    PreparedStatement ps =
      con.prepareStatement(selectStatement);
    ps.setString(1, firstName);
    rs = ps.executeQuery();
    a = new ArrayList();
```

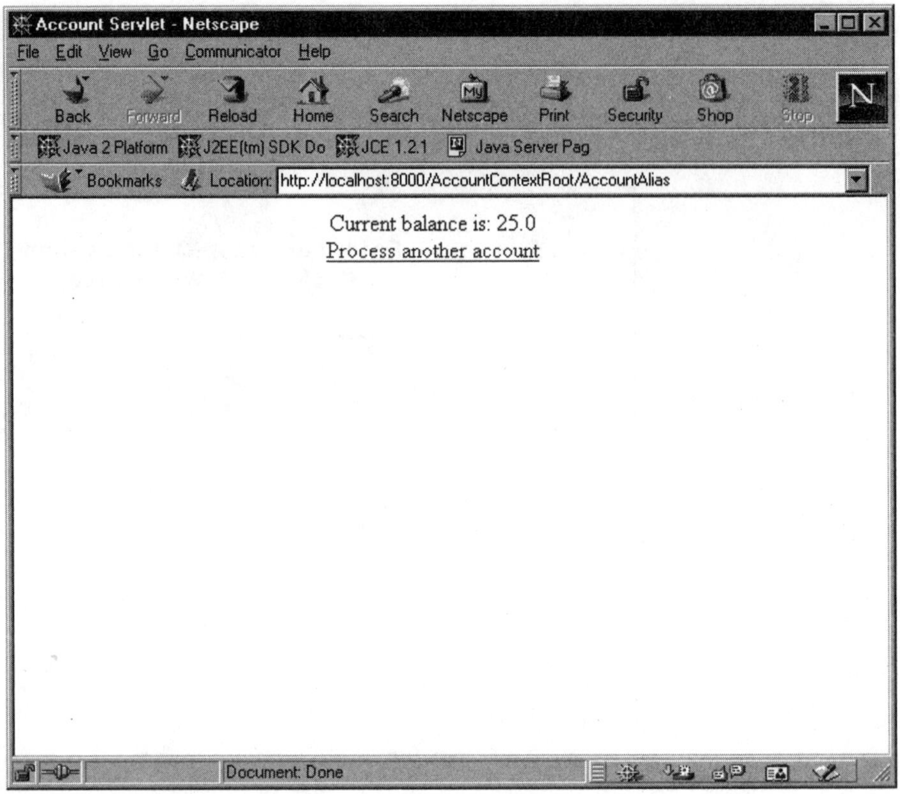

Figure 5-29
The Updated Balance

```
    while (rs.next()) {
      String ssn = rs.getString(1);
      a.add(ssn);
    }
    ps.close();
  }
  catch (SQLException e) {
    throw new FinderException("ejbFindByFirstName " +
      e.getMessage());
  }

  if (a.isEmpty()) {
    throw new ObjectNotFoundException("No rows found.");
  }
  else {
    return a;
  }
}

public Collection ejbFindByLastName(String lastName)
    throws FinderException {
```

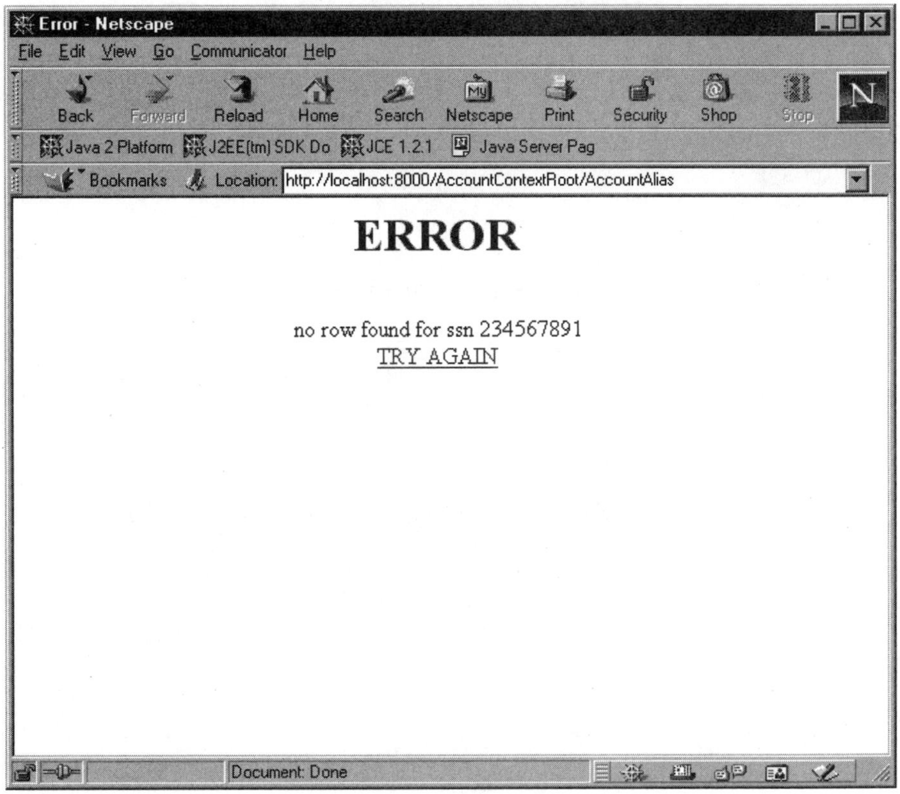

Figure 5-30
An Error Page

```
Error - Netscape                                                    _ □ ✕
File  Edit  View  Go  Communicator  Help

  Back   Forward  Reload   Home  Search  Netscape  Print  Security  Shop   Stop      N

  Java 2 Platform   J2EE(tm) SDK Do   JCE 1.2.1    Java Server Pag

  Bookmarks    Location: http://localhost:8000/AccountContextRoot/AccountAlias         ▼



                            ERROR


                     no row found for ssn 234567891
                              TRY AGAIN










        Document: Done
```

```
String selectStatement =
  "SELECT ssn " +
  "FROM customer WHERE lastname = ? ";

ResultSet rs = null;
ArrayList a;

try {
  PreparedStatement ps =
    con.prepareStatement(selectStatement);
  ps.setString(1, lastName);
  rs = ps.executeQuery();
  a = new ArrayList();
  while (rs.next()) {
    String ssn = rs.getString(1);
    a.add(ssn);
  }
  ps.close();
}
catch (SQLException e) {
  throw new FinderException("ejbFindByLastName " +
```

```
        e.getMessage());
    }


    if (a.isEmpty()) {
      throw new ObjectNotFoundException("No rows found.");
    }
    else {
      return a;
    }
  }

public void ejbRemove() {

    String deleteStatement =
      "DELETE FROM customer WHERE ssn = ? ";

    try {
      PreparedStatement ps =
        con.prepareStatement(deleteStatement);
      ps.setString(1, ssn);
      ps.executeUpdate();
      ps.close();
    }
    catch (SQLException e) {
      throw new EJBException("ejbRemove: " +
        e.getMessage());
    }
  }

public void setEntityContext(EntityContext context) {

    this.context = context;

    try {
      InitialContext ic = new InitialContext();
      DataSource ds = (DataSource) ic.lookup(dbName);
      con = ds.getConnection();
    }
    catch (Exception e) {
      throw new EJBException("Unable to connect to database. " +
        e.getMessage());
    }
  }

public void unsetEntityContext() {

    try {

      con.close();
    }
    catch (SQLException ex) {
      throw new EJBException("unsetEntityContext: " +
        ex.getMessage());
```

```
      }
   }

   public void ejbActivate() {
     ssn = (String)context.getPrimaryKey();
   }

   public void ejbPassivate() {
     ssn = null;
   }

   public void ejbLoad() {

     String selectStatement =
       "SELECT firstname, lastname " +
       "FROM customer WHERE ssn = ? ";

     try {
       PreparedStatement ps =
         con.prepareStatement(selectStatement);
       ps.setString(1, this.ssn);
       ResultSet rs = ps.executeQuery();
       if (rs.next()) {
         this.firstName = rs.getString(1);
         this.lastName = rs.getString(2);
         ps.close();
       }
       else {
         ps.close();
         throw new NoSuchEntityException("Row for ssn " + ssn +
           " not found in database.");
       }
     }
     catch (SQLException ex) {
       throw new EJBException("ejbLoad: " +
         ex.getMessage());
     }
   }

   public void ejbStore() {

     String updateStatement =
       "UPDATE customer SET firstname = ? ," +
       "lastname = ? " +
       "WHERE ssn = ?";

     try {
       PreparedStatement ps =
         con.prepareStatement(updateStatement);
       ps.setString(1, firstName);
       ps.setString(2, lastName);
       ps.setString(3, ssn);
       int rowCount = ps.executeUpdate();
       ps.close();
```

```
        if (rowCount == 0) {
          throw new EJBException("Storing row for ssn " +
            ssn + " failed.");
        }
      }
      catch (SQLException ex) {
        throw new EJBException("ejbLoad: " +
          ex.getMessage());
      }
    }
  }
}
```

The Customer Client

  \Chapter5\code\CustomerClient.java

```java
import java.rmi.RemoteException;
import java.util.Collection;
import java.util.Iterator;
import javax.ejb.CreateException;
import javax.ejb.FinderException;
import javax.naming.Context;
import javax.naming.InitialContext;
import javax.rmi.PortableRemoteObject;
public class CustomerClient {

  public static void main(String[] args) {

    String[] [] custRecs = {
      {"123456789", "Paul", "Tremblett"},
      {"456789123", "Barbara", "Hickey"},
      {"234567891", "Michael", "Munch"},
      {"567891234", "Rosemary", "Griffin"},
      {"345678912", "Roy", "Walsh"},
      {"678912345", "Sharon", "Power"},
      {"123456789", "Paul", "Tremblett"},
      {"789123456", "George", "Jones"},
      {"891234567", "John", "Jones"},
      {"912345678", "Barbara", "Feldon"}};

    CustomerHome home = null;

    try {
      Context initial = new InitialContext();
      Object objref = initial.lookup("MyCustomer");
      home = (CustomerHome)PortableRemoteObject.narrow(objref,
```

```
                    CustomerHome.class);
    }
    catch (Exception e) {
      System.err.println("Caught exception.");
      if (e.getMessage() != null) {
        System.out.println(e.getMessage());
      }
      e.printStackTrace();
    }


System.out.println("--- CREATING RECORDS ---");
for (int i = 0; i < custRecs.length; ++i) {
  try {
    home.create(custRecs[i][0], custRecs[i][1],custRecs[i][2]);
    System.out.println("record created for ssn: " +
      custRecs[i][0]);
  }
  catch (RemoteException e) {
    System.err.println("RemoteException");
  }
  catch (CreateException e) {
    System.out.println("create failed for ssn: " +
      custRecs[i][0]);
  }
}

System.out.println("--- RECORDS CREATED ---");

String[] ln = {"Jones", "Smith"};

for (int i = 0; i < ln.length; ++i) {
  System.out.println("Customers with last name = " + ln[i]);

  try {
    Collection cl = home.findByLastName(ln[i]);
    Iterator iLast = cl.iterator();
    while (iLast.hasNext()) {
      Customer cust = (Customer)iLast.next();
      String ssn = (String)cust.getPrimaryKey();
      String firstName = cust.getFirstName();
      String lastName = cust.getLastName();
      System.out.println(ssn + ": " + firstName + " " +
        lastName);
    }
  }
  catch (FinderException e) {
    System.out.println("** NONE **");
  }
  catch (RemoteException e) {
    System.err.println("RemoteException");
    e.printStackTrace();
  }
}

System.out.println("Customers with first name = Barbara:");
```

```
   try {
     Collection cf = home.findByFirstName("Barbara");
     Iterator iFirst = cf.iterator();
     while (iFirst.hasNext()) {
       Customer cust = (Customer)iFirst.next();
       String ssn = (String)cust.getPrimaryKey();
       String firstName = cust.getFirstName();
       String lastName = cust.getLastName();
       System.out.println(ssn + ": " + firstName + " " +
         lastName);
     }


     }
     catch (RemoteException e) {
       System.err.println("remoteException");
       e.printStackTrace();
     }
   catch (FinderException e) {
     System.out.println("** NONE **");
   }
 }
}
```

The Account Servlet

 On the CD  \Chapter5\code\AccountServlet.java

```
import java.io.*;
import javax.ejb.FinderException;
import javax.naming.InitialContext;
import javax.rmi.PortableRemoteObject;
import javax.servlet.*;
import javax.servlet.http.*;

import Account;
import AccountHome;

public class AccountServlet extends HttpServlet {

  AccountHome home = null;

  public void init() throws ServletException {
    try {
      InitialContext ic = new InitialContext();
      Object objref = ic.lookup("java:comp/env/ejb/Account");
```

```java
        home = (AccountHome)PortableRemoteObject.narrow(objref,
               AccountHome.class);
    }
    catch(Exception e) {
      e.printStackTrace();
        throw new ServletException(e.getMessage());
    }
}

public void doPost(HttpServletRequest req,
                   HttpServletResponse res)
   throws ServletException, IOException {

  Account account;

  String ssn = req.getParameter("ssn");
  String[] transType = req.getParameterValues("transaction");
  String amtParm = req.getParameter("amount");
  res.setContentType("text/html");
  PrintWriter out = res.getWriter();
  try {
    account = home.findByPrimaryKey(ssn);
    double amount = Double.parseDouble(amtParm);
    switch (Integer.parseInt(transType[0])) {
      case 1:
        account.credit(amount);
        break;
      case 2:
        account.debit(amount);
        break;
      default:
        generateErrorPage(out,"INTERNAL ERROR");
    }
    generatePage(out, account.getBalance());
  }
  catch (FinderException e) {
    generateErrorPage(out, e.getMessage());
  }
}

private void generatePage(PrintWriter out, double balance) {

  out.println("<html>");
  out.println("<head>");
  out.println("<title>Account Servlet</title>");
  out.println("</head>");
  out.println("<body>");
  out.println("<center>");
  out.println("Current balance is: " + String.valueOf(balance));
  out.println("<br>");
  out.println("<a href=\"http://localhost:8000" +
    "/AccountContextRoot/UpdateAccount.html\">" +
    "Process another account</a>");
  out.println("<center>");
  out.println("</body>");
  out.println("</html>");
}
```

```
private void generateErrorPage(PrintWriter out, String msg) {
  out.println("<html>");
  out.println("<head>");
  out.println("<title>Error</title>");
  out.println("</head>");
  out.println("<body>");
  out.println("<center>");
  out.println("<H1>");
  out.println("ERROR");
  out.println("</H1>");
  out.println("<br>");
  if (msg != null) {
    out.println(msg);
  }
  else {
    System.out.println("No message text available");
  }
  out.println("<br>");
  out.println("<a href=\"http://localhost:8000" +
    "/AccountContextRoot/UpdateAccount.html\">" +
    "TRY AGAIN</a>");
  out.println("</center>");
  out.println("</body>");
  out.println("</html>");
}

public String getServletInfo() {

  return "Instant EJBs Chapter 5 Example";
}
}
```

Summary

In this chapter, we discussed entity beans and presented two simple examples. We used a standalone client to test one entity bean. We also showed how servlet code could be a client of a bean and use data obtained from the bean to deliver HTML to a user who accessed the servlet using a Web browser.

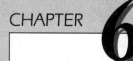

Online Catalog and Inventory

In this chapter:

- Online Catalog
- Inventory Tracking
- JavaServer Pages as a Client
- Delivering WML

The entity beans we developed in the last chapter used bean-managed persistence. In this chapter, we develop beans that use container-managed persistence, use a standalone client to test a catalog bean, and show how JavaServer Pages can also be a client of an inventory bean to deliver content to a desktop browser and a wireless device.

Online Catalog

In the last chapter, we developed two of the most common entity beans encountered in the business world, the customer record and the account record. We now examine two more entity beans: an online catalog entry and an inventory record.

We begin with the simplest form of entry a catalog might have. The three fields it contains are a product identifier (usually a SKU in a real-world application), a product description, and a price.

The Remote Interface

The remote interface, which defines the business methods a client can invoke on the bean, looks like this:

Chapter6\code\CatalogItem.java

```
import javax.ejb.EJBObject;
import java.rmi.RemoteException;

public interface CatalogItem extends EJBObject {
```

```
public void setPrice(double price) throws RemoteException;

public double getPrice() throws RemoteException;

public String getDescription() throws RemoteException;
}
```

The Home Interface

Here is the code for the home interface:

\Chapter6\code\CatalogItemHome.java

```
import java.util.Collection;
import java.rmi.RemoteException;
import javax.ejb.*;

public interface CatalogItemHome extends EJBHome {

    public CatalogItem create(String productId, String description)
        throws RemoteException, CreateException;

    public CatalogItem findByPrimaryKey(String productId)
        throws FinderException, RemoteException;

    public Collection findByDescription(String description)
        throws FinderException, RemoteException;

    public Collection findInRange(double low, double high)
        throws FinderException, RemoteException;
}
```

The home interface defines finder methods whose names begin with find.... Because container-managed persistence is being used, no implementation code is present. This code, as well as the appropriate SQL statements, is implemented by the Application Deployment Tool. In the case of the findByPrimaryKey() method, the complete implementation is provided by the Application Deployment Tool. We will see shortly that we have to supply the WHERE clauses for the findByDescription() and the find-InRange() methods.

The Enterprise Bean

The enterprise bean code looks like this:

\Chapter6\code\CatalogItemBean

```java
import java.util.*;
import javax.ejb.*;

public class CatalogItemBean implements EntityBean {

  public String productID;
  public String description;
  public double price;

  private EntityContext context;

  public String getDescription() {
    return description;
  }

  public double getPrice() {
    return price;
  }

  public void setPrice(double price) {
    this.price = price;
  }

  public String ejbCreate(String productID, String description)
      throws CreateException {

    if (productID == null) {
      throw new CreateException("You must specify a productID.");
    }

    this.productID = productID;
    this.description = description;
    this.price = 0.0;

    return null;
  }

  public void setEntityContext(EntityContext context) {
    this.context = context;
  }

  public void ejbActivate() {
```

```
        productID = (String)context.getPrimaryKey();
    }

    public void ejbPassivate() {
      productID = null;
      description = null;
    }

    public void ejbRemove() {
    }

    public void ejbLoad() {
    }

    public void ejbStore() {
    }

    public void unsetEntityContext() {
    }

    public void ejbPostCreate(String productID, String description) {
    }
  }
```

ejbCreate()

The `ejbCreate()` method takes two arguments: a product identifier and a product description. Since the product identifier serves as the primary key (we will see this when we package and deploy the bean), it must have a nonnull value. If this is not the case, the method throws a *CreateException*. The method saves the values of the two arguments in the corresponding instance variables and initializes the instance variable `price`.

The method returns `null`. This is perfectly OK because with container-managed persistence the container ignores the value returned by the `ejbCreate()` method. The actual insertion of the container-managed fields into the database is performed *after* the `ejbCreate()` method has been invoked.

ejbRemove()

The `ejbRemove()` method, which is the counterpart of `ejbCreate()`, is invoked by the container when a client calls the re-

`move()` method. If you have any processing that must be performed before removal, you should do it in the `ejbRemove()` method. In our case, the method is empty.

ejbLoad()

The container determines when it must refresh the entity bean's state from the underlying database. When such a refresh becomes necessary, the container selects the appropriate row from the database, assigns the row's column values to the corresponding container-managed instance variables and then invokes the `ejbLoad()` method.

In some cases, a transformation is applied to the data retrieved from the database. For example, a monetary amount might be stored in the database as U.S. dollars and converted to another monetary unit, depending on the contents of an environment variable. When such a transformation is necessary, it is performed in the `ejbLoad()` method. Later in this chapter, we see an example of data transformation; however, for this present example, the `ejbLoad()` method is empty.

ejbStore()

The `ejbStore()` method is the counterpart of `ejbLoad()`. When the container determines that it is necessary to synchronize the database with the current state of the bean, it first invokes `ejbStore()` and then updates the database with the current values of any container-managed fields. The `ejbStore()` method performs any required data transformations in the same manner as the `ejbLoad()` method did. Since our `ejbLoad()` method is empty, it makes sense that our `ejbStore()` method is empty as well.

Packaging and Deploying

We compile the above-listed Java code by typing:

```
compileCatalogItem
```

On the CD

\Chapter6\code\compileCatalogItem.bat

We use the Application Deployment Tool to package and deploy our catalog entity bean. The initial procedure, up to and including the General dialog, is the same as the one we used in the previous chapter. The required parameters are shown in Table 6-1.

After we have supplied the appropriate parameters in the General dialog, we click on NEXT> and the Entity Settings dialog is displayed. When we click on the radio button labeled CONTAINER-MANAGED PERSISTENCE in the Entity Setting dialog, the Application Deployment uses reflection to create a list of the public instance variables in *CatalogItemBean* and displays the list as shown in Figure 6-1.

Since we want all of the fields listed to be container-managed, we check all three checkboxes. Next, we enter *java.lang.String* in the entry field labeled "Primary Key Class". Finally, we select *productID* from the drop-down list labeled "Primary Key Field Name". The Entity Settings dialog now looks like Figure 6-2.

When we have completed the Entity Settings dialog, we click on NEXT>. We bypass the next two dialogs by clicking on NEXT> when they appear. When the Resource References dialog is displayed, we click on ADD, causing a partially completed resource reference entry to appear. We complete the entry by typing *jdbc/CatalogDB*

TABLE 6-1	Parameter	Value
Parameters Required to Start Packaging of Catalog Entity Bean	Application File Name	CatalogApp.ear
	DisplayName	CatalogApp
	JAR Display Name	CatalogJAR
	Enterprise Bean Class	CatalogItemBean
	Home Interface	CatalogItemHome
	RemoteInterface	CatalogItem
	Enterprise Bean Display Name	CatalogItemBean

Figure 6-1
Entity Settings Dialog

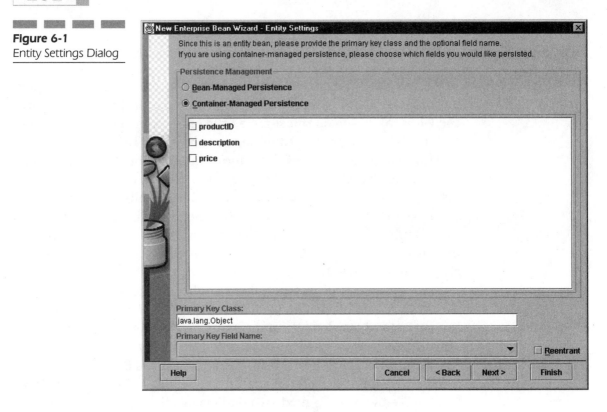

Figure 6-1
Entity Settings Dialog

in the column labeled "Coded Name". The Resource References dialog now looks like Figure 6-3.

After we click on NEXT> in the Resource References dialog, the Security dialog appears. We bypass this dialog by clicking NEXT> and see the Transaction Management dialog, which contains a list of methods and the transaction type assigned to each. We specify a value of *required* for each of the business methods. We do so by locating the row containing the method, clicking on the column in that row labeled "Transaction Type", and selecting *Required* from the resultant drop-down list. When we are finished, the dialog looks like Figure 6-4.

After we click on NEXT> in the Transaction Management dialog, the Review Settings dialog displays the XML that comprises the descriptor. When we are satisfied that the descriptor looks OK, we click on FINISH.

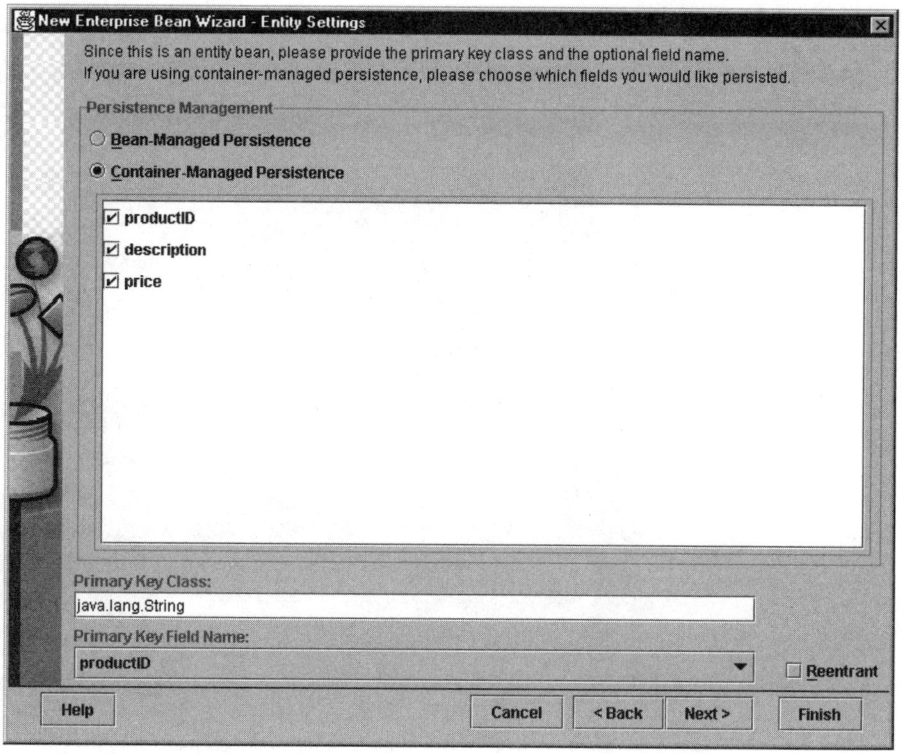

Figure 6-2
Completed Entity Settings Dialog

In the left-hand column of the Application Deployment Tool main window, we expand *CatalogJAR* so that *CatalogItemBean* becomes visible. When we select the tab labeled ENTITY, the Persistence Management panel is displayed as shown in Figure 6-5.

Clicking on the button labeled DEPLOYMENT SETTINGS . . . results in the appearance of the Deployment Settings dialog shown in Figure 6-6.

In the text entry field labeled "Database JNDI Name" we type *jdbc/Cloudscape*. When we tab out of the field, the button labeled GENERATE SQL NOW becomes active (i.e., the text becomes black instead of gray) and the Deployment Settings dialog looks like Figure 6-7. Notice that the checkboxes labeled CREATE TABLE ON DEPLOY and DELETE TABLE ON UNDEPLOY are both checked.

The Application Deployment Tool is now ready to generate the

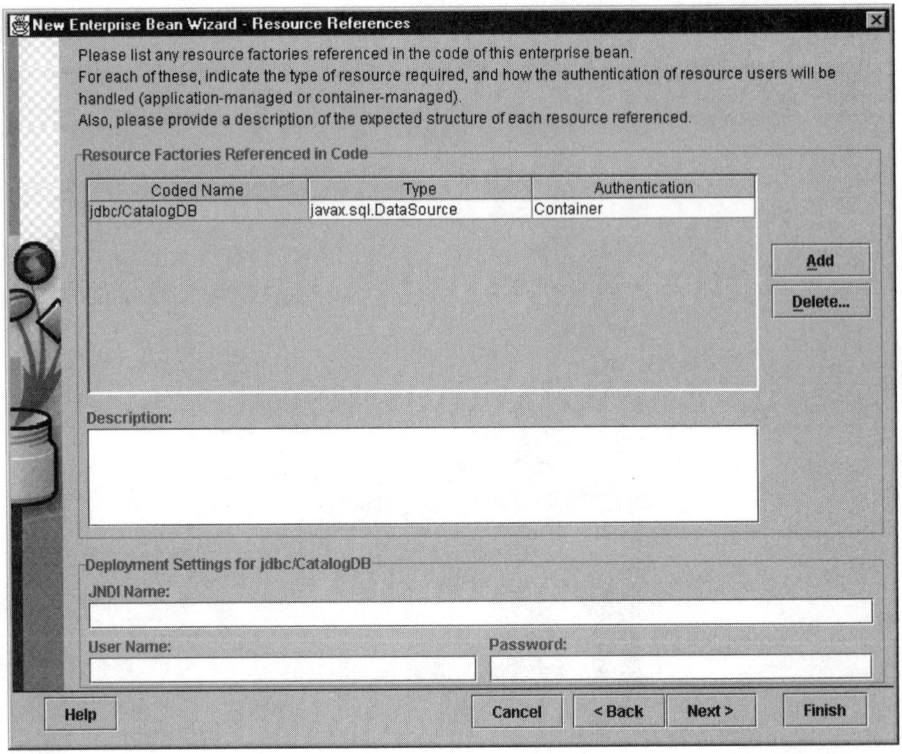

Figure 6-3
Completed Resource
References Dialog

SQL that will manage the database. If the database is not already started, it should be started now, using the command:

```
cloudscape -start
```

After the database has started, we click on the button labeled GENERATE SQL NOW. When SQL generation has begun, a dialog like the one shown in Figure 6-8 is displayed. When we dismiss this dialog, SQL generation proceeds. When it has completed, a dialog like the one shown in Figure 6-9 appears.

When we discussed the home interface, we said that we would have to supply the WHERE clauses for the findByDescription() and findInRange() methods. It is now time to do so. The group box labeled SQL FOR DATABASE ACCESS contains a list of EJB methods from which we select *findByDescription(java.lang.String parameter1)*. When we do so, partial SQL like that shown in Figure 6-10 is displayed.

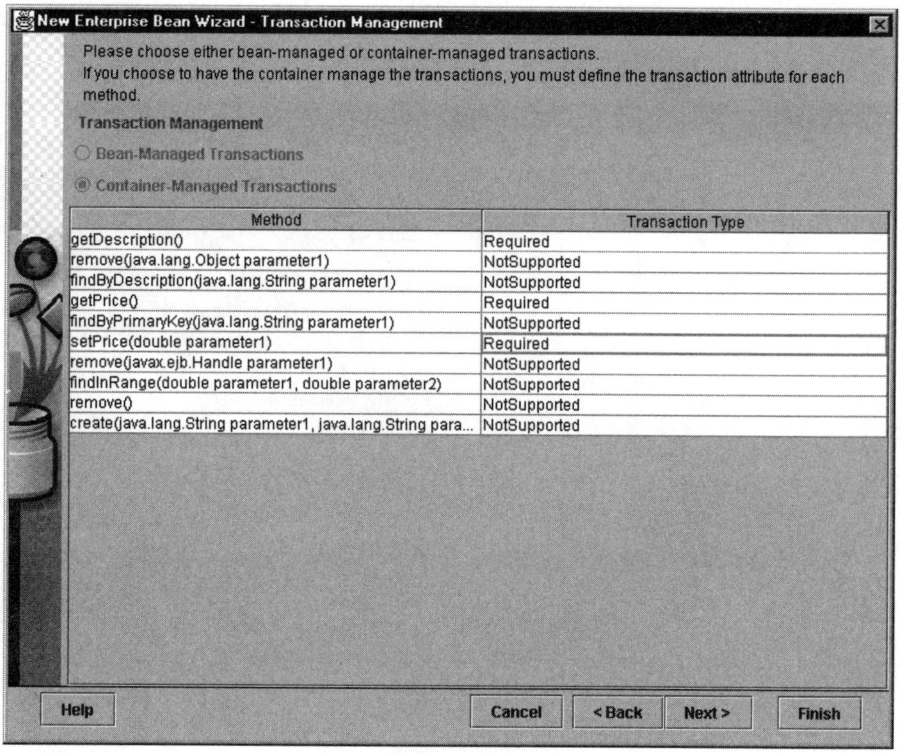

Figure 6-4
Completed Transaction Management
Dialog

We complete the SQL statement by positioning the cursor at the end of the statement and typing

```
WHERE "description" = ?1
```

NOTE: *The double quotes surrounding "description" are important.*

The complete SQL, as shown in Figure 6-11 now reads:

```
SELECT "productID" FROM "CatalogItemBeanTable" WHERE "description"
= ?1
```

We now supply a WHERE clause for *findInRange(double parameter1, double parameter2)*. It reads as follows:

```
WHERE "price" BETWEEN ?1 AND ?2
```

Figure 6-5
Persistence Manage-
ment for CatalogApp

![Application Deployment Tool screenshot showing Persistence Management for CatalogApp. The window titled "Application Deployment Tool: CatalogApp" displays a tree of Local Applications (CatalogApp, CatalogJAR, CatalogIt...) and an inspection panel "Inspecting: CatalogApp.CatalogJAR.CatalogItemBean" with tabs: EJB References, Resource Ref's, Security, Transactions, General, Entity, Environment. The Entity tab is selected showing Persistence Management with radio buttons "Bean-Managed Persistence" and "Container-Managed Persistence" (selected), checkboxes for productID, description, price, a "Deployment Settings..." button, Primary Key Class: java.lang.String, Primary Key Field Name: productID, and a Reentrant checkbox. Below are Servers: localhost and Server Applications with an Undeploy button.]

After all SQL has been completed, we finalize the SQL generation
by clicking on OK.

We are now ready to deploy the application containing our entity
bean. We start the deployment process by selecting *CatalogApp*
from the list of applications displayed in the leftmost column of the
Application Deployment Tool main window and then selecting
"Deploy Application . . ." from the "Tools" drop-down menu. When
the Introduction dialog appears, we check the box labeled RETURN
CLIENT JAR and then click on NEXT>. This results in the appearance
of the JNDI Names dialog. In the column labeled "JNDI Name" we
enter *MyCatalogItem* in the row containing *CatalogItemBean* and
jdbc/Cloudscape in the row containing *jdbc/catalogDB*. At this
point, the dialog box looks like Figure 6-12.

We now click on FINISH to complete the deployment process.

Figure 6-6
Deployment Settings

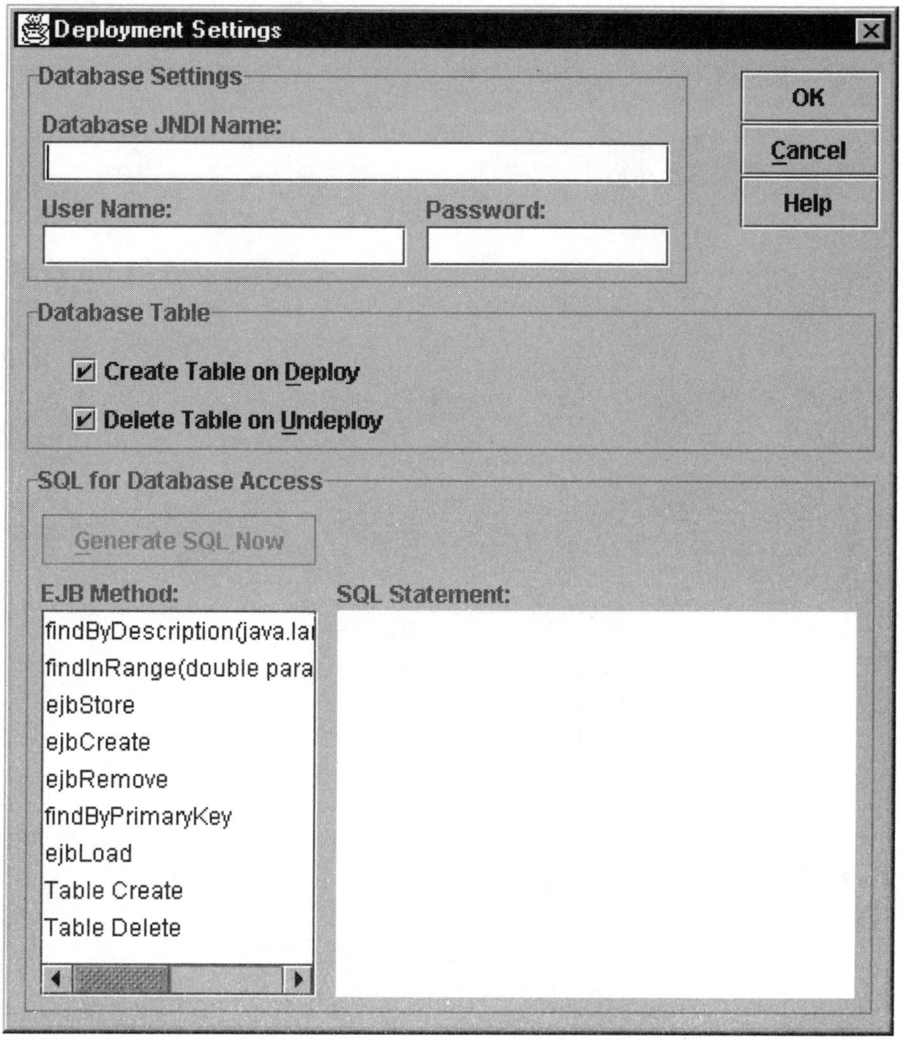

Deployment Settings

Database Settings

Database JNDI Name:

User Name: **Password:**

OK
Cancel
Help

Database Table

☑ **Create Table on Deploy**

☑ **Delete Table on Undeploy**

SQL for Database Access

Generate SQL Now

EJB Method: **SQL Statement:**

findByDescription(java.la
findInRange(double para
ejbStore
ejbCreate
ejbRemove
findByPrimaryKey
ejbLoad
Table Create
Table Delete

The Client

As has been the case with all of the beans we have developed so far,
we now write a simple client to test our new entity bean. Here is
the code:

\Chapter6\code\CatalogClient.java

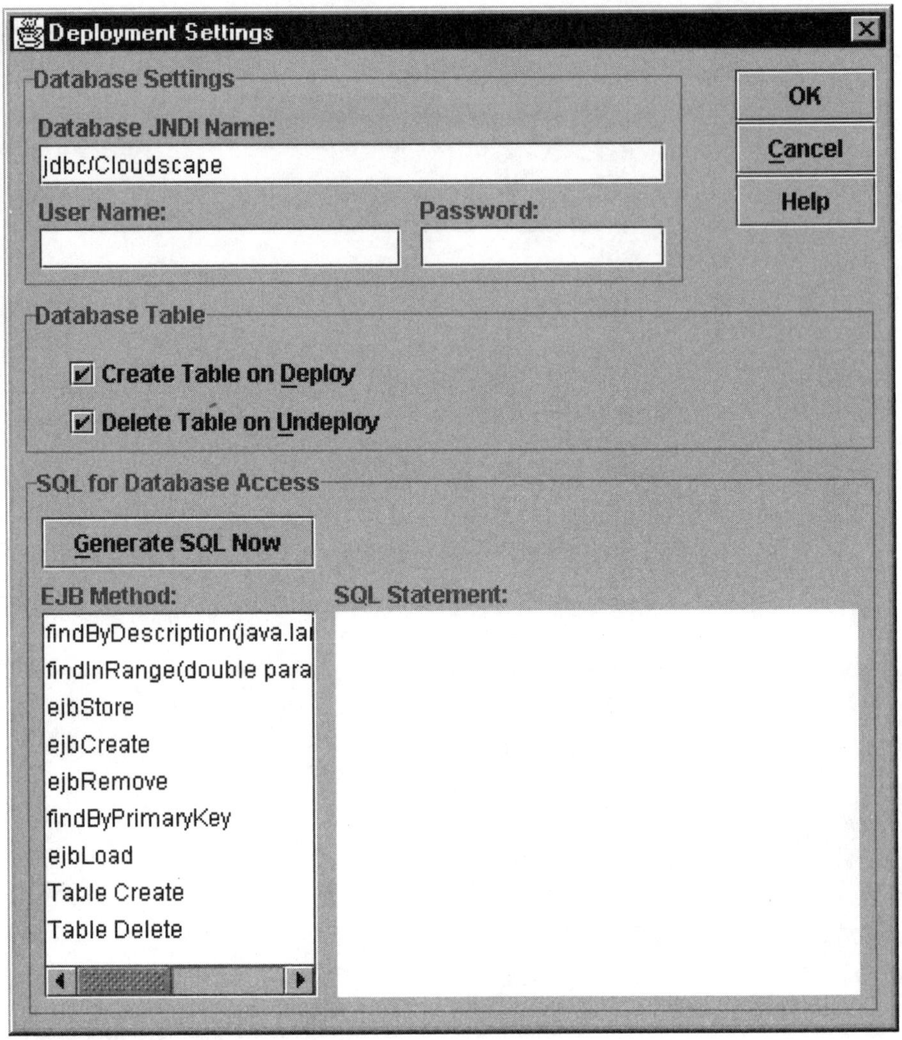

Figure 6-7
Ready to Generate
SQL

Figure 6-7
Ready to Generate
SQL

```
import javax.naming.*;
import javax.rmi.PortableRemoteObject;

public class CatalogClient {

  public static void main(String[] args) {

    String[] [] catalogData = {
      {"111","Formatted Diskettes - Box of 50","9.95"},
      {"222","Diskette Labels - Package of 50","1.59"},
      {"333","Diskette Mailers - Box of 50","8.49"},
```

Figure 6-8
SQL Generation
Notification

```
        {"444","CD-RW 74min/650MB - Box of 50","47.95"},
        {"555","CD Jewel Cases - Box of 50","17.95"}
    };

    final int PRODUCT_ID = 0;
    final int DESCR = 1;
    final int PRICE = 2;

    CatalogItemHome home = null;

    try {
      Context initial = new InitialContext();
      Object objref = initial.lookup("MyCatalogItem");

      home = (CatalogItemHome)PortableRemoteObject.narrow(objref,
          CatalogItemHome.class);
    }
    catch (NamingException e) {
      System.out.println("Caught NamingException");
      e.printStackTrace();
      System.exit(0);
    }

    System.out.println("LOADING DATA");
```

Figure 6-9
Request for Finder
SQL

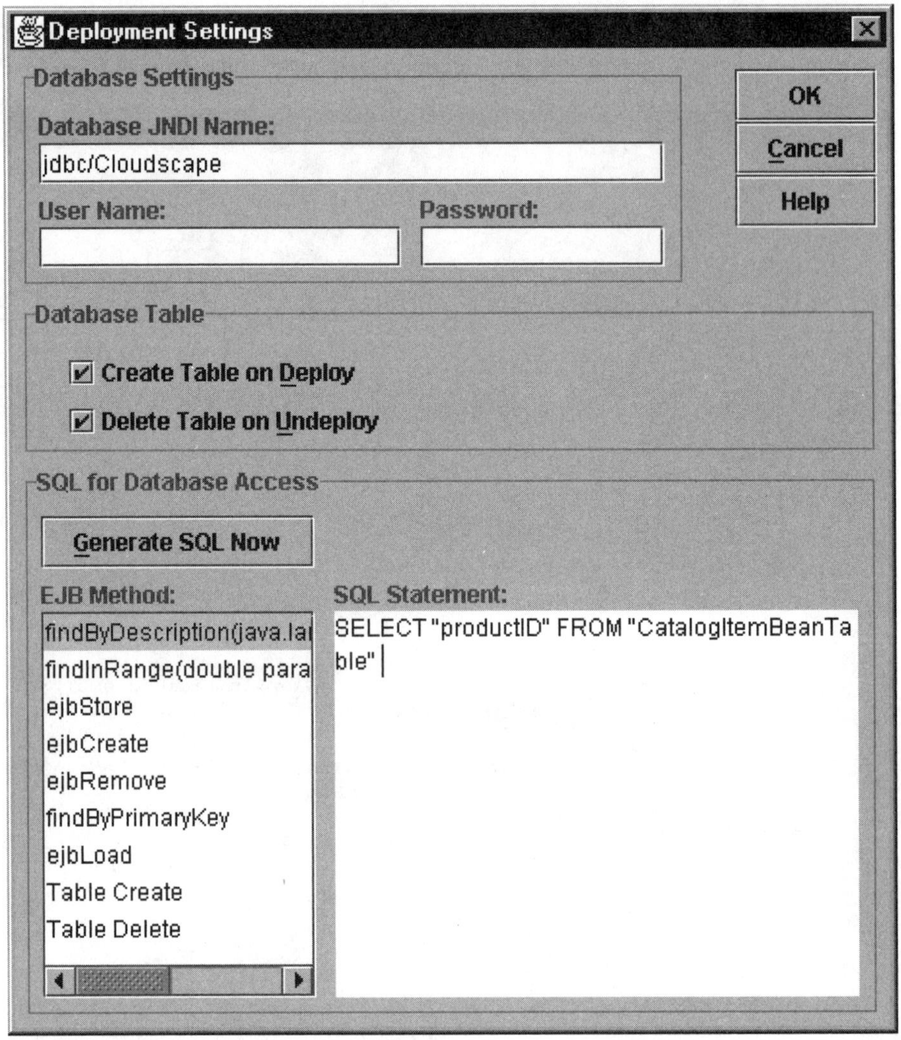

Figure 6-10
Preparing to Complete
SQL

```
         for (int i = 0; i < catalogData.length; ++i) {
           String key = catalogData[i][PRODUCT_ID];
           String desc = catalogData[i][DESCR];
           double price = Double.parseDouble(catalogData[i] [PRICE]);
           try {
             CatalogItem ci = home.create(key,desc);
             ci.setPrice(price);
           }
           catch (Exception e) {
             System.out.println("caught Exception");
             e.printStackTrace();
           }
         }
```

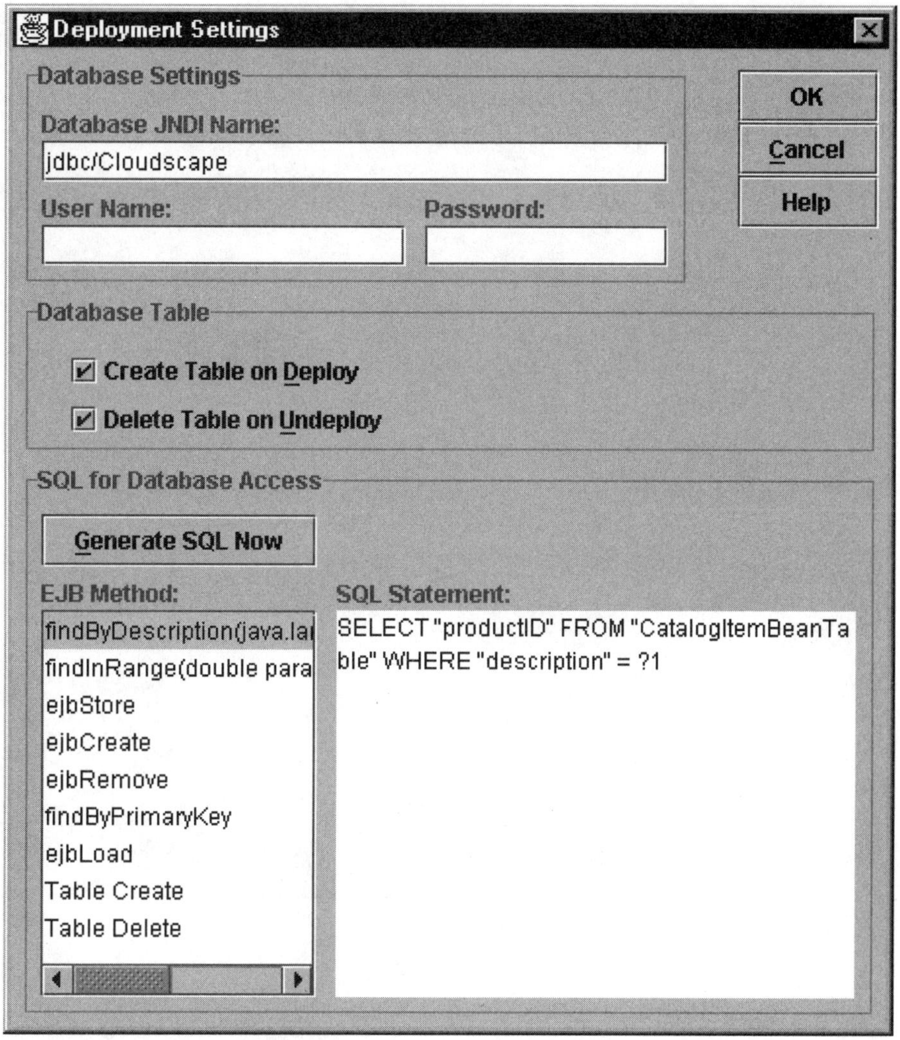

Figure 6-11
Completed SQL

```
                 System.out.println();
                 System.out.println("ACCESSING DATA");

                 for (int i = 0; i < catalogData.length; ++i) {
                   try {
                     CatalogItem prodfound =
                       home.findByPrimaryKey(catalogData[i] [PRODUCT_ID]);
                     System.out.println(prodfound.getDescription() +
                       " ... &" + prodfound.getPrice());
                   }
                   catch (Exception e) {
                     System.out.println("caught exception");
                     e.printStackTrace();
```

Figure 6-12
Specifying JNDI
Names

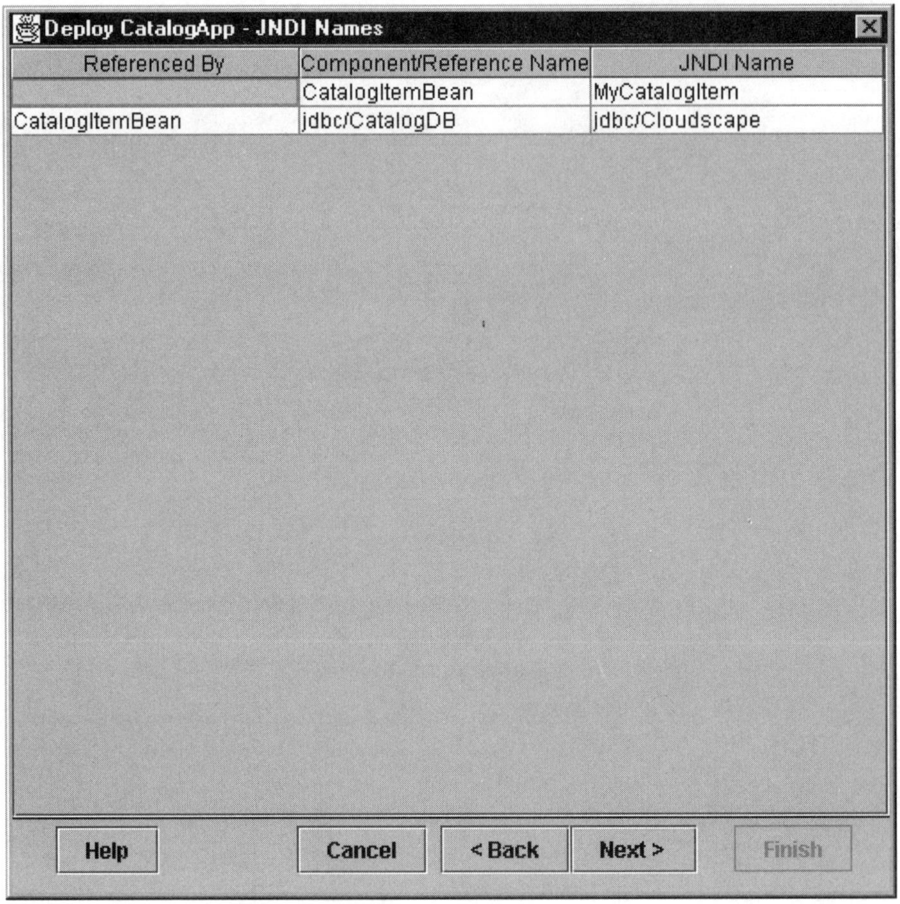

Deploy CatalogApp - JNDI Names		☒
Referenced By	Component/Reference Name	JNDI Name
	CatalogItemBean	MyCatalogItem
CatalogItemBean	jdbc/CatalogDB	jdbc/Cloudscape

Help   Cancel   < Back   Next >   Finish

```
      }
    }

    System.out.println();
    System.out.println("CHECKING PRICES BETWEEN &5 & &10");

    try {
      Collection c = home.findInRange(5.00, 10.00);
      Iterator i = c.iterator();

      while (i.hasNext()) {
        CatalogItem product = (CatalogItem)i.next();
        String productId = (String)product.getPrimaryKey();
        String desc = product.getDescription();
        double price = product.getPrice();
        System.out.println(desc + " ... &" + price);
```

```
        }
      }
      catch (Exception e) {
        System.out.println("caught exception");
        e.printStackTrace();
      }
    }
  }
```

The client program performs the following actions:

- Finds the bean
- Traverses the String array `catalogData`, tokenizing each element into productID, description, and price
- Invokes the `create()` method to create an instance of our entity bean
- Traverses the `catalogData` array, again passing each productID to the `findByPrimaryKey()` method to retrieve the instance of the bean whose key is that productID
- Displays the description and price of each bean thus found
- Uses the `findByRange()` method to obtain a collection of those catalog items whose price is between $5.00 and $10.00 and displays the description and price of each

Running the Client

We execute the client by typing:

```
runCatalogClient
```

\Chapter6\code\runCatalogClient.bat

The client produces results like those shown in Figure 6-13.

If we execute our client a second time, we get results like those shown in Figure 6-14. In Figure 6-7, we noticed that CREATE TABLE ON DEPLOY and DELETE TABLE ON UNDEPLOY were checked. We are now in a position to see the significance of these settings. We first

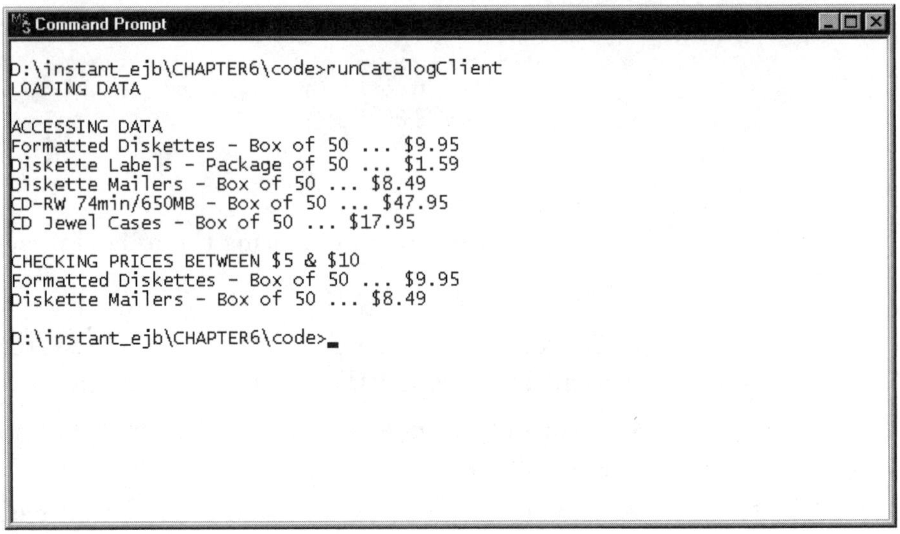

Figure 6-13

Result of Running
CatalogClient

```
Command Prompt                                                    _ □ ×
D:\instant_ejb\CHAPTER6\code>runCatalogClient
LOADING DATA

ACCESSING DATA
Formatted Diskettes - Box of 50 ... $9.95
Diskette Labels - Package of 50 ... $1.59
Diskette Mailers - Box of 50 ... $8.49
CD-RW 74min/650MB - Box of 50 ... $47.95
CD Jewel Cases - Box of 50 ... $17.95

CHECKING PRICES BETWEEN $5 & $10
Formatted Diskettes - Box of 50 ... $9.95
Diskette Mailers - Box of 50 ... $8.49

D:\instant_ejb\CHAPTER6\code>_



```

Figure 6-13
Result of Running
CatalogClient

select *CatalogApp* from the list labeled "Server Applications" at the
bottom of the Application Deployment Tool main window and then
click on the button labeled UNDEPLOY and click on OK in the resulting dialog box. This undeploys the application and deletes the
table. We now repeat the deployment process previously described
by selecting the "Deploy Application . . ." item from the "Tools"

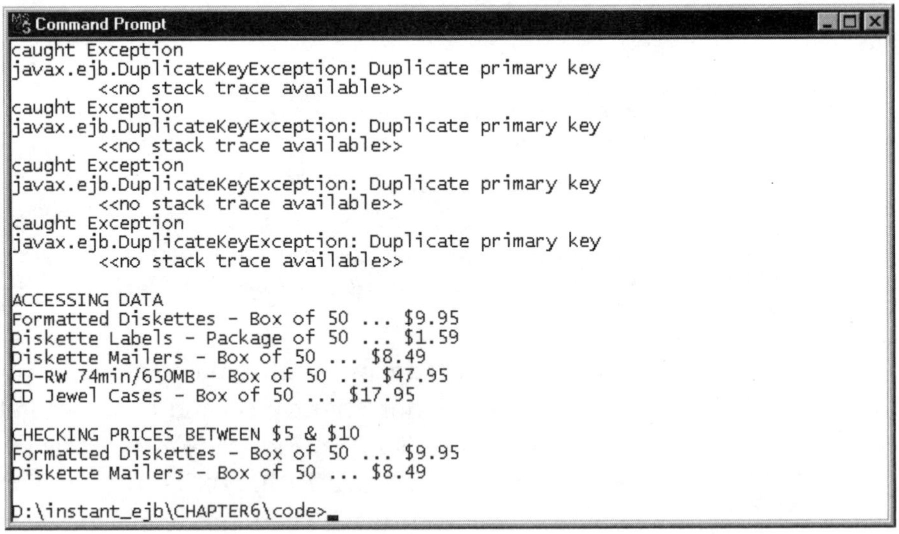

Figure 6-14
Result of Running
CatalogClient a
Second Time

```
Command Prompt                                                    _ □ ×
caught Exception
javax.ejb.DuplicateKeyException: Duplicate primary key
            <<no stack trace available>>
caught Exception
javax.ejb.DuplicateKeyException: Duplicate primary key
            <<no stack trace available>>
caught Exception
javax.ejb.DuplicateKeyException: Duplicate primary key
            <<no stack trace available>>
caught Exception
javax.ejb.DuplicateKeyException: Duplicate primary key
            <<no stack trace available>>

ACCESSING DATA
Formatted Diskettes - Box of 50 ... $9.95
Diskette Labels - Package of 50 ... $1.59
Diskette Mailers - Box of 50 ... $8.49
CD-RW 74min/650MB - Box of 50 ... $47.95
CD Jewel Cases - Box of 50 ... $17.95

CHECKING PRICES BETWEEN $5 & $10
Formatted Diskettes - Box of 50 ... $9.95
Diskette Mailers - Box of 50 ... $8.49

D:\instant_ejb\CHAPTER6\code>_
```

drop-down menu and run the client once more. This time we do not raise a *DuplicateKeyException*. From this we see that the options of creating a table on deployment and deleting it on undeployment are useful.

A Catalog/Inventory Bean

The next bean we develop can be used to provide input both for an online catalog and to track inventory. Unlike the catalog, which used a simple *String* as a key, our inventory bean uses a multipart key whose components are a product identifier and a supplier identifier. In addition to the key components, the bean has instance variables that hold product description, price, quantity on hand, minimum reorder quantity, and a sales brochure.

> **NOTE:** *Good design might dictate that this bean be split into two simpler beans. The purpose of the example is to demonstrate features of a bean rather than to teach proper design.*

The Remote Interface

Here is the code for the remote interface:

\Chapter6\code\ComplexKeyedItem

```
import javax.ejb.EJBObject;
import java.rmi.RemoteException;

public interface ComplexKeyedItem extends EJBObject {

    public String getProductID() throws RemoteException;
```

```
public String getSupplier() throws RemoteException;

public double getPrice() throws RemoteException;

public void setPrice(double price) throws RemoteException;

public String getDescription() throws RemoteException;

public void setDescription(String description)
   throws RemoteException;

public byte[] getSalesBrochure() throws RemoteException;

public void setSalesBrochure(byte[] brochure, int len)
   throws RemoteException;

public int getQuantityOnHand() throws RemoteException;

public void setQuantityOnHand(int quantity)
   throws RemoteException;

public int getMinimumReorderQuantity() throws RemoteException;

public void setMinimumReorderQuantity(int quantity)
   throws RemoteException;
```

The Home Interface

This is the code for the home interface:

\Chapter6\code\ComplexKeyedItemHome

```
import java.util.Collection;
import java.rmi.RemoteException;
import javax.ejb.*;

public interface ComplexKeyedItemHome extends EJBHome {

   public ComplexKeyedItem create(String productId, String supplier)
      throws RemoteException, CreateException;
   public ComplexKeyedItem findByPrimaryKey(CatalogItemKey key)
      throws FinderException, RemoteException;
```

```
public Collection findByProductID(String productID)
   throws FinderException, RemoteException;

public Collection findBySupplier(String supplier)
   throws FinderException, RemoteException;
}
```

The Enterprise Bean

The code for the enterprise bean is somewhat lengthy and is presented at the end of the chapter. We discuss some of the bean's methods here.

ejbCreate()

The `ejbCreate()` method is invoked by the container when a client calls the `create()` method of the home interface. The method initializes the bean's instance variables. The return type of the method is *CatalogItemKey*. We will examine the *CatalogItemKey* class shortly.

NOTE: *The method creates and returns an instance of CatalogItemKey; however, as we mentioned earlier, this returned value is ignored by the container.*

ejbLoad()

When we discussed the `ejbLoad()` method earlier in the chapter, we said that it could be used to transform data after it was retrieved from the database by the container but before it was made available for use by any of the bean's methods. One of the fields of the bean we are developing is a sales brochure that is available to the client as an array of bytes but which is stored in the database in compressed form. If you examine the `ejbLoad()` method in the bean listing at the end of the chapter, you will see that it uses the *java.util.zip* package to decompress the sales-Brochure byte array retrieved from the database and stores the resulting data in the private instance variable unzipped-Brochure. The variable unzippedBrochure is returned by the getSalesBrochure() method but, when we package the bean, we will see that it is not even presented by the Application Deployment Tool as a candidate for container management because it is private and not discovered by reflection.

ejbSave()

The ejbStore() method uses the *java.util.zip* package to compress the data in the unzippedBrochure instance variable and to store the results in salesBrochure, which is managed by the container.

The PrimaryKey Class

For most entity beans, the primary key class is *java.lang.String* or some class in the *java.lang* package. We saw this was true for the *CatalogItem* bean we just developed.

In the bean we are now creating, the primary key is comprised of two components: a product ID and a supplier. Many items in the database can have the same product ID. Each item with the same product ID must have a unique supplier. When primary keys are complex, we can supply our own primary key class, which must meet the following requirements:

- The access control modifier is public.

- All fields are public.

- For container-managed persistence, the field names must match corresponding container-managed fields in the entity bean class.

- The class must have a public default constructor.

- The class must be serializable.

Here is the code for our PrimaryKeyClass:

On the CD   \Chapter6\code\CatalogItemKey

```java
public class CatalogItemKey implements java.io.Serializable {

  public String productID;
  public String supplier;

  public CatalogItemKey() {};

  public CatalogItemKey(String productID, String supplier) {
    this.productID = productID;
    this.supplier =supplier;
  }

  public String getProductID() {
    return productID;
  }

  public void setProductID(String productID) {
    this.productID = productID;
  }

  public String getSupplier() {
    return supplier;
  }

  public void setSupplier(String supplier) {
    this.supplier = supplier;
  }

  public boolean equals(Object other) {

    if (other instanceof CatalogItemKey) {
      return (productID.equals(((CatalogItemKey)other) .productID)
            && supplier.equals(
            ((CatalogItemKey)other).supplier));
    }
    return false;
  }

  public int hashCode() {
    return productID.hashCode();
  }
}
```

Packaging and Deploying

We compile the code by typing the command:

```
compileComplexKeyedItem
```

━ ━ ━ ━ ━ ━ ━ ━ ━ ━ ━ ━ ━ ━ ━ ━ ━

\Chapter6\code\compileComplexKeyedItem.bat

For the most part, the packaging process is identical to the one we followed to package the first bean in this chapter. We discuss only where it differs. The parameters required to package the bean are shown in Table 6-2. When we add `.class` files to the JAR, in addition to *ComplexKeyedItem.class, ComplexKeyedItem-Home.class,* and *ComplexKeyedItemBean.class,* we add *Catalog-ItemKey.class.*

When the Entity Settings dialog is displayed, after we check CON-TAINER-MANAGED PERSISTENCE and check the checkbox next to each of the instance variables, we enter *CatalogItemKey* in the text entry filed labeled "PrimaryKeyClass". We do *not* select a Primary Key Field Name from the drop-down list. Before proceeding, we should make sure the Entity Setting dialog looks like Figure 6-15.

TABLE 6-2

Parameters Required to Package ComplexKeyedItem Bean

Parameter	Value
Application File Name	ComplexKeyApp.ear
DisplayName	ComplexKeyApp
JAR Display Name	ComplexKeyJAR
Enterprise Bean Class	ComplexKeyedItemBean
Home Interface	ComplexKeyedItemHome
RemoteInterface	ComplexKeyedItem
Enterprise Bean Display Name	ComplexKeyedItemBean
Bean Reference Coded Name	ejb/ComplexKeyedItem
Resource Coded Name	jdbc/CatalogDB

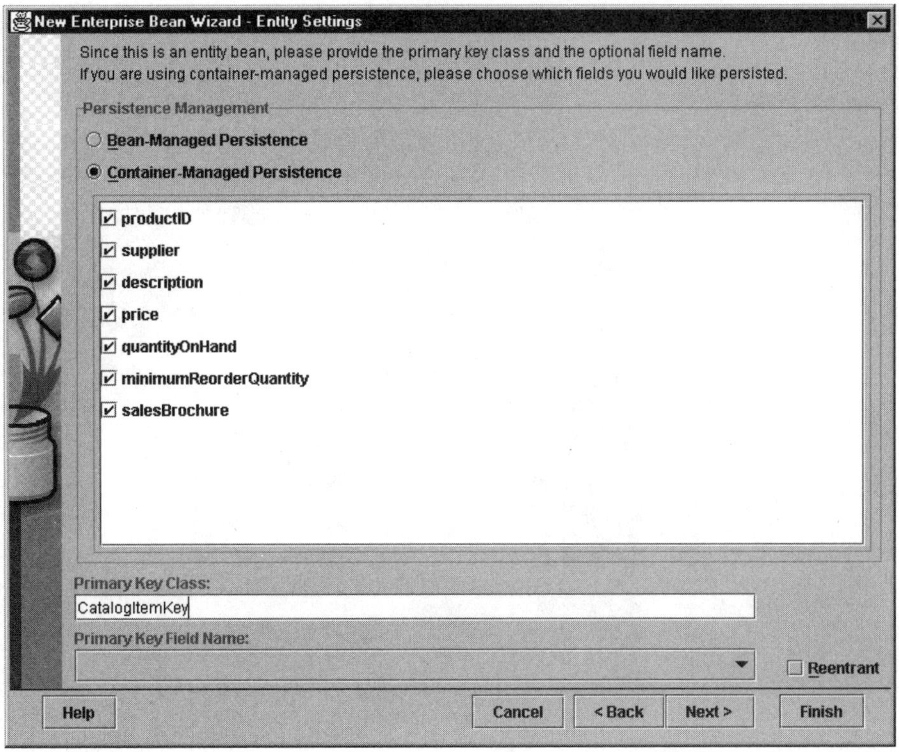

Figure 6-15
Entity Settings Dialog

When the Enterprise Bean References dialog is displayed, in addition to supplying the information shown in Table 6-2, we select *Entity* from the drop-down list in the column labeled "Type". The Enterprise Bean References dialog should then look like Figure 6-16.

When we reach the Transaction Management dialog, we should specify Transaction Types so that the dialog looks like Figure 6-17.

After we have added the bean, we select it and click on the ENTITY tab. We specify *jdbc/Cloudscape* as the Database JNDI Name. After we generate the SQL, we must add the following additional SQL for the finder methods:

1. for *findByProductID*

```
SELECT "productID", "supplier" FROM "ComplexKeyedItemBeanTable"
WHERE
"productID" = ?1
```

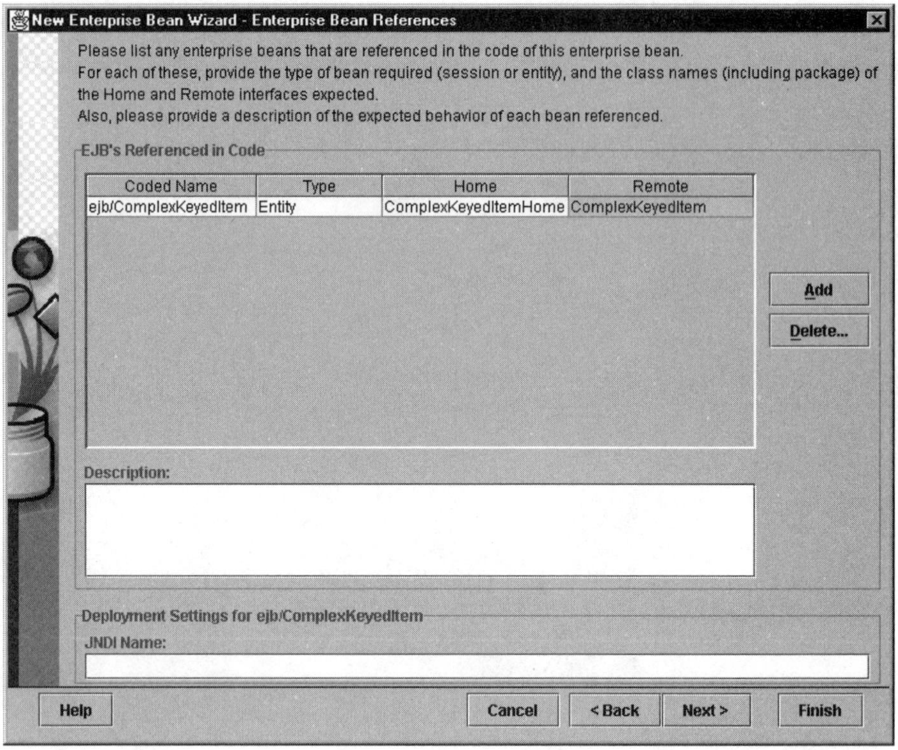

Figure 6-16
Enterprise Bean
References Dialog

2. for *findBySupplier*

```
SELECT "productID", "supplier" FROM "ComplexKeyedItemBeanTable"
WHERE
"supplier" = ?1
```

JavaServer Pages as a Client

In the last chapter, we added servlets to our growing list of clients a bean can have. We will now add JavaServer Pages (JSPs) to that list.

NOTE: *For further information on JavaServer Pages, see "Instant JavaServer Pages" by Paul Tremblett (Osborne / McGraw-Hill, ISBN 0-07-212601-9).*

Figure 6-17
Transaction
Management
Dialog

![New Enterprise Bean Wizard - Transaction Management dialog]

New Enterprise Bean Wizard - Transaction Management

Please choose either bean-managed or container-managed transactions.
If you choose to have the container manage the transactions, you must define the transaction attribute for each method.

Transaction Management

○ Bean-Managed Transactions
◉ Container-Managed Transactions

Method	Transaction Type
getSupplier()	Required
setSalesBrochure([B parameter1, int parameter2)	Required
remove(java.lang.Object parameter1)	NotSupported
getDescription()	Required
remove(javax.ejb.Handle parameter1)	NotSupported
getSalesBrochure()	Required
getProductID()	Required
findByProductID(java.lang.String parameter1)	Required
findBySupplier(java.lang.String parameter1)	Required
setPrice(double parameter1)	Required
remove()	NotSupported
findByPrimaryKey(CatalogItemKey parameter1)	Required
getQuantityOnHand()	Required
setMinimumReorderQuantity(int parameter1)	Required
create(java.lang.String parameter1, java.lang.String para...	Required
setDescription(java.lang.String parameter1)	Required
getPrice()	Required
getMinimumReorderQuantity()	Required
setQuantityOnHand(int parameter1)	Required

Help   Cancel   < Back   Next >   Finish

The application presents two text entry fields into which the user types a product identifier and a supplier. When the user clicks on OK, the description and price of the product matching the key whose components match the specified product identifier and supplier are displayed followed by the sales brochure for the product.

The JSP Pages

The Initial Page
Here is the code for the initial JSP page:

 On the CD

\Chapter6\code\CatalogSearch.jsp

```
<jsp:useBean id="catBean" class="CatalogBean" scope="session" />
<html>
```

```
<body>
<center>
<h1>Catalog Search</h1>
<form method="get"
action="http://localhost:8000/CatalogContextRoot/FindProductsAlias"
>
<table>
  <tr>
    <td>Product ID: </td>
    <td><input name="productID" type="text"></td>
  </tr>
    <tr>
    <td>Supplier: </td>
    <td><input name="supplier" type="text"></td>
  </tr>
</table>
<br>
<br>
<input type="submit" value="GET PRODUCT DATA">
</form>
</center>
</body>
</html>
```

The Results Page

The JSP page that displays the data belonging to the specified products looks like this:

 ━ ━ ━ ━ ━ ━ ━ ━ ━ ━ ━ ━ ━ ━ ━ ━ ━

\Chapter6\code\FindProducts.jsp

```
<%@ page errorPage="FindErrorAlias" %>
<jsp:useBean id="catBean" class="CatalogBean" scope="session" />
<jsp:setProperty name="catBean" property="*" />
<html>
<head>
<title>CatalogSearch</title>
</head>
<body>
<p>
Product ID:
<jsp:getProperty name="catBean" property="productID" />
<p>
Description:
<jsp:getProperty name="catBean" property="description" />
<p>
Supplier:
<jsp:getProperty name="catBean" property="supplier" />
<p>
Price:
```

```
<jsp:getProperty name="catBean" property="price" />
<p>
Brochure:
<jsp:getProperty name="catBean" property="salesBrochure" />
</body>
</html>
```

The Error Page
The following page handles errors:

\Chapter6\code\FindError.jsp

```
<%@ page isErrorPage="true" %>
<jsp:useBean id="catBean" class="CatalogBean" scope="request" />
<html>
<head>
<title>error</title>
</head>
<body>
<p>
<%= exception.getMessage() %>
</body>
</html>
```

The Intermediate JavaBean
JavaServer Pages do not interact with enterprise beans directly;
rather, they use a JavaBean as an intermediary. Here is the code
for the intermediate bean:

\Chapter6\code\CatalogBean

```
import java.rmi.RemoteException;
import javax.ejb.FinderException;
import javax.naming.Context;
import javax.naming.InitialContext;
import javax.rmi.PortableRemoteObject;

public class CatalogBean {

    ComplexKeyedItemHome home;
```

```java
public String productID;
public String supplier;

private String searchProductID;
private String searchSupplier;

public CatalogBean() {
  try {
    Context ic = new InitialContext();
    java.lang.Object objref =
      ic.lookup("java:comp/env/ejb/ComplexKeyedItem");
    home =
      (ComplexKeyedItemHome) PortableRemoteObject.narrow(objref,
        ComplexKeyedItemHome.class);
  }
  catch (Exception e) {
    System.err.println ("Couldn't locate ComplexKeyedItemHome");
    e.printStackTrace();
  }
}

public ComplexKeyedItem findProduct(String productID,
  String supplier)
    throws Exception {
  CatalogItemKey key =
    new CatalogItemKey(productID, supplier);
  try {
    return home.findByPrimaryKey(key);
  }
  catch (FinderException e) {
    throw new Exception("FinderException: " + e.getMessage());
  }
  catch (RemoteException e) {
    throw new Exception("RemoteException: " + e.getMessage());
  }
}

public void setProductID(String productID) {
  this.productID = productID;
}

public String getProductID() {
  return productID;
}

public String getSalesBrochure()
    throws Exception, RemoteException {
  ComplexKeyedItem item =
    findProduct(productID, supplier);
  return new String(item.getSalesBrochure());
}

public String getSupplier()
    throws Exception, RemoteException {
```

```
      ComplexKeyedItem item =
        findProduct(productID, supplier);
      return item.getSupplier();
    }

    public void setSupplier(String supplier) {
      this.supplier = supplier;
    }

    public String getDescription()
        throws Exception, RemoteException {
      ComplexKeyedItem item =
        findProduct(productID, supplier);
      return item.getDescription();
    }

    public double getPrice()
        throws Exception, RemoteException {
      ComplexKeyedItem item =
        findProduct(productID, supplier);
      return item.getPrice();
    }
}
```

CatalogBean defines methods that shadow the business methods in *ComplexKeyedItemBean*. The scope of *CatalogBean* is specified in the JSP as session. In the constructor of *CatalogBean*, the enterprise bean is found and a reference to the home interface is obtained and saved in the instance variable home. Since the scope of *CatalogBean* is specified as session in the JSPs that use it, this instance variable is available for reuse for the life of the browser session. Each of the shadow methods passes the product identifier and supplier to the findProduct() method of *CatalogBean*. This method uses the home reference to get the entity bean instance whose key matches the instance of *CatalogItemKey* constructed from the two arguments and returns the instance. The shadow methods then invoke the appropriate business method against the returned instance.

Packaging and Deploying

At this point, our application looks like Figure 6-18. We are now ready to add the web components and the intermediate JavaBean.

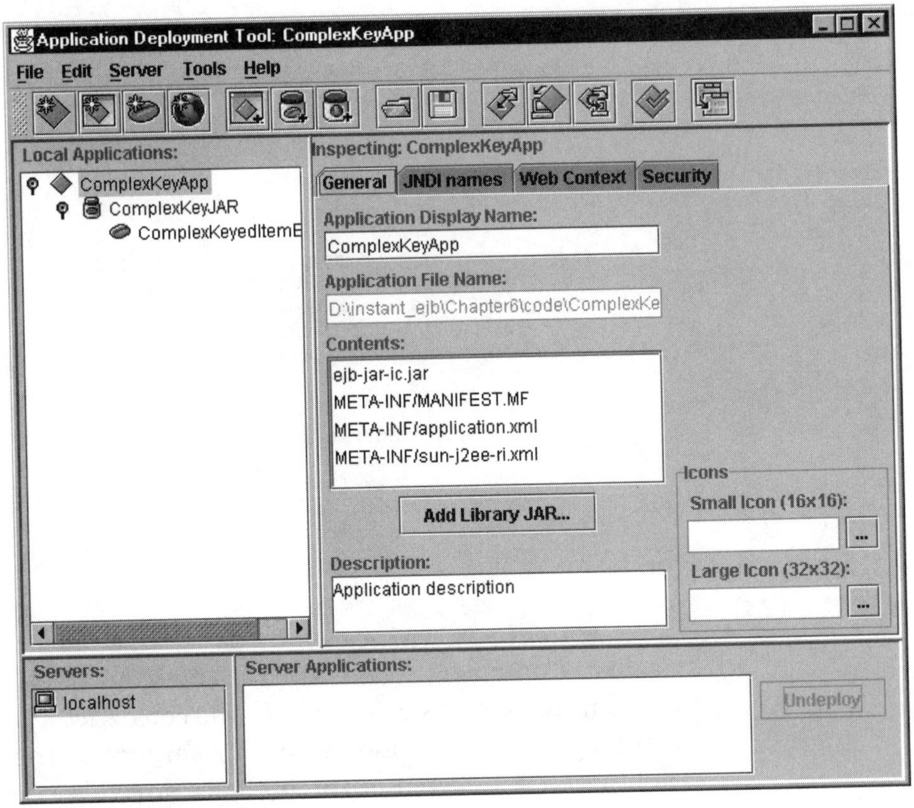

Figure 6-18
Application Prior to
Addition of Web
Components

With *ComplexKeyApp* selected as shown in Figure 6-18, we select
"New Web Component..." from the File drop-down menu. After we
dismiss the Introduction Dialog of the New Web Component Wizard
by clicking "Next>", the WAR File General Properties Dialog is displayed. We type *ComplexKeyWAR* in the text entry field labeled
"WAR Display Name". In the group box labeled "Contents:", we click
on the "Add..." button. When the "Add Content Files" Dialog appears,
we select *CatalogSearch.jsp* and then click the "Add" in the group
box labeled "Files to be Added:". When *CatalogSearch.jsp* appears in
the contents box, we click on "Next>", select *CatalogBean.class*, click
"Add", then click "Finish". The WAR File General Properties Dialog
should now look like Figure 6-19.

After clicking on "Next>", we see the Choose Component Type
Dialog and check the radio button labeled "JSP" so the dialog looks
like Figure 6-20.

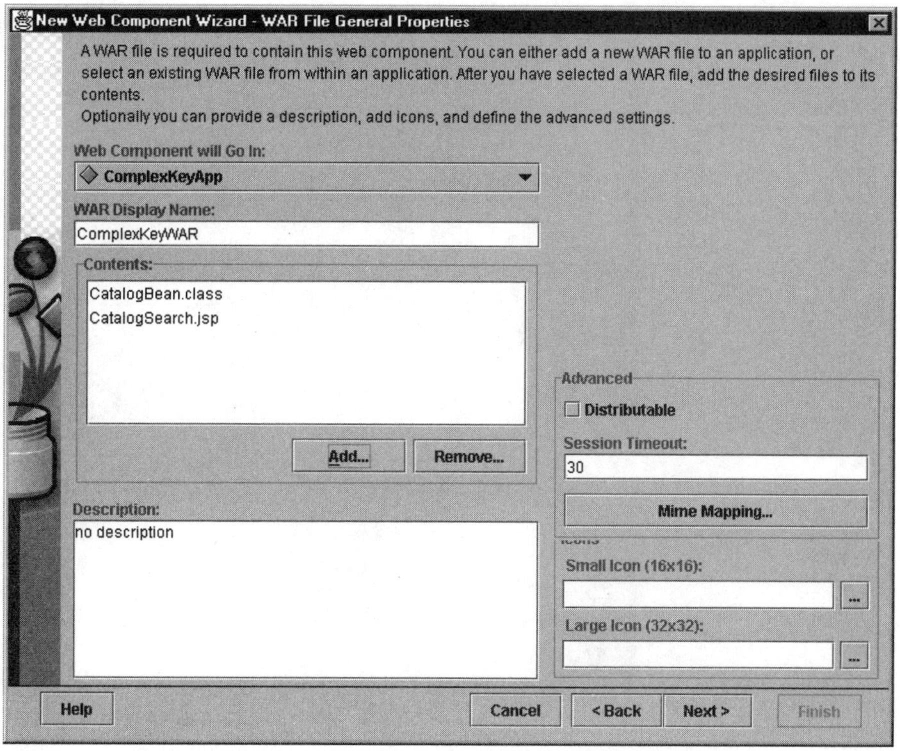

Figure 6-19
WAR File General
Properties Dialog

We now click "Next>" and the Component General Properties Dialog is displayed. We select *CatalogSearch.jsp* from the drop-down list labeled "JSP Filename:"and type *CatalogSearchJSP* in the entry field labeled "Web Component Display Name" so that the Component General Properties Dialog looks like Figure 6-21.

Clicking "Next>" twice in succession bypasses the Component Initialization Parameters Dialog. When the Component Aliases Dialog is displayed, we click on "Add" and enter *CatalogSearchAlias* in the entry field that appears so that the Component Aliases Dialog resembles Figure 6-22.

After dismissing the Component Aliases Dialog by clicking on "Next>", we bypass the Component Security and WAR File Environment dialogs. When the Enterprise Bean References Dialog appears, we click "Add" and then select a type of *entity* and specify values for *Coded Name*, *Home* and *Remote* so that the final appearance of the Enterprise Bean References Dialog looks like Figure 6-23.

Figure 6-20
Choose Component
Type Dialog

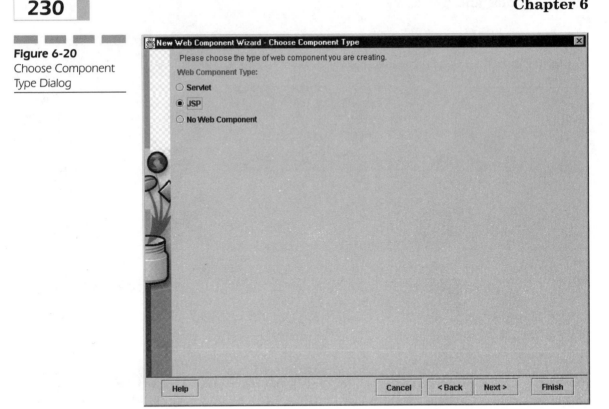

We click "Next>" and enter *jdbc/CatalogDB* as the Coded Name so that the Resource References Dialog resembles Figure 6-24. We then complete the process by clicking on "Finish".

In the Application Deployment Tool main window, we select *ComplexKeyWAR* from the column labeled "Local Applications" and add *FindProducts.jsp* as the next web component using the procedure we just outlined with the exception that we do not need to add *CatalogBean.class*. We then repeat the process for *FindError.jsp*. When we add *FindError.jsp,* we specify no Enterprise Bean References or Resource References. When we are through, the expanded list of applications and components displayed in the Application Deployment Tool main window should look like Figure 6-25.

We are now ready to deploy the application. With *ComplexKeyApp* selected from the list of applications, we select "Deploy Application..." from the Tools drop-down menu. We do not check the

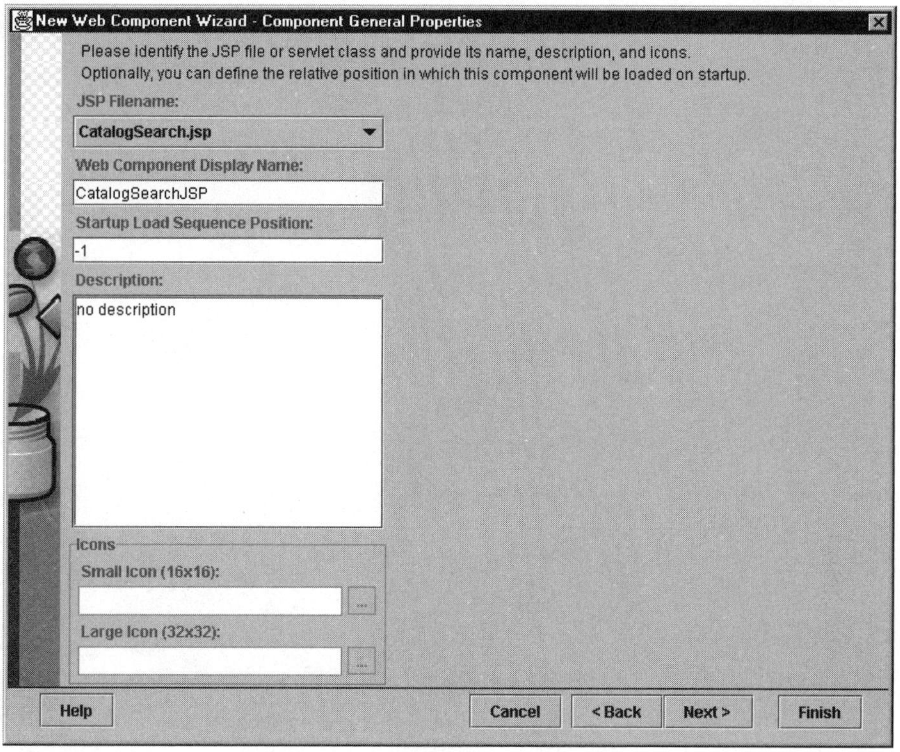

Figure 6-21
Component General
Properties Dialog

New Web Component Wizard - Component General Properties

Please identify the JSP file or servlet class and provide its name, description, and icons.
Optionally, you can define the relative position in which this component will be loaded on startup.

JSP Filename:

CatalogSearch.jsp ▼

Web Component Display Name:

CatalogSearchJSP

Startup Load Sequence Position:

-1

Description:

no description

Icons

Small Icon (16x16):

Large Icon (32x32):

| Help | | Cancel | < Back | Next > | Finish |

checkbox labeled "Return Client Jar" but proceed to the JNDI Names Dialog, which we populate to look like Figure 6-26.

When we click on "Next>", we see the WAR Context Root Dialog. We complete the entry by typing *CatalogContextRoot*. The dialog now looks like Figure 6-27. We complete the process by clicking on "Finish"

Running

Our first order of business is to load the database. We do this using the following code:

On the CD: \Chapter6\code\COmplexKeyDatabaseLoad.java

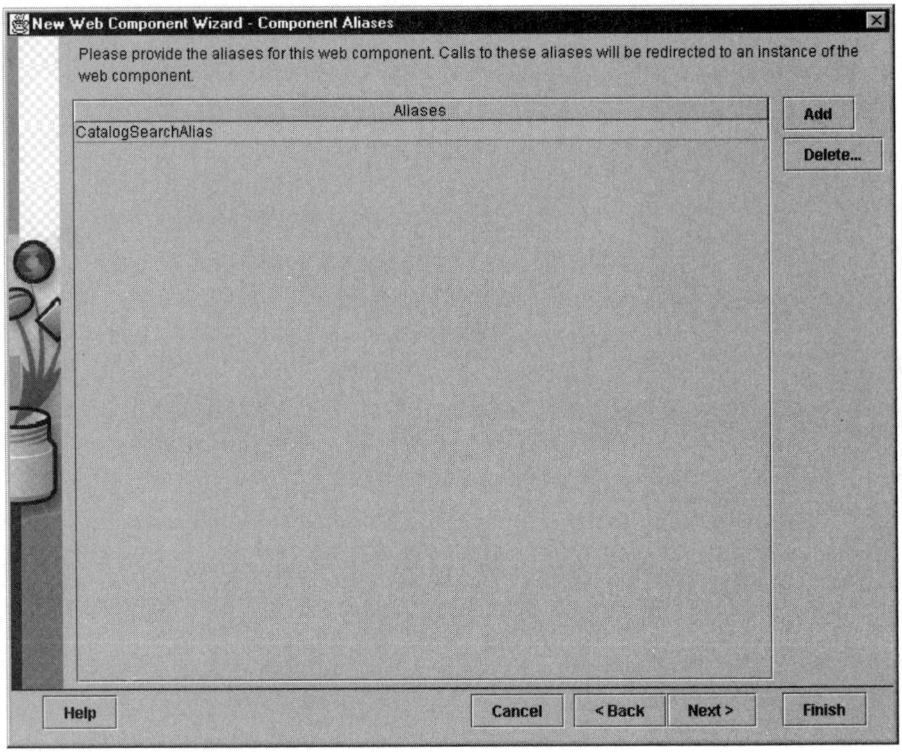

Figure 6-22
Component Aliases
Dialog

Figure 6-22
Component Aliases
Dialog

```java
import java.io.*;
import java.util.*;
import javax.naming.Context;
import javax.naming.InitialContext;
import javax.rmi.PortableRemoteObject;

public class ComplexKeyDatabaseLoad {

  static String desc = null;
  static String fname;
  static byte[] brochure = new byte[0];
  static int brochureLength = 0;

  public static void main(String[] args) {

    BufferedReader br = null;
    String line = null;

    ComplexKeyedItemHome home = null;

    try {
      br = new BufferedReader(new FileReader("CatalogData"));

      Context initial = new InitialContext();
```

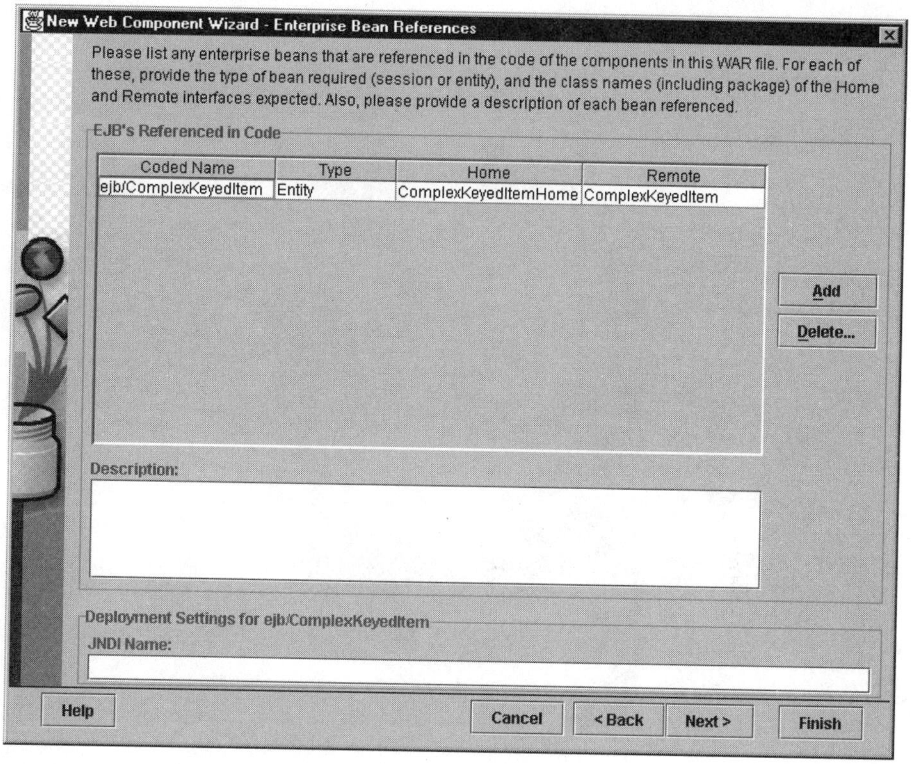

Figure 6-23
Enterprise Bean
References Dialog

```
        Object objref = initial.lookup("MyComplexKeyedItem");

    home =
(ComplexKeyedItemHome)PortableRemoteObject.narrow(objref,
        ComplexKeyedItemHome.class);

        while((line = br.readLine()) != null) {
          createEntry(home, line);
        }
      }
    catch (Exception ex) {
      System.err.println("Caught an exception." );
      System.out.println(ex.getMessage());
      ex.printStackTrace();
    }
  }

public static void createEntry(ComplexKeyedItemHome home,
    String line) throws Exception {

  StringTokenizer st = new StringTokenizer(line,",");
  String productID = st.nextToken();
  String supplier = st.nextToken();
  ComplexKeyedItem ci = home.create(productID, supplier);
```

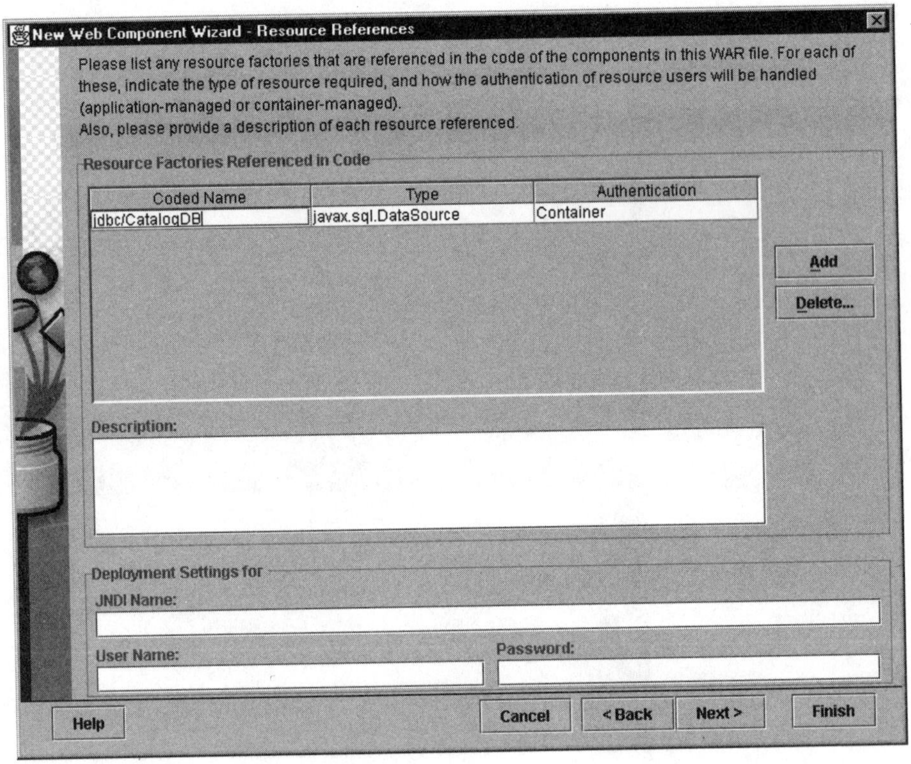

Figure 6-24
Resource References
Dialog

```
      ci.setPrice(Double.parseDouble(st.nextToken()));
      ci.setQuantityOnHand(Integer.parseInt(st.nextToken()));
      ci.setMinimumReorderQuantity(Integer.parseInt(st.nextToken()));
      if (st.hasMoreTokens()) {
        fname = st.nextToken();
        File f = new File(fname);
        int flen = (int)f.length();
        BufferedInputStream bis =
          new BufferedInputStream(new FileInputStream(fname));
        brochure = new byte[flen];
        brochureLength = bis.read(brochure,0,flen);
        bis.close();
        desc = st.nextToken();
      }
      System.out.println("desc: " + desc);
      ci.setDescription(desc);
      ci.setSalesBrochure(brochure,brochureLength);
    }
  }
```

After we compile our database load program, we run it by using
the following batch file:

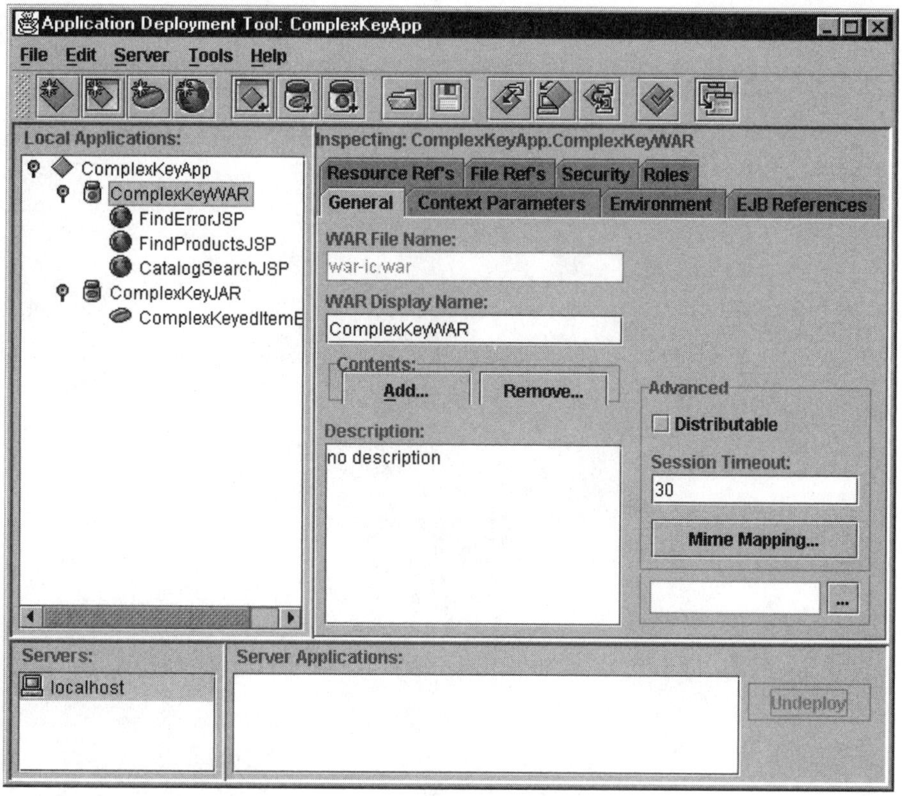

Figure 6-25
Applications and
Components List

We run this batch file by typing the command:

```
runComplexKeyDatabaseLoad
```

From our browser, we open the following URL:

```
http://localhost:8000/CatalogContextRoot/CatalogSearchAlias
```

The initial screen shown in Figure 6-28 is displayed in the browser window.

On the CD: **\Chapter6\code\runComplexKeyDatabaseLoad**

```
@echo off
set J2EE_HOME=c:\j2sdkee1.2.1
set CPATH=.;%J2EE_HOME%\lib\j2ee.jar;ComplexKeyAppClient.jar

java -classpath "%CPATH%" ComplexKeyDatabaseLoad
```

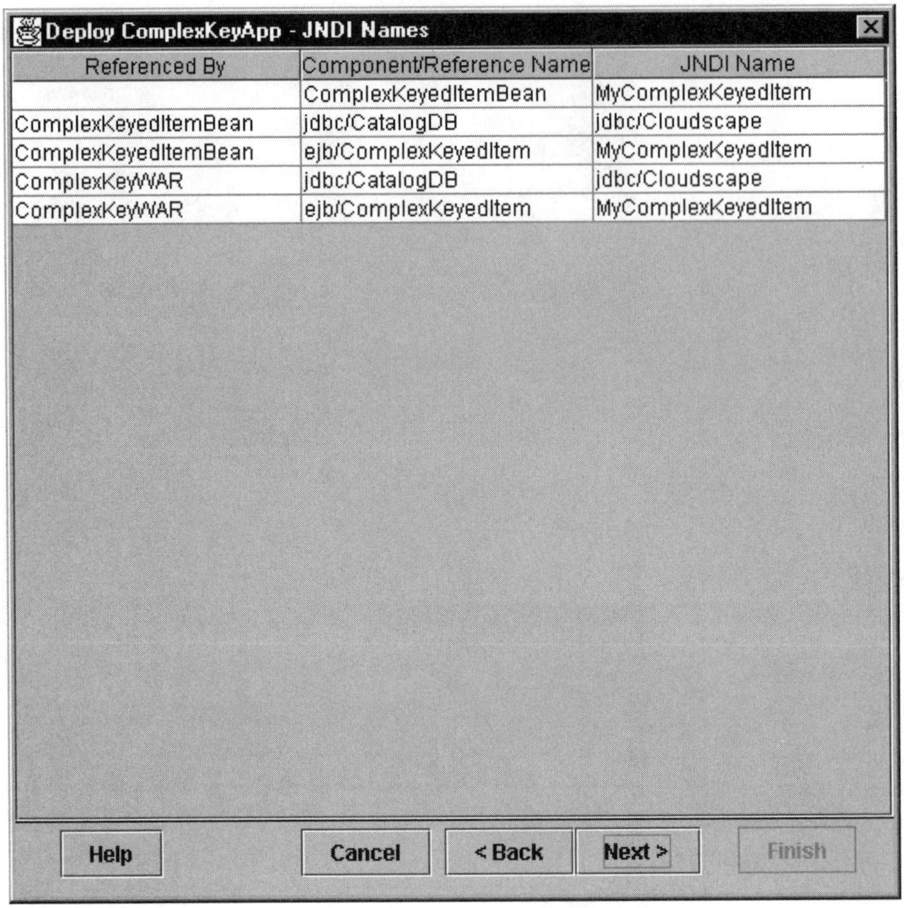

Figure 6-26
JNDI Names Dialog

Deploy ComplexKeyApp - JNDI Names		☒
Referenced By	Component/Reference Name	JNDI Name
	ComplexKeyedItemBean	MyComplexKeyedItem
ComplexKeyedItemBean	jdbc/CatalogDB	jdbc/Cloudscape
ComplexKeyedItemBean	ejb/ComplexKeyedItem	MyComplexKeyedItem
ComplexKeyWAR	jdbc/CatalogDB	jdbc/Cloudscape
ComplexKeyWAR	ejb/ComplexKeyedItem	MyComplexKeyedItem

Help		Cancel	< Back	Next >	Finish

After we enter a value of A12112 for the product ID and a value of S0010 for the supplier, we click on the button labeled "Get Product Data". The search results are shown in Figure 6-29.

Beyond HTML

Although Web browsers on desktop computers are still the most widely used interface to server-based applications, there is a growth in the use of browsers on wireless devices such as cellular phones. To show that JavaServer Pages are not limited to generating HTML and to demonstrate the variety of situations in

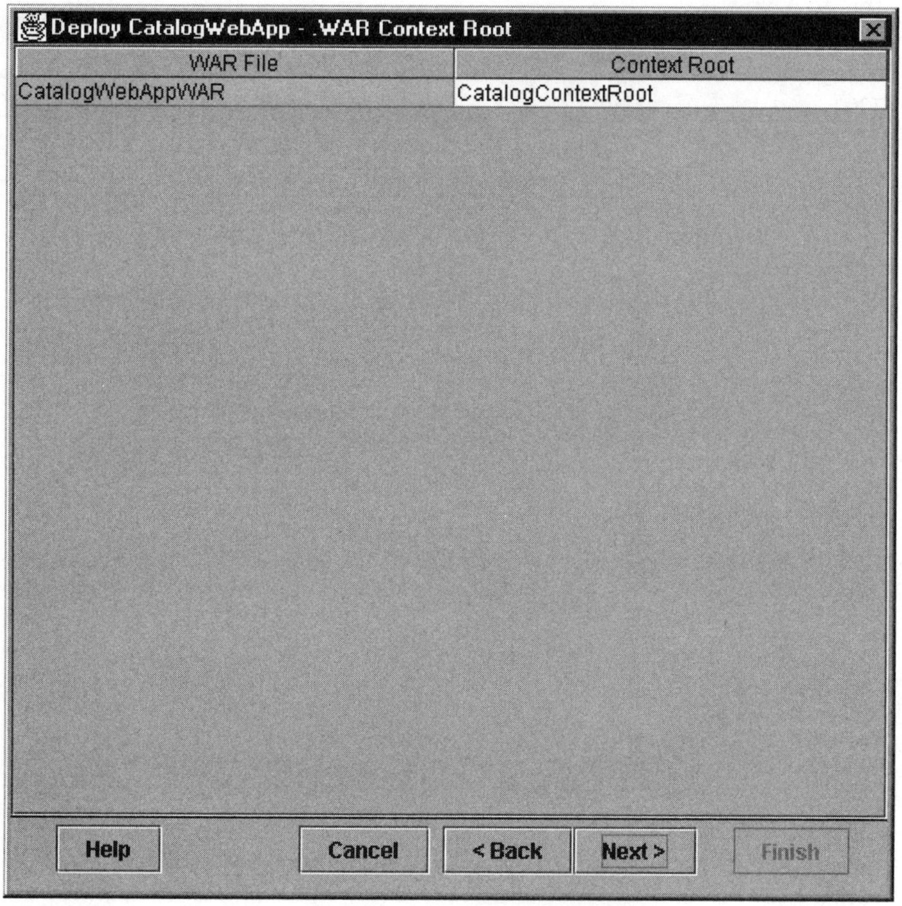

Figure 6-27
Specifying WAR
Context Root

WAR File	Context Root
CatalogWebAppWAR	CatalogContextRoot

Deploy CatalogWebApp - .WAR Context Root

Help Cancel < Back Next > Finish

which EJBs can be used, we will package and deploy an application containing JSP pages that generate WML. By now, you should be sufficiently familiar with the process to try it yourself.

The JSP Pages
The required JavaServer Pages are presented below.

The Initial Page

\Chapter6\code\WirelessCatalogSearch.jsp

Figure 6-28
Catalog Search Initial
Screen

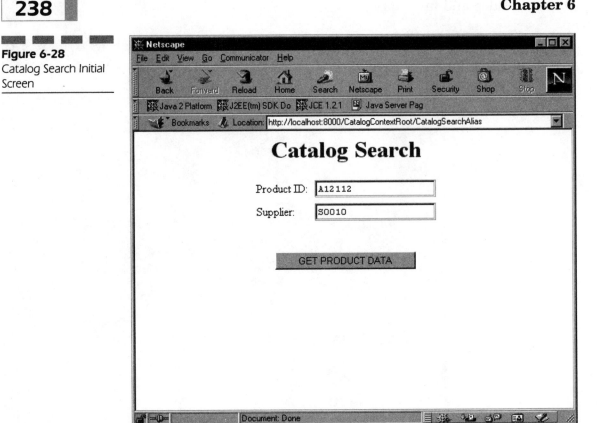

```
<%@ page contentType="text/vnd.wap.wml" %>
<jsp:useBean id="catBean" class="CatalogBean" scope="session" />
<?xml version="1.0"?>
<!DOCTYPE wml PUBLIC "-//WAPFORUM//DTD WML 1.1//EN"
"http://www.wapforum.org/DTD/wml_1.1.xml">

<wml>

<template>
<do type="prev" label="Back">
<prev/>
</do>
</template>

<card id="search" title="Catalog Search">
<p>
<do type="accept" label="Confirm">

  <go
href="http://localhost:8000/WirelessContextRoot/WirelessFindProduct
sAlias?pro
```

Figure 6-29
Search Results

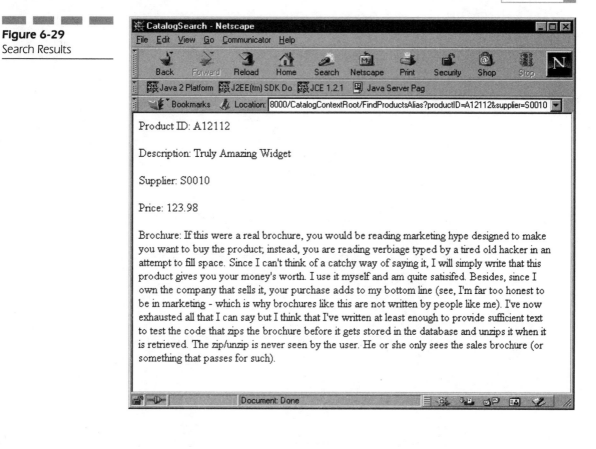

```
ductID=&(productID)&amp;supplier=&(supplier)"/>
</do>
</p>
<p>
Product ID:
<input name="productID"/>
</p>
<p>
Supplier:
<input name="supplier"/>
</p>
</card>
</wml>
```

The Results Page

\Chapter6\code\WirelessFindProducts.jsp

```
<%@ page contentType="text/vnd.wap.wml" %>
<%@ page errorPage="WirelessFindErrorAlias" %>
<jsp:useBean id="catBean" class="CatalogBean" scope="request" />
<jsp:setProperty name="catBean" property="*" />
<?xml version="1.0"?>
<!DOCTYPE wml PUBLIC "-//WAPFORUM//DTD WML 1.1//EN"
"http://www.wapforum.org/DTD/wml_1.1.xml">


<wml>


<template>
<do type="prev" label="Back">
<prev/>
</do>
</template>
<card id="findprod" title="Results">
<p>
Product ID:
<jsp:getProperty name="catBean" property="productID" />
</p>
<p>
Supplier:
<jsp:getProperty name="catBean" property="supplier" />
</p>
<p>
<jsp:getProperty name="catBean" property="price" />
</p>
</card>
</wml>
```

Running the Wireless Application

The easiest way to test wireless applications is to use a WAP
emulator. The one we will use to test the application we just
deployed is Wireless Companion from YOURWAP.com. It is available for free download from *www.yourwap.com*. When we start
the Wireless Companion, we see a display like that shown in Figure 6-30.

After we start the Wireless Companion we enter the URL:

```
http://localhost:8000/WirelessContextRoot/WirelessCatalogSearchAlias
```

As we navigate through the application, the browser will display
screens that look like Figures 6-31 through 6-34.

Figure 6-30
Starting the Cellular
Phone Browser

ComplexKeyedItemBean
Code Listing

\Chapter6\code\ComplexKeyedItem.java

```java
import java.io.*;
import java.util.*;
import java.util.zip.*;
```

Figure 6-31
Initial Screen

```
import javax.ejb.*;

public class ComplexKeyedItemBean implements EntityBean {

    public String productID;
    public String supplier;
    public String description;
    public double price;
    public int quantityOnHand;
    public int minimumReorderQuantity;
    public byte[] salesBrochure;

    private byte[] unzippedBrochure;


    private EntityContext context;
```

Figure 6-32
Preparing to Enter
Product ID

```
private static final String createErrorMessage =
  "You must specify productID and supplier.";


public String getProductID() {
  return productID;
}


public String getSupplier() {
  return supplier;
}


public String getDescription() {
  return description;
}
```

Figure 6-33
Entering Product ID

```
public void setDescription(String description) {
  this.description = description;
}

public double getPrice() {
  return price;
}

public void setPrice(double price) {
  this.price = price;
}

public byte[] getSalesBrochure() {
  return unzippedBrochure;
}
```

Figure 6-34
Query Result

```
public void setSalesBrochure(byte[] brochure, int len) {
  unzippedBrochure = new byte[len];
  System.arraycopy(brochure,0,unzippedBrochure,0,len);
}

public int getQuantityOnHand() {
  return quantityOnHand;
}

public void setQuantityOnHand(int quantity) {
  this.quantityOnHand = quantity;
}

public int getMinimumReorderQuantity() {
```

```java
      return minimumReorderQuantity;
   }

   public void setMinimumReorderQuantity(int quantity) {
      this.minimumReorderQuantity = quantity;
   }

   public CatalogItemKey ejbCreate(String productID,
      String supplier)
        throws CreateException {

      if ((productID == null) || (supplier == null)) {
         throw new CreateException(createErrorMessage);
      }


      this.productID = productID;
      this.supplier = supplier;
      this.price = 0.0;
      this.quantityOnHand = 0;
      this.minimumReorderQuantity = 0;


      return new CatalogItemKey(productID, supplier);
   }

   public void setEntityContext(EntityContext context) {
      this.context = context;
   }

   public void ejbActivate() {
   }

   public void ejbPassivate() {
      productID = null;
      supplier = null;
   }


   public void ejbRemove() {
   }

   public void ejbLoad() {
      if (salesBrochure == null) {
         return;
      }
      try {
         ZipInputStream zis =
            new ZipInputStream(new
              ByteArrayInputStream(salesBrochure));
         ZipEntry ze = zis.getNextEntry();
         byte[] temp = new byte[5000];
         int bytesRead = zis.read(temp,0,5000);
         unzippedBrochure = new byte[bytesRead];
         System.arraycopy(temp,0,unzippedBrochure,0,bytesRead);
```

```
          zis.close();
        }
        catch (IOException e) {
          throw new EJBException(e.getMessage());
        }
      }

    public void ejbStore() {
      if (unzippedBrochure == null) {
        return;
      }
      int len = unzippedBrochure.length;
      try {
        ByteArrayOutputStream bos = new ByteArrayOutputStream();
        ZipOutputStream zos =
          new ZipOutputStream(bos);
        ZipEntry ze = new ZipEntry("brochure");
        zos.putNextEntry(ze);
        zos.write(unzippedBrochure,0,len);
        zos.closeEntry();
        zos.close();
        salesBrochure = bos.toByteArray();
      }
      catch (IOException e) {
        throw new EJBException(e.getMessage());
      }
    }
    public void unsetEntityContext() {
    }
    public void ejbPostCreate(String productID, String supplier) {
    }
  }
```

Summary

In this chapter, we developed and tested entity beans that used container-managed persistence. We showed how JavaServer Pages could be used as a client of an EJB. We used JSPs in a traditional browser setting and on a cellular phone.

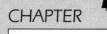

Paul's Roadside Assistance

In this chapter:

- An EJB as a Client of an EJB
- Combining Components to Create Complex Applications
- Additional Technique for Accessing an EJB from a JSP

Up to this point, all of the beans we developed were used either by themselves or in conjunction with a single Web component such as a servlet or a JSP. In the real world, applications are usually complex and involve many components interacting with each other. In this chapter, we examine an application that is more complex than those we have seen in previous chapters. It uses two EJBs, a servlet, a JavaBean, and a number of JSPs to solve a real-world problem.

Paul's Roadside Assistance

The application we will develop is for use by Paul's Roadside Assistance. This business provides a service to which drivers subscribe by paying an annual fee, thus entitling them to roadside assistance if their vehicle becomes disabled.

Upon receipt of a call from a motorist, a truck is dispatched to provide assistance and to make roadside repairs when possible. The truck is equipped with those parts and supplies most likely to be needed to assist a stranded motorist. Those parts and supplies that are not on the truck can be ordered. Truck operators can order parts in one of two ways. They can use their radio to contact a central dispatcher, who takes the order and fills it from the stockroom with the assistance of a browser-based user interface. Optionally, they can use a Web-enabled cellular phone to place the order themselves.

Whenever a truck operator uses parts or supplies from the truck, it is important that the truck be restocked. If a driver uses a gallon of engine coolant, he or she immediately places an order for one gallon to replace it. The item is removed from the stockroom and placed in a bin assigned to the truck. Upon returning to the garage, the very first duty a truck operator must perform is that of restocking the truck from the appropriate bin.

Our Application in Action

The application we develop in this chapter is slightly more complex than those we have seen thus far. We will first observe the interaction between the application and its users. This should prove helpful as we then discuss how the application is constructed.

The Application as Viewed by the Dispatcher

When the dispatcher receives a radio call from a truck operator, he or she types the following URL into the desktop browser:

```
http://localhost:8000/PRA/PQ
```

This sends a request to the *PartsQuery* JSP, which has an alias of *PQ* and which has been deployed in the *PRA* context. The JSP determines that the request is from a browser that supports HTML and forwards the request to *DispatcherRequest.html,* which the browser renders as shown in Figure 7-1.

The `action` attribute of the HTML form in Figure 7-1 has a value of:

```
http://localhost:8000/PRA/WorkDispatcher
```

WorkDirector is an alias for *WorkDirectorServlet.* The servlet uses the value of the selected radio button to determine the resource to which the request should be forwarded. We will first consider the case where the radio button labeled CHECK AVAILABILITY is selected. Since this radio button has a value of *DispatcherQuery,* the request is forwarded to *DispatcherQuery.jsp.* The output produced by this JSP depends on how many of the text entry fields are populated. If the only field into which a value was typed is the

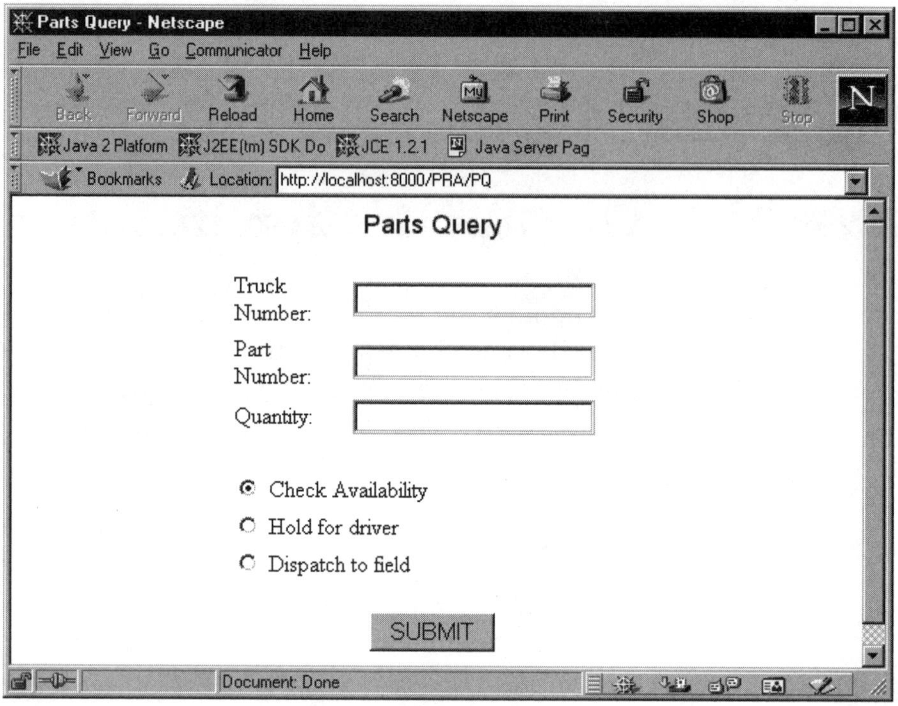

Figure 7-1
Initial Screen Viewed
by the Dispatcher

one labeled "Part Number", the JSP generates HTML that produces the screen shown in Figure 7-2. The dispatcher might enter a query in which only the part number field is completed in answer to the question, "Do we have part number 102010 in stock?"

The next type of query we consider is one in which both the part number field and the quantity field in Figure 7-1 were populated. When this is the case, the output produced by *Dispatcher-Query.jsp* looks like Figure 7-3. The dispatcher might enter this kind of query in response to the question, "Do we have a sufficient quantity of part number 102010 in stock to fill an order for 1 of them?"

If all three text fields in Figure 7-1 are populated, the output from *DispatcherQuery.jsp* looks like Figure 7-4.

The next case we consider is the one in which the dispatcher selects the radio button labeled HOLD FOR DRIVER. Unlike the previous examples, in this case all fields are required. The request is forwarded to *DispatcherHold.jsp,* which generates HTML that pro-

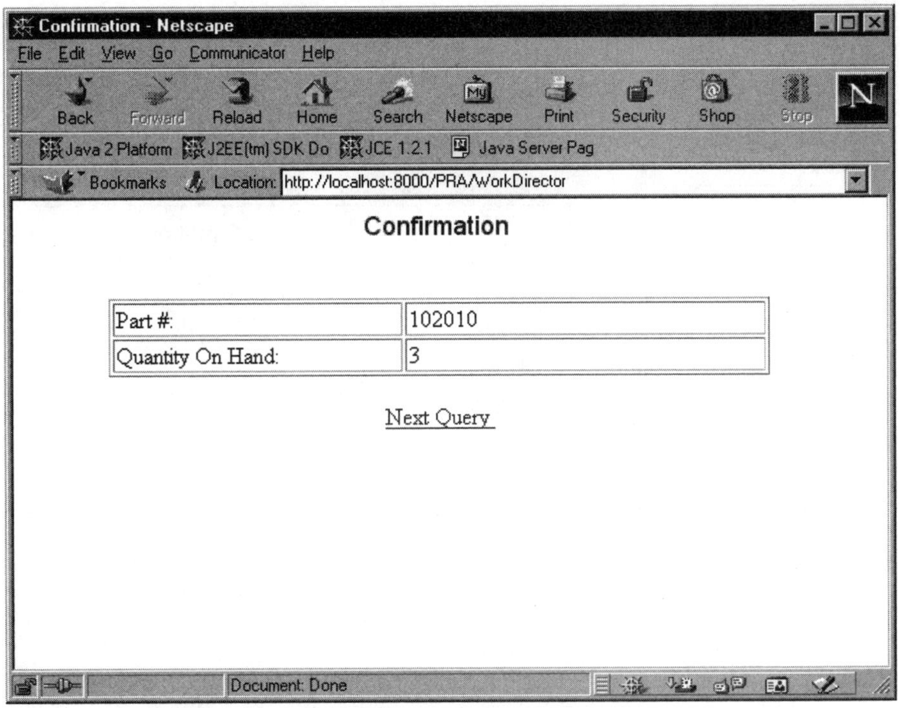

Figure 7-2
Response to Query
Specifying Only Part
Number

duces the screen shown in Figure 7.5. The dispatcher would enter this kind of request if a driver had just replaced a fan belt and had radioed in to make sure that a replacement was available in his or her assigned bin upon return to the garage.

The final case we consider is that in which the radio button labeled DISPATCH TO FIELD is selected. Again, all input fields are mandatory. The output is shown in Figure 7-6. From this screen, the dispatcher can notify the driver of truck number 27, who originated the request, that the part can be expected to arrive at 19:10.

The Application as Viewed by a Driver

A driver initiates a request in exactly the same way the dispatcher does, by typing the following URL:

```
http://localhost:8000/PRA/PQ
```

This sends a request to the *PartsQuery* JSP, which has an alias of *PQ* and which has been deployed in the *PRA* context. The JSP determines that the request is from a wireless device that supports WML and forwards the request to *DriverRequest.jsp*, which the minibrowser in the driver's cellular phone renders as shown in Figure 7-7.

The driver types values into one or more of the input fields and then specifies the desired type of query by selecting a radio button as shown if Figure 7-8.

NOTE: *The actual appearance of the screen will vary according to the type of cellular phone being used. Not all phones will show radio buttons like those shown in Figure 7-8. At the time of writing, the Wireless Companion from YOURWAP.com used to test the code in this book emulated six different models of phones. If you would like to test other models, the Wireless Companion is available for free download from yourwap.com.*

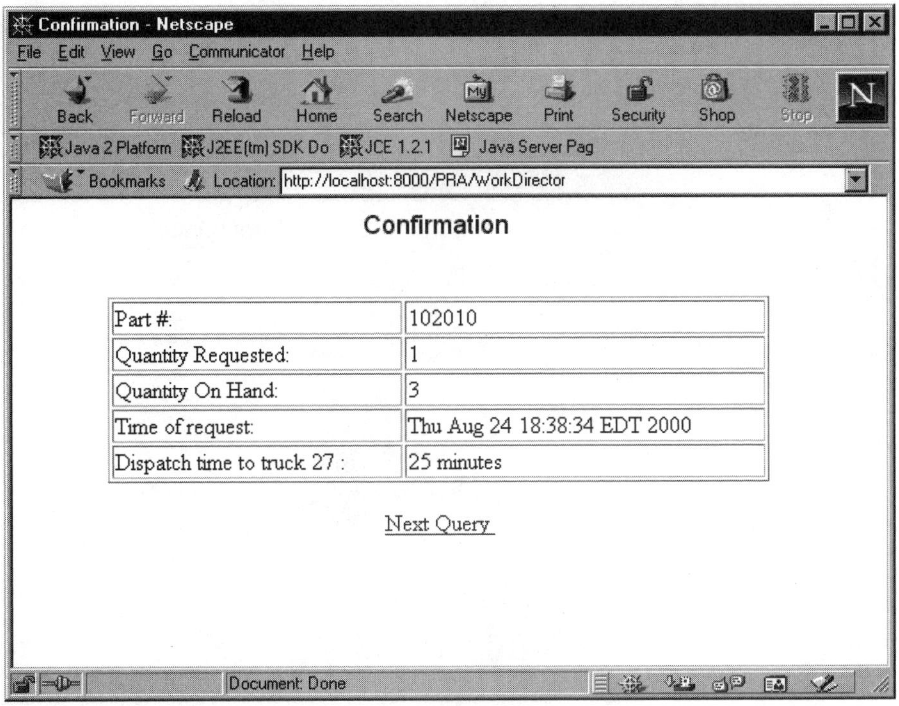

Figure 7-4
Response to Query in
Which All Fields Were
Populated

After the driver has entered the appropriate data and selected the type of query, the request is sent. When the query type is "Check Availability", input is governed by the same rules as queries initiated from a desktop browser. Here, we show only a single query in which all three input fields were populated. The result is shown in Figure 7-9.

Finally, Figures 7-10 and 7-11 show the results of requesting that a part be held for pickup and dispatched to the driver, respectively.

We next examine the application that makes this one operational aspect of Paul's Roadside Assistance possible.

The Stockroom Bean

Since supplies are the lifeblood of our little business, a well-equipped, well-operated stockroom is important; so, the *Stockroom* EJB is the first one we design and implement.

Figure 7-5
Confirmation of
Request to Hold Part
for Driver Pickup

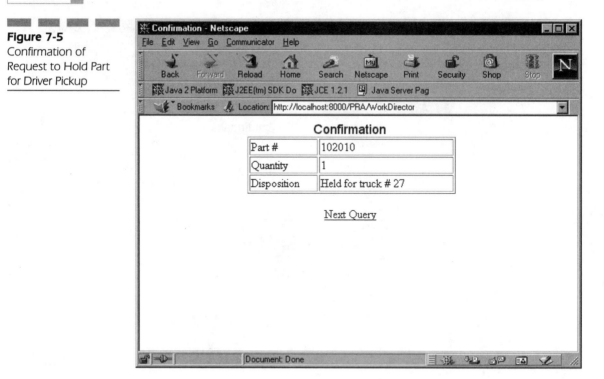

The very name "stockroom" implies a persistent store and so our *Stockroom* EJB is an entity bean. We will use container-managed persistence.

The Remote Interface

The remote interface defines the business methods a client can invoke. We limit such methods to those required to perform the following activities:

- add inventory to the stockroom
- remove inventoried items
- query quantity on hand
- query minimum reorder quantity

Figure 7-6
Confirmation of
Request to Send Part
to Driver

```
Confirmation - Netscape
File  Edit  View  Go  Communicator  Help

Back   Forward   Reload   Home   Search   Netscape   Print   Security   Shop   Stop

Java 2 Platform   J2EE(tm) SDK Do   JCE 1.2.1   Java Server Pag

Bookmarks   Location: http://localhost:8000/PRA/WorkDirector
```

Confirmation

Part #	102010
Quantity	1
Disposition	Sent to truck 27
Estimated arrival time:	Aug 24, 19:10

Next Query

`Document: Done`

- query the number ordered by default when the quantity on hand falls below the minimum reorder quantity

The code for the remote interface is shown below:

\Chapter7\code\Stockroom.java

```java
import javax.ejb.EJBObject;
import java.rmi.RemoteException;

public interface Stockroom extends EJBObject {

    public int getQuantityOnHand()
        throws RemoteException;

    public void setQuantityOnHand(int quantity)
        throws RemoteException;

    public int getMinimumReorderQuantity()
        throws RemoteException;
```

Figure 7-7
Initial Screen Viewed
by a Driver

```
public void setMinimumReorderQuantity(int quantity)
    throws RemoteException;

public int getStandardOrderQuantity()
    throws RemoteException;

public void setStandardOrderQuantity(int quantity)
    throws RemoteException;

public void stock()
    throws RemoteException;

public void stock(int q)
    throws RemoteException;
```

Figure 7-8
Specifying the Query
Type

```
public void take()
    throws RemoteException;

public void take(int q)
    throws RemoteException;
```

The Home Interface

Here is the code for the home interface:

Figure 7-9
Response to Query in
Which All Fields Were
Populated

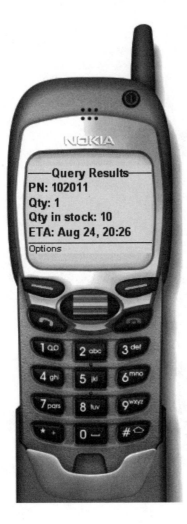

 ***Chapter7\code\StockroomHome**

```
import java.util.Collection;
import java.rmi.RemoteException;
import javax.ejb.*;

public interface StockroomHome extends EJBHome {

    public Stockroom create(String productId)
        throws RemoteException, CreateException;
```

Figure 7-10
Confirmation of
Request to Hold Part
for Pickup

```
        public Stockroom findByPrimaryKey(String productId)
              throws FinderException, RemoteException;
}
```

The Enterprise Bean

The bean code is presented at the end of the chapter. The methods
are self-explanatory and no detailed discussion is required.

Figure 7-11
Confirmation of
Request to Send Part
to Driver

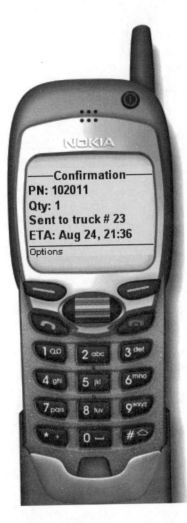

Packaging and Deploying
the Stockroom Bean

As we have already mentioned, the *Stockroom* bean is an entity
bean that uses container-managed persistence. The procedure for
packaging and deploying it is identical to that outlined in Chapter
6 for packaging and deploying the online catalog. The required
parameters are shown in Table 7-1.

We must also remember to do the following:

TABLE 7-1	Parameter	Value
	Application File Name	RoadsideApp.ear
Parameters Required to Package the Stockroom EJB	DisplayName	RoadsideApp
	JAR Display Name	RoadsideJAR
	Enterprise Bean Class	StockroomBean
	Home Interface	StockroomHome
	RemoteInterface	Stockroom
	Enterprise Bean Display Name	StockroomBean

- Specify a transaction type of "Required" for each of the business methods.

- In the Resource References dialog, specify *jdbc/Cloudscape* as the coded name.

- Use the ENTITY tab in the Application Deployment Tool to specify the deployment settings using *jdbc/RoadsideDB*. [We do not need to specify any additional SQL since the only finder method is findByPrimaryKey().]

The PartsManager Bean

Any business that relies on a well-equipped, well-operated stockroom would quickly find itself in shambles if it did not strictly control access to the stockroom. Persons who need items from the stockroom obtain such items not by entering the stockroom and taking the part themselves but rather by asking an authorized person to do so. Our business is no exception and so we design and implement an EJB that accepts requests for supplies and obtains these supplies from the stockroom. We will call this EJB the *PartsManager.*

In the real world, a relationship between a person requesting supplies and the person fulfilling the request exists from the time the request is made to the time the supplies are delivered. The supplier is then free to handle another request from any other person who needs supplies. In our case, no request is conversational and so we make our *PartsManager* a stateless session bean.

The Remote Interface

The listing of the remote interface follows:

\Chapter7\code\PartsManager

```java
import javax.ejb.EJBObject;
import javax.ejb.EJBException;
import java.rmi.RemoteException;

public interface PartsManager extends EJBObject {

  public int getQuantityOnHand(String productID)
     throws RemoteException;

  public void setQuantityOnHand(String productID, int quantity)
     throws RemoteException;

  public int getMinimumReorderQuantity(String productID)
     throws RemoteException;

  public void SetMinimumReorderQuantity(String productID,
    int quantity)
     throws RemoteException;

  public int getStandardOrderQuantity(String productID)
     throws RemoteException;

  public void setStandardOrderQuantity(String productID,
    int quantity)
     throws RemoteException;

  public void take(String productID)
     throws RemoteException;

  public void take(String productID, int quant)
     throws RemoteException;

  public void stock(String productID)
    throws RemoteException;
```

```
public void stock(String productID, int quant)
   throws RemoteException;

public void holdForDriver(String productID,String driverID)
   throws RemoteException, EJBException;

public void holdForDriver(String productID,String driverID, int q)
   throws RemoteException, EJBException;

public void sendToDriver(String productID,String driverID)
   throws RemoteException, EJBException;

public void sendToDriver(String productID,String driverID, int q)
   throws RemoteException, EJBException;

public int getDispatchTime(String productID, String driverID)
   throws RemoteException, EJBException;

}
```

The Home Interface

The home interface looks like this:

\Chapter7\code\PartsManagerHome

```
import java.util.Collection;
import java.rmi.RemoteException;
import javax.ejb.*;

public interface PartsManagerHome extends EJBHome {

    public PartsManager create(String productId)
        throws RemoteException, CreateException;

    public PartsManager create()
        throws RemoteException, CreateException;
}
```

The Enterprise Bean

The complete listing of the enterprise bean is presented at the end of the chapter. When one of the methods of *PartsManagerBean* needs to access data associated with a product, it invokes the get-Stockroom() method passing the product identifier as an argument. The getStockroom() method locates the *Stockroom* entity bean using the findByPrimaryKey() method of its home interface. *PartsManagerBean* can then communicate with *Stockroom* by invoking methods against the instance findByPrimaryKey() returns.

This whole idea of one object communicating with another may not seem like such a big deal on the surface. However, if we consider the case where the *Stockroom* EJB is on one computer and the *PartsManager* EJB is on another, think of all the code we don't have to write. Moving either of the EJBs to a computer other than the one on which it was originally deployed is also a simple task.

Packaging and Deploying the PartsManager Bean

We have already seen how to package a stateless session bean. We place our *PartsManager* bean in *RoadsideJAR* using the parameters shown in Table 7-2. In the Enterprise Bean References dialog, we must also specify a coded name of *ejb/Stockroom* of type "Entity" with the values of *Home* and *Remote* set to "StockroomHome" and "Stockroom", respectively.

TABLE 7-2

Parameters Required to Package and Deploy the Parts-Manager Bean

Parameter	Value
Enterprise Bean Class	PartsManagerBean
Home Interface	PartsManagerHome
RemoteInterface	PartsManager
Enterprise Bean Display Name	PartsManagerBean

The Web Components

Two user interfaces are made available: a Web-enabled cellular phone for drivers and a traditional desktop Web browser for the dispatcher who handles radio calls from drivers who are outside of their cellular phone's coverage area. The WAR file required to implement these user interfaces contains a servlet, a JavaBean, JSPs, and HTML pages. The best way to examine these components and understand how they fit into the overall picture is to follow a request from the time it is entered to the time the results are displayed.

Tracking a Request

All queries, whether they originate from a dispatcher using a browser or from a driver using a Web-enabled cellular phone, are handled by a JavaServer Page that looks like this:

\Chapter7\code\PartsQuery.jsp

```
<%
  String nextPage = null;
  String acceptHeader = request.getHeader("Accept");
  if(acceptHeader.indexOf("text/vnd.wap.wml") < 0) {
    nextPage = "DispatcherRequest.html";
  }
  else {
    nextPage = "DriverRequest.jsp";
  }
%>
<jsp:forward page="<%= nextPage %>" />
```

This JSP determines whether the device from which the request originated is a wireless device. It does so by examining the string returned when the string `Accept` is passed as an argument to the `getHeader()` method. It makes the assumption that a wireless device advertises that it can support a content type of text/vnd.wap.wml. If this is the case, it assigns the script variable nextPage a value of "DriverRequest.jsp"; otherwise, it assigns a value of "DispatcherRequest.html". After nextPage has been assigned a value, the JSP executes the following code:

```
<jsp:forward page="<%= nextPage %>" />
```

This code forwards the request to either *DriverRequest.jsp* or *DispatcherRequest.html,* which generate WML or HTML, respectively.

The PartsQuery JSP

From this point, we will track the two different kinds of requests separately. We begin with the HTTP request from the dispatcher.

A Request from the Dispatcher

Here is the code for DispatcherRequest.html:

\Chapter7\code\DispatcherRequest.html

```
<html>
<head>
  <title>Parts Query</title>
</head>
<body>
  <center>
    <font face="Arial,Helvetica"><font size="+1">
    Parts Query
    </font>
    <br>
    <form method="post" action=
      "http://localhost:8000/PRA/WorkDirector">
      <table COLS=2 WIDTH="50%" >
        <tr>
          <td width="25%">
            Truck Number:
          </td>
```

```
          <td><input type="text" name="tn">
          </td>
        </tr>


      <tr>
        <td width="25%">
          Part Number:
        </td>

        <td>
          <input type="text" name="pn">
        </td>
      </tr>


      <tr>
        <td width="25%">
          Quantity:
        </td>

        <td>
          <input type="text" name="q">
        </td>
      </tr>
    </table>
  <br>
    <table COLS=1 WIDTH="50%" >
      <tr>
        <td width="10%">
          <input type="radio" name="np"
            value="DispatcherQuery.jsp" checked>
          Check Availability
        </td>
      </tr>


      <tr>
        <td>
          <input type="radio" name="np"
            value="DispatcherHold.jsp">
          Hold for driver
        </td>
      </tr>


      <tr>
        <td>
          <input type="radio" name="np"
            value="DispatcherSend.jsp">
          Dispatch to field
        </td>
      </tr>
    </table>
    <p>
    <input type="submit" value="SUBMIT">
  </form>
  </body>
</html>
```

This simple HTML requires no discussion. It is nothing more than a form whose submission sends a request containing the values typed into three text entry fields and the value of one of three radio buttons. As we will see shortly, the value of the selected radio button is used to determine which resource handles the request. The value of the form's `action` attribute is:

```
"http://localhost:8000/PRA/WorkDirector"
```

WorkDirector is an alias for *WorkDirectorServlet,* which has been deployed in the context *PRA.* Here is the listing of `WorkDirectorServlet.java`:

 Chapter7\\code\\WorkDirectorServlet.java

```java
import java.io.IOException;
import javax.servlet.*;
import javax.servlet.http.*;

public class WorkDirectorServlet extends HttpServlet {

  public void doPost (HttpServletRequest req,
    HttpServletResponse res)
      throws ServletException, IOException {

    String url = "/" + req.getParameter("np");
    ServletContext sc = getServletContext();
    RequestDispatcher rd = sc.getRequestDispatcher(url);
    rd.forward(req,res);
  }

  public void doGet (HttpServletRequest req,
                     HttpServletResponse res)
      throws ServletException, IOException {
    doPost (req,res);
  }

  public String getServletInfo() {
    return "Instant EJBs Chapter 7 Example";
  }
}
```

The servlet handles an HTTP GET request by simply invoking the `doPost()` method. This is OK since the processing is identical for both.

The doPost() method is quite simple. It first uses the getParameter() method to obtain the value of the radio button that was selected. All of the radio buttons have the name np (next page). It then prefixes this value with a "/" character; the reason will become apparent shortly.

> **NOTE:** *Perhaps you are wondering why we did not choose a more meaningful name such as* nextPage. *We have already mentioned and discuss later the fact that WorkDirectorServlet also handles requests from wireless devices where transmission rates are lower and longer names carry a higher price tag.*

The next task the doPost() method carries out is that of forwarding the request to the resource corresponding to the value of the parameter np. The mechanism for forwarding requests is the *RequestDispatcher* interface. A *RequestDispatcher* object that acts as a wrapper for the resource located at a given path can be obtained by passing the path to the getRequestDispatcher() method of *ServletContext*. The "/" we prepended to the resource name we obtained earlier using the getParameter() method makes the path relative to the current context root.

After obtaining a *RequestDispatcher* object we invoke its forward() method, passing as parameters the *HttpServletRequest* and *HttpServletResponse* objects that the doPost() method received as parameters.

> **NOTE:** *For more information on the RequestDispatcher interface, see "Instant Java Servlets" by Phil Hanna (ISBN 0072124253, McGraw-Hill).*

The JSPs to which a request can be forwarded are listed at the end of the chapter, with the exception of *DispatcherQuery.jsp*, which is listed immediately below. We discuss only *DispatcherQuery.jsp*; the others are similar.

\Chapter7\code\DispatcherQuery.jsp

```
<%@ page import="java.util.Date" %>
<%@ include file="GetPartsManager.jsp" %>
<%@ page errorPage="DispatcherQueryError.jsp" %>
<jsp:useBean id="qpBean" scope="request"
  class="QueryParms" />
<jsp:setProperty name="qpBean" property="*" />
<html>
<head>
  <title>Confirmation</title>
</head>
<body>
<center>
<font face="Arial,Helvetica"><font size=+1>
Confirmation
<p>
</font></font>
<br>
<table BORDER COLS=2 WIDTH="80%%" >
  <tr>
    <td width="40%">
      Part #:
    </td>


    <td>
      <jsp:getProperty name="qpBean" property="pn" />
    </td>
  </tr>


<%
  if (qpBean.getQ() > 0) {
%>


  <tr>
    <td width="40%">
      Quantity Requested:
    </td>

    <td>
      <jsp:getProperty name="qpBean" property="q" />
    </td>
  </tr>
<%
  }
%>


  <tr>
    <td width="40%">
      Quantity On Hand:
    </td>
```

```
    <td>
      <%= partsManager.getQuantityOnHand(qpBean.getPn()) %>
    </td>
  </tr>

<%
  if (qpBean.getTn() != null) {
%>
  <tr>
    <td width="40%">
      Time of request:
    </td>

    <td>
      <%= new Date() %>
    </td>
  </tr>

  <tr>
    <td width="40%">
      Dispatch time to truck
      <jsp:getProperty name="qpBean" property="tn" />
      :
    </td>

    <td>
      <%= partsManager.getDispatchTime(qpBean.getPn(),
            qpBean.getTn()) %>
      minutes
    </td>
  </tr>
<%
  }
%>
</table>
<br>
<a href="http://localhost:8000/PRA/PQ">
Next Query
</a>
</body>
</html>
```

An examination of *DispatcherQuery.jsp* and the other JSPs to which a request can be dispatched reveals that they all have one line in common. This line is:

```
<%@ include file="GetPartsManager.jsp" %>
```

Here is the code for the included file:

\Chapter7\code\GetPartsManager.jsp

```
<%@ taglib uri="Taglib.tld" prefix="INSTANTEJB" %>
<% PartsManager partsManager = null; %>
<INSTANTEJB:ejb
   jndiName="java:comp/env/ejb/PartsManager"
   homeInterface="PartsManagerHome"
   homeVar="partsManagerHome">
   <% partsManager = partsManagerHome.create(); %>
</INSTANTEJB:ejb>
```

The `taglib` directive in the first line declares that this JSP uses a tag library. It identifies the tag library using the URI "Taglib.tld" and makes the library available to this page using the prefix *INSTANTEJB*.

NOTE: *The JSP Specification defines a tag library as follows:*

■ *A tag library is a collection of actions that encapsulate some functionality to be used from within a JSP page. A tag library is made available to a JSP page via a* `taglib` *directive that identifies the tag library via a URI (Universal Resource Identifier).*

■ *The URI identifying a tag library may be any valid URI as long as it can be used to uniquely identify the semantics of the tag library. A common mechanism is to encode the version of a tag library into its URI.*

■ *The URI identifying the tag library is associated with a Tag Library Description (TLD) file and with tag handler classes.*

The code block bounded by `<INSTANTEJB:ejb>` and `</INSTANTEJB:ejb>` uses the `create()` method of *PartsManagerHome* to obtain a remote interface object, which it stores in the scripting variable `partsManager`. The JSP can use this scripting variable to invoke any of *PartsManager*'s methods.

A tag library is described by a Tag Library Descriptor (TLD).

NOTE: *The JSP Specification defines a tag library as follows:*

■ *The Tag Library Descriptor (TLD) is an XML document that describes a tag library. The TLD for a tag library is used by a JSP container to interpret pages that include* `taglib` *directives referring to that tag library. The TLD is also used by JSP page-authoring tools that will* generate JSP pages that use a library and by authors who do the same manually.

■ *The TLD includes documentation on the library as a whole and on its individual tags, version information on the JSP container and on the tag library, and information on each of the actions defined in the tag library.*

■ *Each action in the library is described by giving its name, the class for its tag handler, optional information on a* TagExtraInfo *class, and information on all the attributes of the action. Each valid attribute is mentioned explicitly, with indication on whether it is mandatory, whether it can accept request-time expressions, and additional information.*

■ *A TLD file is useful as a descriptive mechanism for providing information on a tag library. It has the advantage that it can be read by tools without having to instantiate objects or load classes. The approach we follow conforms to the conventions used in other J2EE technologies.*

■ *The DTD to the tag library descriptor is organized so that interesting elements have an optional ID attribute. This attribute can be used by other documents, like vendor-specific documents, to provide annotations of the TLD information. An alternative approach, although based on XML name spaces that have some interesting properties, was not pursued, in part, for consistency with the rest of the J2EE descriptors.*

■ *The official DTD is described at "http://java.sun.com/j2ee/dtds/web-jsptaglibrary_1_1.dtd"*

Here is the TLD that describes our tag library.

 \Chapter7\code\Taglib.tld

```xml
<?xml version="1.0" encoding="ISO-8859-1" ?>
<!DOCTYPE taglib
        PUBLIC "-//Sun Microsystems, Inc.//DTD JSP Tag Library
1.1//EN"
        "http://java.sun.com/j2ee/dtds/web-jsptaglibrary_1_1.dtd">

<taglib>
  <tlibversion>1.0</tlibversion>
  <jspversion>1.1</jspversion>
  <urn></urn>
  <info>
```

```
        Tag library for EJB support
    </info>

    <tag>
      <name>ejb</name>
      <tagclass>EjbTag</tagclass>
      <teiclass>EjbExtraInfo</teiclass>
      <bodycontent>JSP</bodycontent>
      <info>
        Look up a home and declare enterprise bean.
      </info>

      <attribute>
        <name>jndiName</name>
        <required>true</required>
        <rtexprvalue>true</rtexprvalue>
        <type>String</type>
      </attribute>
      <attribute>
        <name>homeInterface</name>
        <required>true</required>
      </attribute>
      <attribute>
        <name>homeVar</name>
        <required>true</required>
      </attribute>
    </tag>
  </taglib>
```

Within the `<tag>` element, we see that the `<tagclass>` element specifies that the Tag Handler Class is *EjbTag*. The Tag Handler class is used to assist in evaluation of actions during execution of a JSP page. Here is the code for *EjbTag.java:*

Chapter7\\code\\EjbTag.java

```
import javax.rmi.PortableRemoteObject;
import javax.naming.*;
import javax.servlet.jsp.*;
import javax.servlet.jsp.tagext.*;

public class EjbTag extends BodyTagSupport {

    private String jndiName = null;
    private String homeVar = null;
    private String homeInterface = null;

    public EjbTag() {
        super();
    }
```

```
      public void setJndiName (String jndiName) {
         this.jndiName = jndiName;
      }

      public void setHomeVar (String homeVar) {
         this.homeVar = homeVar;
      }

      public void setHomeInterface (String homeInterface) {
         this.homeInterface = homeInterface;
      }

      public void doInitBody() throws JspException {
         try {
           InitialContext ic = new InitialContext();
           Object homeRef = ic.lookup(jndiName);
           homeRef = PortableRemoteObject.narrow(homeRef,
              Class.forName(homeInterface));
           pageContext.setAttribute(homeVar, homeRef);
         }
         catch (NamingException ex) {
           throw new JspTagException("Unable to lookup home:
"+jndiName);
         }
         catch (ClassNotFoundException ex) {
           throw new JspTagException("Class "+homeInterface+" not
              found");
         }
      }
   }
```

Our tag supplies a scripting variable (partsManager) and so we must provide a *TagExtraInfo* class. The <teiclass> element specifies that the *TagExtraInfo* class is *EjbExtraInfo*. Here is the code:

\Chapter7\code\EjbExtraInfo.java

```
import javax.servlet.jsp.*;
import javax.servlet.jsp.tagext.*;

public class EjbExtraInfo extends TagExtraInfo {
  public VariableInfo[] getVariableInfo(TagData data) {
    VariableInfo[] vi = new VariableInfo[] {
      new VariableInfo((String)data.getAttribute("homeVar"),
                       (String)data.getAttribute("homeInterface"),
                       true,
                       VariableInfo.NESTED)
    };
    return vi;
  }
}
```

The scripting variable `partsManager` that was made available by the included code we just examined makes the following code in *DispatcherQuery.jsp* possible:

```
<%= partsManager.getQuantityOnHand(qpBean.getPn()) %>
```

and

```
<%= partsManager.getDispatchTime(qpBean.getPn(),
        qpBean.getTn()) %>
```

Examining *DispatcherQuery.jsp* further, we see the following code:

```
<jsp:useBean id="qpBean" scope="request"
  class="QueryParms" />
<jsp:setProperty name="qpBean" property="*" />
```

The `<jsp:useBean>` action associates an instance of the Java-Bean *QueryParms* with the scripting variable `qpBean`. The `<jsp:setProperty>` action sets the properties in the Bean using all of the request parameters. This technique of using a JavaBean as a holder for parameters is quite common. Here is the code for the JavaBean:

\Chapter7\code\QueryParms.java

```
public class QueryParms {

  String partNumber;
  String truckNumber;
  int quantity;

  public void setPn(String pn) {
    partNumber = pn;
  }

  public String getPn() {
    return partNumber;
  }

  public void setTn(String tn) {
    truckNumber = tn;
  }
```

```
    public String getTn() {
      return truckNumber;
    }

    public void setQ(int q) {
      quantity = q;
    }

    public int getQ() {
      return quantity;
    }
}
```

DispatcherQuery.jsp contains the following code:

```
<%@ page errorPage="DispatcherQueryError.jsp" %>
```

This directive specifies that any exceptions thrown during execution of *DispatcherQuery.jsp* are to be handled by *DispatcherQueryError.jsp,* which looks like this:

***Chapter7\\code\\DispatcherQueryError.jsp*

```
<%@ page isErrorPage="true" %>
<html>
  <head>
    <title>ERROR</title>
  </head>
  <body bgcolor="#ff0000" link="#ffffff"
    vlink="#ffffff" alink="#ffffff">
    <font face="Arial,Helvetica"><font color="#ffffff">
      <font size="+2">
    <center>An error occurred while processing your request.
    <p>
    </font>
    <font size="+1">
    <table width="50%">
      <tr>
        <td>
          <font color="#ffffff" size="+1">
          Please check the data you supplied as input and re-enter
          your request.
          <p>If the problem persists, notify your system
             administrator.
          </font>
        </td>
      </tr>
    </table>
    <p>
    <a href="http://localhost:8000/PRA/DispatcherRequest.html">
    Click here to re-try query.
    </a>
  </body>
</html>
```

This JSP page simply reports that an error has occurred and provides the user with an opportunity to retry the request. You might also consider adding code to print a stack trace to the log file.

A Request from a Driver

When a request is received from a driver who is using a wireless device, *PartsQuery.jsp* forwards the request to *DriverRequest.jsp*. Here is the code:

Chapter7\\code\\DriverRequest.jsp

```
<%@ page contentType="text/vnd.wap.wml" %>
<?xml version="1.0"?>
<!DOCTYPE wml PUBLIC "-//WAPFORUM//DTD WML 1.1//EN"
"http://www.wapforum.org/DTD
/wml_1.1.xml">


<wml>
<card title="Query Info">
<do type="accept" label="Send Query">
  <go method="get"

href="http://localhost:8000/PRA/WorkDirector?tn=&(tn)&amp;pn=&(pn)&
amp;q=&(q)
&amp;np=&(np)" />
</do>
<p>
Truck #:
<input name="tn"/>
</p>
<p>
Part #:
<input name="pn"/>
</p>
<p>
Quantity #:
<input name="q" value="1"/>
</p>
<p>
<select name="np">
<option value="DriverQuery.jsp">Query</option>
<option value="DriverHold.jsp">Hold</option>
<option value="DriverSend.jsp">Dispatch</option>
</select>
```

```
</p>
</card>
</wml>
```

Packaging and Deploying

We place the Web components of our application in *RoadsideWAR* using the "New Web Component . . ." option of the "File" drop-down menu. We specify the name of the WAR file when we add the first component. Since we have already dealt with adding Web components, we will not present a screen-by-screen description here but will simply list the action required in each of the dialogs presented by the "New Web Component" wizard.

The WorkDirector Servlet

TABLE 7-3

Actions and
Parameters for
WorkDirectorServlet

Dialog	Actions
WAR File General Properties	1. Specify *RoadsideWAR* as WAR File Display Name 2. Click on ADD
Add Content Files	1. Select *WorkDirectorServlet.class* 2. Click on ADD 3. Click on NEXT> 4. Select *WorkDirectorServlet.class* 5. Click on ADD 6. Click on FINISH
Choose Component Type	1. Select radio button labeled SERVLET
Component General Properties	1. Select *WorkDirectorServlet* as value of Servlet Class 2. Specify *WorkDirectorServlet* as Web Component Display Name
Component Aliases	1. Click on ADD 2. Enter WorkDirectorServlet as the alias

The QueryParms JavaBean

Dialog	Actions
WAR File General Properties	1. Specify *RoadsideWAR* as WAR File Display Name 2. Click on ADD
WAR File General Properties	1. Verify that WAR Display Name is *RoadsideWAR* 2. Click on ADD
Add Content Files	1. Select *QueryParms.class* 2. Click on ADD 3. Click on NEXT> 4. Select *QueryParms.class* 5. Click on ADD 6. Click on FINISH
Choose Component Type	1. Select *No Web Component* 2. Click on FINISH

The HTML Pages

Dialog	Actions
WAR File General Properties	1. Verify that WAR Display Name is *RoadsideWAR* 2. Click on ADD
Add Content Files	1. Select *DispatcherRequest.html* 2. Click on ADD 3. Click on NEXT> 4. Select *DispatcherRequest.html* 5. Click on ADD 6. Click on FINISH
Choose Component Type	1. Select *No Web Component* 2. Click on FINISH

The GetPartsManager JSP

TABLE 7-6

Actions and
Parameters for
GetPartsManager
JSP

Dialog	Actions
WAR File General Properties	1. Verify that WAR Display Name is *RoadsideWAR* 2. Click on ADD
Add Content Files	1. Select *GetPartsManager.jsp* 2. While holding the CTRL key, select *Taglib.tld* 3. Click on ADD 4. Click on NEXT> 5. Select *EjbTag.class* 6. While holding the CTRL key, select *EjbExtraInfo.class* 7. Click on ADD 8. Click on FINISH
Choose Component Type	1. Select the radio button labeled JSP 2. Click on NEXT>
Component General Properties	1. Select *GetPartsmanager.jsp* from the drop-down list labeled JSP Filename 2. Specify *GetPartsManager* as Web Component Display Name
Enterprise Bean References	1. Click on ADD 2. Enter ejb/PartsManager under the column labeled coded name 3. Select *Entity* from the drop-down list under the column labeled Type 4. Enter PartsManagerHome under the column labeled Home 5. Enter PartsManager under the column labeled Remote 6. Click on FINISH

NOTE: *The procedure for adding this component differs from others we have seen. If the procedure is not followed, an error will be encountered at runtime.*

The PartsQuery JSP

TABLE 7-7

Actions and
Parameters for
PartsQuery JSP

Dialog	Actions
WAR File General Properties	1. Verify that WAR Display Name is *RoadsideWAR* 2. Click on ADD
Add Content Files	1. Select *PartsQuery.jsp* 2. Click on ADD 3. Click on NEXT> 4. Select *PartsQuery.jsp* 5. Click on ADD 6. Click on FINISH
Choose Component Type	1. Click on radio button labeled JSP
Component General Properties	1. Select *PartsQuery.jsp* from the drop-down list labeled JSP Filename 2. Enter PartsQuery as Web Component Display Name
Component Aliases	1. Click on ADD 2. Enter PQ as the alias 3. Click on FINISH

The Error Pages

We package the error pages, *DispatcherQueryError.jsp* and *Driver-QueryError.jsp*, by following the same procedure as we followed to package *PartsQuery.jsp*, with one exception—we do *not* specify an alias.

The Query JSPs

The query JSPs are:

■ *DispatcherQuery.jsp*

- *DispatcherHold.jsp*
- *DispatcherSend.jsp*
- *DriverRequest.jsp*
- *DriverQuery.jsp*
- *DriverHold.jsp*
- *DriverSend.jsp*

We package these by following the same procedure as we followed to package *PartsQuery.jsp*, with one exception—we do not specify an alias.

Deploying the Application

We start the deployment process by selecting "Deploy Application . . ." from the "Tools" drop-down menu. In the Introduction dialog, we do check the box labeled RETURN CLIENT JAR. This JAR file is used by the client that we see in the next section.

The JNDI names we specify are shown in Table 7-8. In the .WAR Context Root dialog, we enter *PRA* as the value of Context Root.

TABLE 7-8

JNDI Names

Referenced By	Component/Reference Name	JNDI Name
	StockroomBean	MyStockroom
StockroomBean	jdbc/RoadsideDB	jdbc/Cloudscape
	PartsManagerBean	MyPartsManager
PartsManagerBean	ejb/Stockroom	MyStockroom
RoadsideWAR	ejb/PartsManager	MyPartsManager

Stocking the Stockroom

Before accepting requests, we populate the *Stockroom* table using the following code:

\Chapter7\code\FillStockroom.java

```java
import java.io.*;
import java.util.*;
import javax.naming.Context;
import javax.naming.InitialContext;
import javax.rmi.PortableRemoteObject;

public class FillStockroom {

  public static void main(String[] args) {

    BufferedReader br = null;

    String line = null;

    StockroomHome home = null;

    try {
      br = new BufferedReader (new FileReader("StockData"));

      Context initial = new InitialContext();
      Object objref = initial.lookup("MyStockroom");

      home = (StockroomHome)PortableRemoteObject.narrow(objref,
          StockroomHome.class);

      while((line = br.readLine()) != null) {
        stockItem(home, line);
      }
    }
    catch (Exception ex) {
      System.err.println("Caught an exception." );
      System.out.println(ex.getMessage());
      ex.printStackTrace();
    }
  }

  public static void stockItem(StockroomHome home,
      String line) throws Exception {
```

```
        StringTokenizer st = new StringTokenizer(line,",");
        String productID = st.nextToken();
        Stockroom sr = home.create(product ID);
        int q = Integer.parseInt (st.nextToken());
        sr.setQuantityOnHand(q);
        q = Integer.parseInt(st.nextToken());
        sr.setMinimumReorderQuantity(q);
        q = Integer.parseInt(st.nextToken());
        sr.setStandardOrderQuantity(q);
    }
}
```

This simple standalone client reads comma-delimited data from the file *StockroomData*, tokenizes each line, creates a *Stockroom* bean using the value of the first token as productID, and sets the value of each of the *Stockroom* bean's instance variables using the remaining tokens.

We execute the *FillStockroom* client by typing the command:

```
fillStockroom
```

This executes the following batch file:

***Chapter7\\code\\fillStockroom.bat*

```
@echo off
set J2EE_HOME=c:\j2sdkee1.2.1
set CPATH=.;%J2EE_HOME%\lib\j2ee.jar;RoadsideAppClient.jar

java -classpath "%CPATH%" FillStockroom
```

Stockroom Enterprise Bean

***Chapter7\\code\\StockroomBean.java*

```
import java.util.*;
import javax.ejb.*;

public class StockroomBean implements EntityBean {
```

```java
public String productID;
public int quantityOnHand;
public int minimumReorderQuantity;
public int standardOrderQuantity;
private EntityContext context;

public String ejbCreate(String productID)
    throws CreateException {

  if (productID == null) {
    throw new CreateException("You must specify a productID.");
  }

  this.productID = productID;

  return null;
}

public void setEntityContext(EntityContext context) {
  this.context = context;
}

public void ejbActivate() {
  productID = (String)context.getPrimaryKey();
}

public void ejbPassivate() {
  productID = null;
}

public void ejbRemove() {
}

public void ejbLoad() {
}

public void ejbStore() {
}

public void unsetEntityContext() {
}

public void ejbPostCreate(String productID) {
}

public int getQuantityOnHand() {
  return quantityOnHand;
}

public void setQuantityOnHand(int q) {
  quantityOnHand = q;
}
```

```java
public int getMinimumReorderQuantity() {
  return minimumReorderQuantity;
}

public void setMinimumReorderQuantity(int q) {
  minimumReorderQuantity = q;
}

public int getStandardOrderQuantity() {
  return standardOrderQuantity;
}

public void setStandardOrderQuantity(int q) {
  standardOrderQuantity = q;
}

public void stock() {
 stock(1);
}

public void stock(int q) {
  quantityOnHand += q;
}

public int take() throws EJBException {
  return take(1);
}

public int take(int q) throws EJBException {
  if ((q == 0) || (quantityOnHand < q)) {
    throw new EJBException("bad quantity");
  }
  quantityOnHand -= q;
  return q;
}
```

PartsManager Enterprise Bean

 \Chapter7\code\PartsManager.java

```java
import javax.rmi.*;
import java.rmi.*;
import java.util.*;
import javax.ejb.*;
import javax.naming.*;
```

```
public class PartsManagerBean implements SessionBean {

    public String productID;
    public float price;
    public int quantityOnHand;
    public int minimumReorderQuantity;
    public int standardOrderQuantity;

    private SessionContext context;

    public void ejbCreate(String productID)
        throws CreateException {

      if (productID == null) {
        throw new CreateException("You must specify a productID.");
      }

      this.productID = productID;
    }

    public void ejbCreate() throws CreateException {
    }

    public void setSessionContext(SessionContext context) {
      this.context = context;
    }

    public void ejbActivate() {
    }

    public void ejbPassivate() {
    }

    public void ejbRemove() {
    }

    public int getQuantityOnHand(String productID)
        throws RemoteException {
      Stockroom sr = getStockroom(productID);
      return sr.getQuantityOnHand();
    }

    public void setQuantityOnHand(String productID, int q)
        throws RemoteException {
      Stockroom sr = getStockroom(productID);
      sr.setQuantityOnHand(q);
    }

    public int getMinimumReorderQuantity(String productID)
        throws RemoteException {
      Stockroom sr = getStockroom(productID);
```

```
      return sr.getMinimumReorderQuantity();
   }

   public void setMinimumReorderQuantity(String productID, int q)
      throws RemoteException {
    Stockroom sr = getStockroom(productID);
    sr.setMinimumReorderQuantity(q);
   }

   public int getStandardOrderQuantity(String productID)
      throws RemoteException {
    Stockroom sr = getStockroom(productID);
    return sr.getStandardOrderQuantity();
   }

   public void setStandardOrderQuantity(String productID, int q)
      throws RemoteException {
    Stockroom sr = getStockroom(productID);
    sr.setStandardOrderQuantity(q);
   }

   public void stock(String poductID)
      throws RemoteException {
    stock(productID, 1);
   }

   public void stock(String productID, int quantity)
      throws RemoteException {
    Stockroom sr = getStockroom(productID);
    sr.stock(quantity);
   }

   public void take(String productID)
      throws RemoteException {
    take(productID, 1);
   }

   public void take(String productID, int quantity)
      throws RemoteException {
    Stockroom sr = getStockroom(productID);
    sr.take(quantity);
   }

   public void holdForDriver(String productID, String truckNumber)
      throws RemoteException,EJBException {
    if (truckNumber == null) {
      throw new EJBException("hold requires truck number");
    }
    holdForDriver(productID, truckNumber, 1);
   }

   public void holdForDriver(String productID, String truckNumber,
    int q)
```

```
      throws RemoteException, EJBException {
   if (truckNumber == null) {
     throw new EJBException("hold requires truck number");
   }
   Stockroom sr = getStockroom(productID);
   sr.take(q);
 }

public void sendToDriver(String productID, String truckNumber)
     throws RemoteException, EJBException {
   if (truckNumber == null) {
     throw new EJBException("field dispatch requires truck
       number");
   }
   sendToDriver(productID, truckNumber, 1);
 }

public void sendToDriver(String productID, String truckNumber,
                         int q)
     throws RemoteException, EJBException {
   if (truckNumber == null) {
     throw new EJBException("field dispatch requires truck
       number");
   }
   Stockroom sr = getStockroom(productID);
   sr.take(q);
 }

public int getDispatchTime(String productID, String truckNumber)
     throws RemoteException, EJBException {
   if (truckNumber == null) {
     throw new EJBException("get dispatch time requires truck
       number");
   }
   return 25;
 }

private Stockroom getStockroom(String productID) {
   try {
     Context initial = new InitialContext();
     Object objref =
       initial.lookup("java:comp/env/ejb/Stockroom");

     StockroomHome home =
       (StockroomHome)PortableRemoteObject.narrow(objref,
         StockroomHome.class);

     return home.findByPrimaryKey(productID);
   }
   catch (NamingException e) {
     throw new EJBException("ERROR 100 - Notify System
       Administrator");
 }

   catch (RemoteException e) {
     throw new EJBException("ERROR 101 - Notify System
       Administrator");
```

```
    }

    catch (Exception e) {
      throw new EJBException("can't find " + productID);
    }
  }
}
```

DispatcherHold.jsp

 \Chapter7\code\DispatcherHold.jsp

```jsp
<%@ include file="GetPartsManager.jsp" %>
<%@ page errorPage="DispatcherQueryError.jsp" %>
<jsp:useBean id="qpBean" scope="request"
  class="QueryParms" />
<jsp:setProperty name="qpBean" property="*" />
<%
  partsManager.holdForDriver(qpBean.getPn(), qpBean.getTn(),
    qpBean.getQ());
%>
<html>
  <head>
    <title>Confirmation</title>
  </head>
  <body>
    <center>
    <font face="Arial,Helvetica"><font size=+1>
    Confirmation
    </font></font>
    <br>
    <table border cols=2 width="50%%" >
      <tr>
        <td width="20%">Part #</td>
        <td>
          <jsp:getProperty name="qpBean" property="pn" />
        </td>
      </tr>
      <tr>
        <td width="20%">Quantity</td>
        <td>
          <jsp:getProperty name="qpBean" property="q" />
        </td>
      </tr>
      <tr>
        <td width="20%">Disposition</td>
        <td>
          Held for truck #
          <jsp:getProperty name="qpBean" property="tn" />
```

```
        </td>
      </tr>
    </table>
    <br>
    <a href="http://localhost:8000/PRA/PQ">Next Query</a>
  </body>
</html>
```

DispatcherSend.jsp

 On The CD   *\Chapter7\code\DispatcherSend.jsp*

```
<%@ page import="java.text.SimpleDateFormat" %>
<%@ page import="java.util.Calendar" %>
<%@ page import="java.util.Date" %>
<%@ page import="java.util.GregorianCalendar" %>
<%@ include file="GetPartsManager.jsp" %>
<%@ page errorPage="DispatcherQueryError.jsp" %>
<jsp:useBean id="qpBean" scope="request"
  class="QueryParms" />
<jsp:setProperty name="qpBean" property="*" />
<html>
  <head>
    <title>Confirmation</title>
  </head>
  <body>
    <center>
    <font face="Arial,Helvetica"><font size=+1>
    Confirmation
    </font></font>
    <br>
    <table BORDER COLS=2 WIDTH="80%%" >
      <tr>
        <td width="30%">Part #</td>
        <td>
          <jsp:getProperty name="qpBean" property="pn" />
        </td>
      </tr>
      <tr>
        <td width="30%">Quantity</td>
        <td>
          <jsp:getProperty name="qpBean" property="q" />
        </td>
      </tr>
      <tr>
        <td width="30%">Disposition</td>
        <td>
          Sent to truck
```

```
              <jsp:getProperty name="qpBean" property="tn" />
          </td>
        </tr>
        <tr>
          <td width="30%">
            Estimated arrival time:
          </td>
          <td>
            <%
              GregorianCalendar cal = new GregorianCalendar();
              int dispTime =
                partsManager.getDispatchTime(qpBean.getPn(),
                  qpBean.getTn());
              cal.add(Calendar.MINUTE,dispTime);
              SimpleDateFormat sdf =
                new SimpleDateFormat ("MMM dd, HH:mm");
            %>
            <%= sdf.format(cal.getTime()) %>
          </td>
        </tr>
      </table>
      <br>
      <a href="http://localhost:8000/PRA/PQ">Next Query</a>
    </body>
</html>
```

DriverQuery.jsp

\Chapter7\code\DriverQuery.jsp

```
<%@ page contentType="text/vnd.wap.wml" %>
<%@ page import="java.text.SimpleDateFormat" %>
<%@ page import="java.util.Calendar" %>
<%@ page import="java.util.Date" %>
<%@ page import="java.util.GregorianCalendar" %>
<%@ include file="GetPartsManager.jsp" %>
<%@ page errorPage="DriverQueryError.jsp" %>
<jsp:useBean id="qpBean" scope="request"
  class="QueryParms" />
<jsp:setProperty name="qpBean" property="*" />
<?xml version="1.0"?>
<!DOCTYPE wml PUBLIC "-//WAPFORUM//DTD WML 1.1//EN"
"http://www.wapforum.org/DTD
/wml_1.1.xml">
<wml>
<card title="Query Results">
<do type="accept" label="Next">
<go href="http://localhost:8000/PRA/PQ" />
</do>
```

```
<p>
PN:
<jsp:getProperty name="qpBean" property="pn" />
</p>
<%
  if (qpBean.getQ() > 0) {
%>
<p>
Qty:
<jsp:getProperty name="qpBean" property="q" />
</p>
<%
  }
%>
<p>
Qty in stock:
<%= partsManager.getQuantityOnHand(qpBean.getPn()) %>
</p>
<%
  if (qpBean.getTn() != null) {
%>
<p>
ETA:
<%
 GregorianCalendar cal = new GregorianCalendar();
 cal.add(Calendar.MINUTE,25);
   SimpleDateFormat sdf = new SimpleDateFormat("MMM dd, HH:mm");
%>
<%= sdf.format(cal.getTime()) %>
</p>
<%
  }
%>
</card>
</wml>
```

DriverHold.jsp

\Chapter7\code\DriverHold.jsp

```
<%@ page contentType="text/vnd.wap.wml" %>
<%@ page import="java.text.SimpleDateFormat" %>
<%@ page import="java.util.Calendar" %>
<%@ page import="java.util.Date" %>
<%@ page import="java.util.GregorianCalendar" %>
<%@ include file="GetPartsManager.jsp" %>
<%@ page errorPage="DriverQueryError.jsp" %>
<jsp:useBean id="qpBean" scope="request"
  class="QueryParms" />
```

```
<jsp:setProperty name="qpBean" property="*" />
<%
  partsManager.holdForDriver(qpBean.getPn(), qpBean.getTn(),
    qpBean.getQ());
%>
<?xml version="1.0"?>
<!DOCTYPE wml PUBLIC "-//WAPFORUM//DTD WML 1.1//EN"
"http://www.wapforum.org/DTD
/wml_1.1.xml">


<wml>


<card title="Confirmation">
<do type="accept" label="Next">
<go href="http://localhost:8000/PRA/PQ" />
</do>
<p>
PN:
<jsp:getProperty name="qpBean" property="pn" />
</p>
<p>
Qty:
<jsp:getProperty name="qpBean" property="q" />
</p>
<p>
Sent to truck #
<jsp:getProperty name="qpBean" property="tn" />
</p>
<p>
ETA:
<%
 GregorianCalendar cal = new GregorianCalendar();
 cal.add(Calendar.MINUTE,25);
   SimpleDateFormat sdf = new SimpleDateFormat("MMM dd, HH:mm");
%>
<%= sdf.format(cal.getTime()) %>
</p>
</card>
</wml>
```

DriverSend.jsp

\Chapter7\code\DriverSend.jsp

```
<%@ page contentType="text/vnd.wap.wml" %>
<%@ page import="java.text.SimpleDateFormat" %>
<%@ page import="java.util.Calendar" %>
<%@ page import="java.util.Date" %>
```

```
<%@ page import="java.util.GregorianCalendar" %>
<%@ include file="GetPartsManager.jsp" %>
<%@ page errorPage="DriverQueryError.jsp" %>
<jsp:useBean id="qpBean" scope="request"
    class="QueryParms" />
<jsp:setProperty name="qpBean" property="*" />
<%
  partsManager.holdForDriver(qpBean.getPn(), qpBean.getTn(),
    qpBean.getQ());
%>
<?xml version="1.0"?>
<!DOCTYPE wml PUBLIC "-//WAPFORUM//DTD WML 1.1//EN"
"http://www.wapforum.org/DTD
/wml_1.1.xml">

<wml>

<card title="Confirmation">
<do type="accept" label="Next">
<go href="http://localhost:8000/PRA/PQ" />
</do>
<p>
PN:
<jsp:getProperty name="qpBean" property="pn" />
</p>
<p>
Qty:
<jsp:getProperty name="qpBean" property="q" />
</p>
<p>
Sent to truck #
<jsp:getProperty name="qpBean" property="tn" />
</p>
<p>
ETA:
<%
 GregorianCalendar cal = new GregorianCalendar();
 cal.add(Calendar.MINUTE,25);
   SimpleDateFormat sdf = new SimpleDateFormat("MMM dd, HH:mm");
%>
<%= sdf.format(cal.getTime()) %>
</p>
</card>
</wml>
```

DriverQueryError.jsp

\Chapter7\code\DriverQueryError.jsp

```
<%@ page contentType="text/vnd.wap.wml" %>
<%@ page errorPage="DriverQueryError.jsp" %>
<jsp:useBean id="qpBean" scope="request"
  class="QueryParms" />
<?xml version="1.0"?>
<!DOCTYPE wml PUBLIC "-//WAPFORUM//DTD WML 1.1//EN"
"http://www.wapforum.org/DTD
/wml_1.1.xml">
<wml>
<card title="ERROR">
<do type="accept" label="Next">
<go href="http://localhost:8000/PRA/PQ" />
</do>
<p>
An error occurred while processing request for part number
<jsp:getProperty name="qpBean" property="pn" />
</p>
<p>
Please check the data you supplied as input and re-enter your
request.
</p>
<p>
If the problem persists, notify your system administrator.
</p>
</card>
</wml>
```

Summary

In this chapter, we saw how multiple EJBs can be used in conjunction with Web components and JavaBeans to develop applications. We also saw how an EJB can be a client of another EJB.

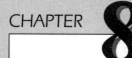

Replenishing the Stockroom

In this chapter:

- An Automated Ordering Procedure
- Transactions
- Bean-managed Transactions
- A JDBC Transaction
- Managing Orders

In this chapter, we identify and address one of the shortcomings of the example we developed in the previous chapter. In so doing, we introduce the concept of transactions and show an example of a JDBC transaction.

And When She Got There, The Cupboard Was Bare

The application we developed in the previous chapter does not fully solve the problem of keeping trucks supplied with the parts and supplies necessary to keep the business running. Consider the case where the driver of truck 22 places an order for 5 of part number 102010. Confirmation of the order is shown in Figure 8-1.

When the driver of another truck subsequently attempts to place an order for part number 102010, the error message shown in Figure 8-2 is displayed.

The driver calls back to the office as instructed in the error message. The dispatcher who receives the call at the office investigates by first checking availability of the part. Examination of the output shown in Figure 8-3 explains the error the second driver encountered: the driver who placed the first order depleted the available supply of part number 102010.

Now that we have identified the shortcoming in our system, we must develop a solution. The solution can be found by examining any of the real-world stockrooms that have operated successfully for years. Whenever a stock clerk removes a part from the supply

Figure 8-1
Truck 22 Places Order
for Part 102010

shelf, he or she updates the quantity on hand. When the quantity on hand reaches or falls below a preestablished minimum reorder quantity, the clerk fills out an order form, which is sent to a warehouse. A shipment containing the requested parts is sent to the stockroom and the stock clerk replenishes the supply.

Rather than trusting a stock clerk to determine whether the quantity on hand has reached or fallen below the minimum reorder quantity, we will automate the ordering process.

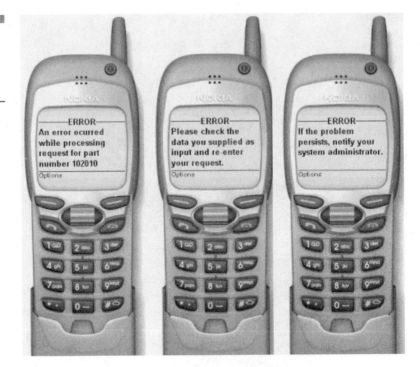

A Smarter Stockroom Bean

To implement our automated ordering process, we must modify the *Stockroom* bean. A complete listing of the modified code can be found at the end of the chapter. The first modification is to the `take()` method, which now looks like this:

```
public int take(int q) throws EJBException {
  int qt = -1;
  if (q <= 0) {
    return qt;
  }
  if (q <= quantityOnHand) {
    qt = q;
    quantityOnHand -= q;
  }
  if (quantityOnHand <= minimumReorderQuantity) {
    placeOrder();
  }
  return qt;
}
```

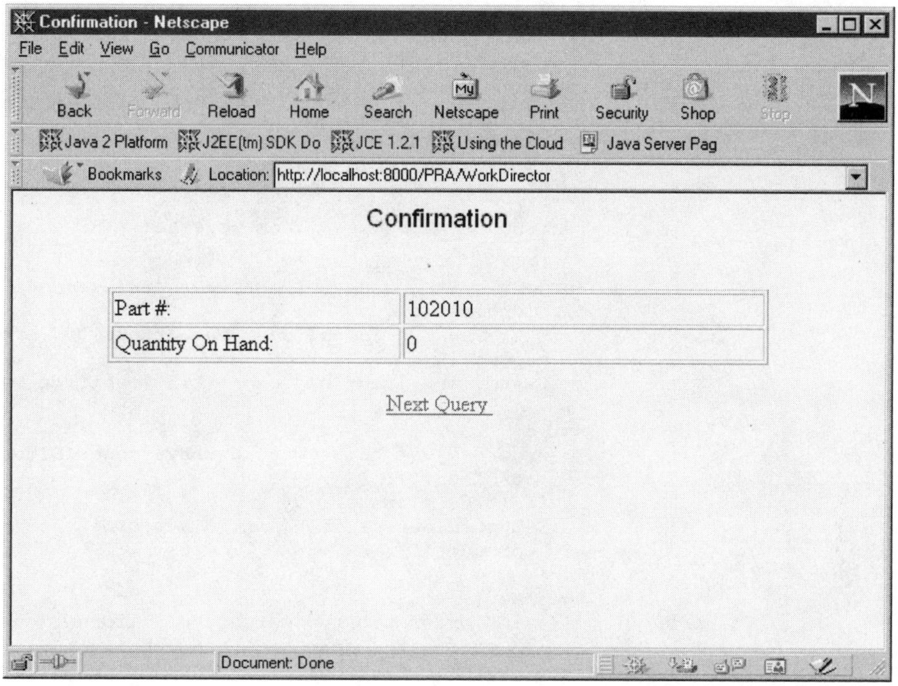

Figure 8-3
Supply of Part 102010
Is Depleted

The method returns a positive integer if the requested quantity of a product can be successfully obtained from the stockroom; otherwise, it returns a negative integer. In our present implementation, if the requested quantity is greater than the quantity currently on hand, the operation fails. In other words, we make no provision for handling a partially filled order accompanied by a back order. If the method determines that a sufficient quantity of the requested part is available, it adjusts the instance variable quantityOnHand. If, after adjustment, the value of the instance variable is less than or equal to minimumReorderQuantity, the placeOrder() method is invoked. Here is the code for that method:

```
private java.sql.Date placeOrder() {

    java.sql.Date deliveryDate = null;

    String[] [] orders = null;
```

```
    try {
      Context initial = new InitialContext();
      Object objref = initial.lookup("java:comp/env/ejb/Warehouse");

      WarehouseHome home =
          (WarehouseHome)PortableRemoteObject.narrow(objref,
          WarehouseHome.class);

    Warehouse warehouse = home.create();

    orders = warehouse.getPastDueOrders(customerID, productID);
    if (orders.length > 0) {
      System.out.println("past due orders for product " +
      productID);
      System.out.println("send email to office manager");
    }
    else {
      orders = warehouse.getOrdersByProductID(customerID,
        productID);
      if (orders.length >0) {
        System.out.println("expediate order for product" +
        productID);
      }
      else {
        int orderNumber = warehouse.fillOrder(customerID,
          productID, standardOrderQuantity);
        System.out.println("order #: " + orderNumber);
        deliveryDate = warehouse.getDeliveryDate(orderNumber);
        System.out.println("delivery date: " + deliveryDate);
      }
    }
    warehouse.remove();
  }
  catch (Exception e) {
    System.err.println("Caught an exception." );
    e.printStackTrace();
  }
  finally {
    return deliveryDate;
  }
}
```

The `placeOrder()` method first gets an instance of the *Warehouse* session bean that we examine in detail shortly. It first invokes this bean's `getPastDueOrders()` method, which returns an array containing those orders that were previously placed and whose promised delivery date has passed. If any such orders exist, as indicated by the length of the returned array being greater than zero, an urgent email is sent to the stockroom manager, who investigates why the shipment is late. In the interest of simplicity, we simply print a message to the system standard output device.

NOTE: *The* customerID *argument that is passed to getPastDue-Orders() is hard coded as* 112112. *Later we see how to avoid such hard coding, so that the same code can be used for multiple stockrooms.*

If there are no past due orders, placeOrder() invokes the getOrdersByProductID() method of the warehouse instance. This method is similar to getOutstandingOrders() but returns a list of orders that have been placed and whose anticipated delivery date has not yet arrived. The reason for this check is to avoid placing multiple orders for the same product. If an order for the requested product is outstanding, we send email to the stockroom manager to request that the order be expedited. We could even send this request directly to the warehouse. For the sake of simplicity, we take the same approach we did before and print a message to the system standard output device.

If we determine that no orders for the product already exist, we place an order by invoking the warehouse instance's fillOrder() method. After we print the order number returned by the fillOrder() method, we pass it as an argument to the getDeliveryDate() method and print the date that is returned.

The placeOrder() method is now finished with the warehouse instance and releases it by invoking the remove() method.

The Warehouse

The *Warehouse* EJB we present here is a session bean that interfaces with the database that reflects the state of the physical warehouse.

The Remote Interface

The remote interface defines the methods that a client can invoke. The code for the remote interface is shown below:

\Chapter8\code\Warehouse.java

```
import javax.ejb.EJBObject;
import java.rmi.RemoteException;
import java.sql.Date;
import java.sql.SQLException;

public interface Warehouse extends EJBObject {

    public int fillOrder(String customerID, String productID,

                         int quantity)
        throws RemoteException;

    public void closeOrder(int orderNumber)
        throws RemoteException;

    public java.sql.Date getDeliveryDate(int orderNumber)
        throws RemoteException;

    public String[] getOrder(int orderNumber)
        throws RemoteException;

    public String[] [] getOutstandingOrders(String customerID)
        throws RemoteException;

    public String[] [] getOrdersByProductID(String customerID,

                                            String productID)

        throws RemoteException;

    public String[] [] getPastDueOrders(String customerID,

                                        String productID)

        throws RemoteException;
}
```

The Home Interface

Here is the code for the home interface:

On The CD   **\Chapter8\code\WarehouseHome.java**

```java
import java.rmi.RemoteException;
import javax.ejb.*;

public interface WarehouseHome extends EJBHome {

    public Warehouse create()
        throws RemoteException, CreateException;
}
```

The Enterprise Bean

The reason we introduced the *Warehouse* bean is to fill orders placed from the stockroom. Filling an order is a multistep process that proceeds as follows:

1. Assign a unique order number that can be used to identify the order throughout its life cycle.

2. Record the data necessary to fill the order. These data consist of:
- the order number mentioned earlier
- the customer who placed the order
- the product being ordered
- the quantity of the product being ordered
- the promised delivery date

3. Update the warehouse inventory to reflect removal of the ordered items.

Either all of the above steps must complete, or none of them at all; otherwise, data integrity is lost. The three steps together are regarded as an indivisible unit of work. The term used to refer to such an indivisible unit of work is a *transaction.*

A successful transaction ends with a *commit,* which consists of saving all of the data modifications made during the transaction. A failed transaction ends with a *rollback,* which reverses the effects of all operations performed during the transaction. At the conclusion of a rollback, all data look exactly like they did before the transaction began.

When we discussed persistence, we saw that J2EE allowed us to choose who would be responsible for managing persistence, the bean or the container. J2EE gives us the same choice when it comes to responsibility for managing transactions. As was the case with persistence, we specify our choice by making declarative statements in the Application Deployment Tool.

NOTE: *A session bean can use bean-managed or container-managed transactions. An entity bean is not permitted to have bean-managed transactions.*

Our *Warehouse* bean is a session bean and we will use bean-managed transactions. When using bean-managed transactions, we must further choose between using JDBC and JTA (Java Transaction API) to manage the transaction. We choose JDBC so we will postpone discussion of JTA until later.

NOTE: *The choice is between using JDBC or JTA to manage the transaction. Choosing JTA in no way precludes use of JDBC operations within the transaction.*

A JDBC transaction is controlled by the transaction manager of the database system. Beans that use a JDBC transaction use the `commit()` and `rollback()` methods of the *javax.sql.Connection* interface. The program does not explicitly specify the beginning of the transaction. The transaction begins implicitly with the first SQL statement following the most recent `commit()`, `rollback()`, or `connect()`. As we already mentioned, if the transaction is successful, it ends with a `commit()`; otherwise, it ends with a `rollback()`. Here is the transaction code from *WarehouseBean*:

```
public int fillOrder (String customerID, String productID,
```

```
      int quantity) {

      int orderNumber = -1;

      try {
        connection.setAutoCommit(false);
        orderNumber = getNextOrderNumber();
        updateOrderItem(customerID, productID, quantity, orderNumber);
        updateInventory(productID, quantity);
        connection.commit();
      }
      catch (Exception ex) {
        try {
          connection.rollback();
          throw new EJBException("Transaction failed: " +
            ex.getMessage());
          }
        catch (SQLException sqx) {
          throw new EJBException("Rollback failed: " +
            sqx.getMessage());
        }
      }
      finally {
        return orderNumber;
      }
    }
```

Inside the first try block, we see the following line:

```
connection.setAutoCommit(false);
```

This method invocation instructs the DBMS that it should not automatically commit every SQL statement. The instance variable `connection` holds a *Connection* to the database identified by the JNDI name `java:comp/env/jdbc/WarehouseDB`. The connection is obtained during execution of the bean's `ejbCreate()` method and each time the bean is activated; it is closed each time the bean is passivated and during execution of the `ejbRemove()` method.

The `fillOrder()` method first obtains an order number that can be assigned to the order. It does so, by invoking `getNextOrderNumber()`. The most recently assigned order number is stored in a table called *ordseqno* in a single row containing a single value. The `getNextOrderNumber()` method executes two SQL statements to increment the value stored in the table and to select the updated number.

The next step in the transaction updates a table called *orderitem*. This update is performed by invoking `updateOrderItem()`, which executes a single SQL statement that inserts a row containing the order number, the customer ID, the product ID, the quantity ordered, and the promised delivery date. In a real-world implementation, the delivery date would be calculated by an algorithm. In our application, we simply add one day to the current date.

The final step in the transaction updates the *inventory* table. This update is performed by invoking `updateInventory()`, which executes an SQL statement that decrements the quantity of the specified product by the specified amount.

If an *SQLException* is thrown by any of the steps, the `catch` block attempts to invoke the `rollback()` method on the connection. If no exception is thrown, `fillOrder()` invokes `commit()` on the connection.

The PartsManager Bean

The *PartsManager* EJB is modified to enable communication with the *Warehouse* EJB. The listing of the modified *PartsManager* is shown at the end of the chapter.

Packaging and Deploying

The differences between the application is this chapter and the one in Chapter 7 are:

- The *PartsManager* EJB communicates with a *Warehouse* EJB as well as a *Stockroom* EJB; therefore, in the EJB References dialog, we add the following entry:

Coded Name	Type	Home	Remote
ejb/Warehouse	Session	WarehouseHome	Warehouse

■ The application contains an additional EJB, the *Warehouse* EJB. It is a stateful session bean that uses bean-managed transactions. In the Resource References dialog, we add the following entry:

Coded Name	Type	Authentication
jdbc/WarehouseDB	javax.sql.DataSource	Container

■ To support managing the stockroom, which we discuss later, the WAR file contains one additional HTML file and five additional JSPs. These are:
  - ■ *ManageStockroom.html*
  - ■ *GetOrders.jsp*
  - ■ *ViewOrder.jsp*
  - ■ *CloseOrder.jsp*
  - ■ *OrderListEmpty.jsp*
  - ■ *ProcessShipment.jsp*

Listings of these additional files can be found at the end of the chapter.

Preparing to Run

Before running our application that accesses the stockroom and the warehouse, we must first populate the database tables. We have already seen the code that fills the stockroom and we use the same code in this chapter. We use the following SQL to fill the warehouse:

\Chapter8\code\fillWarehouse.sql

```
drop table inventory;

create table inventory
(productID char(6),
quantity decimal(5));
```

```
insert into inventory
values ('102010', 500),
        ('102011', 500),
        ('102012', 500),
        ('102013', 500),
        ('102014', 500),
        ('102015', 500),
        ('102016', 500),
        ('102017', 500),
        ('102018', 500);

drop table orderitem;

create table orderitem
(orderNumber integer,
customerID char(6),
productID char(6),
quantity integer,
deliveryDate date);

drop table ordnoseq;

create table ordnoseq
(orderNumber integer);

insert into ordnoseq
values(2000100001);

exit;
```

We execute these SQL statements by typing the command:

```
fillWarehouse
```

This executes the batch file *fillWarehouse.bat*.

\Chapter8\code\fillWarehouse.bat

Observing Our Application in Action

We have already seen the kind of output our Roadside Assistance application produces, so we will show no further screen shots.

Instead, we will observe what is displayed in the window from which we started the J2EE Server (assuming it was started using `j2ee -verbose`).

When we place an order for a quantity of 10 of part number 102010, we see the following output:

```
order #: 2000100002
delivery date: 2000-09-10
```

Since we have already examined the code for the modified *Stockroom* and discussed the fact that we would use `System.out.println()` statements to record events related to ordering, the preceding output shows that our automated ordering process is working. It has detected that the quantity of part 102010 on hand is at or below the minimum reorder quantity and an order has been placed to the warehouse.

If we place a second request for the same part, the `placeOrder()` method determines that an outstanding order exists and the following output is displayed:

```
expediate order for product 102010
```

If we set the system clock ahead to a point beyond the promised delivery date (Don't forget to set it back!), we see the following output displayed when we attempt to request part 102010 from the stockroom

```
past due orders for product 102010
send email to office manager
```

NOTE: *The modified Stockroom EJB simply implements the mechanism for automatically placing orders. It does not handle receipt of shipments from the warehouse. This means that, if we make the same requests for parts we showed at the beginning of the chapter, although the automated order process generates orders, we will see the same error messages in our browser or cellular phone. You might want to add code to receive orders and restock the stockroom.*

Managing the Stockroom

In addition to modifying the *Stockroom* EJB to implement auto-mated ordering, we also included modifications that enable management of the stockroom. Management of the stockroom consists of such activities as tracking orders that have been placed to the warehouse, receiving shipments from the warehouse, updating the stockroom database to reflect receipt of ordered items, and closing out orders.

We test the stockroom management facility by accessing the following URL:

```
http://localhost:8000/CH8/ManageStockroom.html
```

This results in the appearance of the screen shown in Figure 8-4.

If we select the radio button labeled GET OUTSTANDING ORDERS, the *PartsManager* bean obtains a list of orders from the bean and displays them as shown in Figure 8-5.

If we select one order from the list and click on the radio button

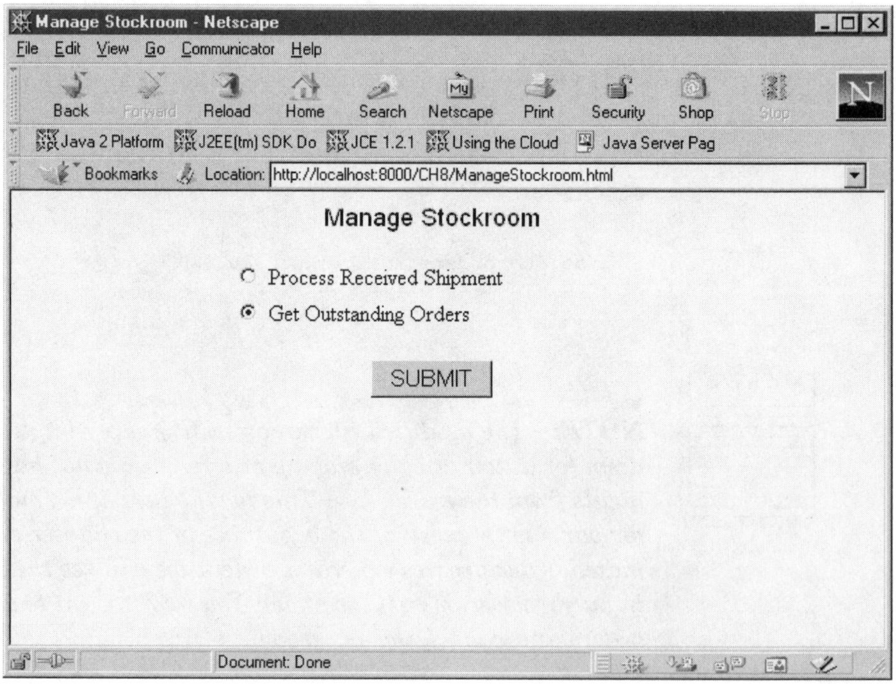

Figure 8-4
Stockroom Management Initial Screen

Figure 8-5

List of Outstanding
Orders

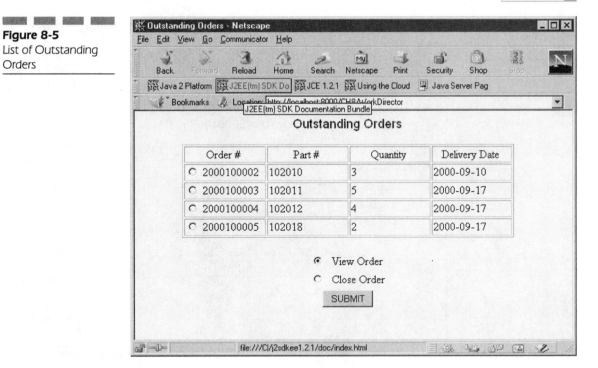

labeled VIEW ORDER, the *PartsManager* bean gets that order from
the *Warehouse* bean and displays it as shown in Figure 8-6.

We did not implement code to receive a shipment and restock the
stockroom. If we had, after processing the shipment we would close
the order by selecting the appropriate radio button. Confirmation
of closing is displayed as shown in Figure 8-7.

With one order now closed, when we request the list of outstanding orders, it contains one less order, as we can see from Figure 8-8. When all orders have been closed, the message shown in
Figure 8-9 is displayed.

The Revised Stockroom Bean

\Chapter8\code\StockroomBean.java

Figure 8-6
Order Details

```
 Order - Netscape                                                    _ □ ×
File  Edit  View  Go  Communicator  Help

  Back    Forward   Reload    Home    Search   Netscape   Print   Security   Shop

  Java 2 Platform    J2EE(tm) SDK Do   JCE 1.2.1   Using the Cloud    Java Server Pag

   Bookmarks    Location: http://localhost:8000/CH8/WorkDirector

                       Order # 2000100002


          Customer ID:      112112
          Part #:           102010
          Quantity:         3
          Delivery Date:    2000-09-10


              ⦿ Close Order ◯ View Outstanding Odrers
                         SUBMIT


    =□=              Document: Done
```

```java
import java.util.*;
import java.sql.*;
import javax.ejb.*;
import javax.naming.Context;
import javax.naming.InitialContext;
import javax.rmi.PortableRemoteObject;


public class StockroomBean implements EntityBean {

  public String productID;
  public int quantityOnHand;
  public int minimumReorderQuantity;
  public int standardOrderQuantity;


  private String customerID = "112112";


  private EntityContext context;


  public String ejbCreate(String productID)
      throws CreateException {

    if (productID == null) {
      throw new CreateException("You must specify a productID.");
```

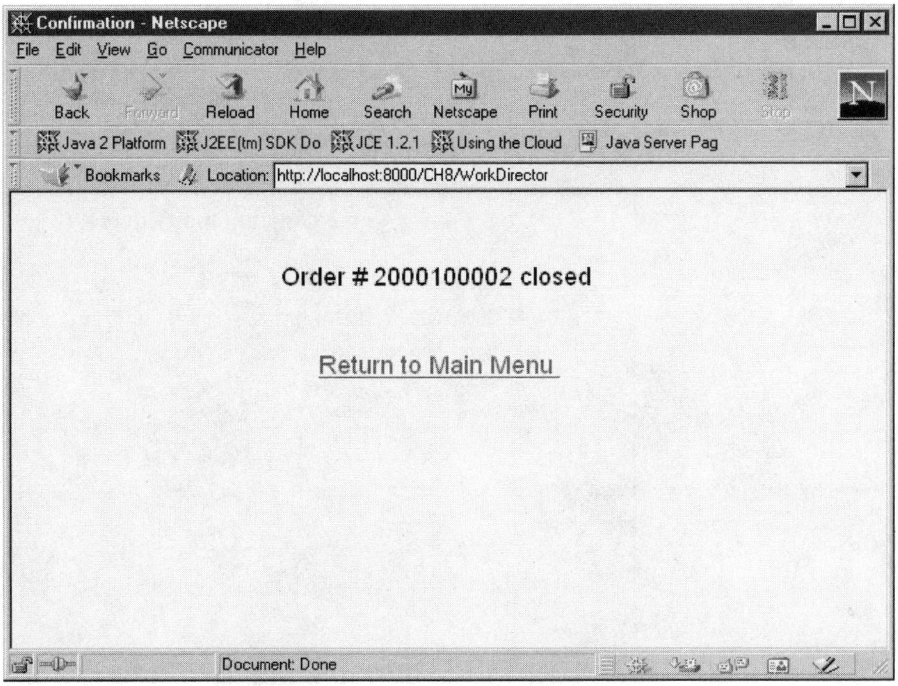

Figure 8-7
Confirmation of Clos-
ing an Order

```
      }

      this.productID = productID;

      return null;
   }

   public void setEntityContext(EntityContext context) {
      this.context = context;
   }

   public void ejbActivate() {
      productID = (String)context.getPrimaryKey();
   }

   public void ejbPassivate() {
      productID = null;
   }

   public void ejbRemove() {
   }

   public void ejbLoad() {
   }
```

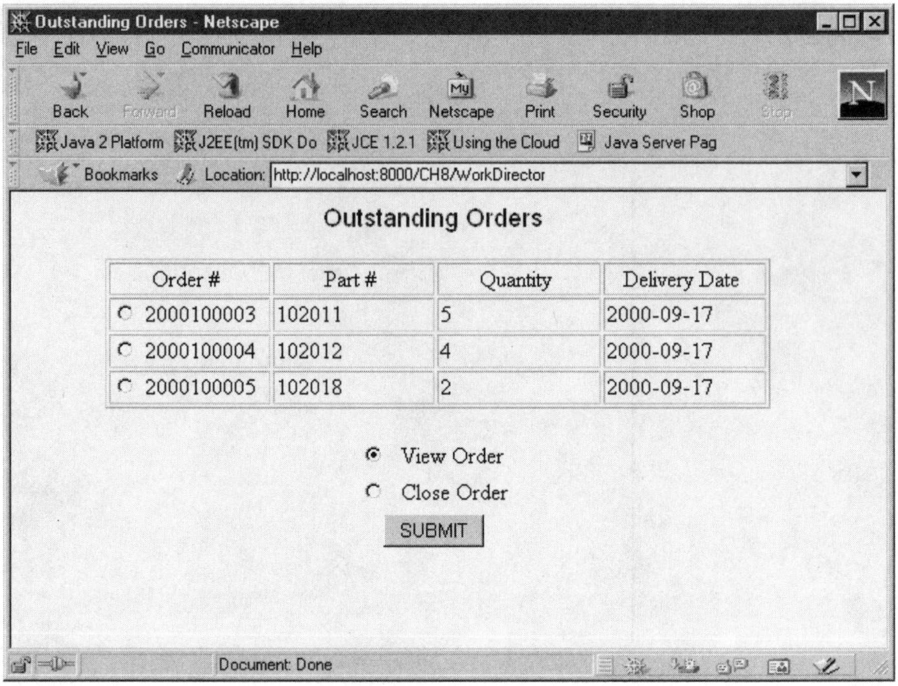

Figure 8-8

Order List After Closing an Order

```
public void ejbStore() {
}

public void unsetEntityContext() {
}

public void ejbPostCreate(String productID) {
}

public int getQuantityOnHand() {
  return quantityOnHand;
}

public void setQuantityOnHand(int q) {
  quantityOnHand = q;
}

public int getMinimumReorderQuantity() {
  return minimumReorderQuantity;
}

public void setMinimumReorderQuantity(int q) {
  minimumReorderQuantity = q;
}
```

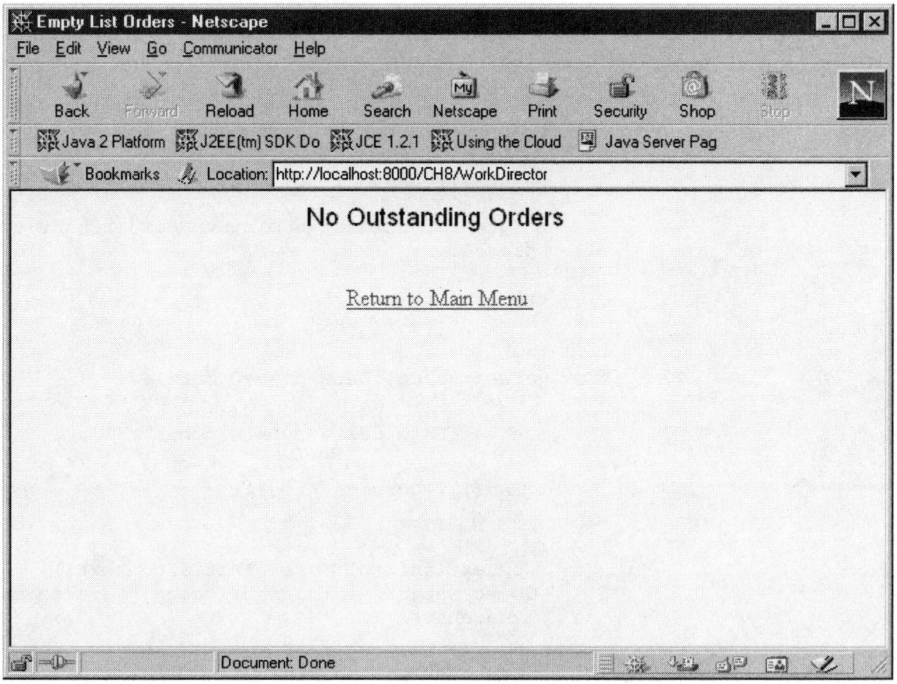

Figure 8-9
After Closing All
Orders

```
public int getStandardOrderQuantity() {
  return standardOrderQuantity;
}

public void setStandardOrderQuantity(int q) {
  standardOrderQuantity = q;
}

public void stock() {
  stock(1);
}

public void stock(int q) {
  quantityOnHand += q;
}

public void stock(int q, int orderNumber) {
  quantityOnHand += q;
  closeOrder();
}

public int take() throws EJBException {
  return take(1);
}
```

```
public int take(int q) throws EJBException {
  int qt = -1;
  if (q <= 0) {
    return qt;
  }
  if (q <= quantityOnHand) {
    qt = q;
    quantityOnHand -= q;
  }
  if (quantityOnHand <= minimumReorderQuantity) {
    placeOrder();
  }
    return qt;
}

private java.sql.Date placeOrder() {

  java.sql.Date deliveryDate = null;

  String[] [] orders = null;

  try {
    Context initial = new InitialContext();
    Object objref = initial.lookup("java:comp/env/ejb/
      Warehouse");

    WarehouseHome home =
      (WarehouseHome)PortableRemoteObject.narrow(objref,
        WarehouseHome.class);

    Warehouse warehouse = home.create();

    orders = warehouse.getPastDueOrders(customerID, productID);
    if (orders.length > 0) {
      System.out.println("past due orders for product " +
      productID);
      System.out.println("send email to office manager");
    }
    else {
      orders = warehouse.getOrdersByProductID(customerID,
        productID);
      if (orders.length >0) {
        System.out.println("expediate order for product" +
          productID);
      }
      else {
        int orderNumber = warehouse.fillOrder(customerID,
          productID, standardOrderQuantity);
        System.out.println("order #: " + orderNumber);
        deliveryDate = warehouse.getDeliveryDate(orderNumber);
        System.out.println("delivery date: " + deliveryDate);
      }
    }
    warehouse.remove();
  }
```

```
    catch (Exception e) {
      System.err.println("Caught an exception." );
      e.printStackTrace();
    }
    finally {
      return deliveryDate;
```

The Warehouse Bean

 On the CD

\Chapter8\code\WarehouseBean.java

```java
import java.text.*;
import java.util.*;
import javax.ejb.*;
import java.sql.*;
import javax.sql.*;
import javax.naming.*;

public class WarehouseBean implements SessionBean {

  private SessionContext context;
  private Connection connection;
  private String dbName = "java:comp/env/jdbc/WarehouseDB";

  public int fillOrder (String customerID, String productID,
    int quantity) {

    int orderNumber = -1;

    try {
      connection.setAutoCommit(false);
      orderNumber = getNextOrderNumber();
      updateOrderItem(customerID, productID, quantity,
          orderNumber);
      updateInventory(productID, quantity);
      connection.commit();
    }
    catch (Exception ex) {
      try {
        connection.rollback();
        throw new EJBException("Transaction failed: " +
          ex.getMessage());
        }
      catch (SQLException sqx) {
```

```java
        throw new EJBException("Rollback failed: " +
          sqx.getMessage());
      }
    }
    finally {
      return orderNumber;
    }
  }


  public void closeOrder(int orderNumber) {
    String deleteStatement =
      "DELETE FROM orderitem WHERE orderNumber = ? ";

    try {
      PreparedStatement preparedStatement =
        connection.prepareStatement(deleteStatement);

      preparedStatement.setInt(1, orderNumber);

      ResultSet rs = preparedStatement.executeQuery();

      preparedStatement.close();
    }
    catch (SQLException e) {
      System.out.println("SQLException " + e.getMessage());
      throw new EJBException
        ("Unable to close order due to SQLException: " +
          e.getMessage());
    }
  }

  public String[] [] getPastDueOrders(String customerID,
      String productID) {

    String[] [] orders = null;

    String selectStatement =
      "SELECT orderNumber, productID, quantity, deliveryDate " +
      "FROM orderitem WHERE customerID = ? " +
      "AND productID = ? " +
      "AND deliveryDate < current_date";

    try {
      PreparedStatement preparedStatement =
        connection.prepareStatement(selectStatement);

      preparedStatement.setString(1, customerID);
      preparedStatement.setString(2, productID);

      ResultSet rs = preparedStatement.executeQuery();

      Vector v = new Vector();
```

```
      while (rs.next()) {
        String[] s = new String[4];
        for (int i = 0; i < 4; ++i) {
          s[i] = rs.getString(i+1);
        }
        v.addElement(s);
      }

      preparedStatement.close();

      orders = new String[v.size()][4];

      for (int i = 0; i < v.size(); ++i) {
        String[] s = (String[])v.elementAt(i);
          for (int j = 0; j < 4; ++j) {
          orders[i][j] = s[j];
        }
      }
    }
    catch (SQLException e) {
      System.out.println("SQLException " + e.getMessage());
      throw new EJBException
        ("Unable to get past due orders due to SQLException: " +
          e.getMessage());
    }
    finally {
      return orders;
    }
  }

  public String[] [] getOutstandingOrders(String customerID) {

    String[] [] orders = null;

    String selectStatement =
      "SELECT orderNumber, productID, quantity, deliveryDate " +
      "FROM orderitem WHERE customerID = ? ";

    try {
      PreparedStatement preparedStatement =
        connection.prepareStatement(selectStatement);

      preparedStatement.setString(1, customerID);

      ResultSet rs = preparedStatement.executeQuery();

      Vector v = new Vector();

      while (rs.next()) {
        String[] s = new String[4];
        for (int i = 0; i < 4; ++i) {
          s[i] = rs.getString(i+1);
        }
```

```
      v.addElement(s);
    }


    preparedStatement.close();


    orders = new String[v.size()][4];


    for (int i = 0; i < v.size(); ++i) {
      String[] s = (String[])v.elementAt(i);
        for (int j = 0; j < 4; ++j) {
        orders[i][j] = s[j];
      }
    }
  }
  catch (SQLException e) {
    System.out.println("SQLException " + e.getMessage());
    throw new EJBException
      ("Unable to get outstanding orders due to SQLException: " +
        e.getMessage());
  }
  finally {
    return orders;
  }
}


public String[] [] getOrdersByProductID(String customerID,
  String productID) {


  String[] [] orders = null;


  String selectStatement =
    "SELECT orderNumber, productID, quantity, deliveryDate " +
    "FROM orderitem WHERE customerID = ? " +
    "AND productID = ?";


    try {
      PreparedStatement preparedStatement =
        connection.prepareStatement(selectStatement);


      preparedStatement.setString(1, customerID);
      preparedStatement.setString(2, productID);


      ResultSet rs = preparedStatement.executeQuery();


      Vector v = new Vector();


      while (rs.next()) {
        String[] s = new String[4];
        for (int i = 0; i < 4; ++i) {
          s[i] = rs.getString(i+1);
        }
```

```
        v.addElement(s);
      }


    preparedStatement.close();


    orders = new String[v.size()][4];


    for (int i = 0; i < v.size(); ++i) {
      String[] s = (String[])v.elementAt(i);
        for (int j = 0; j < 4; ++j) {
        orders[i][j] = s[j];
      }
    }
  }
  catch (SQLException e) {
    System.out.println("SQLException " + e.getMessage());
    throw new EJBException
      ("Unable to get orders due to SQLException: " +
      e.getMessage());
  }
  finally {
    return orders;
  }
}


public String[] getOrder(int orderNumber) {

  String selectStatement =
    "SELECT customerID, productID, quantity, deliveryDate " +
    "FROM orderitem WHERE orderNumber = ? ";

  String[] order = new String[4];

  try {
    PreparedStatement preparedStatement =
      connection.prepareStatement(selectStatement);

    preparedStatement.setInt(1, orderNumber);

    ResultSet rs = preparedStatement.executeQuery();

    while (rs.next()) {
      for (int i = 0; i < 4; ++i) {
        order[i] = rs.getString(i+1);
      }
    }

    preparedStatement.close();
  }
  catch (SQLException e) {
    System.out.println("SQLException " + e.getMessage());
    throw new EJBException
```

```
            ("Unable to get order due to SQLException: " +
              e.getMessage());
      }
    finally {
      return order;
    }
}

public java.sql.Date getDeliveryDate(int orderNumber) {

    java.sql.Date deliveryDate = null;

    String selectStatement =
      "SELECT deliveryDate " +
      "FROM orderitem WHERE orderNumber = ? ";

    try {

      PreparedStatement preparedStatement =
        connection.prepareStatement(selectStatement);

      preparedStatement.setInt(1, orderNumber);

      ResultSet rs = preparedStatement.executeQuery();

      if (rs.next()) {
        deliveryDate = rs.getDate(1);
      }

      preparedStatement.close();
    }
    catch (SQLException e) {
      System.out.println("SQLException " + e.getMessage());
      throw new EJBException
        ("Unable to get delivery date due to SQLException: " +
          e.getMessage());
    }
    finally {
      return deliveryDate;
    }
}

public void ejbCreate() throws CreateException {

    try {
      makeConnection();
    }
    catch (Exception ex) {
      throw new CreateException(ex.getMessage());
    }
}
```

```java
public void ejbRemove() {

  try {
    connection.close();
  }
  catch (SQLException ex) {
    throw new EJBException(ex.getMessage());
  }
}

public void ejbActivate() {

  try {
    makeConnection();
  }
  catch (Exception ex) {
    throw new EJBException(ex.getMessage());
  }
}

public void ejbPassivate() {

  try {
    connection.close();
  }
  catch (SQLException ex) {
    throw new EJBException(ex.getMessage());
  }
}

public void setSessionContext(SessionContext context) {

  this.context = context;

}

public WarehouseBean() {}

private void updateOrderItem(String customerID,
  String productID,

                            int quantity, int orderNumber)

  throws SQLException {

GregorianCalendar cal = new GregorianCalendar();
cal.add(Calendar.DAY_OF_WEEK,1);
java.sql.Date deliveryDate =
  new java.sql.Date(cal.getTime().getTime());

String updateStatement =
  "INSERT INTO orderitem VALUES" +
  " (?,?,?,?,?)";
```

```
    PreparedStatement preparedStatement =
      connection.prepareStatement(updateStatement);

    preparedStatement.setInt(1, orderNumber);
    preparedStatement.setString(2, customerID);
    preparedStatement.setString(3, productID);
    preparedStatement.setInt(4, quantity);
    preparedStatement.setDate(5, deliveryDate);
    preparedStatement.executeUpdate();
    preparedStatement.close();
}

private void updateInventory(String productID, int quantity)
    throws SQLException {

  String updateStatement =
    "UPDATE inventory " +
    "SEt quantity = quantity - ? " +
    "WHERE productID = ?";

  PreparedStatement preparedStatement =
    connection.prepareStatement(updateStatement);

  preparedStatement.setInt(1, quantity);
  preparedStatement.setString(2, productID);
  preparedStatement.executeUpdate();
  preparedStatement.close();
}

private void makeConnection()
    throws NamingException, SQLException {

  InitialContext ic = new InitialContext();
  DataSource ds = (DataSource) ic.lookup(dbName);
  connection = ds.getConnection();
}

public int getNextOrderNumber()
    throws SQLException {

  String setNext = "UPDATE ordnoseq " +
    "SET orderNumber = orderNumber + 1";

  String getNext = "SELECT orderNumber FROM ordnoseq";

  int n = 0;

  PreparedStatement ps1 = connection.prepareStatement(setNext);
  PreparedStatement ps2 = connection.prepareStatement(getNext);
  ps1.executeUpdate();
  ResultSet rs = ps2.executeQuery();
  rs.next();
```

```
        n = rs.getInt(1);
        rs.close();
        ps1.close();
        ps2.close();
        return n;
    }
}
```

The Revised PartsManager Bean

```
import javax.rmi.*;
import java.rmi.*;
import java.util.*;
import javax.ejb.*;
import javax.naming.*;

public class PartsManagerBean implements SessionBean {

    public String productID;
    public int quantityOnHand;
    public int minimumReorderQuantity;
    public int standardOrderQuantity;

    private SessionContext context;

    public void ejbCreate(String productID)
        throws CreateException {

      if (productID == null) {
        throw new CreateException("You must specify a productID.");
      }

      this.productID = productID;
    }

    public void ejbCreate() throws CreateException {
    }

    public void setSessionContext(SessionContext context) {
      this.context = context;
    }

    public void ejbActivate() {
    }

    public void ejbPassivate() {
    }
```

```
public void ejbRemove() {
}

public int getQuantityOnHand(String productID)
  throws RemoteException {
  Stockroom sr = getStockroom(productID);
  return sr.getQuantityOnHand();
}

public void setQuantityOnHand(String productID, int q)
    throws RemoteException {
  Stockroom sr = getStockroom(productID);
  sr.setQuantityOnHand(q);
}

public int getMinimumReorderQuantity(String productID)
    throws RemoteException {
  Stockroom sr = getStockroom(productID);
  return sr.getMinimumReorderQuantity();
}

public void setMinimumReorderQuantity(String productID, int q)
    throws RemoteException {
  Stockroom sr = getStockroom(productID);
  sr.setMinimumReorderQuantity(q);
}

public int getStandardOrderQuantity(String productID)
    throws RemoteException {
  Stockroom sr = getStockroom(productID);
  return sr.getStandardOrderQuantity();
}

public void setStandardOrderQuantity(String productID, int q)
    throws RemoteException {
  Stockroom sr = getStockroom(productID);
  sr.setStandardOrderQuantity(q);
}

public void stock(String productID)
    throws RemoteException {
  stock(productID, 1);
}

public void stock(String productID, int quantity)
    throws RemoteException {
  Stockroom sr = getStockroom(productID);
  sr.stock(quantity);
}

public void take(String productID)
    throws RemoteException {
  take(productID, 1);
}
```

```
public void take(String productID, int quantity)
    throws RemoteException {
  Stockroom sr = getStockroom(productID);
  sr.take(quantity);
}

public void holdForDriver(String productID, String truckNumber)
    throws RemoteException,EJBException {
  if (truckNumber == null) {
    throw new EJBException("hold requires truck number");
  }
  holdForDriver(productID, truckNumber, 1);
}

public void holdForDriver(String productID, String truckNumber,
                          int q)
    throws RemoteException, EJBException {
  if (truckNumber == null) {
    throw new EJBException("hold requires truck number");
  }
  Stockroom sr = getStockroom(productID);
  if (sr.take(q) < 0) {
    throw new EJBException("not available");
  }
}

public void sendToDriver(String productID, String truckNumber)
    throws RemoteException, EJBException {
  if (truckNumber == null) {
    throw new EJBException("field dispatch requires truck
      number");
  }
  sendToDriver(productID, truckNumber, 1);
}

public void sendToDriver(String productID, String truckNumber,
     int q)
    throws RemoteException, EJBException {
  if (truckNumber == null) {
    throw new EJBException("field dispatch requires truck
      number");
  }
  Stockroom sr = getStockroom(productID);
  if (sr.take(q) < 0) {
    throw new EJBException("not available");
  }
}

public int getDispatchTime(String productID, String truckNumber)
    throws RemoteException, EJBException {
  if (truckNumber == null) {
    throw new EJBException("get dispatch time requires truck
      number");
  }
  return 25;
}
```

```
public String[] getOrder(int orderNumber) {
  String[] order = new String[4];
  try {
    Context initial = new InitialContext();
    Object objref = initial.lookup("java:comp/env/ejb/
      Warehouse");

    WarehouseHome home =
      (WarehouseHome)PortableRemoteObject.narrow(objref,
        WarehouseHome.class);

    Warehouse warehouse = home.create();
    order = warehouse.getOrder(orderNumber);
    warehouse.remove();
  }
  catch (Exception e) {
    System.out.println("Caught an exception");
    e.printStackTrace();
  }
  finally {
    return order;
  }
}

public String[] [] getOutstandingOrders(String customerID) {
  String[] [] orders = null;
  try {
    Context initial = new InitialContext();
    Object objref =
      initial.lookup("java:comp/env/ejb/Warehouse");

    WarehouseHome home =
      (WarehouseHome)PortableRemoteObject.narrow(objref,
        WarehouseHome.class);

    Warehouse warehouse = home.create();
    orders = warehouse.getOutstandingOrders(customerID);
    warehouse.remove();
  }
  catch (Exception e) {
    System.out.println("Caught an exception");
    e.printStackTrace();
  }
  finally {
    return orders;
  }
}
public void closeOrder(int orderNumber) {
  try {
    Context initial = new InitialContext();
    Object objref =
      initial.lookup("java:comp/env/ejb/Warehouse");

    WarehouseHome home =
      (WarehouseHome)PortableRemoteObject.narrow(objref,
        WarehouseHome.class);
```

```java
      Warehouse warehouse = home.create();
      warehouse.closeOrder(orderNumber);
      warehouse.remove();
    }
    catch (Exception e) {
      System.out.println("Caught an exception");
      e.printStackTrace();
    }
  }

  private Stockroom getStockroom(String productID) {
    try {
      Context initial = new InitialContext();
      Object objref =
        initial.lookup("java:comp/env/ejb/Stockroom");

      StockroomHome home =
        (StockroomHome)PortableRemoteObject.narrow(objref,
          StockroomHome.class);

      return home.findByPrimaryKey(productID);
    }
    catch (NamingException e) {
      throw new EJBException("ERROR 100 - Notify System
        Administrator");
    }

    catch (RemoteException e) {
      throw new EJBException("ERROR 101 - Notify System
        Administrator");
    }

    catch (Exception e) {
      throw new EJBException("can't find " + productID);
    }
  }
}
```

ManageStockroom.html

 \Chapter8\code\ManageStockroom.html

```html
<html>
<head>
  <title>Manage Stockroom</title>
</head>
```

```
<body>
  <center>
    <font face="Arial,Helvetica"><font size="+1">
    Manage Stockroom
    </font>
    <br>
    <form method="post" action=
      "http://localhost:8000/CH8/WorkDirector">
      <table COLS=1 WIDTH="50%" >
        <tr>
          <td width="25%">
            <input type="radio" name="np"
              value="ProcessShipment.jsp" checked>
            Process Received Shipment
          </td>
        </tr>

        <tr>
          <td>
            <input type="radio" name="np"
              value="GetOrders.jsp">
            Get Outstanding Orders
          </td>
        </tr>
      </table>
      <p>
      <input type="submit" value="SUBMIT">
    </form>
  </body>
</html>
```

GetOrders.jsp

 \Chapter8\code\GetOrders.jsp

```
<%@ include file="GetPartsManager.jsp" %>
<jsp:useBean id="qpBean" scope="request"
  class="QueryParms" />
<jsp:setProperty name="qpBean" property="*" />
<%
  String[] [] orders = partsManager.getOutstandingOrders("112112");
  if (orders.length == 0) {
%>
<jsp:forward page="OrderListEmpty.jsp" />
<%
```

```
      }
%>
<html>
<head>
 <title>Outstanding Orders</title>
</head>
<body>
<center>
<font face="Arial,Helvetica"><font size=+1>
<p>
Outstanding Orders
</font></font>
<br>
<form method="post" action=
  "http://localhost:8000/CH8/WorkDirector">
<table BORDER COLS=4 WIDTH="80%" >
  <tr>
    <td align="center" width="25%">
      Order #
    </td>
    <td align="center" width="25%">
      Part #
    </td>
    <td align="center" width="25%">
      Quantity
    </td>
    <td align="center" width="25%">
      Delivery Date
    </td>
  </tr>
<% for (int i = 0; i < orders.length; ++i) {
%>
  <tr>
    <td>
      <input type="radio" name="orderNumber"
        value="<%= orders[i][0] %>">
      <%= orders[i][0] %>
    </td>
<%
    for (int j = 1; j < 4; ++j) {
%>
    <td width="25%">
      <%= orders[i][j] %>
    </td>
<%
    }
%>
  </tr>
<%
  }
%>
</table>
<br>
<table>
  <tr>
    <td>
      <input type="radio" name="np" value="ViewOrder.jsp" checked>
```

```
      </td>
      <td>
        View Order
      </td>
    </tr>
    <tr>
      <td>
        <input type="radio" name="np" value="CloseOrder.jsp">
      </td>
      <td>
        Close Order
      </td>
    </tr>
</table>
<input type="submit" value="SUBMIT"
</form>
</body>
</html>
```

ViewOrder.jsp

 \Chapter8\code\ViewOrder.jsp

```
<%@ include file="GetPartsManager.jsp" %>
<jsp:useBean id="qpBean" scope="request"
  class="QueryParms" />
<jsp:setProperty name="qpBean" property="*" />
<%
  String[] order = partsManager.getOrder(qpBean.getOrderNumber());
%>
<html>
<head>
  <title>Order</title>
</head>
<body>
<center>
<font face="Arial,Helvetica"><font size=+1>
Order #
<jsp:getProperty name="qpBean" property="orderNumber" />
<p>
</font></font>
<br>
<table BORDER COLS=2 WIDTH="80%%" >
  <tr>
    <td width="20%">
```

```
        Customer ID;
      </td>

    <td>
      <%= order[0] %>
    </td>
  </tr>


  <tr>
    <td width="20%">
      Part #:
    </td>

    <td>
      <%= order[1] %>
    </td>
  </tr>


  <tr>
    <td width="20%">
      Quantity:
    </td>

    <td>
      <%= order[2] %>
    </td>
  </tr>


  <tr>
    <td width="20%">
      Delivery Date:
    </td>

    <td>
      <%= order[3] %>
    </td>
  </tr>

</table>
<br>
<form method="post" action=
  "http://localhost:8000/CH8/WorkDirector">
<input type="hidden" name="orderNumber"
  value="<jsp:getProperty name="qpBean" property="orderNumber" />"
<table>
  <tr>
    <td>
      <input type="radio" name="np" value="CloseOrder.jsp" checked>
    </td>
    <td>
      Close Order
    </td>
  </tr>
```

```
    <tr>
      <td>
        <input type="radio" name="np" value="GetOrders.jsp">
      </td>
      <td>
        View Outstanding Odrers
      </td>
    </tr>
</table>
<br>
<input type="submit" value="SUBMIT"
</form>
</body>
</html>
```

CloseOrder.jsp

 On the CD

\Chapter8\code\CloseOrder.jsp

```
<%@ include file="GetPartsManager.jsp" %>
<jsp:useBean id="qpBean" scope="request"
  class="QueryParms" />
<jsp:setProperty name="qpBean" property="*" />
<%
    partsManager.closeOrder(qpBean.getOrderNumber());
%>
<html>
<head>
  <title>Confirmation</title>
</head>
<body>
<center>
<font face="Arial,Helvetica"><font size=+1>
<br>
<br>
Order #
<jsp:getProperty name="qpBean" property="orderNumber" />
closed
<br>
<br>
<br>
<a href="http://localhost:8000/CH8/ManageStockroom.html">
Return to Main Menu
</a>
</center>
</body>
</html>
```

OrderListEmpty.jsp

 On the CD

\Chapter8\code\OrderListEmpty.jsp

```
<html>
<head>
  <title>Empty List Orders</title>
</head>
<body>
<center>
<font face="Arial,Helvetica"><font size=+1>
<p>
No Outstanding Orders
</font></font>
<br>
<br>
<br>
<a href="http://localhost:8000/CH8/ManageStockroom.html">
Return to Main Menu
</a>
</center>
</body>
</html>
```

 ## ProcessShipment.jsp

On the CD

\Chapter8\code\ProcessShipment.jsp

```
<html>
<head>
  <title>Process Received Shipment</title>
</head>
<body>
<center>
<font face="Arial,Helvetica"><font size="+1">
Process Received Shipment
</font>
<br>
<br>
```

```
THIS FUNCTION IS NOT YET IMPLEMENTED
<br>
<br>
<a href="http://localhost:8000/CH8/ManageStockroom.html">
Return to main menu
</a>
</font>
</center>
</body>
</html>
```

Summary

In this chapter, we discussed the concept of a transaction and used a bean-managed JDBC transaction to implement the warehouse component of an automated ordering process.

The relative ease with which we extended the functionality of our original Roadside Assistance serves as testimony to the contribution EJBs make to the development process.

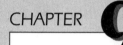

The Automatic
Teller Machine

In this chapter:

- The ATM
- A Bean-Managed JTA Transaction

In the last chapter we used a JDBC transaction. In this chapter we use the Java Transaction API (JTA) to implement a simple Automatic Teller Machine (ATM).

The ATM

The basic steps one performs when using an ATM are:

- Provide identification (a magnetic card plus a Personal Identification Number, or PIN)
- Select the type of transaction
- Specify a monetary amount (except when the transaction is an inquiry)
- Initiate the transaction

We will use a browser to simulate an ATM. Instead of inserting a magnetic card on which our account number has been recorded and then entering a PIN (the "something you have, something you know" approach to security), we will simply enter an account number. The transactions we will allow are:

- withdraw cash from checking
- withdraw cash from savings
- query checking balance
- query savings balance
- transfer money from checking to savings
- transfer money from savings to checking

We will use a single JSP that handles the display and an intermediate JavaBean that interacts with the ATM bean to carry out the transactions.

The Remote Interface

The code for the remote interface is shown below:

\Chapter9\code\Atm.java

```java
import javax.ejb.EJBObject;
import java.rmi.RemoteException;

public interface Atm extends EJBObject {

  public void withdrawFromChecking(double amount)
    throws RemoteException;

  public void withdrawFromSavings(double amount)
    throws RemoteException;

  public void transferFromCheckingToSavings(double amount)
    throws RemoteException;

  public void transferFromSavingsToChecking(double amount)
    throws RemoteException;

  public double getCheckingBalance()
    throws RemoteException;

  public double getSavingsBalance()
    throws RemoteException;

  public String getCustomerName()
    throws RemoteException;
}
```

The Home Interface

The home interface is listed below:

\Chapter9\code\AtmHome.java

```java
import java.rmi.RemoteException;
import javax.ejb.*;
```

```
public interface AtmHome extends EJBHome {

    public Atm create(String id)
        throws RemoteException, CreateException;
}
```

The Enterprise Bean

The complete listing of the *ATM* EJB is shown at the end of the chapter. It uses the Java Transaction API (JTA). Unlike a JDBC transaction, which is controlled by the DBMS, a JTA transaction is controlled by the J2EE transaction manager.

A JTA transaction uses the *UserTransaction* interface, which contains methods that allow an application to explicitly manage transaction boundaries. We will see how transaction boundaries are demarcated by examining a single method, withdrawFrom-Checking(). The other methods are similar. Here is the code:

```
public void withdrawFromChecking(double amount) {

    UserTransaction userTransaction =
        context.getUserTransaction();

    try {
        userTransaction.begin();
        updateChecking(-amount);
        machineBalance -= amount;
        putCashInMachine(machineBalance);
        userTransaction.commit();
    }
    catch (Exception e) {
        try {
            userTransaction.rollback();
        }
        catch (SystemException se) {
            throw new EJBException
                ("Rollback failed: " + se.getMessage());
        }
        throw new EJBException
            ("Transaction failed: " + e.getMessage());
    }
}
```

The method first obtains the transaction demarcation interface by invoking the getUserTransaction() interface on the *Session-*

Context object that was saved in the bean's setSessionContext() method. We can see that the transaction is started explicitly by invocation of the begin() method. Within the confines of the transaction, the method then invokes two methods within its own class to update the tables containing checking account data and the amount of cash in the ATM machine. After the updates have been applied, the commit() method is invoked. If any exceptions are thrown, they are caught by a catch block, which invokes the rollback() method.

The JSP

All of the ATM transactions are handled by a single JavaServer Page, which is listed at the end of the chapter. This page uses an intermediate JavaBean to communicate with the EJB, a technique we have already seen. The JSP starts by using the <jsp:setProperty> action to save all of the data from the HTML form that called it in instance variables of the intermediate JavaBean. Next, from within a scriptlet, it invokes the performTransaction() method of the intermediate JavaBean. Finally, it presents the checking and/or savings balance(s) returned by the performTransaction() method.

Packaging and Deploying

We begin by compiling the EJB and the intermediate JavaBean used by the JSP. We use *compileAtm.bat* to do the former and accomplish the latter by simply typing:

```
javac AtmIntermediateBean
```

 ■ ■ ■ ■ ■ ■ ■ ■ ■ ■ ■ ■ ■ ■ ■

\Chapter9\code\compileAtm.bat

Packaging involves the following:

- Create an application with an application file name of *AtmApp.ear* and application display name of *AtmApp*.

- Add a JAR file named *AtmJAR*.

- Add the *Atm* EJB to the JAR file using the following parameters:
  - `Display Name`—AtmBean
  - `Bean Type`—stateful session
  - `Enterprise Bean Class`—AtmBean
  - `Home Interface`—AtmHome
  - `Remote Interface`—Atm
  - Resource References
    1. `Coded Name`—jdbc/AtmDB
    2. `Type`—javax.sql.DataSource
    3. `Authentication`—Container

- Add a WAR file named *AtmWAR*.

- Add *AtmTransaction.jsp* to the WAR file with an alias of *DoTransaction*. Include the JavaBean named *AtmIntermediate-Bean* following the same procedure as we did in Chapter 6 for the *CatalogBean*.

- Add *ATM.html* to the WAR file specifying "No Web Component" as the `Component Type`.

- Select the WAR file and then use the EJB REFERENCES tab to add an entry with values of *ejb/Atm* for `Coded Name`, *Entity* for `Type`, *AtmHome* for `Home`, and *Atm* for `Remote`.

When we deploy the application, we specify the following JNDI names:

Referenced by	Component/Reference Name	JNDI Name
	AtmBean	MyAtm
AtmBean	jdbc/AtmDB	jdbc/Cloudscape
AtmWAR	ejb/Atm	MyAtm

We specify *CH9* as the Web Context.

The Database

The database contains four tables. The first, named *customer,* is used to hold customer information. Its primary key is a unique customer identifier. The customer names we will see displayed later are also stored in this table. Two tables, *checking* and *savings,* are used to hold the current balance for checking accounts and savings accounts, respectively. The keys in these tables must appear in the *customer* table. The fourth table, *machinefunds,* contains a single row that holds the amount of cash in the machine.

We create and populate the tables using the following SQL:

\Chapter8\code\createATM.sql

```
drop table savings;
drop table checking;
drop table customer;

create table customer
(id char(6) constraint pk_customer primary key,
name_first varchar(15),
name_last varchar(25));

insert into customer
values ('121212', 'John', 'Johnson'),
       ('131313', 'Susan', 'Smith'),
       ('141414', 'James', 'Jackson');

create table checking
(id char(6) ,
balance decimal(10,2),
constraint fk_checking foreign key(id) references customer(id));

insert into checking
values ('121212', 500.00),
       ('131313', 725.00),
       ('141414', 820.00);

create table savings
(id char(6),
balance decimal(10,2),
constraint fk_savings foreign key(id) references customer(id));

insert into savings
values ('121212', 25500.00),
```

```
                ('131313', 15225.00),
                ('141414', 17255.00);

drop table machinefunds;
create table machinefunds
(amount decimal(10,2),
time_stamp date);

insert into machinefunds
values (10000.00, current_date);

exit;
```

We execute the SQL using *createAtm.bat*.

 ■ ■ ■ ■ ■ ■ ■ ■ ■ ■ ■ ■ ■ ■ ■ ■ ■ ■ ■

\Chapter8\code\createAtm.bat

Running Our Application

We access the ATM using the following URL:

```
http://localhost:8000/CH9/ATM.html
```

When the first screen appears, we enter a customer ID of 121212 and specify an amount of $100 as shown in Figure 9-1. We select the radio button labeled WITHDRAW FROM CHECKING.

When the transaction has completed successfully, output like that shown in Figure 9-2 is displayed.

If the customer only wishes to determine an account's current balance, it is not necessary to enter an amount. Figure 9-3 demonstrates such an inquiry. When the transaction has completed successfully, Figure 9-4 is displayed.

One last transaction the customer can make involves no disbursement of funds but transfers funds between the customer's checking and savings accounts. Such a transaction is initiated as shown in Figure 9-5. Upon successful completion of this transaction, output like that shown in Figure 9-6 is displayed.

Figure 9-1
Customer 121212
Withdraws $100 from
Checking

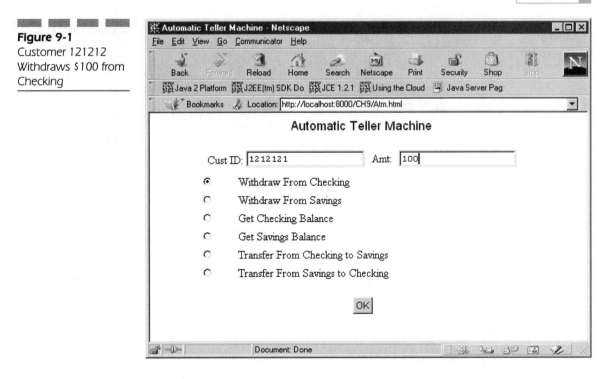

AtmBean

\Chapter9\code\AtmBean.java

```java
import java.util.*;
import javax.ejb.*;
import java.sql.*;
import javax.sql.*;
import javax.naming.*;
import javax.transaction.*;


public class AtmBean implements SessionBean {
private String customerId;
private double machineBalance;
private SessionContext context;
private Connection con;
private String dbName = "java:comp/env/jdbc/AtmDB";


public void withdrawFromChecking(double amount) {
```

Figure 9-2
Cash Disbursement
and Current Balance

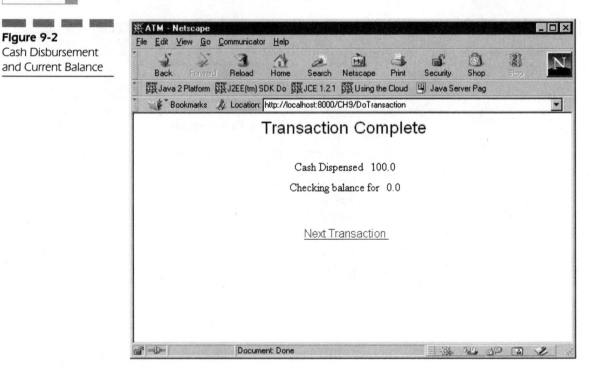

```
UserTransaction userTransaction =
  context.getUserTransaction();


try {
  userTransaction.begin();
  updateChecking(-amount);
  machineBalance -= amount;
  putCashInMachine(machineBalance);
  userTransaction.commit();
}
catch (Exception e) {
  try {
    userTransaction.rollback();
  }
  catch (SystemException se) {
    throw new EJBException
      ("Rollback failed: " + se.getMessage());
    }
    throw new EJBException
      ("Transaction failed: " + e.getMessage());
  }
}


public void withdrawFromSavings(double amount) {
```

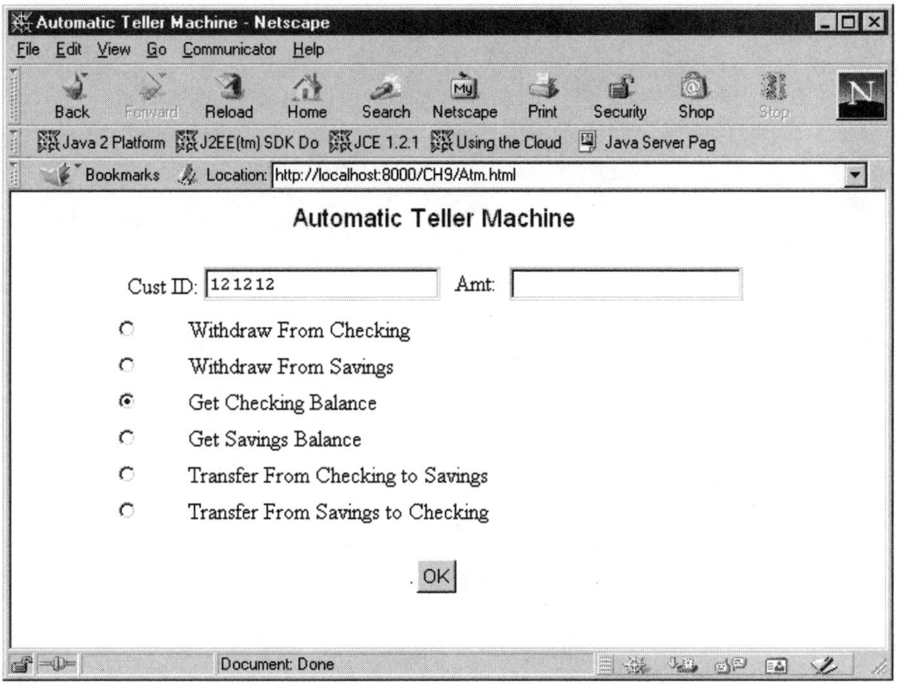

Figure 9-3
Customer 121212
Determines Balance of
Checking Account

```
UserTransaction userTransaction = context.getUserTransaction();

try {
  userTransaction.begin();
  updateSavings(-amount);
  machineBalance -= amount;
  putCashInMachine(machineBalance);
  userTransaction.commit();
}
catch (Exception e) {
  try {
    userTransaction.rollback();
  }
  catch (SystemException se) {
    throw new EJBException
      ("Rollback failed: " + se.getMessage());
    }
    throw new EJBException
      ("Transaction failed: " + e.getMessage());
  }
}

public void transferFromCheckingToSavings(double amount) {

  UserTransaction userTransaction = context.getUserTransaction();
```

Figure 9-4
Checking Account
Balance

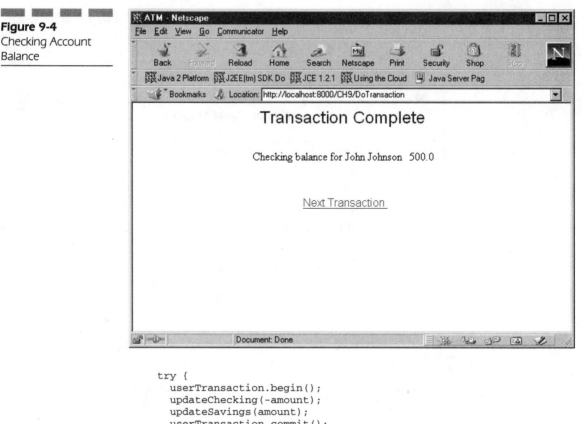

```
    try {
      userTransaction.begin();
      updateChecking(-amount);
      updateSavings(amount);
      userTransaction.commit();
    }
    catch (Exception e) {
      try {
        userTransaction.rollback();
      }
      catch (SystemException se) {
        throw new EJBException
          ("Rollback failed: " + se.getMessage());
      }
      throw new EJBException
        ("Transaction failed: " + e.getMessage());
    }
  }

  public void transferFromSavingsToChecking(double amount) {

    UserTransaction userTransaction = context.getUserTransaction();

    try {

      userTransaction.begin();
```

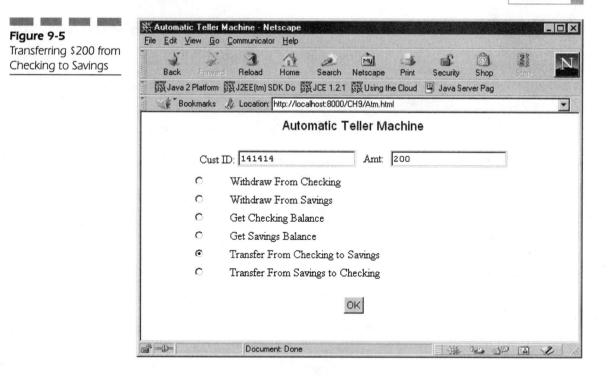

Figure 9-5
Transferring $200 from
Checking to Savings

```
      updateSavings(-amount);

      updateChecking(amount);

      userTransaction.commit();

    }

    catch (Exception e) {

      try {

        userTransaction.rollback();

      }

      catch (SystemException se) {

        throw new EJBException

          ("Rollback failed: " + se.getMessage());
```

Figure 9-6
Account Balances
After Transfer of Funds

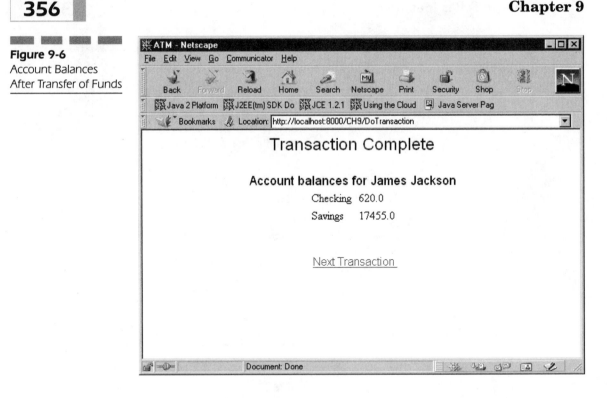

```
        }

    throw new EJBException

        ("Transaction failed: " + e.getMessage());

    }

}

public double getCheckingBalance() {

    try {

    return selectFromChecking();

    }

    catch (SQLException e) {

    throw new EJBException ("Unable to get balance: " +
```

```
                    e.getMessage());

    }

}

public double getSavingsBalance() {

  try {
    return selectFromSavings();
  }
  catch (SQLException e) {
      throw new EJBException ("Unable to get balance: " +
        e.getMessage());
  }
}

public void ejbCreate(String id) throws CreateException {
  String selectStatement =
    "SELECT amount " +
    "FROM machinefunds " +
    "WHERE time_stamp = " +
    "(SELECT max(time_stamp) FROM machinefunds)";

  customerId = id;

  try {
    makeConnection();

    PreparedStatement ps =
      con.prepareStatement(selectStatement);

    ResultSet rs = ps.executeQuery();

    if (rs.next()) {
      machineBalance = rs.getDouble(1);
      ps.close();
    }
    else {
    ps.close();
    throw new EJBException
      ("Row for id " + customerId + " not found.");
    }
  }
  catch (Exception e) {
    throw new CreateException(e.getMessage());
  }
}

public void ejbRemove() {

  try {
    con.close();
```

```
    }
    catch (SQLException ex) {
      throw new EJBException(ex.getMessage());
    }
  }

  public void ejbActivate() {

    try {
      makeConnection();
    }
    catch (Exception e) {
      throw new EJBException(e.getMessage());
    }
  }

  public void ejbPassivate() {

    try {
      con.close();
    }
    catch (SQLException e) {
      throw new EJBException(e.getMessage());
    }
  }

  public void setSessionContext(SessionContext context) {
    this.context = context;
  }

  private void makeConnection()
      throws NamingException, SQLException {

    InitialContext ic = new InitialContext();
    DataSource ds = (DataSource) ic.lookup(dbName);
    con = ds.getConnection();
  }

  private void updateChecking(double amount)
      throws SQLException {

    String updateStatement =
      "UPDATE checking SET balance = balance + ? " +
      "WHERE id = ?";

    PreparedStatement ps =
      con.prepareStatement(updateStatement);

    ps.setDouble(1, amount);
    ps.setString(2, customerId);
    ps.executeUpdate();
    ps.close();
  }
```

```java
private void updateSavings(double amount)
    throws SQLException {

  String updateStatement =
    "UPDATE savings SET balance = balance + ? " +
    "WHERE id = ?";

  PreparedStatement ps =
    con.prepareStatement(updateStatement);

  ps.setDouble(1, amount);
  ps.setString(2, customerId);
  ps.executeUpdate();
  ps.close();
}

private void putCashInMachine(double amount)
    throws SQLException {

  String insertStatement =
    "INSERT INTO machinefunds values " +
    "( ? , current_date )";

  PreparedStatement ps =
    con.prepareStatement(insertStatement);

  ps.setDouble(1, amount);
  ps.executeUpdate();
  ps.close();
}

private double selectFromChecking() throws SQLException {

  String selectStatement =
    "SELECT balance " +
    "FROM checking " +
    "WHERE id = ?";

  PreparedStatement ps =
    con.prepareStatement(selectStatement);

  ps.setString(1, customerId);
  ResultSet rs = ps.executeQuery();

  if (rs.next()) {
    double result = rs.getDouble(1);
    ps.close();
    return result;
  }
  else {
    ps.close();
    throw new EJBException
```

```
            ("Row for id " + customerId + " not found.");
    }
}


public String getCustomerName() throws SQLException {

    String selectStatement =
      "SELECT name_first,name_last " +
      "FROM customer " +
      "WHERE id = ?";

    PreparedStatement ps =
      con.prepareStatement(selectStatement);

    ps.setString(1, customerId);
    ResultSet rs = ps.executeQuery();

    if (rs.next()) {
      StringBuffer sb = new StringBuffer(rs.getString(1));
      sb.append(" ");
      sb.append(rs.getString(2));
      ps.close();
      return sb.toString();
    }
    else {
      ps.close();
      throw new EJBException
        ("Row for id " + customerId + " not found.");
    }
}

private double selectFromSavings() throws SQLException {

    String selectStatement =
      "SELECT balance " +
      "FROM savings " +
      "WHERE id = ?";

    PreparedStatement ps =
      con.prepareStatement(selectStatement);

    ps.setString(1, customerId);
    ResultSet rs = ps.executeQuery();

    if (rs.next()) {
      double result = rs.getDouble(1);
      ps.close();
      return result;
      }
      else {
        ps.close();
        throw new EJBException
          ("Row for id " + customerId + " not found.");
```

```
      }
    }
  }
```

AtmIntermediateBean

 \Chapter8\code\AtmIntermediateBean.java

```java
import javax.naming.*;
import javax.rmi.*;

public class AtmIntermediateBean {

  private double checkingBalance = 0.0;
  private double savingsBalance = 0.0;

  private String customerId;
  private String customerName;
  private double amount = 0.0;

  private int transaction;

  static final int WITHDRAW_FROM_CHECKING = 1;
  static final int WITHDRAW_FROM_SAVINGS = 2;
  static final int GET_CHECKING_BALANCE = 3;
  static final int GET_SAVINGS_BALANCE = 4;
  static final int TRANSFER_FROM_CHECKING_TO_SAVINGS = 5;
  static final int TRANSFER_FROM_SAVINGS_TO_CHECKING = 6;

  public AtmIntermediateBean() {
  }

  public String getCustomerName() {
    return customerName;
  }

  public int getTransaction() {
    return transaction;
  }

  public void setTransaction(int transaction) {
    this.transaction = transaction;
  }
```

```java
public double getCheckingBalance() {
  return checkingBalance;
}

public double getSavingsBalance() {
  return savingsBalance;
}

public double getAmount() {
  return amount;
}

public void setAmount(double amount) {
  this.amount = amount;
}

public String getCustomerId() {
  return customerId;
}

public void setCustomerId(String customerId) {
  this.customerId = customerId;
}

public void performTransaction() throws Exception {

  try {
    Context initial = new InitialContext();
    Object objref =
    initial.lookup("java:comp/env/ejb/Atm");
  AtmHome home =
    (AtmHome)PortableRemoteObject.narrow(objref,
    AtmHome.class);
  Atm atm = home.create(customerId);

  customerName = atm.getCustomerName();

  switch (transaction) {
    case WITHDRAW_FROM_CHECKING:
      atm.withdrawFromChecking(amount);
      checkingBalance = atm.getCheckingBalance();
      break;
    case WITHDRAW_FROM_SAVINGS:
      atm.withdrawFromSavings(amount);
      savingsBalance = atm.getSavingsBalance();
      break;
    case GET_CHECKING_BALANCE:
      checkingBalance = atm.getCheckingBalance();
      break;
    case GET_SAVINGS_BALANCE:
      savingsBalance = atm.getSavingsBalance();
      break;
    case TRANSFER_FROM_CHECKING_TO_SAVINGS:
      atm.transferFromCheckingToSavings(amount);
```

```
            checkingBalance = atm.getCheckingBalance();
            savingsBalance = atm.getSavingsBalance();
            break;
        case TRANSFER_FROM_SAVINGS_TO_CHECKING:
            atm.transferFromSavingsToChecking(amount);
            checkingBalance = atm.getCheckingBalance();
            savingsBalance = atm.getSavingsBalance();
            break;
        default:
            System.err.println("Caught an exception." );
            throw new Exception("internal error");
        }
      atm.remove();
    }
    catch (Exception e) {
        System.err.println("Caught an exception." );
        e.printStackTrace();
    }
  }
}
```

AtmTransaction.jsp

 \Chapter9\code\AtmTransaction.jsp

```
<jsp:useBean id="atmBean" class="AtmIntermediateBean"
  scope="request" />
<jsp:setProperty name="atmBean" property="*" />
<%
   atmBean.performTransaction();
%>
<html>
<head>
<title>ATM</title>
</head>
<body>
<center>
<font face="Arial, Helvetica"><font size="+2">
Transaction Complete
<br>
<br>
</font>
<font size="+1">
<%
   int transaction = atmBean.getTransaction();
   if ((transaction == 1) || (transaction == 2))
```

```
%>
<table>
<tr>
<td>
  Cash Dispensed
</td>
<td>
<jsp:getProperty name="atmBean" property="amount" />
</td>
</tr>
</table>
<%
  }

  switch (transaction) {
    case 1:
    case 3:
%>
<table>
  <tr>
    <td>
      Checking balance for
      <jsp:getProperty name="atmBean" property="customerName" />
    </td>
    <td>
      <jsp:getProperty name="atmBean" property="checkingBalance" />
    </td>
  </tr>
</table>
<%
    break;
    case 2:
    case 4:
%>
<table>
  <tr>
    <td>
      Savings balance for
      <jsp:getProperty name="atmBean" property="customerName" />
    </td>
    <td>
      <jsp:getProperty name="atmBean" property="savingsBalance" />
    </td>
  </tr>
</table>
<%
    break;
    case 5:
    case 6:
%>
    Account balances for
    <jsp:getProperty name="atmBean" property="customerName" />
    <br>
<table>
  <tr>
    <td>
      Checking
```

```
        </td>
        <td>
          <jsp:getProperty name="atmBean" property="checkingBalance" />
        </td>
      </tr>
      <tr>
        <td>
          Savings
        </td>
        <td>
          <jsp:getProperty name="atmBean" property="savingsBalance" />
        </td>
      </tr>
    </table>
    <%
          break;
      }
    %>
    <br>
    <br>
    </font>
    <a href="http://localhost:8000/CH9/Atm.html">
    Next Transaction
    </a>
    </font>
    </center>
    </body>
    </html>
```

 ## ATM.html

 On The CD   *\Chapter8\code\ATM.html*

```
    <html>
    <head>
      <title>Automatic Teller Machine</title>
    </head>
    <body>
    <font face="Arial,Helvetica"><font size="+1">
    <center>
    Automatic Teller Machine
    </font></font>
    <form method="post" action=
      "http://localhost:8000/CH9/DoTransaction">
    <table>
    <tr>
```

```
<td>
Cust ID:
<input type="text" name="customerId">
</td>
<td>
Amt:
</td>
<td>
<input type="text" name="amount">
</td>
</tr>
</table>
<table width="80%">
  <tr>
    <td>
      <input type="radio" name="transaction" value=1 checked>
    </td>
    <td>
      Withdraw From Checking
    </td>
  </tr>
  <tr>
    <td>
      <input type="radio" name="transaction" value=2 >
    </td>
    <td>
      Withdraw From Savings
    </td>
  </tr>
  <tr>
    <td>
      <input type="radio" name="transaction" value=3 >
    </td>
    <td>
      Get Checking Balance
    </td>
  </tr>
  <tr>
    <td>
      <input type="radio" name="transaction" value=4 >
    </td>
    <td>
      Get Savings Balance
    </td>
  </tr>
  <tr>
    <td>
      <input type="radio" name="transaction" value=5 >
    </td>
    <td>
      Transfer From Checking to Savings
    </td>
  </tr>
  <tr>
    <td>
      <input type="radio" name="transaction" value=6 >
    </td>
    <td>
```

```
            Transfer From Savings to Checking
        </td>
      </tr>
  </table>
  <table>
    <tr>
      <td>
        Customer ID:
      </td>
      <td>
        <input type="text" name="customerID">
      </td>
    </tr>
      <td>
        Amount:
      </td>
      <td>
        <input type="text" name="amount">
      </td>
    </tr>
  <br>
  <input type="submit" value="OK">
</form>
</center>
</body>
</html>
```

 ## Summary

In this chapter we developed an application that uses bean-managed JTA transactions.

Another Approach to the ATM

In this chapter:

- Container-Managed Transactions
- Transaction Attributes
- An Alternate Implementation of an ATM
- Rollback
- Synchronization

We have seen bean-managed transactions that use JDBC and JTA. In this chapter, we expand our coverage of transactions to include container-managed transactions.

Container-Managed Transactions

When a bean uses container-managed transactions, the transaction boundaries are set by the EJB container and not by the bean. Because of this, beans that use container-managed transactions tend to be easier to develop. Unlike bean-managed transactions, which can be used only by session beans, container-managed transactions can be used by both session and entity beans.

In most implementations, the container begins a transaction before the method associated with the transaction begins and ends the transaction just before the method returns. Once a transaction has begun, no other transaction can be started; in other words, nesting is not permitted. Does this mean that we have to be constantly aware of such a restriction as we write each method? Do we have to keep track of whether the method is associated with a transaction and whether a method we wish to call is associated with a transaction so we can avoid breaking this no nesting rule? The answer is no; the container takes care of things. Before invoking a method, the container takes whatever actions are necessary to properly manage transactions.

Consider the case shown in Figure 10-1. The client, *Bean1,* is executing `businessMethodA()`, which is associated with a trans-

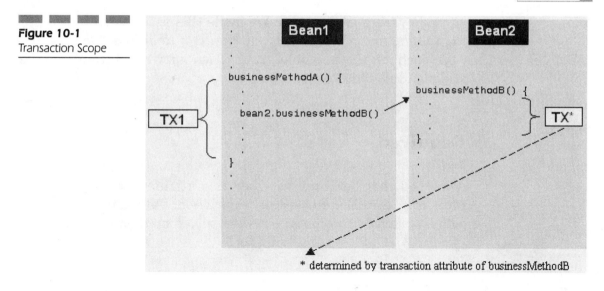

Figure 10-1
Transaction Scope

action. It invokes `businessMethodB()` in *Bean2*. Before invoking `businessMethodB()`, the container uses its transaction attribute to decide which of the following will happen:

- `businessMethodB()` executes within the scope of the transaction of `businessMethodA()`

- `businessMethodB()` executes within a new transaction

- `businessMethodB()` executes outside of any transaction

- `businessMethodB()` does not execute; an exception is thrown

Transaction Attributes

We associate a method with a transaction by assigning the method a transaction attribute in the Transaction Management dialog of the Application Deployment Tool. We have already assigned transaction attributes in earlier chapters. When we did so, we simply stated that the best way to maintain consistency between the state of a bean's instance variables and the underlying data store was to associate any method that used the instance variable with a transaction. We made this association by assigning the method a transaction attribute of *Required*. We now discuss each of the possible transaction attributes that can be assigned to a method.

Required

A method that has been assigned this attribute must *always* be invoked within the scope of a transaction. Table 10-1 shows the actions taken by the container when such a method is invoked.

Requires New

A method that has been assigned this attribute must always be invoked within the context of a *new* transaction. Table 10-2 shows the actions taken by the container when such a method is invoked.

Mandatory

A method that has been assigned this attribute can be invoked *only* by a client that supplies a transaction context. Table 10-3 shows the actions taken by the container when such a method is invoked.

TABLE 10-1

Container's Response to Required Attribute

Client Has No Transaction in Effect	Client Has Transaction in Effect
1. Creates a new transaction	1. Invokes the method within the client's transaction context
2. Invokes the method within the context of the new transaction	
3. Terminates the new transaction	
4. Returns to the client	

	Client Has No Transaction in Effect	Client Has Transaction in Effect
TABLE 10-2 Container's Response to Requires New Attribute	1. Creates a new transaction 2. Invokes the method within the context of the new transaction 3. Terminates the new transaction 4. Returns to the client	1. Suspends the client's transaction 2. Creates a new transaction 3. Invokes the method within the context of the new transaction 4. Terminates the new transaction 5. Resumes the client's transaction 6. Returns to the client

Not Supported

A method that has been assigned this attribute must *never* execute within a transaction. Table 10-4 shows the actions taken by the container when such a method is invoked.

Supports

A method that has been assigned this attribute can be invoked within the context of a transaction context supplied by a client. Table 10-5 shows the actions taken by the container when such a method is invoked.

	Client Has No Transaction in Effect	Client Has Transaction in Effect
TABLE 10-3 Container's Response to Mandatory Attribute	1. Throws a TransactionRequiredException to the client	1. Invokes the method within client's transaction context

	Client Has No Transaction in Effect	Client Has Transaction in Effect
TABLE 10-4 Container's Response to Not Supported Attribute	1. Invokes the method 2. Returns to the client	1. Suspends the client's transaction 2. Invokes the method 3. Resumes the client's transaction 4. Returns to the client

Never

A method that has been assigned this attribute can *never* be invoked within a transaction. Table 10-6 shows the actions taken by the container when such a method is invoked.

Figure 10-2 summarizes the transaction attributes and scope discussed earlier.

> **NOTE:** *In those cases where T2 Transactional Context is listed as "NONE", it means that the method does not execute with a transaction controlled by the container. The method might still be controlled by the transaction manager of the DBMS.*

The ATM

Now that we have discussed container-managed transactions, we will examine an EJB that uses them. The EJB is an alternate implementation of the Automatic Teller Machine we developed in

	Client Has No Transaction in Effect	Client Has Transaction in Effect
TABLE 10-5 Container's Response to Supports Attribute	1. Invokes the method with no transaction context	1. Invokes the method within the client's transaction context

TABLE 10-6	**Client Has No Transaction in Effect**	**Client Has Transaction in Effect**
Container's Response to *Never* Attribute	1. Invokes the method	1. Throws a RemoteException to the client

the last chapter and will use the same interface. To differentiate between the two implementations, we will call this one *AtmCmt*.

The Remote Interface

Here is the code for the remote interface:

On The CD ▬ ▬ ▬ ▬ ▬ ▬ ▬ ▬ ▬ ▬ ▬ ▬ ▬ ▬ ▬ ▬ ▬ ▬
\Chapter10\code\AtmCmt.java

Figure 10-2
Summary of Transaction Attributes and Scope

T2 Transaction Attribute	Client Transaction	T2 Transactional Context
Required	NONE / T1	T2 / T1
Requires New	NONE / T1	T2 / T2
Mandatory	NONE / T1	ERROR / T1
Not Supported	NONE / T1	NONE / NONE
Supports	NONE / T1	NONE / T1
Never	NONE / T1	NONE / ERROR

```
import javax.ejb.EJBObject;
import java.rmi.RemoteException;

public interface AtmCmt extends EJBObject {

  public void withdrawFromChecking(double amount)
    throws RemoteException, NegativeBalanceException;

  public void withdrawFromSavings(double amount)
    throws RemoteException, NegativeBalanceException;

  public void transferFromCheckingToSavings(double amount)
    throws RemoteException, NegativeBalanceException;

  public void transferFromSavingsToChecking(double amount)
    throws RemoteException, NegativeBalanceException;

  public double getCheckingBalance()
    throws RemoteException;

  public double getSavingsBalance()
    throws RemoteException;

  public String getCustomerName()
    throws RemoteException;
}
```

The Home Interface

The code for the home interface is as follows:

\Chapter10\code\AtmCmtHome.java

```
import java.rmi.RemoteException;
import javax.ejb.EJBHome;
import javax.ejb.CreateException;

public interface AtmCmtHome extends EJBHome {

  public AtmCmt create(String id)
      throws RemoteException, CreateException;
}
```

The Enterprise Bean

The enterprise bean code is listed in its entirety at the end of the chapter. We will list some of the methods as we now discuss some important aspects of the bean.

Rollback

Rollback in a bean using container-managed transactions is *always* handled by the container. Whether rollback occurs depends on the type of exception that is thrown. If a system exception is thrown, rollback is automatic. If an application exception is thrown, rollback is not automatic. When the application catches an application exception, it can use the `setRollbackOnly()` method of the *EJB-Context* interface to mark the transaction for rollback. Once this method has been invoked within a transaction, the only possible outcome for the transaction is rollback. As we see when we examine the `transferFromCheckingToSavings()` method shortly, the `setRollbackOnly()` method does not necessarily have to be invoked within a `catch` block but can be invoked at any time.

In light of what we just said about rollback in a container-managed transaction, let's examine the `transferFromCheckingToSavings()` method of *AtmCmtBean*. Here is the code:

```
public void transferFromCheckingToSavings(double amount)
    throws NegativeBalanceException {

  checkingBalance -= amount;
  savingsBalance += amount;

  try {
    updateChecking(checkingBalance);
    if (checkingBalance < 0.00) {
      context.setRollbackOnly();
      throw new NegativeBalanceException();
    }
    updateSavings(savingsBalance);
  }
  catch (SQLException e) {
    throw new EJBException
```

```
        ("Transaction failed due to SQLException: " +
          e.getMessage());
    }
}
```

The method first deducts the amount to be transferred from `checkingBalance` and adds the corresponding amount to `savingsBalance`. It then invokes the `updateChecking()` method passing the new balance as an argument. The `updateChecking()` method looks like this:

```
private void updateChecking(double amount) throws SQLException {

    String updateStatement =
      "UPDATE checking SET balance = ? " +
      "WHERE id = ?";

    PreparedStatement ps =
      connection.prepareStatement(updateStatement);

    ps.setDouble(1, amount);
    ps.setString(2, customerId);
    ps.executeUpdate();
    ps.close();
}
```

If the SQL UPDATE statement executed by `updateChecking()` fails, the method throws an *SQLException*, which is caught by the invoking method `transferFromCheckingToSavings()`. To ensure that the transaction is rolled back automatically, the `catch` block in `transferFromCheckingToSavings()` creates and throws an *EJBException,* using the message text obtained from the *SQLException*. Since *EJBException* is a system exception, rollback is automatic.

If `updateChecking()` returns successfully, the invoking method tests whether `checkingBalance` has become negative. If it has, `transferFromCheckingToSavings()` invokes the `setRollbackOnly()` method. From this point on, the current transaction is permanently marked for rollback by the container.

Since rollback is only automatic when a system exception is thrown, it is important that we know which exceptions are system exceptions. Table 10-7 classifies each of the exceptions in the *javax.ejb* package. In addition to those exceptions that are listed in

TABLE 10-7

Exceptions Thrown
by the `javax.ejb`
Package

Method	Exception	Type
ejbCreate	CreateException	Application
ejbFindByPrimaryKey (and all other finder methods)	ObjectNotFoundException	Application
ejbRemove	RemoveException	Application
ejbLoad	NoSuchEntityException	System
ejbStore	NoSuchEntityException	System
all other methods	EJBException	System

the table as application exceptions, any exception not found in the table should be regarded as an application exception.

The SessionSynchronization Interface

A bean that uses container-managed transactions can optionally implement the *SessionSynchronization* interface. When it chooses to implement this interface, it must provide implementations of the methods defined by the interface. These methods represent points in the life of a transaction and are invoked by the container. The methods are `afterBegin()`, `beforeCompletion()`, and `afterCompletion()`.

The `afterBegin()` method is invoked immediately before the container invokes the business method associated with the transaction. Here is the `afterBegin()` method of *AtmCmtBean:*

```
public void afterBegin() {

  try {
    checkingBalance = selectFromChecking();
    savingsBalance = selectFromSavings();
  }
  catch (SQLException e) {
    throw new EJBException("afterBegin Exception: " +
      e.getMessage());
  }
}
```

The code contained in this method is typical of what one finds in most `afterBegin()` implementations; it loads instance variables from the database.

The container invokes `beforeCompletion()` after all code in the business method has executed but before committing the transaction. This provides one final opportunity for the session bean to invoke the `setRollbackOnly()` method to roll back the transaction. Some applications also use this method to update the database from the instance variables. The `beforeCompletion()` method of our *AtmCmtBean* is empty.

The container invokes `afterCompletion()` when the transaction has completed. The method is invoked with a single argument. This argument is a `boolean`, which has a value of `true` if the transaction was committed and `false` if the transaction was rolled back. Here is the `afterCompletion()` method of our *AtmCmtBean:*

```
public void afterCompletion(boolean committed) {

   if (committed == false) {
     try {
       checkingBalance = selectFromChecking();
       savingsBalance = selectFromSavings();
     }
     catch (SQLException e) {
       throw new EJBException("afterCompletion SQLException: " +
            e.getMessage());
     }
   }
}
```

If the argument committed has a value of `false`, the instance variables `checkingBalance` and `savingsBalance` are refreshed from the database. This is necessary since instance variables of the session bean are not managed as part of the transaction and so can become out of synch with the values in the database.

Don't Mess Around with Jim

Invoking certain methods would interfere with transaction boundaries set by the container; such methods should never be invoked from a bean that is using container-managed transactions. Table 10-8 lists these methods.

Packaging and Deploying

Before packaging the application, we compile the Java code using *compileAtmCmt.bat.* We also compile the intermediate JavaBean *AtmCmtIntermediateBean.java* and *NegativeBalanceException .java.* Finally, we should note that the class specified in the <use-Bean> action in *AtmTransaction.jsp* is *AtmCmtIntermediate-Bean.*

\Chapter10\code\AtmCmtIntermediateBean.java
\Chapter10\code\AtmTransaction.jsp
\Chapter10\code\NegativeBalanceException.java

NOTE: *The listings for AtmCmtIntermediateBean and AtmTransaction are not shown since they are so similar to code we have already seen. NegativeBalanceException is a simple extension of Exception. Code for all of these can be found on the CD.*

TABLE 10-8	**Interface**	**Method**
Methods Not Allowed in Container-Managed Transactions	ejb.EJBContext	getUserTransaction
	java.sql.Connection	commit
	java.sql.Connection	setAutoCommit
	java.sql.Connection	rollback
	javax.transaction.UserTransaction	ALL

The procedure for packaging the application is the same as we used in Chapter 9. The differences are:

- when we add the three bean components, we also add *NegativeBalanceException.class*

- in the Transaction Management dialog, we specify Bean-Managed transactions and assign each of the business methods an attribute of *Required*

- the Coded Name, Home, and Remote specified in the EJB Reference are *AtmCmt* instead of *Atm*

- When we deploy the application, we specify a Web Context of *CH10*

Running the Application

Since the user interface is the same as the one used in Chapter 9, we will not show any of the output here. The only difference in running the application is the URL used to access it. The new URL is:

```
http://localhost:8000/CH10/Atm.html
```

AtmCmtBean.java

\Chapter10\code\AtmCmtBean.java

```
import java.util.*;
import javax.ejb.*;
import java.sql.*;
import javax.sql.*;
import javax.naming.*;
```

```java
public class AtmCmtBean
    implements SessionBean, SessionSynchronization {

    private String customerId;
    private String customerName;
    private double checkingBalance;
    private double savingsBalance;
    private SessionContext context;
    private Connection connection;
    private String dbName = "java:comp/env/jdbc/AtmDB";

    public void withdrawFromChecking(double amount)
        throws NegativeBalanceException {

      checkingBalance -= amount;

      try {
        updateChecking(checkingBalance);
        if (checkingBalance < 0.00) {
          context.setRollbackOnly();
          throw new NegativeBalanceException();
        }
      }
      catch (SQLException e) {
        throw new EJBException
          ("Transaction failed due to SQLException: " +
            e.getMessage());
      }
    }

    public void withdrawFromSavings(double amount)
        throws NegativeBalanceException {

      savingsBalance -= amount;

      try {
        updateSavings(savingsBalance);
        if (savingsBalance < 0.00) {
          context.setRollbackOnly();
          throw new NegativeBalanceException();
        }
      }
      catch (SQLException e) {
        throw new EJBException
          ("Transaction failed due to SQLException: " +
            e.getMessage());
      }
    }

    public void transferFromCheckingToSavings(double amount)
        throws NegativeBalanceException {
```

```
    checkingBalance -= amount;
    savingsBalance += amount;

    try {
      updateChecking(checkingBalance);
      if (checkingBalance < 0.00) {
        context.setRollbackOnly();
        throw new NegativeBalanceException();
      }
      updateSavings(savingsBalance);
    }
    catch (SQLException e) {
      throw new EJBException
        ("Transaction failed due to SQLException: " +
        e.getMessage());
    }
  }


  public void transferFromSavingsToChecking(double amount)
      throws NegativeBalanceException {

    savingsBalance -= amount;
    checkingBalance += amount;

    try {
      updateSavings(checkingBalance);
      if (savingsBalance < 0.00) {
        context.setRollbackOnly();
        throw new NegativeBalanceException();
      }
      updateChecking(checkingBalance);
    }
    catch (SQLException e) {
      throw new EJBException
        ("Transaction failed due to SQLException: " +
          e.getMessage());
    }
  }


  public double getCheckingBalance() {
    return checkingBalance;
  }


  public double getSavingsBalance() {
    return savingsBalance;
  }


  public String getCustomerName() {
    return customerName;
  }


  public void ejbCreate(String id) throws CreateException {
```

```
        customerId = id;


    try {
      makeConnection();
      checkingBalance = selectFromChecking();
      savingsBalance = selectFromSavings();
      customerName = selectFromCustomer();
    }
    catch (Exception e) {
      throw new CreateException(e.getMessage());
    }
  }


  public void ejbRemove() {

    try {
      connection.close();
    }
    catch (SQLException e) {
      throw new EJBException("ejbRemove SQLException: " +
        e.getMessage());
    }
  }


  public void ejbActivate() {

    try {
      makeConnection();
    }
    catch (Exception e) {
      throw new EJBException("ejbActivate Exception: " +
        e.getMessage());
    }
  }


  public void ejbPassivate() {

    try {
      connection.close();
    }
    catch (SQLException e) {
      throw new EJBException("ejbPassivate Exception: " +
        e.getMessage());
    }
  }

  public void setSessionContext(SessionContext context) {
    this.context = context;
  }

  public void afterBegin() {
```

```
        try {
          checkingBalance = selectFromChecking();
          savingsBalance = selectFromSavings();
        }
        catch (SQLException e) {
          throw new EJBException("afterBegin Exception: " +
            e.getMessage());
        }
    }


    public void beforeCompletion() {
    }


    public void afterCompletion(boolean committed) {

      if (committed == false) {
        try {
          checkingBalance = selectFromChecking();
          savingsBalance = selectFromSavings();
        }
        catch (SQLException e) {
          throw new EJBException("afterCompletion SQLException: " +
            e.getMessage());
        }
      }
    }


    private void updateChecking(double amount) throws SQLException {

      String updateStatement =
        "UPDATE checking SET balance = ? " +
        "WHERE id = ?";


      PreparedStatement ps =
        connection.prepareStatement(updateStatement);


      ps.setDouble(1, amount);
      ps.setString(2, customerId);
      ps.executeUpdate();
      ps.close();
    }


    private void updateSavings(double amount) throws SQLException {

      String updateStatement =
        "UPDATE savings SET balance = ? " +
        "WHERE id = ?";


      PreparedStatement ps =
        connection.prepareStatement(updateStatement);
```

```
      ps.setDouble(1, amount);
      ps.setString(2, customerId);
      ps.executeUpdate();
      ps.close();
  }


  private double selectFromChecking() throws SQLException {

    String selectStatement =
      "SELECT balance " +
      "FROM checking WHERE id = ? ";

    PreparedStatement ps =
      connection.prepareStatement(selectStatement);

    ps.setString(1, customerId);

    ResultSet rs = ps.executeQuery();

    if (rs.next()) {
      double result = rs.getDouble(1);
      ps.close();
      return result;
    }
    else {
      ps.close();
      throw new EJBException
        ("Row for id " + customerId + " not found.");
    }
  }


  private double selectFromSavings() throws SQLException {

    String selectStatement =
      "SELECT balance " +
      "FROM savings WHERE id = ? ";
    PreparedStatement ps =
      connection.prepareStatement(selectStatement);

    ps.setString(1, customerId);

    ResultSet rs = ps.executeQuery();

    if (rs.next()) {
      double result = rs.getDouble(1);
      ps.close();
      return result;
    }
    else {
```

```
        ps.close();
        throw new EJBException
          ("Row for id " + customerId + " not found.");
    }
}


private String selectFromCustomer() throws SQLException {


    String selectStatement =
      "SELECT name_first, name_last " +
      "FROM customer WHERE id = ? ";
    PreparedStatement ps =
      connection.prepareStatement(selectStatement);


    ps.setString(1, customerId);
```

Figure 10-3
Summary of Types of
Transactions

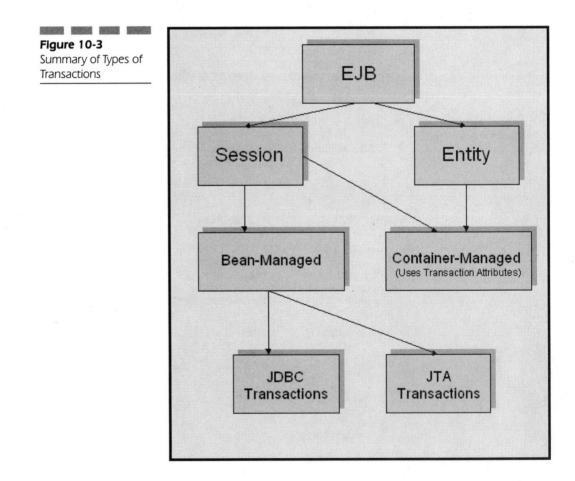

```
      ResultSet rs = ps.executeQuery();

   if (rs.next()) {
      StringBuffer sb = new StringBuffer(rs.getString(1));
      sb.append(rs.getString(2));
      ps.close();
      return sb.toString();
   }
   else {
      ps.close();
      throw new EJBException
        ("Row for id " + customerId + " not found.");
   }
}


private void makeConnection()
    throws NamingException, SQLException {

   InitialContext ic = new InitialContext();
   DataSource ds = (DataSource) ic.lookup(dbName);
   connection = ds.getConnection();
   }
}
```

Summary

This chapter rounded out our discussion of transactions that started in Chapter 8. Figure 10-3 summarizes what we covered in Chapters 8 through 10.

CHAPTER

Customization Without Compilation

In this chapter:

- Environment Entries
- Changing a Tax Rate
- Using a Tax Table

When we developed our *Warehouse* EJB, we used a hard-coded constant as a customer ID when we placed an order from the stockroom. If we wanted to use the code in a different stockroom, we would first have to modify it. In this chapter, we see how J2EE allows us to customize runtime data without changing the source code.

Environment Entries

The vehicle used to perform customization of EJBs is the environment entry. An environment entry is a name–value pair. It is stored in the enterprise bean's deployment descriptor by the Application Deployment Tool.

A Simple Tax Bean

Many business applications involve calculation of sales tax. We would not want every developer in our company writing his or her own version of code that calculates a state sales tax so we might develop a tax bean whose remote interface contains a single method, `applyTax()`. The bean code that implements this method uses two data items, the amount to be taxed and the tax rate that should be applied. The first of these is supplied by the caller. The second can be either hard-coded or determined at run time.

The evils of hard-coding require no discussion. We will now see how to determine the tax rate at run time using an environment entry.

The Remote Interface

The remote interface, which defines the single business method `applyTax()`, is listed below:

\Chapter11\code\SimpleTax.java

```
import javax.ejb.EJBObject;
import java.rmi.RemoteException;

public interface SimpleTax extends EJBObject {

   public double applyTax(double amount) throws RemoteException;
}
```

The Home Interface

The code for the home interface looks like this:

\Chapter11\code\SimpleTaxHome.java

```
import java.io.Serializable;
import java.rmi.RemoteException;
import javax.ejb.CreateException;
import javax.ejb.EJBHome;

public interface SimpleTaxHome extends EJBHome {

   SimpleTax create() throws RemoteException, CreateException;
}
```

The Enterprise Bean

The code that merits the most attention in this chapter is the code that implements the applyTax() method. It looks like this:

On The CD

\Chapter11\code\SimpleTaxBean.java

```java
import javax.ejb.*;
import javax.naming.*;

public class SimpleTaxBean implements SessionBean {

  public double applyTax(double amount) {
    try {

      Context initial = new InitialContext();
      Context environment =
        (Context)initial.lookup("java:comp/env");

      Double taxRate = (Double)environment.lookup("Tax Rate");

      return amount * (1.00 + taxRate.doubleValue());

    }
    catch (NamingException e) {
      throw new EJBException("NamingException: " + e.getMessage());
    }
  }

  public void ejbCreate() {
  }

  public void ejbRemove() {
  }

  public void ejbActivate() {
  }

  public void ejbPassivate() {
  }

  public void setSessionContext(SessionContext sc) {
  }
}
```

The `applyTax()` method locates the environment naming context by using `lookup()` with `java:comp/env` as a parameter. A subsequent invocation of `lookup()` on the environment obtains the value of the entry whose name is *"Tax Rate"*. This value is used as the tax rate.

Packaging and Deploying

Our bean is a stateless session bean that we package using the parameters shown in Table 11-1.

As we step through the packaging process using the NEXT> button, when we get to the Environment Entries dialog, we click on ADD and populate an entry that looks like Figure 11-1.

We enter values in the columns labeled "Code Name" and "Value"; we select the value in the column labeled "Type" from a drop-down list.

The Client

The client does nothing more than get an instance of the bean and invoke its `applyTax()` method, passing it a value supplied as a command line argument. The code looks like this:

TABLE 11-1

Parameters Required to Package SimpleTaxApp

Parameter	Value
Application File Name	SimpleTaxApp.ear
Application Display Name	SimpleTaxApp
JAR Display Name	SimpleTaxJAR
Enterprise Bean Class	SimpleTaxBean
Home Interface	SimpleTaxHome
Remote Interface	SimpleTax
JNDI Name	MySimpleTax

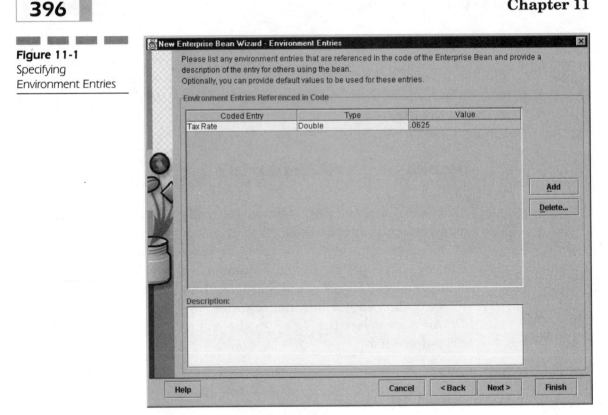

 \Chapter11\code\SimpleTaxClient.java

```java
import javax.naming.*;
import javax.rmi.PortableRemoteObject;

public class SimpleTaxClient {

  public static void main(String[] args) {

    double amount = 0.0;

    if (args.length != 1) {

      exit("Error: requires an argument");

    }
```

```
      try {
        amount = Double.parseDouble(args[0]);
      }
      catch (NumberFormatException e) {
        exit(args[0] + " is not a acceptable value");
      }


      if (amount <= 0) {
        exit("amount must be positive");
      }


      try {
        Context initial = new InitialContext();
        Object objref = initial.lookup("MySimpleTax");

        SimpleTaxHome home =
          (SimpleTaxHome)PortableRemoteObject.narrow(objref,
            SimpleTaxHome.class);


        SimpleTax taxBean = home.create();


        double totalCost = taxBean.applyTax(amount);
        System.out.println("total cost of item = " +
          String.valueOf(totalCost));


      }
      catch (Exception e) {
        System.err.println("Caught an unexpected exception!");
        e.printStackTrace();
      }
    }


  private static void exit(String msg) {
    System.out.println(msg);
    System.exit(0);
  }
}
```

Running the Client

Figure 11-2 shows output from running the client twice. The first time, no command line argument is specified and an error is displayed. The second time, the result of applying a tax of 6.25% is displayed.

Figure 11-2
Running
SimpleTaxClient

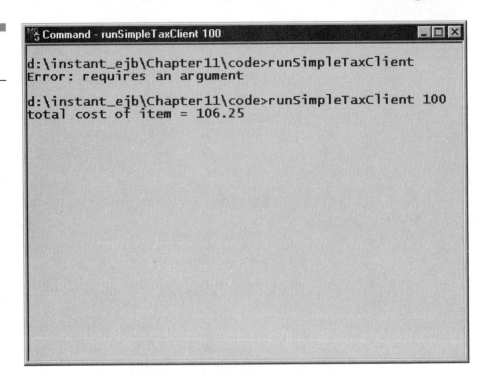

```
 Command - runSimpleTaxClient 100                          _ □ X

d:\instant_ejb\Chapter11\code>runSimpleTaxClient
Error: requires an argument

d:\instant_ejb\Chapter11\code>runSimpleTaxClient 100
total cost of item = 106.25
```

Tax from a Tax Table

Specifying a tax rate using an environment entry eliminates the
need for hard coding. The approach we took, however, leaves something to be desired. If the person deploying the bean enters an
incorrect value for the tax rate, it might not be noticed for quite
some time (perhaps even during a tax audit). If the tax rate
changes, each installation that has deployed the bean must be notified, the change must be made (with the same risk of error we just
mentioned), and the bean must be redeployed.

A better approach might be to create a database containing the
tax rate for each of the 50 states, using the two-character state
abbreviation as the key to the database. Instead of specifying a tax
rate during deployment, we specify a state abbreviation. At runtime, the tax bean uses the two-character code to look up the tax. If
an incorrect abbreviation is typed during deployment, the runtime

code will not find a row in the database and will report an exception. Since tax rates are changed in the database, redeployment is unnecessary when such a change is made.

The TaxTable Bean

The *TaxTable* bean is an entity bean that uses bean-managed persistence and container-managed transactions. Its three components are presented below.

The Remote Interface

The single method defined in the remote interface is getTaxPercent(). The code for the remote interface is as follows:

\Chapter11\code\TaxTable.java

```
import javax.ejb.EJBObject;
import java.rmi.RemoteException;

public interface TaxTable extends EJBObject {

    public double getTaxRate()
        throws RemoteException;
}
```

The Home Interface

Here is the code for the home interface:

\Chapter11\code\TaxTableHome.java

```
import java.util.Collection;
import java.rmi.RemoteException;
import javax.ejb.*;

public interface TaxTableHome extends EJBHome {

    public TaxTable create(String state, double taxRate)
        throws RemoteException, CreateException;

    public TaxTable findByPrimaryKey(String state)
        throws FinderException, RemoteException;
}
```

The Enterprise Bean

The complete listing of the enterprise bean can be found at the end of the chapter. It is similar to the *CustomerRecord* bean we developed in Chapter 5.

Accessing the Tax Table

The tax table is hidden from an application that needs to calculate tax. Such an application creates an instance of *BetterTaxBean,* invokes its applyTax() method as many times as necessary, and then removes the instance. The tax rate, obtained from the tax table, is stored in an instance variable of the instance of *BetterTaxBean.* We will now see how *BetterTaxBean* gets the tax rate from the tax table.

The Remote Interface

As was the case with the simpler bean we saw earlier, the remote interface contains the single method applyTax(). Here is the remote interface code:

\Chapter11\code\BetterTax.java

```
import javax.ejb.EJBObject;
import java.rmi.RemoteException;

public interface BetterTax extends EJBObject {

  public double applyTax(double amount) throws RemoteException;
}
```

The Home Interface

Here is the code for the home interface:

\Chapter11\code\BetterTaxHome.java

```
import java.io.Serializable;
import java.rmi.RemoteException;
import javax.ejb.CreateException;
import javax.ejb.EJBHome;

public interface BetterTaxHome extends EJBHome {

  BetterTax create() throws RemoteException, CreateException;
}
```

The Enterprise Bean

Here is the code for the enterprise bean:

\Chapter11\code\BetterTaxBean.java

```
import javax.naming.Context;
import javax.naming.InitialContext;
```

```java
import javax.naming.NamingException;
import javax.rmi.PortableRemoteObject;
import javax.ejb.*;

public class BetterTaxBean implements SessionBean {

  SessionContext context;

  double taxRate = 0.0;

  public void ejbCreate() throws CreateException {

    String state = null;

    try {
      InitialContext initial = new InitialContext();
      Context environment =
        (Context)initial.lookup("java:comp/env");

      state = (String)environment.lookup("State");
    }
    catch (NamingException e) {
      throw new EJBException("NamingException: " + e.getMessage());
    }

    try {
      Context ctx = new InitialContext();
      Object objref = ctx.lookup("MyTaxTable");

      TaxTableHome home =
        (TaxTableHome)PortableRemoteObject.narrow(objref,
          TaxTableHome.class);

      TaxTable taxTable = home.findByPrimaryKey(state);
      taxRate = taxTable.getTaxRate();
    }
    catch (Exception ex) {
      System.err.println("Caught an exception." );
      ex.printStackTrace();
    }
  }

  public double applyTax(double amount) {
    return amount * (1.00 + taxRate);
  }

  public void ejbRemove() {
  }
```

```
    public void ejbActivate() {
    }

    public void ejbPassivate() {
    }

    public void setSessionContext(SessionContext sc) {
      this.context = sc;
    }
}
```

The `ejbCreate()` method uses gets the value of an environment entry whose coded name is "*State*". It passes this value of the `findByPrimaryKey()` method of the *TaxTable* bean and then invokes the `getTaxRate()` method against the bean that is returned and stores the value that is returned in the instance variable `taxRate`.

The `applyTax()` method uses the value stored in `taxRate`.

Packing and Deploying

Since packaging and deployment involves nothing new, we will simply use the "Open Application . . ." option from the "File" dropdown menu of the Application Deployment Tool to open `Better-TaxApp.ear`. If we select *BetterTaxBean* and then click on the ENVIRONMENT tab, we see an environment entry with a coded name of "*State*", a type of "*String*", and a value of "*NY*".

The Client

Here is the code for the client:

***Chapter11\\code\\BetterTaxClient.java*

```
import java.util.*;
import javax.naming.Context;
import javax.naming.InitialContext;
import javax.rmi.PortableRemoteObject;

public class BetterTaxClient {

  public static void main(String[] args) {

    double amount = 0.0;

    if (args.length != 1) {
      exit("Error: requires an argument");
    }

    try {
      amount = Double.parseDouble(args[0]);
    }
    catch (NumberFormatException e) {
      exit("Error: " + args[0] + " is not an acceptable value");
    }

   if (amount <=0) {
      exit("Error: amount must be positive");
    }

    try {
      Context initial = new InitialContext();
      Object objref = initial.lookup("MyBetterTax");

      BetterTaxHome home =
        (BetterTaxHome)PortableRemoteObject.narrow(objref,
          BetterTaxHome.class);

      BetterTax taxer = home.create();

      System.out.println("total cost = " +
        taxer.applyTax(amount));

      taxer.remove();
    }
    catch (Exception e) {
      System.err.println("Caught an unexpected exception!");
      e.printStackTrace();
    }
  }

  private static void exit(String msg) {
    System.out.println(msg);
```

```
        System.exit(0);
    }
}
```

Running the Client

Before running the client, we populate the tax table database using *createTaxTable.bat*. The required SQL is contained in *createTaxTable.sql*.

\Chapter11\code\createTaxTable.bat
\Chapter11\code\createTaxTable.sql

When we run the client using *runBetterTaxClient.bat,* we observe output like that shown in Figure 11-3.

\Chapter11\code\runBetterTaxClient.bat

Figure 11-3
Output from
BetterTaxCient

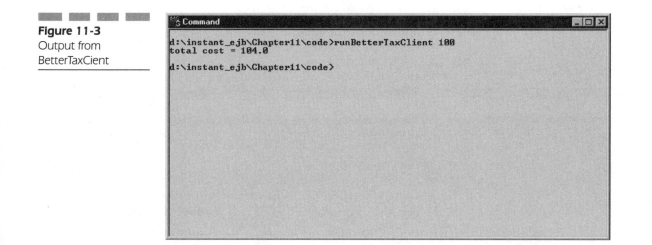

```
d:\instant_ejb\Chapter11\code>runBetterTaxClient 100
total cost = 104.0

d:\instant_ejb\Chapter11\code>
```

TaxTable Enterprise Bean

 \Chapter11\code\TaxTableBean.java

```java
import java.sql.*;
import javax.ejb.*;
import javax.naming.*;
import javax.sql.*;


public class TaxTableBean implements EntityBean {

  private String state;
  private double taxRate;
  private EntityContext context;
  private Connection con;
  private String dbName = "java:comp/env/jdbc/TaxTableDB";

  private static final String connectionFailure =
    "Unable to connetc to database";

  public double getTaxRate() {
    return taxRate;
  }

  public String ejbCreate(String state, double taxRate)
      throws CreateException {

    String insertStatement =
      "INSERT INTO taxtable VALUES ( ? , ? )";

    try {
      PreparedStatement ps =
        con.prepareStatement(insertStatement);

      ps.setString(1, state);
      ps.setDouble(2, taxRate);

      ps.executeUpdate();
      ps.close();
    }
    catch (SQLException e) {
      throw new CreateException("Error inserting state: "
        + state + ". " + e.getMessage());
    }
```

```
      this.state = state;
      this.taxRate = taxRate;

   return state;
   }


   public String ejbFindByPrimaryKey(String primaryKey)
      throws FinderException {

      boolean found;

      String selectStatement =
        "SELECT state " +
        "FROM taxtable WHERE state = ? ";

      try {
        PreparedStatement ps =
          con.prepareStatement(selectStatement);
        ps.setString(1, primaryKey);

        ResultSet rs = ps.executeQuery();
        found = rs.next();
        ps.close();
        if (found) {
          return primaryKey;
         }
        else {
          throw new ObjectNotFoundException
            ("no row found for state " + primaryKey);
        }
      }
      catch (SQLException e) {
        throw new FinderException(e.getMessage());
      }
   }


   public void ejbRemove() {
      String deleteStatement =
        "DELETE FROM taxtable WHERE state = ? ";
      try {
        PreparedStatement ps =
          con.prepareStatement(deleteStatement);

        ps.setString(1, state);
        ps.executeUpdate();
        ps.close();
      }
      catch (SQLException e) {
        throw new EJBException("ejbRemove: " +
          e.getMessage());
      }
   }


   public void setEntityContext(EntityContext context) {
```

```java
  this.context = context;
  try {
    InitialContext ic = new InitialContext();
    DataSource ds = (DataSource) ic.lookup(dbName);
    con = ds.getConnection();
  }
  catch (NamingException e) {
    throw new EJBException(connectionFailure + e.getMessage());
  }
  catch (SQLException e) {
    throw new EJBException(connectionFailure + e.getMessage());
  }
}

public void unsetEntityContext() {

  try {
    con.close();
  }
  catch (SQLException ex) {
    throw new EJBException("unsetEntityContext: " +
      ex.getMessage());
  }
}

public void ejbActivate() {

  state = (String)context.getPrimaryKey();
}

public void ejbPassivate() {

  state = null;
}

public void ejbLoad() {

  String selectStatement =
    "SELECT taxRate " +
    "FROM taxtable WHERE state = ? ";

  try {
    PreparedStatement ps =
      con.prepareStatement(selectStatement);

    ps.setString(1, this.state);

    ResultSet rs = ps.executeQuery();

    if (rs.next()) {
      this.taxRate = rs.getDouble(1);
      ps.close();
    }
```

```
        else {
          ps.close();
          throw new NoSuchEntityException("Row for state " + state +
            " not found in database.");
        }
      }
      catch (SQLException e) {
        throw new EJBException("ejbLoad: " + e.getMessage());
      }
    }

  public void ejbStore() {

      String updateStatement =
        "UPDATE taxtable SET taxRate = ? " +
        "WHERE state = ?";

      try {
        PreparedStatement ps =
          con.prepareStatement(updateStatement);

        ps.setDouble(1, taxRate);
        ps.setString(2,state);
        int rowCount = ps.executeUpdate();
        ps.close();

        if (rowCount == 0) {
          throw new EJBException("Storing row for state " +
            state + " failed.");
        }
      }
      catch (SQLException e) {
        throw new EJBException("ejbLoad: " + e.getMessage());
      }
    }

  public void ejbPostCreate(String state, double taxRate) {
    }
  }
```

Summary

In this chapter, we saw how we can use environment entries to achieve customization without compilation.

CHAPTER 12

Authentication and Authorization

In this chapter:

- The J2EE Approach to Security
- Authentication
- Using the Realm Tool
- Authorization

Up to this point, the only time we dealt with the issue of security was when we developed a J2EE application client in Chapter 4. Security consisted of limiting access to the application to a user who could supply a user ID and password that the J2EE server could validate. In the real business world, this would be woefully inadequate. If all that is required to run an application is to supply a valid user ID and password, any valid user could run every application deployed on the server. In this chapter, we see how the security offered by J2EE extends far beyond authenticating a user and see how easy it is for every EJB we develop to take advantage of that security.

The J2EE Approach to Security

A J2EE server uses security attributes declared in the Application Deployment Tool to enforce security. The declarative approach offers the same advantages in the area of security that we have already seen in other areas. It enables the programmer who writes the bean code to concentrate on business logic and it allows the administrator of the J2EE server to perform customization at deployment time.

The two levels at which the J2EE server enforces security are authentication and authorization.

Authentication

Authentication is the process by which we prove our identity. We can do this by presenting one or more of the following:

1. something we know
2. something we have
3. something we are

The first of these, something we know, is usually a password. The second is quite often a token, that is, a pseudo-random number generated by code embedded in a miniature device or card that has been synchronized with an authentication server. The third can take the form of a unique physical characteristic such as the image derived by scanning a palm or retina.

The J2EE server delivered with the reference implementation used to develop the EJBs in this book uses a user ID and password to perform authentication. We saw in Chapter 4 that one valid user ID is *guest,* which has a password of *guest123.* Neither the NT system on which the EJBs in the book were developed nor the Linux system on which many of them were tested has a system user called *guest.* J2EE users and system users belong to different realms.

NOTE: *The security mechanisms discussed in this chapter are specific to the J2EE server delivered as part of the reference implementation. Commercial implementations are free to use any security mechanisms they choose, including those of the operating system on which they run. When such is the case, a J2EE user may be synonymous with a system user.*

A *realm* is a group of users whose access to and use of controlled resources are governed by a common authentication policy. J2EE provides authentication for users in two realms: the *default* realm and the *certificate* realm. Here we only discuss the default realm.

The default realm can be divided into groups. A *group* is a category of users who have something in common. Consider, for example, the Roadside Assistance application we developed in Chapter 7 and expanded in Chapter 8. Users of this application fall into two categories: those who issue queries and order parts and those who are responsible for maintaining the stockroom. These two categories of users could be assigned to two groups. A user is allowed to belong to more than one group. The person responsible for maintaining the stockroom will occasionally need to issue a query, an activity associated with the group to which the drivers and the dispatcher belong. It makes sense, then, that he or she should belong to both groups.

Creating Groups and Users

We create groups and users with the Realm Tool. To begin, we invoke the tool with no options by simply typing the command `realmtool`. This results in a display of all allowable options as shown in Figure 12-1.

If we invoke the tool with the `-show` option, the realm names are listed as shown in Figure 12-2. This verifies the statement we made earlier that J2EE provides authentication for users in two realms, the default realm and the certificate realm.

We can obtain a list of all users in the default realm by typing the command `realmtool -list default`. The output is shown in Figure 12-3.

Figure 12-1
Realm Tool Options

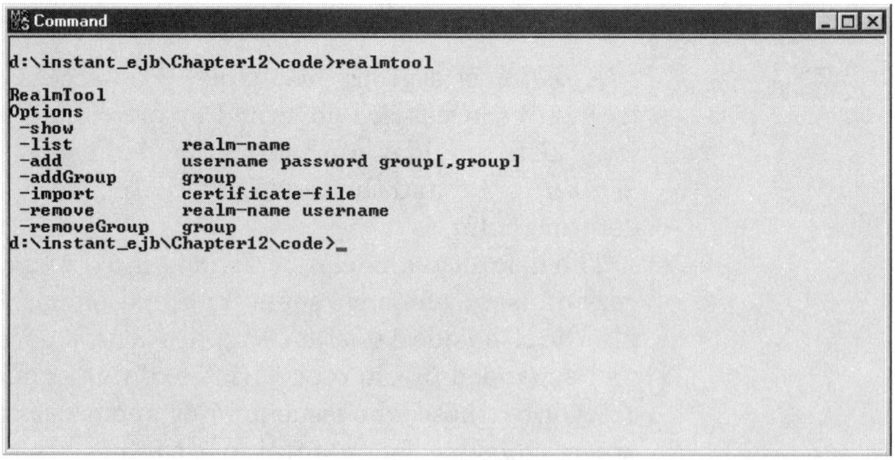

```
d:\instant_ejb\Chapter12\code>realmtool

RealmTool
Options
 -show
 -list          realm-name
 -add           username password group[,group]
 -addGroup      group
 -import        certificate-file
 -remove        realm-name username
 -removeGroup   group
d:\instant_ejb\Chapter12\code>_
```

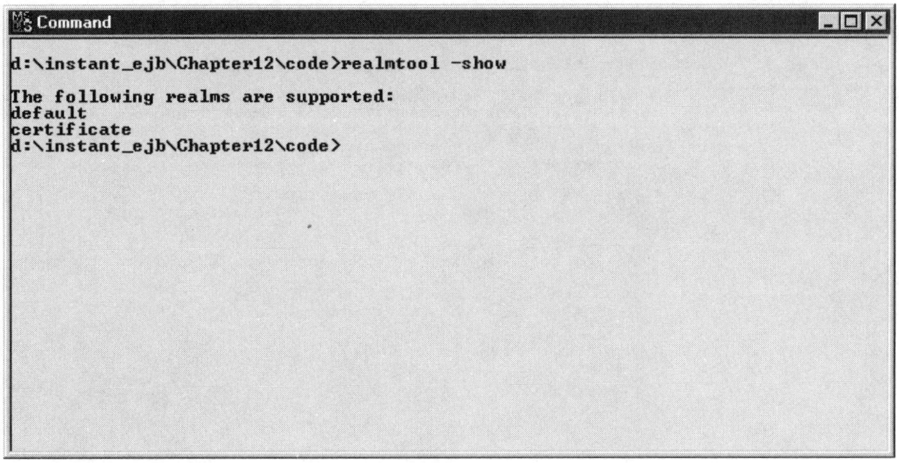

Figure 12-2
Obtaining a List of
J2EE Realms

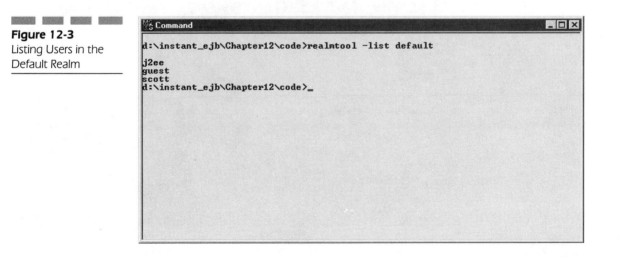

```
d:\instant_ejb\Chapter12\code>realmtool -show

The following realms are supported:
default
certificate
d:\instant_ejb\Chapter12\code>
```

We add a user by invoking the tool with the -add option. The full
syntax is:

```
realmtool -add <username password group[,group]>
```

NOTE: *The syntax "group[,group]" indicates that a user can be assigned
to multiple groups.*

Figure 12-3
Listing Users in the
Default Realm

```
d:\instant_ejb\Chapter12\code>realmtool -list default

j2ee
guest
scott
d:\instant_ejb\Chapter12\code>_
```

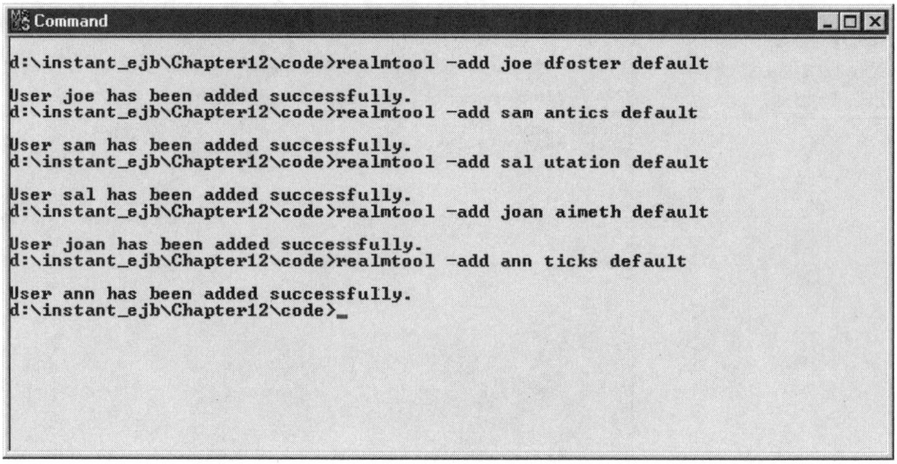

Figure 12-4
Adding Users

```
Command                                                                    _ □ ×
d:\instant_ejb\Chapter12\code>realmtool -add joe dfoster default

User joe has been added successfully.
d:\instant_ejb\Chapter12\code>realmtool -add sam antics default

User sam has been added successfully.
d:\instant_ejb\Chapter12\code>realmtool -add sal utation default

User sal has been added successfully.
d:\instant_ejb\Chapter12\code>realmtool -add joan aimeth default

User joan has been added successfully.
d:\instant_ejb\Chapter12\code>realmtool -add ann ticks default

User ann has been added successfully.
d:\instant_ejb\Chapter12\code>_
```

Figure 12-4 shows how we add several users and Figure 12-5 reflects these additions.

If we want to create a group, we use the -addGroup option. Figure 12-6 shows how we create a group called *incrowd* and add users to it. Figure 12-7 shows the latest user listing.

Before we see how to use the group we just created, we need to create one more group called *topclearance* and add the user *paul* to

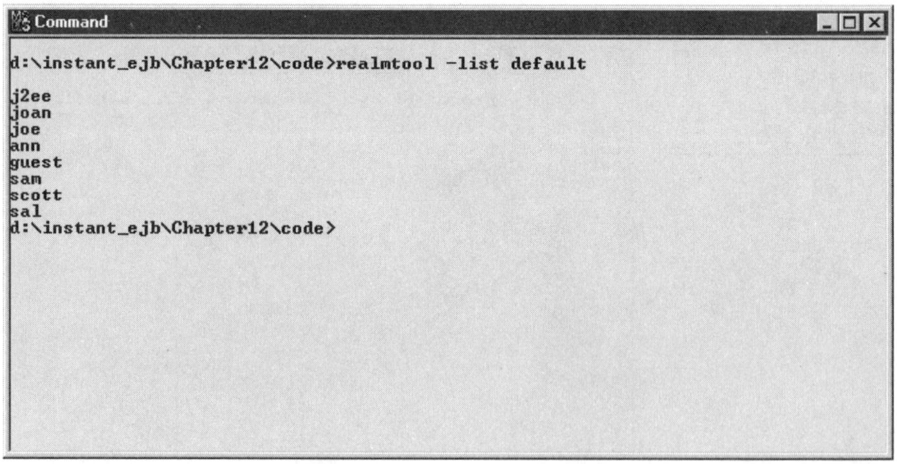

Figure 12-5
The Expanded
User List

```
Command                                                                    _ □ ×
d:\instant_ejb\Chapter12\code>realmtool -list default

j2ee
joan
joe
ann
guest
sam
scott
sal
d:\instant_ejb\Chapter12\code>
```

Figure 12-6
Creating and
Populating the
incrowd Group

Figure 12-6
Creating and
Populating the
incrowd Group

```
d:\instant_ejb\Chapter12\code>realmtool -addGroup incrowd

Group incrowd has been added successfully.
d:\instant_ejb\Chapter12\code>realmtool -add ellie bluejay incrowd

User ellie has been added successfully.
d:\instant_ejb\Chapter12\code>realmtool -add josephine why42 incrowd

User josephine has been added successfully.
d:\instant_ejb\Chapter12\code>realmtool -add mike_z creeque incrowd

User mike_z has been added successfully.
d:\instant_ejb\Chapter12\code>realmtool -add paul lv67ilbh incrowd

User paul has been added successfully.
d:\instant_ejb\Chapter12\code>realmtool -add rebekah luvchem incrowd

User rebekah has been added successfully.
d:\instant_ejb\Chapter12\code>realmtool -add sanjoy ismile4u incrowd

User sanjoy has been added successfully.
d:\instant_ejb\Chapter12\code>_
```

the new group. The sequence of commands we use to accomplish this task is:

```
realmtool -addGroup topclearance
realmtool -remove paul
realmtool -add paul lv67ilbh incrowd,topclearance
```

Figure 12-7
The Latest User Listing

```
d:\instant_ejb\Chapter12\code>realmtool -list default

ann
joe
sanjoy
guest
paul
sam
josephine
sal
ellie
j2ee
scott
rebekah
joan
mike_z
d:\instant_ejb\Chapter12\code>_
```

Authorization

Now that we have created and populated two groups, we are ready to explore the second aspect of security, authorization. We begin by writing a simple stateless session bean that we will use as our test vehicle.

The Remote Interface

The remote interface defines three business methods. The code looks like this:

\Chapter12\code\SecurityTest.java

```java
import javax.ejb.EJBObject;
import java.rmi.RemoteException;

public interface SecurityTest extends EJBObject {

  public String getPublicData() throws RemoteException;
  public String getNotSoPublicData() throws RemoteException;
  public String getSensitiveData() throws RemoteException;
}
```

The Home Interface

The home interface is shown below.

\Chapter12\code\SecurityTestHome.java

```java
import java.io.Serializable;
import java.rmi.RemoteException;
import javax.ejb.CreateException;
import javax.ejb.EJBHome;
```

```
public interface SecurityTestHome extends EJBHome {

   SecurityTest create() throws RemoteException, CreateException;
}
```

The Enterprise Bean

This is the code for the enterprise bean.

\Chapter12\code\SecurityTestBean.java

```
import javax.naming.Context;
import javax.naming.InitialContext;
import javax.naming.NamingException;
import javax.rmi.PortableRemoteObject;
import javax.ejb.*;

public class SecurityTestBean implements SessionBean {

  SessionContext context;

  String publicData = "Anybody is allowed to see this";
  String notSoPublicData = "A few are allowed to see this";
  String sensitiveData = "Access to this must be REALLY
    restricted";

  public void ejbCreate() throws CreateException {
  }

  public String getPublicData() {
    return publicData;
  }

  public String getNotSoPublicData() {
    return notSoPublicData;
  }

  public String getSensitiveData() {
    return sensitiveData;
  }
```

```
    public void ejbRemove() {
    }

    public void ejbActivate() {
    }

    public void ejbPassivate() {
    }

    public void setSessionContext(SessionContext sc) {
      this.context = sc;
    }
}
```

We compile the three components using *compileSecurityTest.bat*.

\Chapter12\code\compileSecurityTest.bat

A Client

The client code we use to obtain an instance of our bean and invoke its methods is shown below:

\Chapter12\code\SecurityTestClient.java

```
import java.util.*;
import javax.naming.Context;
import javax.naming.InitialContext;
import javax.rmi.PortableRemoteObject;


public class SecurityTestClient {

  public static void main(String[] args) {
```

```
try {
  Context initial = new InitialContext();
  Object objref = initial.lookup("MySecurityTest");

  SecurityTestHome home =
    (SecurityTestHome)PortableRemoteObject.narrow(objref,
      SecurityTestHome.class);

  SecurityTest securityTest = home.create();

  System.out.println();
  System.out.println("attempting to access public data");
  String publicData = securityTest.getPublicData();
  System.out.println("got public data = it's as follows:");
  System.out.println(publicData);

  System.out.println();
  System.out.println("attempting to access not so public
    data");
  String notSoPublicData = securityTest.getNotSoPublicData();
  System.out.println("got not so public data - it's as
    follows:");
  System.out.println(notSoPublicData);

  System.out.println();
  System.out.println("attempting to access sensitive data");
  String sensitiveData = securityTest.getSensitiveData();
  System.out.println("got sensitive data - it's as follows:");
  System.out.println(sensitiveData);
  System.out.println();

  securityTest.remove();
}
catch (Exception e) {
  System.err.println("Caught an unexpected exception!");
  e.printStackTrace();
}
  }
}
```

Packaging and Deploying

Since we are now familiar with packaging and deploying a bean as simple as the *SecurityTest* bean, in the interest of time, we will simply open the application from the CD. To do so, we select the "Open Application . . ." option from "File" drop-down menu of the Application Deployment Tool and open *SecurityTestApp.ear*. When we deploy the application, we must click the checkbox labeled RETURN CLIENT JAR.

On The CD   *\Chapter12\code\SecurityTestApp.ear*

Running the J2EE Client

We start the J2EE client by typing:

```
runclient -client SecurityTestAppClient.jar -name
SecurityTestClient
```

After the startup message shown in Figure 12-8 is displayed, a Login dialog pops up. We enter one of the user IDs we just created (and the associated password) so the dialog looks like Figure 12-9.

Figure 12-8
SecurityTestClient
Startup

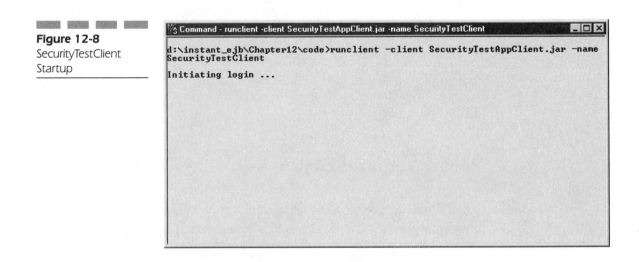

```
Command - runclient -client SecurityTestAppClient.jar -name SecurityTestClient

d:\instant_ejb\Chapter12\code>runclient -client SecurityTestAppClient.jar -name
SecurityTestClient

Initiating login ...
```

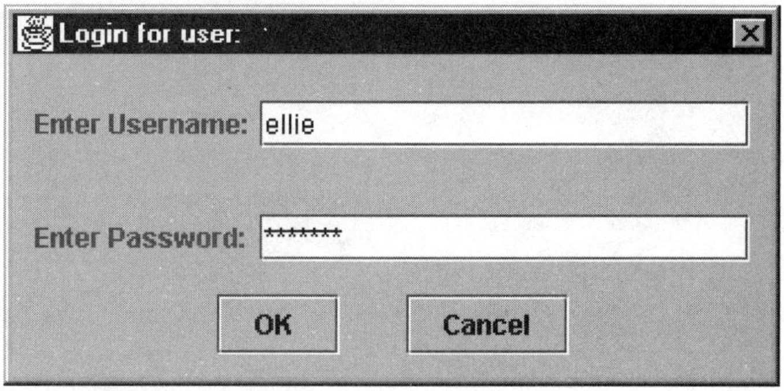

Figure 12-9
SecurityTestClient
Login Dialog

Figure 12-9
SecurityTestClient
Login Dialog

When we click on the OK button, the output shown in Figure 12-10 is displayed. The client ran successfully and all the bean's methods were invoked.

Introducing Security

The output displayed in Figure 12-10 demonstrates two things:

1. the client ran successfully
2. all of the bean's methods were successfully invoked

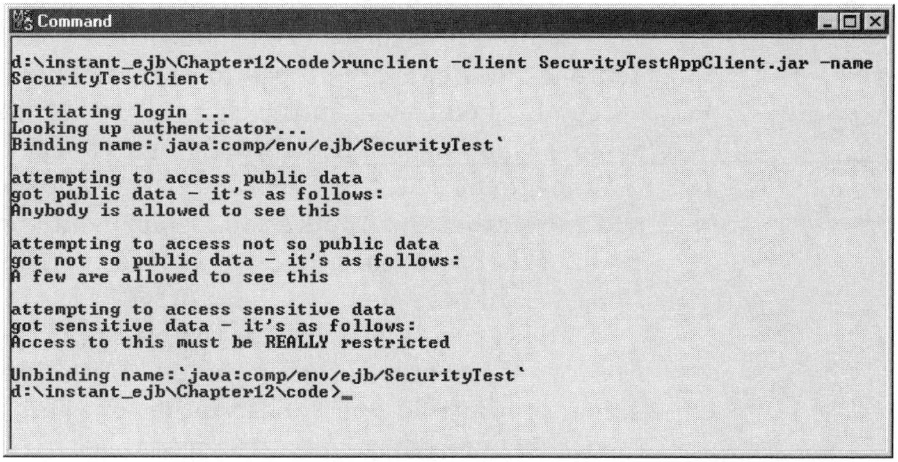

Figure 12-10
Output from
SecurityTestClient

```
d:\instant_ejb\Chapter12\code>runclient -client SecurityTestAppClient.jar -name
SecurityTestClient

Initiating login ...
Looking up authenticator...
Binding name:`java:comp/env/ejb/SecurityTest`

attempting to access public data
got public data - it's as follows:
Anybody is allowed to see this

attempting to access not so public data
got not so public data - it's as follows:
A few are allowed to see this

attempting to access sensitive data
got sensitive data - it's as follows:
Access to this must be REALLY restricted

Unbinding name:`java:comp/env/ejb/SecurityTest`
d:\instant_ejb\Chapter12\code>_
```

Figure 12-11
Selecting the SECURITY
Tab for the Application

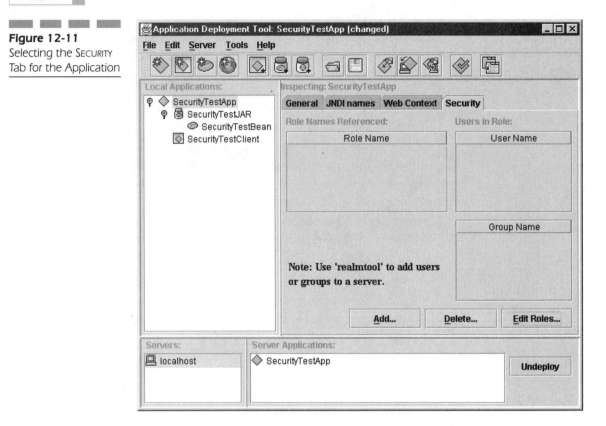

If we run the client using any of the user IDs shown in Figure 12-7, we observe identical results. We now see how to construct and then tighten a security net around the application. We do so by defining roles, mapping these roles to the J2EE users and groups we established earlier in the chapter, and limiting access to those persons who are defined as belonging to a particular role.

We begin by selecting *SecurityTestApp* and clicking on the SECURITY tab so that the Application Deployment Tool looks like Figure 12-11. When we click on the button in Figure 12-11 labeled ADD . . . , the screen shown in Figure 12-12 is displayed.

To create a role, we click on the button in Figure 12-12 labeled ADD. . . . We populate the empty entry that appears by typing a name for the role and a description of what the role is for. We repeat this procedure to create three roles:

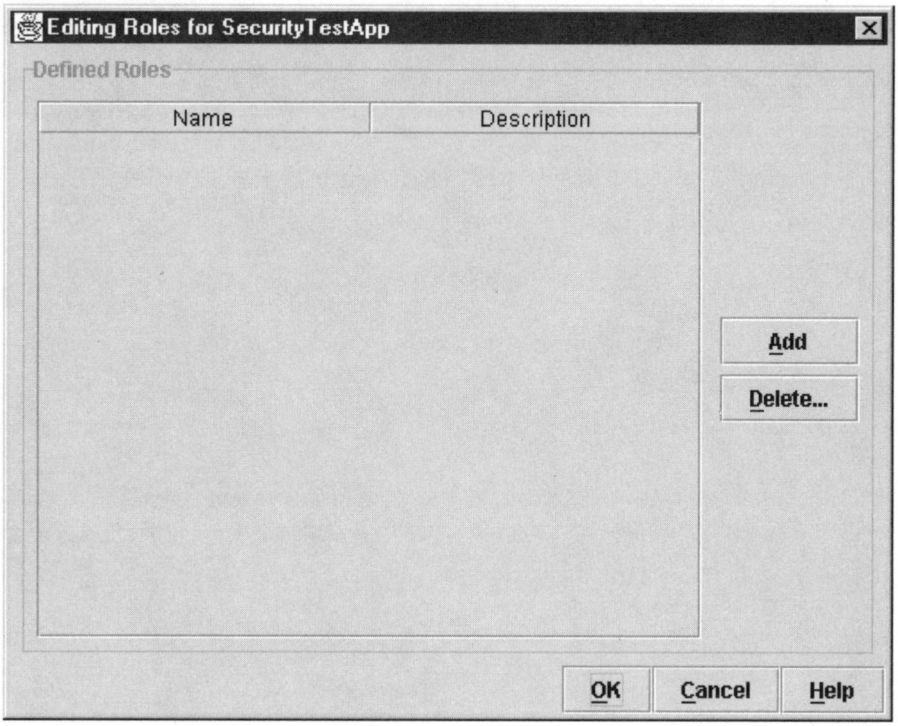

Figure 12-12
Editing Roles for
SecurityTestApp

1. Untrusted Users

2. Level 1 Clearancce

3. Top Secret Clearance

When we have completed the three entries and the dialog looks like Figure 12-13, we click on the button labeled OK and the Application Deployment Tool looks like Figure 12-14.

We are now ready to assign users to the roles. We do so by first selecting the role to which we will be adding users (we start with "*Untrusted Users*") and then clicking on the ADD . . . button. In the dialog that appears, we select the user and/or group we wish to add to the role. We will add the user *joe* and the entire group *incrowd*. (See Figure 12-15.) After we have made our selections, we click on the OK button and notice that the "Untrusted Users" role reflects the additions as shown in Figure 12-16.

Figure 12-13
Adding Roles

```
Editing Roles for SecurityTestApp                               [X]
┌─Defined Roles──────────────────────────────────────────────────
│  ┌──────────────────────────┬──────────────────────────────┐
│  │          Name            │         Description           │
│  ├──────────────────────────┼──────────────────────────────┤
│  │ Untrusted Users          │ The least privileged         │
│  │ Level 1 Clearance        │ The more privileged          │
│  │ Top Secret Clearance     │ Be stingy with this one       │
│  └──────────────────────────┴──────────────────────────────┘
│                                                    ┌─────────┐
│                                                    │   Add   │
│                                                    └─────────┘
│                                                    ┌─────────┐
│                                                    │ Delete..│
│                                                    └─────────┘
│
│
│
│                                    ┌──────┐ ┌────────┐ ┌──────┐
│                                    │  OK  │ │ Cancel │ │ Help │
│                                    └──────┘ └────────┘ └──────┘
```

We complete setting up the roles as follows:

1. add the group *topclearance* to *"Untrusted Users"*

2. add the groups *incrowd* and *topclearance* to *"Level 1 Clearance"*

3. add the user *paul* to *"Top Secret Clearance"*

NOTE: *At first, it might seem strange to add all members of* incrowd *and* topclearance *to* "Untrusted Users"*. Upon thinking about it further, we realize that the roles we have defined in this case correspond to increasing levels of trust and users in any role in the hierarchy must be granted not only the privileges associated with their own level of trust but also the privileges associated with all lower levels of trust.*

This hierarchical model is peculiar to the example we are exploring in this chapter. A hierarchical model is by no means mandatory.

Figure 12-14
After Adding Roles

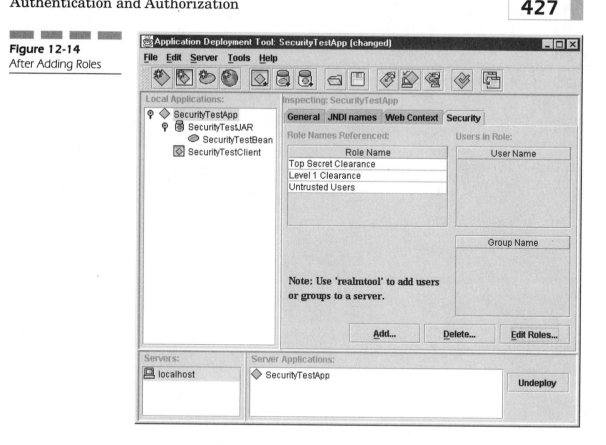

The final step consists of defining which roles are permitted to invoke the bean's methods. We do this by selecting the bean so that it is highlighted in the leftmost column of the Application Deployment Tool (we must expand the Jar so the bean is visible) and clicking on the SECURITY tab. When we do so, a dialog like the one shown in Figure 12-17 is displayed. We notice that the bean's methods are listed in the leftmost column and that there is one column for each of the roles we defined with an empty checkbox for each of the bean's methods. When a checkbox is unchecked, the bean method in the first column of the row containing the checkbox can be invoked by anybody. When the checkbox is checked, only a client belonging to the role listed at the top of the

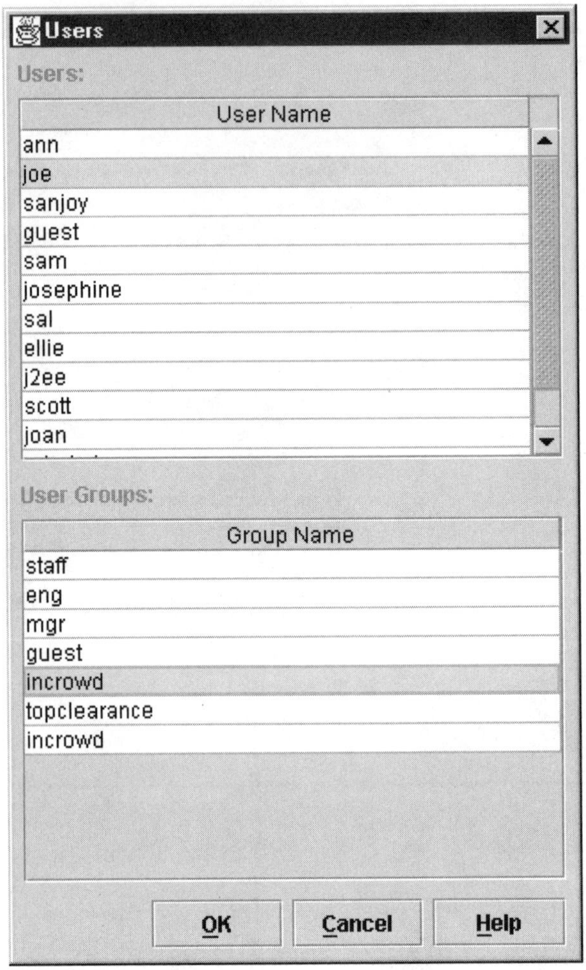

Figure 12-15
Assigning a User and
a Group to a Role

![Users dialog window. Title bar reads "Users". Section "Users:" with a table of User Names: ann, joe, sanjoy, guest, sam, josephine, sal, ellie, j2ee, scott, joan. Section "User Groups:" with a table of Group Names: staff, eng, mgr, guest, incrowd, topclearance, incrowd. Buttons at bottom: OK, Cancel, Help.]

column containing the checkbox can invoke the method. We grant access to the `getSensitivedata()` method to users in the "Top Secret Clearance" role by checking the appropriate checkbox; similarly, we grant access to the `getPublicData()` method to users of all three roles we defined. We also grant access to the `getNotSoPublicdata()` method to the "Level 1 Clearance" and "Top Secret Clearance" roles. The last method is not shown because it is beyond the scroll range shown but is reached by scrolling.

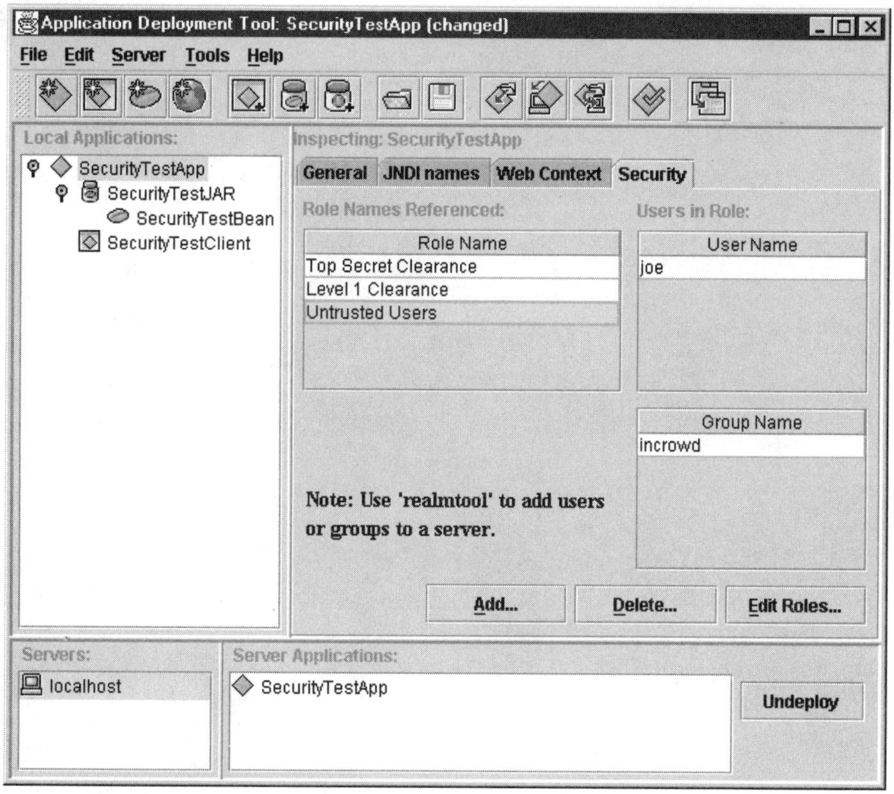

Figure 12-16
The Untrusted Users
Role After the
Addition

Proving That It Works

The best way to demonstrate the security we have imposed is to run the client several times using different user IDs as shown in Table 12-1. We run the client using *runSecurityTestClient.bat*.

TABLE 12-1

Parameters Required
to Test Security
Setup

User ID	Password	Output
guest	guest123	Figure 12-18
joe	dfoster	Figure 12-19
rebekah	luvchem	Figure 12-20
paul	lv67ilbh	Figure 12-21

Figure 12-17
Defining Method
Permissions

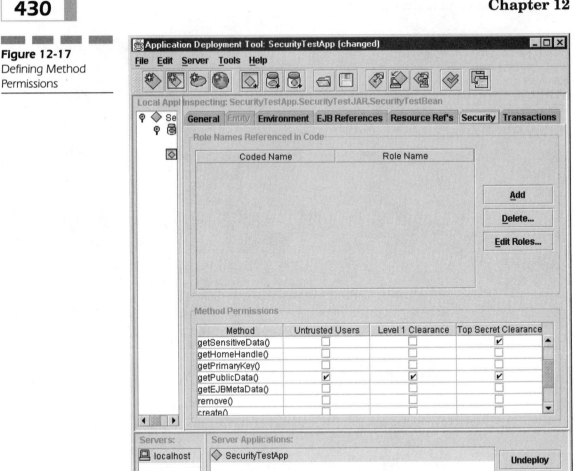

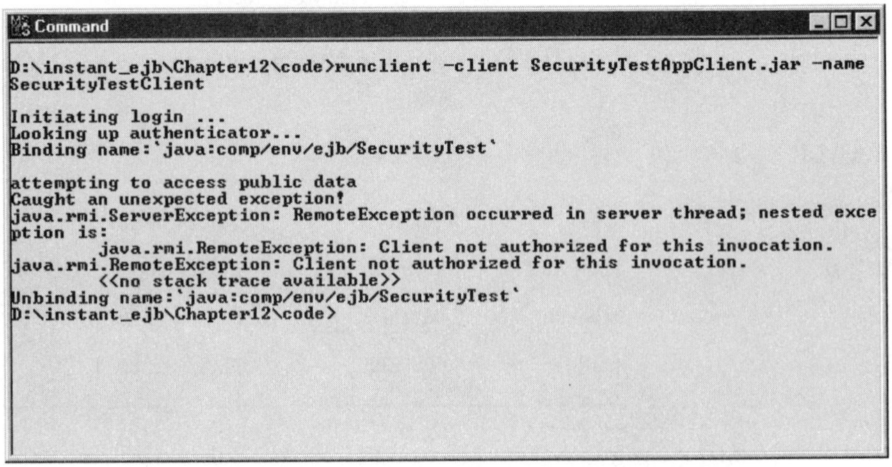

Figure 12-18
User Outside Defined
Roles

Figure 12-19
User in Untrusted
Users Role

```
Command                                                                    _ □ X

D:\instant_ejb\Chapter12\code>runclient -client SecurityTestAppClient.jar -name
SecurityTestClient

Initiating login ...
Looking up authenticator...
Binding name:`java:comp/env/ejb/SecurityTest`

attempting to access public data
got public data - it's as follows:
Anybody is allowed to see this

attempting to access not so public data
Caught an unexpected exception!
java.rmi.ServerException: RemoteException occurred in server thread; nested exce
ption is:
        java.rmi.RemoteException: Client not authorized for this invocation.
java.rmi.RemoteException: Client not authorized for this invocation.
        <<no stack trace available>>
Unbinding name:`java:comp/env/ejb/SecurityTest`
D:\instant_ejb\Chapter12\code>
```

\Chapter12\code\runSecurityTestClient.bat

We can change everything we just did declaratively using the
Application Deployment Tool without ever touching the code. This
includes adding or removing users from a role or even increasing or
decreasing the number of roles.

Figure 12-20
User in Level 1
Clearance Role

```
Command                                                                    _ □ X

D:\instant_ejb\Chapter12\code>runclient -client SecurityTestAppClient.jar -name
SecurityTestClient

Initiating login ...
Looking up authenticator...
Binding name:`java:comp/env/ejb/SecurityTest`

attempting to access public data
got public data - it's as follows:
Anybody is allowed to see this

attempting to access not so public data
got not so public data - it's as follows:
A few are allowed to see this

attempting to access sensitive data
Caught an unexpected exception!
java.rmi.ServerException: RemoteException occurred in server thread; nested exce
ption is:
        java.rmi.RemoteException: Client not authorized for this invocation.
java.rmi.RemoteException: Client not authorized for this invocation.
        <<no stack trace available>>
Unbinding name:`java:comp/env/ejb/SecurityTest`
D:\instant_ejb\Chapter12\code>
```

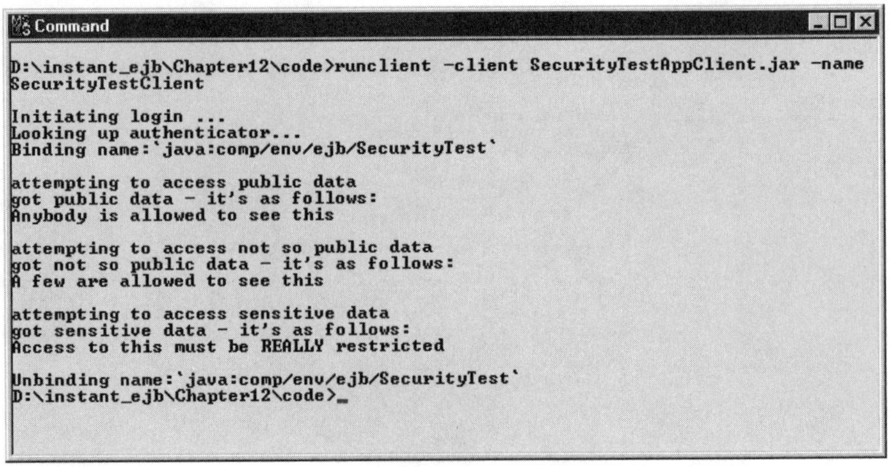

Figure 12-21
User in Top Secret
Clearance Role

```
  Command                                                    _ □ ×

D:\instant_ejb\Chapter12\code>runclient -client SecurityTestAppClient.jar -name
SecurityTestClient

Initiating login ...
Looking up authenticator...
Binding name:`java:comp/env/ejb/SecurityTest`

attempting to access public data
got public data - it's as follows:
Anybody is allowed to see this

attempting to access not so public data
got not so public data - it's as follows:
A few are allowed to see this

attempting to access sensitive data
got sensitive data - it's as follows:
Access to this must be REALLY restricted

Unbinding name:`java:comp/env/ejb/SecurityTest`
D:\instant_ejb\Chapter12\code>_
```

Summary

In this chapter, we saw how access to beans could be controlled at
the method level. We saw how J2EE security was handled declaratively and we developed a test case to demonstrate a small test
suite.

Sending Email from an EJB

In this chapter:

- The Mailer Bean
- Sending Email

When we developed the automated ordering process in Chapter 8, we included code that detected conditions under which email should be sent. We said then that, in the interest of simplicity, we would simply print a message to the system output device. In this chapter, we see how to send email from an EJB.

The Mailer Bean

The mailer bean we develop in this chapter uses JNDI to find an object of type *javax.mail.Session*. The mechanism we use is identical to the one we used to locate a database resource (i.e., we link a coded name representing the resource to a JNDI name and use the `lookup()` method, which returns the resource).

After we have obtained the *Session* object, we instantiate an object of type *MimeMessage*, invoke its setter methods to provide content, and pass the message object as an argument to the static method `send()` of *javax.mail.Transport*. The `send()` method initiates delivery of the message.

The Remote Interface

The remote interface, which contains the single business method `sendEmail()`, is listed below:

\Chapter13\code\Mailer.java

```
import javax.ejb.EJBObject;
import java.rmi.RemoteException;
```

```
public interface Mailer extends EJBObject {

  public void sendEmail(String recipient) throws RemoteException;
}
```

The Home Interface

Here is the home interface:

\Chapter13\code\MailerHome.java

```
import java.io.Serializable;
import java.rmi.RemoteException;
import javax.ejb.CreateException;
import javax.ejb.EJBHome;

public interface MailerHome extends EJBHome {

    Mailer create() throws RemoteException, CreateException;
}
```

The Enterprise Bean

The enterprise bean is shown below:

\Chapter13\code\MailerBean.java

```
import java.util.*;
import javax.ejb.*;
import javax.mail.*;
import javax.activation.*;
import javax.mail.internet.*;
import javax.naming.*;

public class MailerBean implements SessionBean {

    SessionContext sc;
    private static final String mailer = "JavaMailer";

    public void sendEmail(String recipient) {
```

```
      try {
        Context initial = new InitialContext();
        Session session =
          (Session) initial.lookup("java:comp/env/MailSession");

        Message msg = new MimeMessage(session);
        msg.setFrom();

        msg.setRecipients(Message.RecipientType.TO,
          InternetAddress.parse(recipient, false));

        msg.setSubject("Past Due Order");

        String messageText = "Order #: 2000100002" + '\n' +
          "Part #: 102010" + '\n' +
          "Qty: 10" + '\n' +
          "Scheduled Delivery Date:2000-09-10 ";

        msg.setText(messageText);

        msg.setHeader("X-Mailer", mailer);
        msg.setSentDate(new Date());

        Transport.send(msg);

        System.out.println("Mail sent");
      }
      catch(Exception e) {
        throw new EJBException(e.getMessage());
      }
    }

    public MailerBean() {
    }

    public void ejbCreate() {
    }

    public void ejbRemove() {
    }

    public void ejbActivate() {
    }

    public void ejbPassivate() {
    }

    public void setSessionContext(SessionContext sc) {
    }
  }
```

Packaging and Deploying

We package the stateless session bean using the parameters shown in Table 13-1.

When we reach the Resource References dialog, we click on the ADD button and populate the entry that appears. We type a value into the column labeled "Coded Name" and select the values in the other two columns from drop-down lists. In earlier examples, we simply left the column labeled "Type" as it appeared. Here, when we select "javax.mail.Session", a new group box labeled DEPLOYMENT SETTINGS FOR MAILSESSION appears. We populate the fields in this group box so that the contents are as shown in Figure 13-1.

NOTE: *For* From: *and* Host: *you must specify actual values from a functioning SMTP server. The* User Name *must be a valid NT user name. If you try to run the client code using the values shown in Figure 13-1, the program will fail.*

Finally, we select *MailerApp* from the leftmost column of the Application Deployment Tool and specify JNDI names as shown in Table 13-2.

TABLE 13-1	Parameter	Value
Parameters Required to Package Mailer-Bean	Application File Name	MailerApp.ear
	Application Display Name	MailerApp
	Jar File Name	MailerAppJAR
	Enterprise Bean Class	MailerBean
	Home Interface	MailerHome
	Remote Interface	Mailer
	Enterprise Bean Display Name	MailerBean

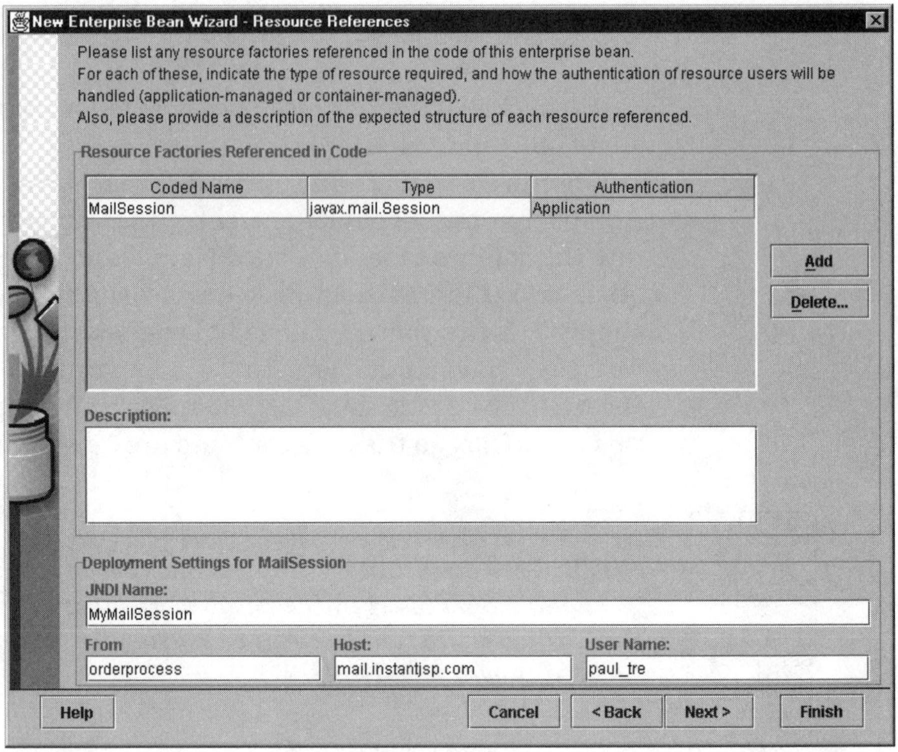

Figure 13-1
Resource References
for MailSession

New Enterprise Bean Wizard - Resource References

Please list any resource factories referenced in the code of this enterprise bean.
For each of these, indicate the type of resource required, and how the authentication of resource users will be
handled (application-managed or container-managed).
Also, please provide a description of the expected structure of each resource referenced.

Resource Factories Referenced in Code

Coded Name	Type	Authentication
MailSession	javax.mail.Session	Application

Add
Delete...

Description:

Deployment Settings for MailSession
JNDI Name:
MyMailSession

From	Host:	User Name:
orderprocess	mail.instantjsp.com	paul_tre

Help   Cancel   < Back   Next >   Finish

A Simple Client

In the interest of simplicity, we will use a standalone client to test
our *Mailer* bean. After we have tested it, we can then incorporate it
into the placeOrder() method of *StockRoomBean* in Chapter 8.
Here is the code for the client:

TABLE 13-2

JNDI Names

Referenced by	Component/Reference Name	JNDI Name
	MailerBean	MyMailer
MailerBean	MailSession	MyMailSession

`\Chapter13\code\MailerClient.java`

```java
import javax.naming.Context;
import javax.naming.InitialContext;
import javax.rmi.PortableRemoteObject;
import Mailer;
import MailerHome;

public class MailerClient {

  public static void main(String[] args) {
    try {
      String recipient = "manager@********.com";

      Context initial = new InitialContext();
      Object objref = initial.lookup("MyMailer");

      MailerHome home =
        (MailerHome)PortableRemoteObject.narrow(objref,
          MailerHome.class);

      Mailer mailer = home.create();
      mailer.sendEmail(recipient);

    }
    catch (Exception e) {
      System.err.println("Caught an unexpected exception!");
      e.printStackTrace();
    }
  }
}
```

NOTE: *You must modify the line that reads:* `String recipient =`
`"manager@********.com";` *The asterisks should be replaced by a valid*
domain name.

Running the Client

We run the client using *runMailerClient.bat*

Figure 13-2
Email Received by
Stockroom Manager

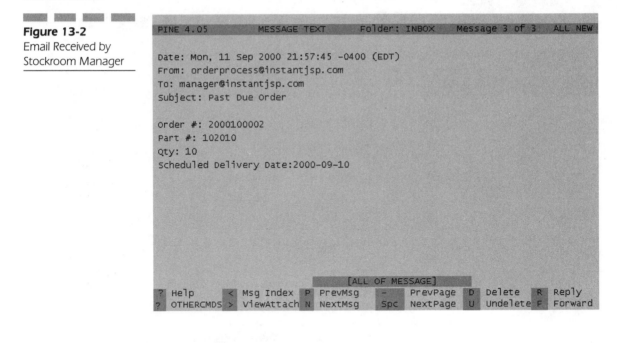

```
PINE 4.05          MESSAGE TEXT     Folder: INBOX    Message 3 of 3    ALL NEW

Date: Mon, 11 Sep 2000 21:57:45 -0400 (EDT)
From: orderprocess@instantjsp.com
To: manager@instantjsp.com
Subject: Past Due Order

Order #: 2000100002
Part #: 102010
Qty: 10
Scheduled Delivery Date:2000-09-10




                                      [ALL OF MESSAGE]
? Help      < Msg Index  P PrevMsg   -    PrevPage  D Delete    R Reply
? OTHERCMDS > ViewAttach N NextMsg   Spc  NextPage  U Undelete  F Forward
```

\Chapter13\code\runMailerClient.bat

When the program runs, the message "Mail Sent" is displayed on the standard output device and we see it in the window in which we started the J2EE server (assuming we used the -verbose option). The recipient named in the client code receives a message like the one shown in Figure 13-2.

Summary

In this chapter, we saw how to send email from an Enterprise JavaBean. We also saw that the bean could be customized to use any SMTP server without changing the code.

 \Chapter13\code\MailerClient.java

```java
import javax.naming.Context;
import javax.naming.InitialContext;
import javax.rmi.PortableRemoteObject;
import Mailer;
import MailerHome;

public class MailerClient {

  public static void main(String[] args) {
    try {
      String recipient = "manager@********.com";

      Context initial = new InitialContext();
      Object objref = initial.lookup("MyMailer");

      MailerHome home =
        (MailerHome)PortableRemoteObject.narrow(objref,
          MailerHome.class);

      Mailer mailer = home.create();
      mailer.sendEmail(recipient);

    }
    catch (Exception e) {
      System.err.println("Caught an unexpected exception!");
      e.printStackTrace();
    }
  }
}
```

NOTE: *You must modify the line that reads:* String recipient = *"manager@********.com"; The asterisks should be replaced by a valid domain name.*

Running the Client

We run the client using *runMailerClient.bat*

Figure 13-2
Email Received by
Stockroom Manager

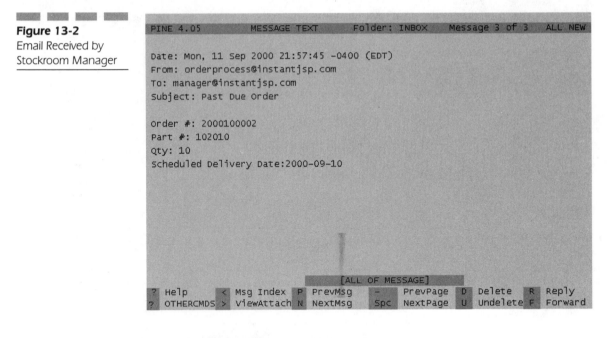

```
PINE 4.05          MESSAGE TEXT      Folder: INBOX    Message 3 of 3    ALL NEW

Date: Mon, 11 Sep 2000 21:57:45 -0400 (EDT)
From: orderprocess@instantjsp.com
To: manager@instantjsp.com
Subject: Past Due Order

order #: 2000100002
Part #: 102010
Qty: 10
Scheduled Delivery Date:2000-09-10




                             [ALL OF MESSAGE]
? Help     <  Msg Index   P  PrevMsg    -    PrevPage   D  Delete    R  Reply
? OTHERCMDS > ViewAttach  N  NextMsg   Spc   NextPage   U  Undelete  F  Forward
```

\Chapter13\code\runMailerClient.bat

When the program runs, the message "Mail Sent" is displayed on the standard output device and we see it in the window in which we started the J2EE server (assuming we used the -verbose option). The recipient named in the client code receives a message like the one shown in Figure 13-2.

Summary

In this chapter, we saw how to send email from an Enterprise JavaBean. We also saw that the bean could be customized to use any SMTP server without changing the code.

CHAPTER **14**

Thinking
Outside
the Box

In this chapter:

■ Remote Monitoring of a Jar File

As we pointed out from the very beginning, Enterprise JavaBeans are all about business logic in a distributed environment. The term *business* usually brings to mind such activities as interest rate calculations, bank transactions, and other activities related to some kind of commerce. Perhaps a better definition of business logic might be any code that performs a task that contributes to the successful operation of our enterprise.

In this chapter, we consider an example that, although perhaps somewhat contrived, demonstrates that beans can be used to perform tasks outside the realm of traditional business procedures but are, nonetheless, an important part of the enterprise.

The Jar File Monitor

Let us suppose that we have a critical application deployed and operational on one of our enterprise servers. We receive a call from the project manager asking us to provide her with a tool to monitor the Jar file in which the components that comprise the application are stored. She wants to issue a query from her desktop that will display the names of all the components in the application and the date/time they were last modified. There are many ways to tackle the problem but, since we now know how to use EJBs, we decide to develop a *JarFileMonitor* bean and provide her with a client that uses our bean.

The Remote Interface

The remote interface is shown below:

\Chapter14\code\RemoteJarMonitor.java

```
import java.io.IOException;
import java.util.jar.JarEntry;
import javax.ejb.EJBObject;
import java.rmi.RemoteException;
import MiniJarEntry;

public interface RemoteJarMonitor extends EJBObject {

    public MiniJarEntry[] getEntries() throws RemoteException;

}
```

The single method in the remote interface returns an array of objects of type *MiniJarEntry*. The code for class *MiniJarEntry* is as follows:

\Chapter14\code\MiniJarEntry.java

```
import java.io.Serializable;
import java.util.Date;

public class MiniJarEntry implements Serializable {
    private String name;
    private long size;
    private Date time;

    MiniJarEntry() {
    }

    public String getName() {
        return name;
    }

    public long getSize() {
        return size;
    }

    public Date getTime() {
        return time;
    }
```

```
public void setName(String name) {
  this.name = name;
}


public void setSize(long size) {
  this.size = size;
}


public void setTime(long time) {
  this.time = new Date(time);
}
}
```

The three private instance variables hold the name of a *Jar-Entry,* the size of the entry, and a `long`, representing the date/time the entry was modified. The *MiniJarEntry* class implements *java.io.Serializable*. All objects that are transferred be-tween components in a distributed environment must be capable of being serialized. If we tried to write a version of the remote inter-face whose `getEntries()` method was defined as returning an array of *JarEntry* objects, it would compile, although the corre-sponding `getEntries()` method in the bean code would throw an exception at runtime. Our solution is to use the *MiniJarEntry* class, which is serializable. When we discuss the bean code, we will see how its `getEntries()` method creates and returns an instance of *MiniJarEntry*.

The Home Interface

Here is the code for the home interface:

 \Chapter14\code\RemoteJarMonitorHome.java

```
import java.io.Serializable;
import java.rmi.RemoteException;
import javax.ejb.CreateException;
import javax.ejb.EJBHome;
```

```
public interface RemoteJarMonitorHome extends EJBHome {

  RemoteJarMonitor create()
    throws RemoteException, CreateException;
}
```

The Enterprise Bean

The code for the enterprise bean follows:

\Chapter14\code\RemoteJarMonitorBean.java

```
import java.util.*;
import java.util.jar.*;
import java.util.zip.*;
import javax.naming.*;
import javax.ejb.*;
import java.net.*;
import java.io.*;


import MiniJarEntry;

public class RemoteJarMonitorBean implements SessionBean {

  private JarFile jarFile = null;

  public MiniJarEntry[] getEntries() {
    Context context;
    URL url;
    JarURLConnection connection;

    try {
      context = new InitialContext();
      url = (URL)context.lookup("java:comp/env/url/MyURL");
      connection = (JarURLConnection)url.openConnection();
      jarFile = (JarFile)connection.getJarFile();
      Vector v = new Vector();
      for (Enumeration e = jarFile.entries();
          e.hasMoreElements();) {
        v.add((JarEntry)e.nextElement());
      }
      MiniJarEntry[] jeArray = new MiniJarEntry[v.size()];
```

```
        for (int i = 0; i < v.size(); ++i) {
          JarEntry je = (JarEntry)v.elementAt(i);
          jeArray[i] = new MiniJarEntry();
          jeArray[i].setName(je.getName());
          jeArray[i].setSize(je.getSize());
          jeArray[i].setTime(je.getTime());
        }
        return jeArray;
      }
      catch (Exception e) {
        throw new EJBException(e.getMessage());
      }
    }


    public void ejbCreate() {
      }


    public void ejbRemove() {
      }


    public void ejbActivate() {
    }


    public void ejbPassivate() {
    }


    public void setSessionContext(SessionContext sc) {
    }
  }
```

We see that the `getEntries()` method passes `java:comp/env/url/MyURL` to the `lookup()` method to find a resource. This is the same mechanism we used in the previous chapter to find a mail session. The resource we find is the URL to which *url/MyURL* is mapped. When we package and deploy the bean shortly, we will see that this URL is "jar:http://localhost:8000/monitor/Test.jar!/". From the syntax, we know this is a JAR URL. When we invoke `openConnection()` against it, a *JarURLConnection* is returned. We get the Jar file by invoking the `getJarFile()` method against this connection. The remainder of the code in `getEntries()` obtains information about each entry in the Jar file and uses the setter methods to store the information in an instance of *MiniJarEntry*. All instances of *MiniJarEntry*—one for each entry in the Jar file—are stored in an array and this array is returned to the caller of `getEntries()`.

Packaging and Deploying

Before we begin the packaging and deployment procedure, we first create a test Jar file that we can monitor. The Jar file we create contains the components of the *RemoteJarMonitor* bean. Under normal conditions, it would contain all the components of some application. We create our simple Jar file using the command:

```
jar -cvf Test.jar RemoteJarMon*.class
```

We package our *RemoteJarMonitor* as a stateless session bean using the parameters shown in Table 14-1.

When we reach the Resource References dialog, we click on ADD and populate the entry that appears. We type *url/MyURL* into the first field, select *java.net.URL* from the drop-down list in the second column and select *Container* from the drop-down list in the third column. When *java.net.URL* is selected from the drop-down list in the second column, a group box labeled DEPLOYMENT SETTINGS FOR *url/MyURL* appears. In the entry field labeled :URL:" we type *jar:http:localhost:8000/jarcontext/Test.jar!/*. The completed dialog looks like Figure 14-1.

Under normal conditions, the Jar file we are monitoring would be deployed in its own application. For convenience, we simply create a War file in *RemoteJarMonitorApp* and add the *Test.jar* file we created earlier to it.

We now start deployment, during which we specify the JNDI names shown in Table 14-2. Additionally, we must specify *jar-context* as the context root for the War file.

	Parameter	Value
TABLE 14-1 Parameters for Packaging RemoteJarMonitor Bean	Application File Name	RemoteJarMonitorApp.ear
	Application Display Name	RemoteJarMonitorApp
	JAR Display Name	RemoteMonitorJar
	Enterprise Bean Class	RemoteJarMonitorBean
	Home Interface	RemoteJarMonitorHome
	Remote Interface	RemoteJarMonitor

Figure 14-1

Specifying Resource
References for
RemoteJarMonitor
Bean

```
Application Deployment Tool: RemoteJarMonitorApp                    _ □ X
File   Edit   Server   Tools   Help

Local Applications: Inspecting: RemoteJarMonitorApp.RemoteMonitorWar.RemoteJarMonitorBean
  ♀ ◇ RemoteJar      EJB References   Resource Ref's   Security   Transactions
      🗐 Remote           General            Entity              Environment
    ♀ 🗐 Remote      ┌Resource Factories Referenced in Code──────────────────────
      ✎ Rem          ┌──────────────┬──────────────┬──────────────┐   ┌────────┐
  ♀ ◇ RemoteJar      │ Coded Name   │   Type       │ Authentication│   │  Add   │
    ♀ 🗐 Remote      │ url/MyURL    │ java.net.URL │ Container     │   └────────┘
      ✎ Rem          │              │              │               │   ┌────────┐
      🗐 Remote      └──────────────┴──────────────┴──────────────┘   │ Delete...│
                                                                       └────────┘
                     Description:
                     ┌──────────────────────────────────────────┐
                     │                                          │
                     └──────────────────────────────────────────┘
                     ┌Deployment Settings for url/MyURL──────────────
                     URL:
                     ┌──────────────────────────────────────────┐
   ◄ ▒▒▒▒  ►         │ jar:http://localhost:8000/monitor/Test.jar!/│
                     └──────────────────────────────────────────┘
  Servers:           Server Applications:
  🖳 localhost        ◇ RemoteJarMonitorApp                          ┌────────┐
                                                                     │Undeploy│
                                                                     └────────┘
```

The Client

The client we develop is a simple standalone client for which the
code looks like this:

On the CD

\Chapter14\code\RemoteJarMonitorClient.java

TABLE 14-2

JNDI Names

Referenced By	Component/Reference Name	JNDI Name
	RemoteJarMonitorBean	MyRemoteJarMonitor
RemoteJarMonitorBean	url/MyURL	jar:http://localhost:8000/ jarcontext/Test.jar!/

```
import java.util.*;
import java.util.jar.JarEntry;
import javax.naming.Context;
import javax.naming.InitialContext;
import javax.rmi.PortableRemoteObject;

import RemoteJarMonitor;
import RemoteJarMonitorHome;

import MiniJarEntry;

public class RemoteJarMonitorClient {

  public static void main(String[] args) {
    try {
      Context initial = new InitialContext();
      Object objref = initial.lookup("MyRemoteJarMonitor");

      RemoteJarMonitorHome home =
        (RemoteJarMonitorHome)PortableRemoteObject.narrow(objref,
          RemoteJarMonitorHome.class);

      RemoteJarMonitor remoteJarMonitor = home.create();
      MiniJarEntry[cb je = remoteJarMonitor.getEntries();
      System.out.println();
      for (int i = 0; i < je.length; ++i) {
        System.out.println("Entry: " + je[i].getName());
        System.out.println(" Size: " + je[i].getSize());
        System.out.println(" Date: " + je[i].getTime());
        System.out.println();
      }
    }
    catch (Exception e) {
      System.err.println("Caught an unexpected exception!");
      e.printStackTrace();
    }
  }
}
```

Running the Client

We run the client using *runRemoteJarMonitorClient*.

 ▬ ▬ ▬ ▬ ▬ ▬ ▬ ▬ ▬ ▬ ▬ ▬ ▬ ▬ ▬ ▬ ▬ ▬
\Chapter14\code\runRemoteJarMonitorClient.bat

The first time we run the client, we see output similar to that shown in Figure 14-2.

Figure 14-2
Output from Remote-
JarMonitorClient

```
Command                                                          _ □ X
d:\instant_ejb\Chapter14\code>runRemoteJarMonitor

Entry: META-INF/
  Size: 0
  Date: Sat Sep 30 21:34:22 EDT 2000

Entry: META-INF/MANIFEST.MF
  Size: 68
  Date: Sat Sep 30 21:34:24 EDT 2000

Entry: RemoteJarMonitor.class
  Size: 234
  Date: Sat Sep 30 21:33:08 EDT 2000

Entry: RemoteJarMonitorBean.class
  Size: 2445
  Date: Sat Sep 30 21:33:08 EDT 2000

Entry: RemoteJarMonitorHome.class
  Size: 272
  Date: Sat Sep 30 21:33:08 EDT 2000

d:\instant_ejb\Chapter14\code>
```

If we use *compileRemoteJarMonitor.bat* to recompile the three components of *RemoteJarMonitor,* redeploy *RemoteJarMonitorApp,* and run the client again, we see that the output shows new date/time stamps as shown in Figure 14-3.

NOTE: *The updated version of* Test.jar *may not be detected until the server is stopped and restarted.*

Figure 14-3
After Jar File
Modification

```
Command                                                          _ □ X
  Size: 0
  Date: Sat Sep 30 22:52:08 EDT 2000

Entry: META-INF/MANIFEST.MF
  Size: 68
  Date: Sat Sep 30 22:52:08 EDT 2000

Entry: RemoteJarMonitor.class
  Size: 234
  Date: Sat Sep 30 22:12:28 EDT 2000

Entry: RemoteJarMonitorBean.class
  Size: 2445
  Date: Sat Sep 30 22:12:28 EDT 2000

Entry: RemoteJarMonitorClient.class
  Size: 1974
  Date: Sat Sep 30 22:50:28 EDT 2000

Entry: RemoteJarMonitorHome.class
  Size: 272
  Date: Sat Sep 30 22:12:28 EDT 2000

d:\instant_ejb\Chapter14\code>_
```

Summary

In this chapter, we developed an EJB to perform a task that is somewhat different from what we would normally classify as *business* logic. We did this to show that the solution to many problems can be found in Enterprise JavaBeans.

CHAPTER **15**

So What's the Price?

In this chapter:

- Deriving Crude Timings
- Demonstrating What Takes So Much Time
- A User's View of Performance

By now it should be clear that EJBs do indeed make a developer's job easier. Like any tool or environment that helps the developer, EJBs are subjected to the question "So what's the price we pay at execution time?" We do not in any way pretend that a single chapter in an introductory book on EJBs can provide a comprehensive answer to this question. We can, however, perform some simple measurements that give us some insight into the performance of EJBs.

Our First Look at EJB Performance

We start our crude performance measurement by developing a simple stateful session bean that contains a single instance variable and a method that increments it. We capture the current time at strategic points in the code and use the captured values to determine elapsed time.

NOTE: *Simple reporting of timestamps at various points during the execution of a program is not a very scientific way of measuring performance; however, it is easy to implement and serves our immediate purpose in this chapter.*

The Remote Interface

Here is the code for the remote interface:

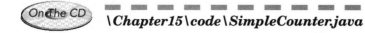

\Chapter15\code\SimpleCounter.java

```java
import javax.ejb.EJBObject;

import java.rmi.RemoteException;

public interface SimpleCounter extends EJBObject {

  public int next() throws RemoteException;
}
```

The Home Interface

The home interface is listed below:

\Chapter15\code\SimpleCounterHome.java

```java
import java.io.Serializable;
import java.rmi.RemoteException;
import javax.ejb.CreateException;
import javax.ejb.EJBHome;

public interface SimpleCounterHome extends EJBHome {

    SimpleCounter create()
      throws RemoteException, CreateException;
}
```

The Enterprise Bean

The enterprise bean looks like this:

\Chapter15\code\SimpleCounterBean.java

```java
import java.rmi.RemoteException;
import javax.ejb.CreateException;
import javax.ejb.SessionBean;
import javax.ejb.SessionContext;

public class SimpleCounterBean implements SessionBean {
```

```
  int counter;

  public int next() {
    return ++counter;
  }

  public void ejbCreate() throws CreateException {
    counter = 0;
  }
  public void ejbRemove() {}
  public void ejbActivate() {}
  public void ejbPassivate() {}
  public void setSessionContext(SessionContext sc) {}
}
```

Packaging and Deploying

We compile the bean by typing `compileSimpleCounter`.

 \Chapter15\code\compileSimpleCounter.bat

To allow us to concentrate on our goal of measuring performance, we simply load the application from the prepackaged .ear file using the "Open Application . . ." option in the "File" drop-down menu.

 \Chapter15\code\SimpleTimingApp.ear

This file contains beans and Web components for the remainder of this chapter.

The Client

We use a simple standalone client, which is listed below.

 \Chapter15\code\SimpleCounterClient.java

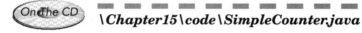

On The CD *\Chapter15\code\SimpleCounter.java*

```java
import javax.ejb.EJBObject;

import java.rmi.RemoteException;

public interface SimpleCounter extends EJBObject {

  public int next() throws RemoteException;
}
```

The Home Interface

The home interface is listed below:

On The CD *\Chapter15\code\SimpleCounterHome.java*

```java
import java.io.Serializable;
import java.rmi.RemoteException;
import javax.ejb.CreateException;
import javax.ejb.EJBHome;

public interface SimpleCounterHome extends EJBHome {

    SimpleCounter create()
      throws RemoteException, CreateException;
}
```

The Enterprise Bean

The enterprise bean looks like this:

On The CD *\Chapter15\code\SimpleCounterBean.java*

```java
import java.rmi.RemoteException;
import javax.ejb.CreateException;
import javax.ejb.SessionBean;
import javax.ejb.SessionContext;

public class SimpleCounterBean implements SessionBean {
```

```
int counter;

public int next() {
  return ++counter;
}

public void ejbCreate() throws CreateException {
  counter = 0;
}
public void ejbRemove() {}
public void ejbActivate() {}
public void ejbPassivate() {}
public void setSessionContext(SessionContext sc) {}
}
```

Packaging and Deploying

We compile the bean by typing `compileSimpleCounter`.

\Chapter15\code\compileSimpleCounter.bat

To allow us to concentrate on our goal of measuring performance, we simply load the application from the prepackaged .ear file using the "Open Application . . ." option in the "File" drop-down menu.

\Chapter15\code\SimpleTimingApp.ear

This file contains beans and Web components for the remainder of this chapter.

The Client

We use a simple standalone client, which is listed below.

\Chapter15\code\SimpleCounterClient.java

```
import java.util.Date;
import javax.naming.Context;
import javax.naming.InitialContext;
import javax.rmi.PortableRemoteObject;

import SimpleCounter;
import SimpleCounterHome;

public class SimpleCounterClient {

  public static void main(String[] args) {

    int iterations = 0;

    if (args.length != 1) {
      abort("requires one argument");
    }

    try {
      iterations = Integer.parseInt (args[0]);
    }
    catch (NumberFormatException e) {
      abort(args[0] + " is not a valid integer");
    }

    if (iterations <= 0) {
      abort("iteration count must be positive");
    }

    long started = new Date().getTime();

    try {
      Context initial = new InitialContext();
      Object objref = initial.lookup("MySimpleCounter");

      long completedLookup = new Date().getTime();

      SimpleCounterHome home =
        (SimpleCounterHome)PortableRemoteObject.narrow(objref,
        SimpleCounterHome.class);

      long gotHomeInterface = new Date().getTime();

      SimpleCounter counter = home.create();

      long createdInstance = new Date().getTime();

      for (int i = 0; i < iterations; ++i) {
        counter.next();
      }
```

```
            long ended = new Date().getTime();

            System.out.println("lookup took " +
                (completedLookup - started) + " milliseconds");

            System.out.println("getting home interface took " +
                (gotHomeInterface - completedLookup) + " milliseconds");

            System.out.println("creating bean took " +
                (createdInstance - gotHomeInterface) + " milliseconds");

            System.out.println(iterations + " iterations took " +
                (ended - createdInstance) + " milliseconds");

            System.out.println("total elapsed time was " +
                (ended - started) + " milliseconds");
        }
        catch (Exception ex) {
            System.err.println("Caught an unexpected exception!");
            ex.printStackTrace();
        }
    }

    private static void abort(String message) {
        System.out.println("Program terminating");
        System.out.println(message);
        System.exit(0);
    }
}
```

Running

We compile the client by typing `compileSimpleCounterClient`.

\Chapter15\code\compileSimpleCounterClient.bat

When we run the client by typing `runSimpleCounterClient`, we observe the output shown in Figure 15-1.

\Chapter15\code\runSimpleCounterClient.bat

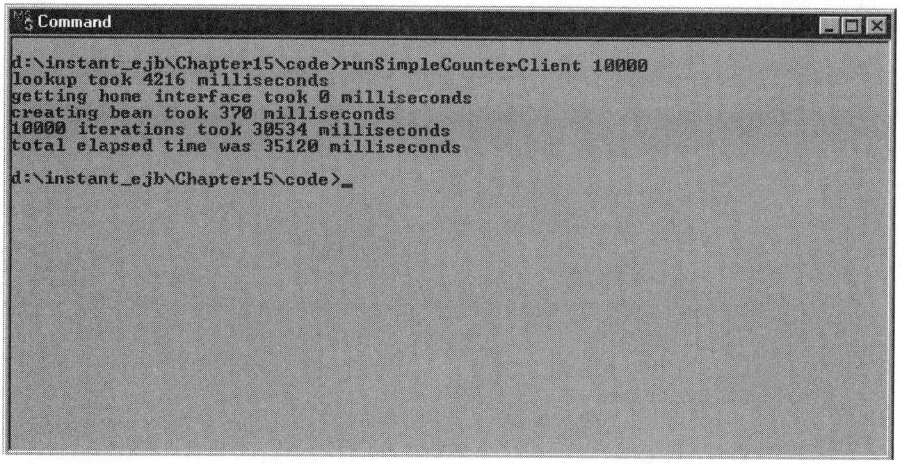

Figure 15-1
Output from
SimpleCounterClient

```
Command                                                                    _ □ ×
d:\instant_ejb\Chapter15\code>runSimpleCounterClient 10000
lookup took 4216 milliseconds
getting home interface took 0 milliseconds
creating bean took 370 milliseconds
10000 iterations took 30534 milliseconds
total elapsed time was 35120 milliseconds

d:\instant_ejb\Chapter15\code>_
```

We are probably not too surprised that the lookup takes in
excess of 4 seconds the first time we run the client. We might also
conclude that the smaller figures for subsequent lookups in Figure
15-2 are the result of caching, although this is purely empirical. We
may not find the time required to create the bean excessive. The
figure that might raise our eyebrows in the 30 seconds required to
increment the counter 10000 times; that equates to .3 seconds per
increment—quite slow even for the 266-MHz Pentium II on which
the code was run.

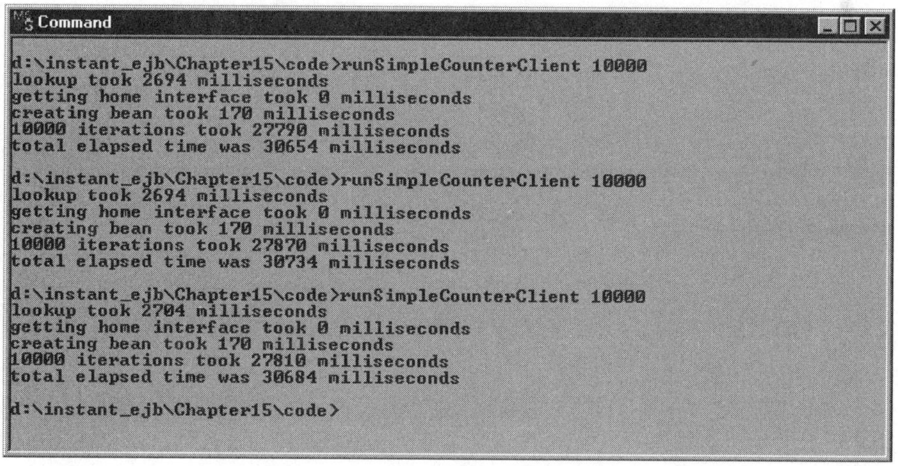

Figure 15-2
Three Subsequent
Executions of
SimpleCounterClient

```
Command                                                                    _ □ ×
d:\instant_ejb\Chapter15\code>runSimpleCounterClient 10000
lookup took 2694 milliseconds
getting home interface took 0 milliseconds
creating bean took 170 milliseconds
10000 iterations took 27790 milliseconds
total elapsed time was 30654 milliseconds

d:\instant_ejb\Chapter15\code>runSimpleCounterClient 10000
lookup took 2694 milliseconds
getting home interface took 0 milliseconds
creating bean took 170 milliseconds
10000 iterations took 27870 milliseconds
total elapsed time was 30734 milliseconds

d:\instant_ejb\Chapter15\code>runSimpleCounterClient 10000
lookup took 2704 milliseconds
getting home interface took 0 milliseconds
creating bean took 170 milliseconds
10000 iterations took 27810 milliseconds
total elapsed time was 30684 milliseconds

d:\instant_ejb\Chapter15\code>
```

Trying a Non-EJB Version

We now step outside the world of EJB and write the counter program using a simple Java program that creates an instance of a class we call NonBeanCounter and invokes its next() method a specified number of times. Here is the code:

On the CD

\Chapter15\code\NonBeanCounter.java

```java
import java.util.Date;

public class NonBeanCounter {

  int counter;

  public NonBeanCounter() {
    counter = 0;
  }

  public int next() {
    return ++counter;
  }

  public static void main(String[] args) {
    int iterations = 0;

    if (args.length != 1) {
      abort("requires one argument");
    }

    try {
      iterations = Integer.parseInt(args[0]);
    }
    catch (NumberFormatException e) {
      abort(args[0] + " is not a valid integer");
    }

    if (iterations <= 0) {
      abort("iteration count must be positive");
    }

    NonBeanCounter counter = new NonBeanCounter();
```

```
long start = new Date().getTime();

for (int i = 0; i < iterations; ++i) {
  counter.next();
}

long elapsedTime = new Date().getTime() - start;

System.out.println(iterations + " iterations in " +
  elapsedTime + " milliseconds");
}

private static void abort(String message) {
  System.out.println("Program terminating");
  System.out.println(message);
  System.exit(0);
}
}
```

Running the Simple Version

When we compile the non-EJB version using `javac NonBean-Counter.java` and run it by typing `java NonBeanCounter 10000`, we observe the output shown in Figure 15-3.

Figure 15-3
Output from
Non-EJB
Counting Program

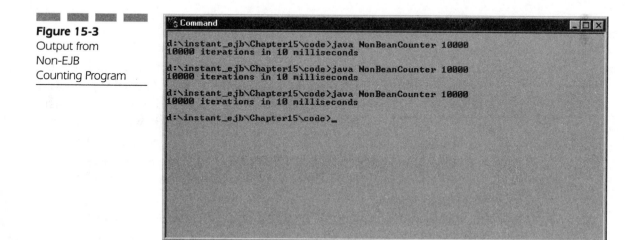

Drawing Some Conclusions

Before we conclude from the experiment we just performed that EJBs are too slow to be of value, we should consider the following:

- If we use the wrong tool to do a job, we shouldn't blame the tool. It would make as much sense to develop an enterprise bean to perform such a trivial task as counting as it would to use a million-dollar ICBM to shoot skeet.

- A more equitable comparison might be obtained by using a version of the non-EJB counter than is RMI-enabled. You might want to try it as an additional exercise.

- There's more to performance than speed. A rowboat might be easier to maneuver than a battleship and might require only a reasonable amount of elbow grease rather than thousands of gallons of diesel fuel. If we had to cross the ocean facing enemy fire, would a rowboat be our vessel of choice?

Reducing the Network Penalty

Enterprise JavaBeans use RMI. Every method invocation effectively results in the transfer of a serialized form of a stack frame across the network. In the experiment we just performed, the simple example was operating at the speed at which the JVM executed byte code. The EJB version had additional dependencies—the speed of the network and the amount of traffic it was carrying. It would seem that one way to improve performance is to reduce the number of network transfers. The next example, although perhaps somewhat contrived, attempts to demonstrate one way we can accomplish this.

The example is a simple program that adds all of the integers from 1 to a specified upper limit. We could take either of the following approaches:

■ store a running sum in an instance variable to which an add() method adds the number specified in its argument and invoke this method repetitively

■ pass a single number to an add() method that performs all of the additions within a single invocation and returns the sum

We opt to use the latter approach.

The Remote Interface

The remote interface is as follows:

\Chapter15\code\SimpleAdder.java

```java
import javax.ejb.EJBObject;
import java.rmi.RemoteException;

public interface SimpleAdder extends EJBObject {

  public long add(int iterations)
    throws RemoteException;
}
```

The Home Interface

Here is the home interface:

\Chapter15\code\SimpleAdderHome.java

```java
import java.io.Serializable;
import java.rmi.RemoteException;
import javax.ejb.CreateException;
import javax.ejb.EJBHome;

public interface SimpleAdderHome extends EJBHome {
  SimpleAdder create()
    throws RemoteException, CreateException;
}
```

The Enterprise Bean

The enterprise bean looks like this:

On the CD **\Chapter15\code\SimpleAdderBean.java**

```java
import java.rmi.RemoteException;
import javax.ejb.CreateException;
import javax.ejb.SessionBean;
import javax.ejb.SessionContext;

public class SimpleAdderBean implements SessionBean {

  public long add(int iterations) {
    long sum = 0;
    for (int i = 1; i <= iterations; ++i) {
      sum += i;
    }
    return sum;
  }

  public void ejbCreate() throws CreateException {
  }

  public void ejbRemove() {}
  public void ejbActivate() {}
  public void ejbPassivate() {}
  public void setSessionContext(SessionContext sc) {}
}
```

Packaging and Deploying

As we have already mentioned, the EJB used in this example is included in the .ear file we already loaded.

The Client

Here is the listing for the simple standalone client:

On the CD

\Chapter15\code\SimpleAdderClient.java

```java
import java.util.Date;

import javax.naming.Context;
import javax.naming.InitialContext;
import javax.rmi.PortableRemoteObject;

import SimpleAdder;
import SimpleAdderHome;

public class SimpleAdderClient {

  public static void main(String[] args) {

    int iterations = 0;

    if (args.length != 1) {
      abort("requires one argument");
    }

    try {
      iterations = Integer.parseInt(args[0]);
    }
    catch (NumberFormatException e) {
      abort(args[0] + " is not a valid integer");
    }

    if (iterations <= 0) {
      abort("iteration count must be positive");
    }

    long started = new Date().getTime();

    try {
      Context initial = new InitialContext();
      Object objref = initial.lookup("MySimpleAdder");

      long completedLookup = new Date().getTime();

      SimpleAdderHome home =
        (SimpleAdderHome)PortableRemoteObject.narrow(objref,
        SimpleAdderHome.class);

      long gotHomeInterface = new Date().getTime();

      SimpleAdder adder = home.create();

      long createdInstance = new Date().getTime();
```

```
        adder.add(iterations);

        long ended = new Date().getTime();

        System.out.println("lookup took " +
          (completedLookup - started) + " milliseconds");      .

        System.out.println("getting home interface took " +
          (gotHomeInterface - completedLookup) + " milliseconds");

        System.out.println("creating bean took " +
          (createdInstance - gotHomeInterface) + " milliseconds");

        System.out.println("accumulation took " +
          (ended - createdInstance) + " milliseconds");

        System.out.println("total elapsed time was " +
          (ended - started) + " milliseconds");
      }
    catch (Exception ex) {
      System.err.println("Caught an unexpected exception!");
      ex.printStackTrace();
    }
  }

  private static void abort(String message) {
    System.out.println("Program terminating");
    System.out.println(message);
    System.exit(0);
  }
}
```

Running

When we run the client using `runSimpleAdderClient`, we observe the output shown in Figure 15-4.

 \Chapter15\code\runSimpleAdderClient.bat

Once More Without the EJB

We now examine a program that performs the accumulation without using an EJB.

Figure 15-4
Output from
SimpleAdderClient

```
Command                                                                    _ □ ×
d:\instant_ejb\Chapter15\code>runSimpleAdderClient 10000
lookup took 2814 milliseconds
getting home interface took 0 milliseconds
creating bean took 260 milliseconds
accumulation took 30 milliseconds
total elapsed time was 3104 milliseconds

d:\instant_ejb\Chapter15\code>runSimpleAdderClient 10000
lookup took 2724 milliseconds
getting home interface took 0 milliseconds
creating bean took 120 milliseconds
accumulation took 10 milliseconds
total elapsed time was 2854 milliseconds

d:\instant_ejb\Chapter15\code>runSimpleAdderClient 10000
lookup took 2744 milliseconds
getting home interface took 0 milliseconds
creating bean took 120 milliseconds
accumulation took 10 milliseconds
total elapsed time was 2874 milliseconds

d:\instant_ejb\Chapter15\code>_
```

\Chapter15\code\NonBeanAdder.java

```java
import java.util.Date;

public class NonBeanAdder {

  public NonBeanAdder() {
  }

  public long add(int iterations) {
    long sum = 0;
    for (int i = 1; i <= iterations; ++i) {
      sum += i;
    }
    return sum;
  }

  public static void main(String[] args) {

    int iterations = 0;

    if (args.length != 1) {
      abort("requires one argument");
    }

    try {
      iterations = Integer.parseInt(args[0]);
    }
    catch (NumberFormatException e) {
      abort(args[0] + " is not a valid integer");
    }
```

```
  if (iterations <= 0) {
    abort("iteration count must be positive");
  }

  NonBeanAdder adder = new NonBeanAdder();

  long start = new Date().getTime();

  long sum = adder.add(iterations);
  System.out.println("sum = " + sum);

  long elapsedTime = new Date().getTime() - start;

  System.out.println(iterations + " iterations in " +
    elapsedTime + " milliseconds");
}

private static void abort(String message) {
  System.out.println("Program terminating");
  System.out.println(message);
  System.exit(0);
}
}
```

Running the Non-EJB Version

After we compile the simple version using `javac NonBeanAdder.java`, we run it using `java NonBeanAdder` and observe the output shown in Figure 15-5.

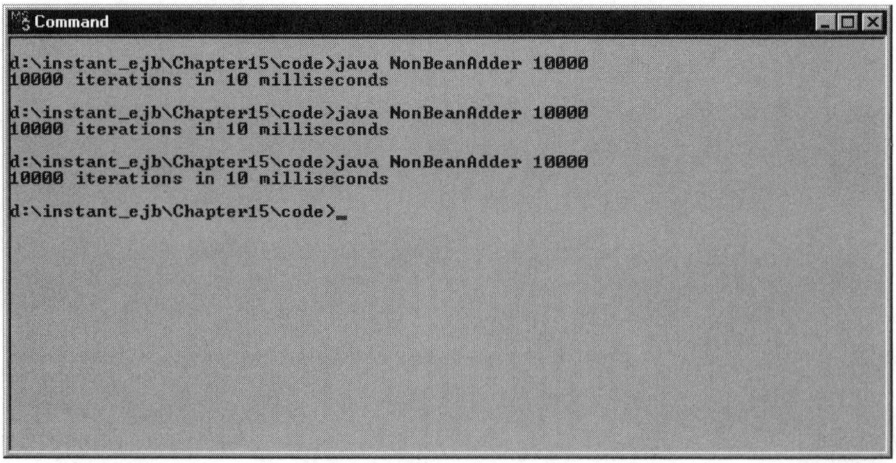

Figure 15-5
Output from
NonBeanAdder

```
d:\instant_ejb\Chapter15\code>java NonBeanAdder 10000
10000 iterations in 10 milliseconds

d:\instant_ejb\Chapter15\code>java NonBeanAdder 10000
10000 iterations in 10 milliseconds

d:\instant_ejb\Chapter15\code>java NonBeanAdder 10000
10000 iterations in 10 milliseconds

d:\instant_ejb\Chapter15\code>_
```

Analyzing What We Observed

As we might have expected, the performance of the non-EJB version was the same as what we observed in the first example. The EJB version, however, performed much better. The lesson we should learn is that remote method invocation is indeed expensive. This can be verified by RMI-enabling the non-EJB version.

A User's Perspective

Although the statistics we just gathered—crude as they are— might be of value to those responsible for building infrastructure and developing applications, a user views things somewhat differently. A user sees performance in terms of how long he or she has to watch an hourglass icon between the time a button is clicked and the time the next screen appears. The next two examples attempt to show the difference between the EJB and non-EJB solution as perceived by a user.

Each example begins with an HTML page that accepts an integer and sends it as part of a request to a JavaServer Page. The JSP uses a `<jsp:setProperty/>` action to save the integer in an instance variable of a JavaBean. It then invokes the JavaBean's `add()` method to sum all of the numbers between 1 and the specified value. The `add()` method in the JavaBean used by the first example is a shadow method that invokes the `add()` method of an EJB. The `add()` method used by the second JavaBean performs the accumulation itself.

The Intermediate JavaBean

Here is the code for the intermediate JavaBean we use in our first example.

\Chapter15\code\IntermediateAdderBean

```java
import java.rmi.RemoteException;

import javax.ejb.FinderException;
import javax.naming.Context;
import javax.naming.InitialContext;
import javax.rmi.PortableRemoteObject;

import SimpleAdder;
import SimpleAdderBean;
import SimpleAdderHome;

public class IntermediateAdderBean {

  private int iterations;

  SimpleAdder adder;

  public IntermediateAdderBean() {
    try {
      Context ic = new InitialContext();
      java.lang.Object objref =
        ic.lookup("java:comp/env/ejb/SimpleAdder");
      SimpleAdderHome home =
        (SimpleAdderHome) PortableRemoteObject.narrow(objref,
          SimpleAdderHome.class);
      adder = home.create();
    }
    catch (Exception e) {
      System.err.println ("Couldn't locate SimpleAdderHome");
      e.printStackTrace();
    }
  }

  public void setIterations(int iterations) {
    this.iterations = iterations;
  }

  public int getIterations() {
    return iterations;
  }

  public long add() throws Exception {
    try {
      return adder.add(iterations);
    }
    catch (RemoteException e) {
      throw new Exception(e.getMessage());
    }
  }
}
```

As we will see when we examine the JSP that uses this JavaBean, the scope of the bean is "session". We perform the lookup, find the home interface, and create the instance of the EJB in the constructor to avoid having to perform these high overhead operations each time the bean is used.

The JSP

The JSP, which contains strategically placed timestamps, looks like this:

\Chapter15\code\AddUsingEJB.jsp

```jsp
<%@ page import="java.util.*" %>
<%@ page import="java.text.*" %>
<%@ page errorPage="AddError" %>
<jsp:useBean id="adderJavaBean" class="IntermediateAdderBean"
  scope="session" />
<%
  SimpleDateFormat sdf =
    new SimpleDateFormat("dd MMM yyyy hh:mm:ss.SSS");
  String sdt = sdf.format(new Date());
  long start = new Date().getTime();
  long answer = adderJavaBean.add();
%>
<html>
<head>
<title>Add Results</title>
</head>
<body>
<%= sdt %>
<br>
<jsp:setProperty name="adderJavaBean" property="*" />
Iterations:
<jsp:getProperty name="adderJavaBean" property="iterations"/>
<p>
Sum:
<%= answer %>
<p>
<%= new Date().getTime() - start %>
<p>
<%
  String edt = sdf.format(new Date());
%>
<%= edt %>
<%= new Date() %>
<p>
```

```
<a href="http://localhost:8000/Timing/AddUsingEJB.html">
Next Test
</a>
</body>
</html>
```

The HTML

The data entry form presented to the user comes from the following HTML:

\Chapter15\code\AddUsingEJB.html

```
<html>
<head>
<title>Timing Using EJB</title>
</head>
<body>
<center>
<h1>Simple Timing Test Using EJB</h1>
<form method="post"
action="http://localhost:8000/Timing/AddUsingEJB">
<table>
  <tr>
    <td>Iterations: </td>
    <td><input name="iterations" type="text"></td>
  </tr>
</table>
<br>
<br>
<input type="submit" value="Perform Addition">
</form>
</center>
</body>
</html>
```

Running the First Web-based Example

We access our first Web-based example by entering the following URL:

```
http://localhost:8000/Timing/AddUsingEjb.html
```

The screen that appears looks like Figure 15-6 after we enter a value of 10000. When we click on the button labeled PERFORM ADDITION, we observe the output shown in Figure 15-7. After we click on NEXT TEST and enter a value of 1000000, we see the output shown in Figure 15-8.

A Simpler JavaBean

The JavaBean we use in our second Web-based example is simpler. It looks like this:

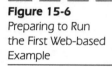

\Chapter15\code\IntermediateAdderBeanNoEJB.java

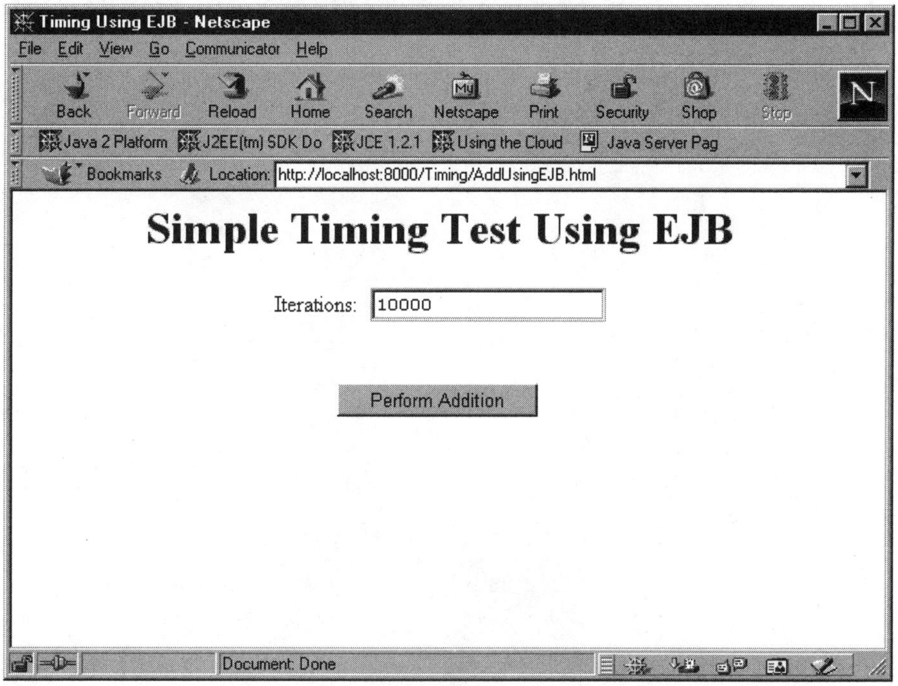

Figure 15-6
Preparing to Run
the First Web-based
Example

Timing Using EJB - Netscape

File Edit View Go Communicator Help

Back Forward Reload Home Search Netscape Print Security Shop Stop

Java 2 Platform J2EE (tm) SDK Do JCE 1.2.1 Using the Cloud Java Server Pag

Bookmarks Location: http://localhost:8000/Timing/AddUsingEJB.html

Simple Timing Test Using EJB

Iterations: 10000

Perform Addition

Document: Done

Figure 15-7
Timing for 10000
Iterations

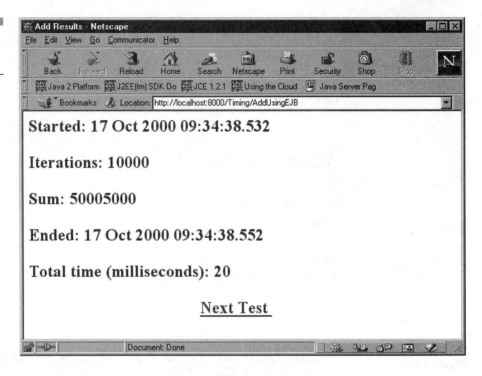

```
public class IntermediateAdderBeanNoEJB {

  private int iterations;

  public IntermediateAdderBeanNoEJB() {
  }

  public void setIterations(int iterations) {
    this.iterations = iterations;
  }

  public int getIterations() {
    return iterations;
  }

  public long add() throws Exception {
    long sum = 0;
    for (int i = 1; i <= iterations; ++i) {
      sum += i;
    }
    return sum;
  }
}
```

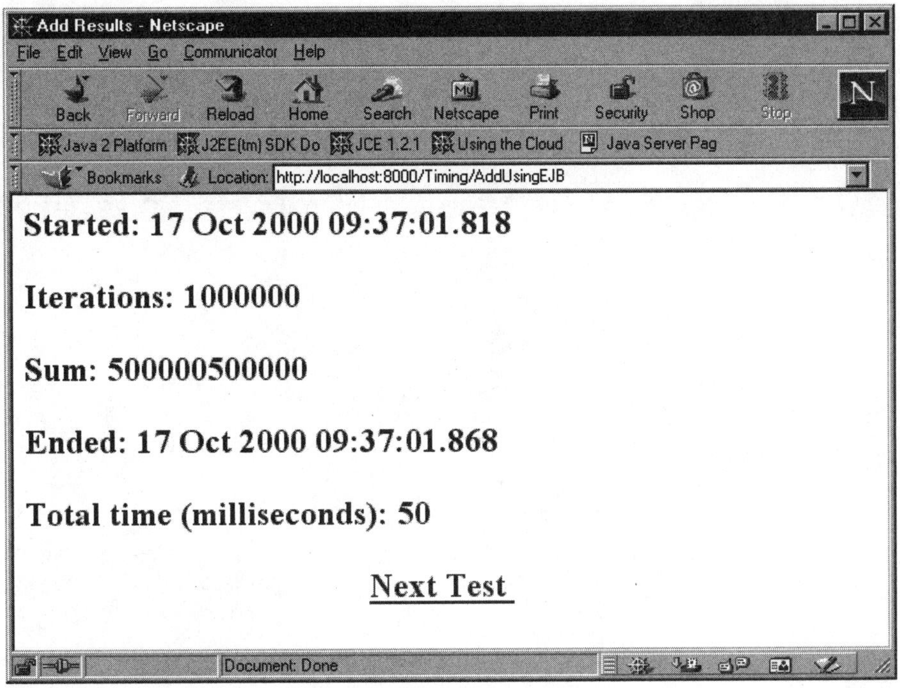

Figure 15-8
Timing for 1000000
Iterations

> **Add Results - Netscape**
>
> File Edit View Go Communicator Help
>
> Back | Forward | Reload | Home | Search | Netscape | Print | Security | Shop | Stop | N
>
> Java 2 Platform | J2EE(tm) SDK Do | JCE 1.2.1 | Using the Cloud | Java Server Pag
>
> Bookmarks | Location: http://localhost:8000/Timing/AddUsingEJB |
>
> ## Started: 17 Oct 2000 09:37:01.818
>
> ## Iterations: 1000000
>
> ## Sum: 500000500000
>
> ## Ended: 17 Oct 2000 09:37:01.868
>
> ## Total time (milliseconds): 50
>
> <u>Next Test</u>
>
> Document: Done

The JSP

Here is the JSP for the second Web-based example:

\Chapter15\code\AddWithoutEJB.jsp

```
<%@ page import="java.util.*" %>
<%@ page import="java.text.*" %>
<%@ page errorPage="AddError" %>
<jsp:useBean id="adderJavaBean" class="IntermediateAdderBeanNoEJB"
  scope="session" />
<jsp:setProperty name="adderJavaBean" property="*" />
<%
  SimpleDateFormat sdf =
    new SimpleDateFormat("dd MMM yyyy hh:mm:ss.SSS");
  Date start = new Date();
  String sdt = sdf.format(start);
  long answer = adderJavaBean.add();
%>
<html>
<head>
```

```
<title>Add Results</title>
</head>
<body>
<h2>
Started:
<%= sdt %>
<p>
Iterations:
<jsp:getProperty name="adderJavaBean" property="iterations"/>
<p>
Sum:
<%= answer %>
<p>
<%
  Date end = new Date();
%>
<p>
<%
  String edt = sdf.format(new Date());
%>
Ended:
<%= edt %>
<p>
Total time (milliseconds):
<%= end.getTime() - start.getTime() %>
<p>
<center>
<a href="http://localhost:8000/Timing/Add.html">
Next Test
</a>
</center>
</body>
</html>
```

The HTML

The HTML looks like this:

\Chapter15\code\AddWithoutEJB.html

```
<html>
<head>
<title>Timing Without EJB</title>
</head>
<body>
<center>
<h1>Simple Timing Test Without EJB</h1>
<form method="post"
action="http://localhost:8000/Timing/AddWithoutEJB">
<table>
  <tr>
    <td>Iterations: </td>
```

```
        <td><input name="iterations" type="text"></td>
      </tr>
    </table>
    <br>
    <br>
    <input type="submit" value="Perform Addition">
  </form>
</center>
</body>
</html>
```

Running the Second Web-based Example

We access our second Web-based example by entering the following URL:

```
http://localhost:8000/Timing/AddWithoutEjb.html
```

The screen that appears looks like Figure 15-9 after we enter a value of 10000. When we click on the button labeled PERFORM ADDITION, we observe the output shown in Figure 15-10. After we click

Figure 15-9
Preparing to Run the
Second Web-based
Example

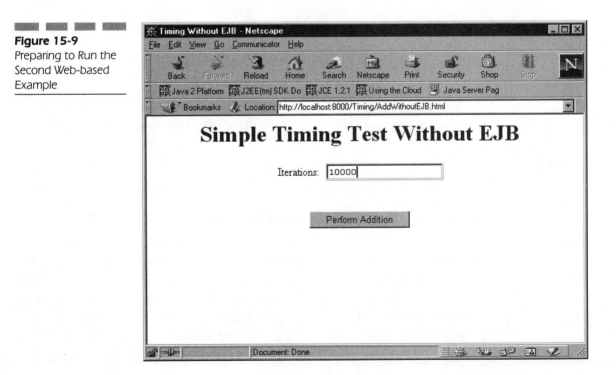

Figure 15-10
Timing for 10000
Iterations

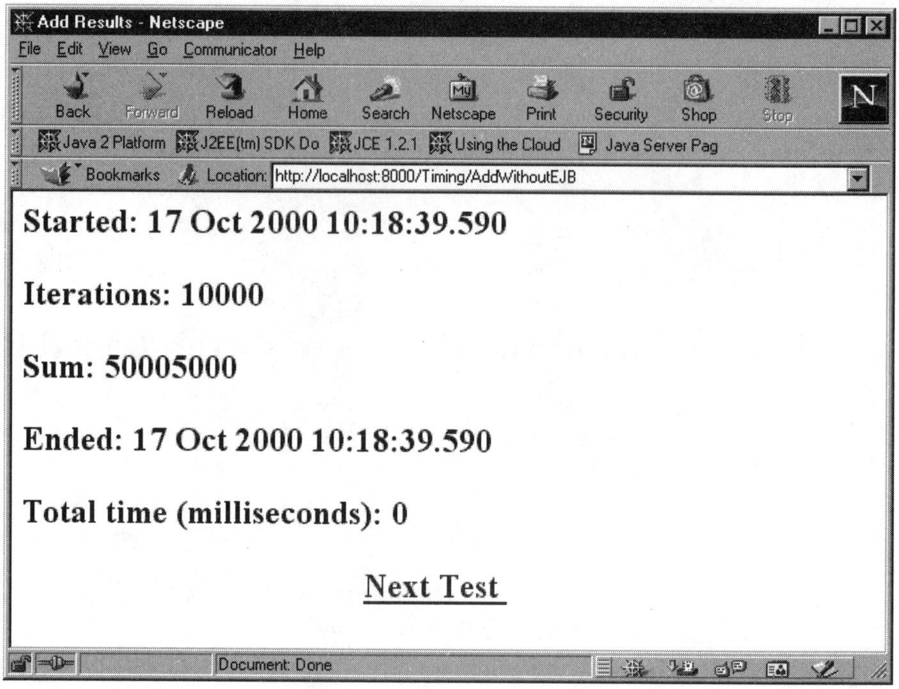

on NEXT TEST and enter a value of 1000000, we see the output shown in Figure 15-11.

NOTE: *The time of zero milliseconds reflects the fact that the clock resolution is not fine enough for this kind of time measurement.*

Analyzing What We Observed

Although the reported timings show that the non-EJB version takes less time, this is not necessarily our perception. In an environment where accumulating the numbers is intermixed with the transmission of a request to a server, the dispatching of that request, the execution of the JSP, the transmission of the response back to the browser, and the rendering of the HTML page by the

Figure 15-11
Timing for 1000000
Iterations

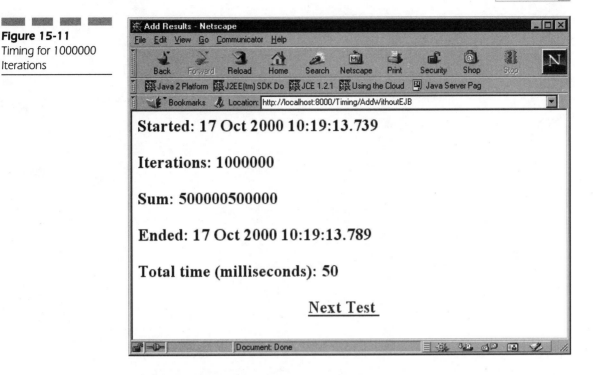

browser, the difference between the two versions is not so notice-able. Suddenly, the results we observed when we ran the earlier examples in the chapter don't seem so discouraging.

Summary

In this chapter, we learned that EJBs do indeed carry a price tag. The intention of the chapter is not to show EJBs in a negative light but rather to prove that there's some truth to the old saying "There is no such thing as a free lunch."

If we considered an application that uses EJBs to perform trans-actions against a number of databases and wrote that same appli-cation by hand in such a way that all of the transactions passed the ACID test, we would find that the difference in performance might not be so pronounced. We would also find that the EJB version would be easier to develop and maintain.

Improving Database Performance Using a Helper Class

In this chapter:

- A Multiline Order
- A Helper Class

In the previous chapter, we learned that we should use an enterprise bean only when it is the proper tool for the job. We also learned that performance improves when we reduced the number of remote method invocations. In this chapter, we put what we learned into practice.

A Multiline Order

If we wanted to develop a system that handled orders from customers, the order might contain:

- A string that uniquely identifies the order
- A string that identifies the customer who placed the order
- One or more lines, each of which contains:
    - An integer that identifies the line within the order
    - A string that uniquely identifies the order
    - A string that identifies an item that was ordered
    - An integer that shows the quantity that was ordered
    - The unit price of the item

We might design our application to use two tables to hold such data. These tables have a one-to-many relationship as shown in Figure 16-1. Each order can contain one or more order lines.

Figure 16-1
Two Tables
Representing a
Multiline Order

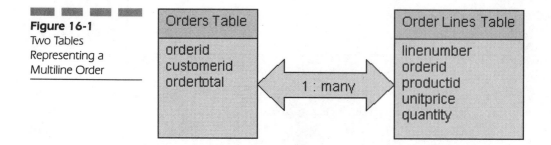

For testing purposes, we populate the two tables with one order of nine lines and another of seven lines. We do this by typing the command createOrderTables.

\Chapter16\code\createOrderTables.bat

The batch file invokes the *ij* utility, which takes its input from the following file:

\Chapter16\code\createOrderTables.sql

```
drop table orderlines;
drop table orders;

create table orders
(orderid char(5) constraint pk_order primary key,
customerid char(5),
ordertotal decimal(10,2));

insert into orders
values ('12345', '12121');

insert into orders
values ('23456', '23232');

create table orderlines
(linenumber integer,
orderid char(5),
productid char(5),
unitprice decimal(10,2),
quantity integer,
constraint fk_orderid
foreign key (orderid)
references orders(orderid));

insert into orderlines
values (1, '12345', '10001', 69.00, 1);
insert into orderlines
values (2, '12345', '10220', 12.00, 2);
insert into orderlines
values (3, '12345', '20101', 15.00, 1);
insert into orderlines
values (4, '12345', '62201', 18.00, 1);
insert into orderlines
values (5, '12345', '43112', 112.00, 3);
insert into orderlines
values (6, '12345', '82001', 23.00, 1);
```

```
insert into orderlines
values (7, '12345', '11223', 88.00, 1);
insert into orderlines
values (8, '12345', '77665', 52.00, 1);
insert into orderlines
values (9, '12345', '12114', 17.00, 4);

insert into orderlines
values (1, '23456', '82001', 23.00, 2);
insert into orderlines
values (2, '23456', '43112', 112.00, 2);
insert into orderlines
values (3, '23456', '77665', 52.00, 1);
insert into orderlines
values (4, '23456', '12114', 17.00, 1);
insert into orderlines
values (5, '23456', '43112', 112.00, 3);
insert into orderlines
values (6, '23456', '82001', 23.00, 2);
insert into orderlines
values (7, '23456', '11223', 88.00, 1);

exit;
```

Now let's consider what is required to retrieve all of the information from an order so that we can display it in an HTML table. We would first find the row in the *orders* table that contains the string that identifies the order we wish to display. We would then issue a query to retrieve all of the rows in the *orderlines* table that contain the order identifier.

Our first inclination might be to map both tables to entity beans; however, based on what we learned in the previous chapter, we ask ourselves whether this is the proper approach. If we use entity beans to represent both tables, the process of retrieving an order would be:

- get the requested order using the `findByPrimaryKey()` method against the *Order* EJB

- use a *finder* method such as `findByOrderID()` to get a collection of those rows in the *OrderLine* EJB that belong to the requested order

- pass each of the keys in the collection to the `findByPrimaryKey()` method of the *OrderLine* EJB

The time required for the last of these operations would degrade performance, especially if the order contained a large number of lines.

An alternate approach is to represent the *orders* table as an entity bean and handle the order lines using a *helper* class.

The Helper Class

Our helper class is a simple Java class containing an instance variable for what would have been each column in a database row. It has a constructor as well as getter and setter methods for each of the instance variables. The listing looks like this:

\Chapter16\code\OrderLine.java

```java
public class OrderLine implements java.io.Serializable {

    private String productID;
    private int lineNumber;
    private int quantity;
    private double unitPrice;
    private String orderID;

    public OrderLine(String productID, int lineNumber, int quantity,
        double unitPrice, String orderID) {

        this.productID = productID;
        this.lineNumber = lineNumber;
        this.quantity = quantity;
        this.unitPrice = unitPrice;
        this.orderID = orderID;
    }

    public String getProductID() {
        return productID;
    }

    public int getQuantity() {
        return quantity;
    }

    public double getUnitPrice() {
        return unitPrice;
    }

    public int getLineNumber() {
        return lineNumber;
    }
```

```
        public String getOrderID() {
           return orderID;
        }
     }
```

Using the Helper Class

The helper class is used by the *MultiLineOrder* EJB. Its three components are presented below.

The Remote Interface

The remote interface looks like this:

 Chapter16\code\MultiLineOrder.java

```
import java.util.ArrayList;
import javax.ejb.EJBObject;
import java.rmi.RemoteException;

public interface MultiLineOrder extends EJBObject {

  public ArrayList getOrderLines()
    throws RemoteException;

  public String getCustomerID()
    throws RemoteException;

  public double getOrderTotal()
    throws RemoteException;
}
```

The Home Interface

The listing for the home interface is as follows:

\Chapter16\code\MultiLineOrderHome.java

```java
import java.util.ArrayList;
import java.util.Collection;
import java.rmi.RemoteException;
import javax.ejb.*;

public interface MultiLineOrderHome extends EJBHome {

    public MultiLineOrder create(String orderID, String customerID,
        double orderTotal, ArrayList orderLines)
          throws RemoteException, CreateException;

    public MultiLineOrder findByPrimaryKey(String orderID)
        throws FinderException, RemoteException;

    public Collection findByProductID(String productID)

        throws FinderException, RemoteException;

}
```

The Enterprise Bean

The listing for the enterprise bean is lengthy and so is presented at the end of the chapter. The methods in which we are most interested are the ones that use the helper class. These are `ejbLoad()` and `ejbStore()`, which are invoked by the container, because when we deploy the application we assign an attribute of required to the business methods. Let's examine the `ejbLoad()` method.

```java
public void ejbLoad() {

    String selectFromOrders =
      "SELECT customerid, ordertotal FROM orders " +
      "WHERE orderid = ? .";

    String selectFromOrderLines =
      "SELECT linenumber, productid, unitprice, quantity " +
      "FROM orderlines WHERE orderid = ? " +
      "ORDER BY linenumber";

    try {
      PreparedStatement ps =
        connection.prepareStatement(selectFromOrders);
```

```
        ps.setString(1, orderID);

        ResultSet rs = ps.executeQuery();

        if (rs.next()) {
          customerID = rs.getString(1);
          orderTotal = rs.getDouble(2);
          ps.close();
        }
        else {
          ps.close();
          throw new NoSuchEntityException("No database row for " +
            orderID);
        }
        ps = connection.prepareStatement(selectFromOrderLines);
        ps.setString(1, orderID);
        rs = ps.executeQuery();
        int lines = 0;
        orderLines = new ArrayList();
        while (rs.next()) {
          int itemNumber = rs.getInt(1);
          String productID = rs.getString(2);
          double unitPrice = rs.getDouble(3);
          int quantity = rs.getInt(4);
          orderLines.add(itemNumber - 1,
            new OrderLine(productID, itemNumber, quantity,
                          unitPrice, orderID));
          lines++;
        }
        ps.close();

        if (lines == 0) {
          throw new NoSuchEntityException("No items for orderID " +
            orderID +
            " found in database.");
        }
      }
    catch (Exception e) {
      throw new EJBException("ejbLoad: " +
        e.getMessage());
    }
  }
```

The method gets the specified order by executing the SQL statement:

```
"SELECT customerid, ordertotal FROM orders " +
    "WHERE orderid = ? ";
```

It then gets all of the lines belonging to that order by executing the SQL statement:

```
"SELECT linenumber, productid, unitprice, quantity " +
    "FROM orderlines WHERE orderid = ? " +
    "ORDER BY linenumber";
```

Finally, the method iterates through the *ResultSet* returned by the last query and for each row returned creates an instance of *OrderLine* (the helper class) and adds it to the *ArrayList* held in the instance variable `orderLines`.

The advantage of this approach is that, since we do it all within `ejbLoad()`, we have already incurred the overhead of invoking an EJB method. The cost of retrieving n lines of an order is the time required to execute the single SQL statement and populate the *ArrayList* with the n items returned by the query. If we had chosen to represent the order lines as an entity bean, the cost would have been:

$$n * (\text{method invocation time} + \text{SQL execution time})$$

The Client

We use a simple Web-based client. It presents an HTML page containing a form with a single entry field, into which the user types the ID of the order to be retrieved. The resulting request is processed by a JSP that uses an intermediate JavaBean to retrieve the order and all of its lines.

The HTML

Here is the code for the HTML page:

\Chapter16\code\GetOrder.html

```
<html>
<head>
<title>Display Order</title>
</head>
<body>
<center>
<h1>Display Order</h1>
<form method="post" action="http://localhost:8000/CH16/GetOrder">
<table>
  <tr>
    <td>Order ID: </td>
    <td><input name="orderID" type="text"></td>
  </tr>
</table>
<br>
<br>
<input type="submit" value="Display Order">
</form>
</center>
</body>
</html>
```

The JSP

The JavaServer Page that processes the request and displays the order looks like this:

 \Chapter16\code\GetOrder.jsp

```
<%@ page import="java.util.ArrayList" %>
<%@ page import="java.util.ListIterator" %>
<jsp:useBean id="orderBean" class="IntermediateOrderBean"
  scope="session" />
<jsp:setProperty name="orderBean" property="orderID" />
<html>
<head>
<title>Order</title>
</head>
<body>
<center>
<b>
Order #
<jsp:getProperty name="orderBean" property="orderID" />
</b>
<table border>
<tr>
<td>
<b>Item #</b>
</td>
```

```
<td>
<b>Product ID</b>
</td>
<td>
<b>Quantity</b>
</td>
<td>
<b>UnitPrice</b>
</td>
</tr>
<%
  ArrayList orderLines = orderBean.getOrderLines();
  ListIterator iterator = orderLines.listIterator(0);
  while (iterator.hasNext()) {
%>
<tr>
<%
    OrderLine line = (OrderLine)iterator.next();
%>
<td>
<%= line.getLineNumber() %>
</td>
<td>
<%= line.getProductID() %>
</td>
<td>
<%= line.getQuantity() %>
</td>
<td>
<%= line.getUnitPrice() %>
</td>
</tr>
<%
    }
%>
</table>
<br>
<br>
<a href="http://localhost:8000/CH16/GetOrder.html">
Get Another Order
</a>
</center>
</body>
</html>
```

The Intermediate JavaBean

Here is the intermediate JavaBean that is used by the JSP:

\Chapter16\code\IntermediateOrderBean.java

```java
import java.util.ArrayList;
import java.rmi.RemoteException;

import javax.ejb.FinderException;
import javax.naming.Context;
import javax.naming.InitialContext;
import javax.rmi.PortableRemoteObject;

import MultiLineOrder;
import MultiLineOrderBean;
import MultiLineOrderHome;

public class IntermediateOrderBean {

  private MultiLineOrder order;
  private MultiLineOrderHome orderHome;
  private String orderID;

  public IntermediateOrderBean() {
    try {
      Context ic = new InitialContext();
      java.lang.Object objref =
        ic.lookup("java:comp/env/ejb/MultiLineOrder");
      orderHome =
        (MultiLineOrderHome) PortableRemoteObject.narrow(objref,
          MultiLineOrderHome.class);
    }
    catch (Exception e) {
      System.err.println ("Unable to locate MultiLineOrderHome");
      e.printStackTrace();
    }
  }

  public void setOrderID(String orderID) {
    this.orderID = orderID;
  }

  public String getOrderID() {
    return orderID;
  }

  public double getOrderTotal() throws Exception {
    try {
      order = orderHome.findByPrimaryKey(orderID);
      return order.getOrderTotal();
    }
    catch (FinderException e) {
      throw new Exception (e.getMessage());
    }
  }

  public ArrayList getOrderLines() throws Exception {
    try {
      order = orderHome.findByPrimaryKey(orderID);
```

```
            return order.getOrderLines();
        }
        catch (FinderException e) {
            throw new Exception (e.getMessage());
        }
    }
}
```

Packaging and Deploying

As we did in the previous chapter, we simply load the application from *HelperClassDemoApp.ear* using the "Open Application" item in the Application Deployment Tool's "File" drop-down menu item.

\Chapter16\code\HelperClassDemoApp.ear

Running the Client

We run our application by accessing the following URL:

```
http://localhost:8000/CH16/GetOrder.html
```

After we type the order ID into the entry field, the page looks like Figure 16-2.

When we click on "Display Order", we see the output shown in Figure 16-3.

MultiLineOrderBean.java

\Chapter16\code\MultiLineOrder.java

```java
import java.sql.*;
import java.util.*;
import javax.sql.*;
```

Figure 16-2
Specifying an Order
to Retrieve

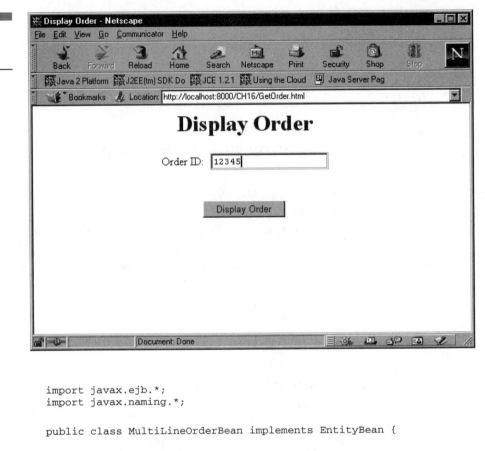

```
import javax.ejb.*;
import javax.naming.*;


public class MultiLineOrderBean implements EntityBean {

  private String orderID;
  private ArrayList orderLines;
  private String customerID;
  private double orderTotal;
  private Connection connection;
  private String dbName = "java:comp/env/jdbc/MultiLineOrderDB";
  private EntityContext context;

  public ArrayList getOrderLines() {
    return orderLines;
  }

  public String getCustomerID() {
    return customerID;
  }

  public double getOrderTotal() {
    return orderTotal;
  }
```

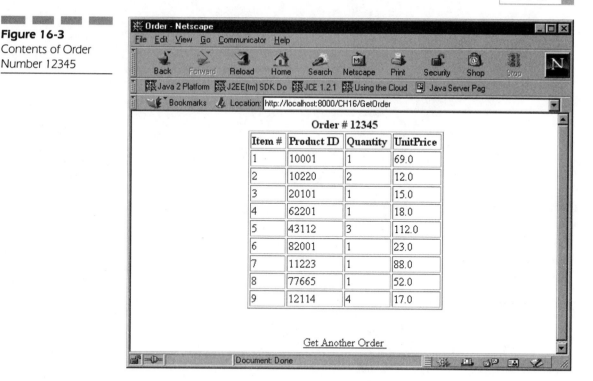

Figure 16-3
Contents of Order
Number 12345

```java
public String ejbCreate(String orderID, String customerID,
   double orderTotal, ArrayList orderLines)
     throws CreateException {

   String insertIntoOrders =
     "INSERT INTO orders VALUES ( ? , ? , ? )";

   String insertIntoLineItems =
     "INSERT INTO orderlines VALUES ( ? , ? , ? , ? , ? )";

   try {
     PreparedStatement ps =
       connection.prepareStatement(insertIntoOrders);

     ps.setString(1, orderID);
     ps.setString(2, customerID);
     ps.setDouble(3, orderTotal);

     ps.executeUpdate();
     ps.close();
     for (int i = 0; i < orderLines.size(); i++) {
       OrderLine line = (OrderLine)orderLines.get(i);
       ps = connection.prepareStatement(insertIntoLineItems);
```

```
        ps.setInt(1, line.getLineNumber());
        ps.setString(2, line.getOrderID());
        ps.setString(3, line.getProductID());
        ps.setDouble(4, line.getUnitPrice());
        ps.setInt(5, line.getQuantity());

        ps.executeUpdate();
        ps.close();
      }
    }
    catch (Exception e) {
      throw new EJBException("ejbCreate: " + e.getMessage());
    }


    this.orderID = orderID;
    this.customerID = customerID;
    this.orderTotal = orderTotal;
    this.orderLines = orderLines ;


    return orderID;
  }


public String ejbFindByPrimaryKey(String primaryKey)
    throws FinderException {


    String selectStatement =
      "SELECT orderid FROM orders WHERE orderid = ? ";


    boolean found;


    try {
      PreparedStatement ps =
        connection.prepareStatement(selectStatement);
      ps.setString(1, primaryKey);

      ResultSet rs = ps.executeQuery();
      found = rs.next();
      ps.close();
    }
    catch (Exception e) {
      throw new EJBException("ejbFindByPrimaryKey: " +
        e.getMessage());
    }


    if (found) {
      return primaryKey;
    }
    else {
      throw new ObjectNotFoundException
        ("Row for id " + primaryKey + " not found.");
    }
  }
```

```java
public Collection ejbFindByProductID(String productID)
   throws FinderException {

  String selectStatement =
    "SELECT DISTINCT orderid FROM orderlines"
    " WHERE productid = ? ";

  try {
    PreparedStatement ps =
      connection.prepareStatement(selectStatement);

    ps.setString(1, productID);
    ResultSet rs = ps.executeQuery();
    ArrayList al = new ArrayList();

    while (rs.next()) {
      String orderID = rs.getString(1);
      al.add(orderID);
    }

    ps.close();

    if (al.isEmpty()) {
      throw new ObjectNotFoundException("No rows found.");
    }
    else {
      return al;
    }
  }
  catch (Exception e) {
    throw new EJBException("ejbFindByProductID " +
      e.getMessage());
  }
}

public void ejbRemove() {

  String deleteFromOrders =
    "DELETE FROM orders WHERE orderid = ?";

    String deleteFromOrderLines =
      "DELETE FROM orderlines WHERE orderid = ?";

  try {
    PreparedStatement ps =
      connection.prepareStatement(deleteFromOrders);

    ps.setString(1, orderID);
    ps.executeUpdate();
    ps.close();
    ps = connection.prepareStatement(deleteFromOrderLines);
    ps.setString(1, orderID);
    ps.executeUpdate();
```

```java
      ps.close();
    }
    catch (Exception ex) {
      throw new EJBException("ejbRemove: " +
        ex.getMessage());
    }
  }

  public void setEntityContext(EntityContext context) {

    this.context = context;
    try {
      InitialContext ic = new InitialContext();
      DataSource ds = (DataSource) ic.lookup(dbName);
      connection = ds.getConnection();
    }
    catch (Exception ex) {
      throw new EJBException("Unable to connect to database. " +
        ex.getMessage());
    }
  }

  public void unsetEntityContext() {
    try {
      connection.close();
    }
    catch (SQLException ex) {
      throw new EJBException("unsetEntityContext: " +
        ex.getMessage());
    }
  }

  public void ejbActivate() {
    orderID = (String)context.getPrimaryKey();
  }

  public void ejbPassivate() {
    orderID = null;
  }

  public void ejbLoad() {

    String selectFromOrders =
      "SELECT customerid, ordertotal FROM orders " +
      "WHERE orderid = ? ";

    String selectFromOrderLines =
      "SELECT linenumber, productid, unitprice, quantity " +
      "FROM orderlines WHERE orderid = ? " +
      "ORDER BY linenumber";

    try {
      PreparedStatement ps =
        connection.prepareStatement(selectFromOrders);

      ps.setString(1, orderID);
```

```java
        ResultSet rs = ps.executeQuery();

        if (rs.next()) {
          customerID = rs.getString(1);
          orderTotal = rs.getDouble(2);
          ps.close();
        }
        else {
          ps.close();
          throw new NoSuchEntityException("No database row for " +
            orderID);
        }
        ps = connection.prepareStatement(selectFromOrderLines);
        ps.setString(1, orderID);
        rs = ps.executeQuery();

        int lines = 0;
        orderLines = new ArrayList();
        while (rs.next()) {
          int itemNumber = rs.getInt(1);
          String productID = rs.getString(2);
          double unitPrice = rs.getDouble(3);
          int quantity = rs.getInt(4);
          orderLines.add(itemNumber - 1,
            new OrderLine(productID, itemNumber, quantity,
                          unitPrice, orderID));
          lines++;
        }
        ps.close();

        if (lines == 0) {
          throw new NoSuchEntityException("No items for orderID " +
            orderID +
            " found in database.");
        }
      }
      catch (Exception e) {
        throw new EJBException("ejbLoad: " +
          e.getMessage());
      }
    }

    public void ejbStore() {

      String updateOrders =
        "UPDATE orders SET customerid = ? ," +
        "ordertotal = ? " + "WHERE orderid = ?";

      String updateOrderLines =
        "UPDATE orderlines SET productid = ? ," +
        "unitprice = ? , quantity = ? " +
        "WHERE orderid = ? AND linenumber = ?";

      try {
        PreparedStatement ps =
          connection.prepareStatement(updateOrders);
```

```
      ps.setString(1, customerID);
      ps.setDouble(2, orderTotal);
      ps.setString(3, orderID);
      int rowCount = ps.executeUpdate();
      ps.close();

      if (rowCount == 0) {
        throw new EJBException("Storing row for orderID " +
          orderID + " failed.");
      }
      for (int i = 0; i < orderLines.size(); i++) {
        OrderLine line = (OrderLine)orderLines.get(i);
        ps = connection.prepareStatement(updateOrderLines);
        ps.setString(1, line.getProductID());
        ps.setDouble(2, line.getUnitPrice());
        ps.setInt(3, line.getQuantity());
        ps.setString(4, orderID);
        ps.setInt(5, line.getLineNumber());
        rowCount = ps.executeUpdate();
        ps.close();

        if (rowCount == 0) {
          throw new EJBException("Storing itemNumber " +
            line.getLineNumber() +
            "for orderID " + orderID + " failed.");
        }
      }
    }
    catch (Exception e) {
      throw new EJBException("ejbLoad: " +
        e.getMessage());
    }
  }

  public void ejbPostCreate(String orderID, String customerID,
      double orderTotal, ArrayList orderLines) { }
}
```

Summary

In this chapter, we learned that we should not automatically use enterprise beans for everything; rather, we should use EJBs where it is appropriate to do so. We also saw that EJBs can be used in conjunction with other components written in Java.

APPENDIX A

The EJB API

This Appendix describes each interface in the EJB API. The interfaces are presented in alphabetical order. For each interface, the hierarchy is given as well as a description, a method summary, and a detailed description of each method. The description of the interfaces is followed by a similar description of each possible exception.

Interface Summary

EJBContext	The EJBContext interface provides an instance with access to the container-provided runtime context of an enterprise Bean instance.
EJBHome	The EJBHome interface is extended by all enterprise Bean's home interfaces.
EJBMetaData	The EJBMetaData interface allows a client to obtain the enterprise Bean's meta-data information.
EJBObject	The EJBObject interface is extended by all enterprise Bean's remote interfaces.
EnterpriseBean	The EnterpriseBean interface must be implemented by every enterprise Bean class.
EntityBean	The EntityBean interface is implemented by every entity enterprise Bean class.
EntityContext	The EntityContext interface provides an instance with access to the container-provided runtime context of an entity enterprise Bean instance.
Handle	The Handle interface is implemented by all EJB object handles.
HomeHandle	The HomeHandle interface is implemented by all home object handles.

SessionBean	The SessionBean interface is implemented by every session enterprise Bean class.
SessionContext	The SessionContext interface provides access to the runtime session context that the container provides for a session enterprise Bean instance.
SessionSynchronization	The SessionSynchronization interface allows a session Bean instance to be notified by its container of transaction boundaries.

Interface EJBContext

public interface **EJBContext**

The EJBContext interface provides an instance with access to the container-provided runtime context of an enterprise Bean instance.

This interface is extended by the SessionContext and Entity-Context interfaces to provide additional methods specific to the enterprise Bean type.

Method Summary

java.security.Identity	**getCallerIdentity()** **Deprecated.** *Use Principal getCallerPrincipal() instead.*
java.security.Principal	**getCallerPrincipal()** Obtain the java.security.principal that identifies the caller.
EJBHome	**getEJBHome()** Obtain the enterprise bean's home interface.
java.util.properties	**getEnvironment()** **Deprecated.** *Use the JNDI naming context java:comp/env to access enterprise bean's environment* instead.
boolean	**getRollbackOnly()** Test if the transaction has been marked for rollback only.

UserTransaction	**getUserTransaction()** Obtain the transaction demarcation interface.
boolean	**isCallerInRole(java.security.Identity role)** **Deprecated.** *Use boolean isCallerInRole(String roleName) instead.*
boolean	**isCallerInRole(java.lang.String roleName)** Test if the caller has a given security role.
void	**setRollbackOnly()** Mark the current transaction for rollback.

Method Detail

getCallerIdentity
public java.security.Identity **getCallerIdentity**()

> ### Deprecated.
>
> *Use Principal getCallerPrincipal().*
>
> ### Returns:
>
> The Identity object that identifies the caller.

getCallerPrincipal
public java.security.Principal **getCallerPrincipal**()

> Obtain the java.security.Principal that identifies the caller.
>
> ### Returns:
>
> The Principal object that identifies the caller.

getEJBHome
public EJBHome **getEJBHome**()

> Obtain the enterprise bean's home interface.
>
> ### Returns:
>
> The enterprise bean's home interface.

getEnvironment
public java.util.Properties **getEnvironment**()

Deprecated.

Use the JNDI naming context java:comp/env to access the enterprise bean's environment.

Returns:

The environment properties for the enterprise bean. If the enterprise bean has no environment properties, an empty java.util.Properties object is returned. This method will never return null.

getRollbackOnly
public boolean **getRollbackOnly**()

throws java.lang.IllegalStateException

Test if the transaction has been marked for rollback only. An enterprise bean instance can use this operation, for example, to test after an exception has been caught, whether it is fruitless to continue computation on behalf of the current transaction. Only enterprise beans with container-managed transactions are allowed to use this method.

Returns:

True if the current transaction is marked for rollback, false otherwise.

Throws:

java.lang.IllegalStateException—The Container throws the exception if the instance is not allowed to use this method (i.e., the instance is of a bean with bean-managed transactions).

getUserTransaction
public UserTransaction **getUserTransaction**()

throws java.lang.IllegalStateException

Obtain the transaction demarcation interface. Only enterprise beans with bean-managed transactions are allowed to use the UserTransaction interface. As entity beans must always use container-managed transactions, only session beans with bean-managed transactions are allowed to invoke this method.

Returns:

The UserTransaction interface that the enterprise bean instance can use for transaction demarcation.

Throws:

java.lang.IllegalStateException—The Container throws the exception if the instance is not allowed to use the UserTransaction interface (i.e., the instance is of a bean with container-managed transactions).

isCallerInRole
public boolean **isCallerInRole**(java.security.Identity role)

Deprecated.

Use boolean isCallerInRole(String roleName) instead.
Test if the caller has a given role.

This method is deprecated in EJB 1.1. The enterprise bean should use the isCallerInRole(String roleName) instead.

Parameters:

role—The java.security.Identity of the role to be tested.

Returns:

True if the caller has the specified role.

isCallerInRole
public booolean **isCallerInRole**(java.lang.String roleName)

Test if the caller has a given security role.

Parameters:

roleName—The name of the security role. The role must be one of the security roles that is defined in the deployment descriptor.

Returns:

True if the caller has the specified role.

setRollbackOnly
public void **setRollbackOnly**()

throws java.lang.IllegalStateException

Mark the current transaction for rollback. The transaction will become permanently marked for rollback. A transaction marked for rollback can never commit. Only enterprise beans with container-managed transactions are allowed to use this method.

Throws:

java.lang.IllegalStateException—The Container throws the exception if the instance is not allowed to use this method (i.e., the instance is of a bean with bean-managed transactions).

Interface EJBHome

public interface **EJBHome**

extends java.rmi.Remote

The EJBHome interface is extended by all enterprise Bean's home interfaces. An enterprise Bean's home interface defines the methods that allow a client to create, find, and remove EJB objects.

Each enterprise Bean has a home interface. The home interface must extend the javax.ejb.EJBHome interface, and define the enterprise Bean type specific create and finder methods (session Beans do not have finders).

The home interface is defined by the enterprise Bean provider and implemented by the enterprise Bean container.

Method Summary

EJBMetaData	**getEJBMetaData()** Obtain the EJBMetaData interface for the enterprise bean.
HomeHandle	**getHomeHandle()** Obtain a handle for the home object.
void	**remove(Handle handle)** Remove an EJB object identified by its handle.
void	**remove(java.lang.Object primaryKey)** Remove an EJB object identified by its primary key.

Method Detail

getEJBMetaData
public EJBMetaData **getEJBMetaData**()

throws java.rmi.RemoteException

Obtain the EJBMetaData interface for the enterprise Bean. The EJBMetaData interface allows the client to obtain information about the enterprise Bean.

The information obtainable via the EJBMetaData interface is intended to be used by tools.

Returns:

The enterprise Bean's EJBMetaData interface.

Throws:

java.rmi.RemoteException—Thrown when the method failed because of a system-level failure.

getHomeHandle
public HomeHandle **getHomeHandle**()

throws java.rmi.RemoteException

Obtain a handle for the home object. The handle can be used at later time to reobtain a reference to the home object, possibly in a different Java Virtual Machine.

Returns:

A handle for the home object.

Throws:

java.rmi.RemoteException—Thrown when the method failed because of a system-level failure.

remove
public void **remove**(Handle handle)

throws java.rmi.RemoteException,RemoveException

Remove an EJB object identified by its handle.

Throws:

RemoveException—Thrown if the enterprise Bean or the container does not allow the client to remove the object.

java.rmi.RemoteException—Thrown when the method failed because of a system-level failure.

remove

public void **remove**(java.lang.Object primaryKey)

throwsjava.rmi.RemoteException,RemoveException

Remove an EJB object identified by its primary key.

This method can be used only for an entity bean. An attempt to call this method on a session bean will result in RemoteException.

Throws:

RemoveException—Thrown if the enterprise Bean or the container does not allow the client to remove the object.

java.rmi.RemoteException—Thrown when the method failed because of a system-level failure.

Interface EJBMetaData

public interface **EJBMetaData**

The EJBMetaData interface allows a client to obtain the enterprise Bean's meta-data information. The meta-data is intended for development tools used for building applications that use deployed enterprise Beans, and for clients using a scripting language to access the enterprise Bean.

Note that the EJBMetaData is not a remote interface. The class that implements this interface (this class is typically generated by container tools) must be serializable, and must be a valid RMI/IDL value type.

Method Summary

EJBHome   **getEJBHome**()
Obtain the home interface for the enterprise Bean.

java.lang.Class	**getHomeInterfaceClass()** Obtain the Class object for the Bean's home interface.
java.lang.Class	**getPrimaryKeyClass()** Obtain the Class object for the enterprise Bean's primary key class.
java.lang.Class	**getRemoteInterfaceClass()** Obtain the Class object for the enterprise Bean's remote interface.
boolean	**isSession()** Test if the enterprise Bean's type is *session*.
boolean	**isStatelessSession()** Test if the enterprise Bean's type is *stateless session*.

Method Detail

getEJBHome
public EJBHome **getEJBHome**()

Obtain the home interface of the enterprise Bean.

Returns:

A handle for the home interface.

getHomeInterfaceClass
public java.lang.Class **getHomeInterfaceClass**()

Obtain the Class object for the enterprise Bean's home interface.

Returns:

The Class object for the home interface.

getPrimaryKeyClass
public java.lang.Class **getPrimaryKeyClass**()

Obtain the Class object for the enterprise Bean's primary key class.

Returns:

The Class object for the primary key class.

getRemoteInterfaceClass
public java.lang.Class **getRemoteInterfaceClass**()

Obtain the Class object for the enterprise Bean's remote interface.

Returns:

The Class object for the remote interface.

isSession
public boolean **isSession**()

Test if the enterprise Bean's type is "session".

Returns:

True if the type of the enterprise Bean is session bean.

isStatelessSession
public boolean **isStatelessSession**()

Test if the enterprise Bean's type is "stateless session".

Returns:

True if the type of the enterprise Bean is stateless session.

Interface EJBObject

public interface **EJBObject**

extends java.rmi.remote

The EJBObject interface is extended by all enterprise Bean's remote interface. An enterprise Bean's remote interface provides the client's view of an EJB object. An enterprise Bean's remote interface defines the business methods callable by a client.

Each enterprise Bean has a remote interface. The remote interface must extend the javax.ejb.EJBObject interface and define the enterprise Bean specific business methods.

The enterprise Bean's remote interface is defined by the enterprise Bean provider and implemented by the enterprise Bean container.

MethodSummary

EJBHome	**getEJBHome()** Obtain the enterprise Bean's home interface.
Handle	**gethandle()** Obtain a handle for the EJB object.
java.lang.Object	**getPrimaryKey()** Obtain the primary key of the EJB object.
boolean	**isIdentical(EJBObject obj)** Test if a given EJB object is identical to the invoked EJB object.
void	**remove()** Remove the EJB object.

Method Detail

getEJBHome
public EJBHome **getEJBHome()**

throws java.rmi.RemoteException

Obtain the enterprise Bean's home interface. The home interface defines the enterprise Bean's create, finder, and remove operations.

Returns:

A reference to the enterprise Bean's home interface.

Throws:

java.rmi.RemoteException—Thrown when the method failed because of a system-level failure.

getHandle
public Handle **getHandle**()

throws java.rmi.RemoteException

Obtain a handle for the EJB object. The handle can be used at later time to reobtain a reference to the EJB object, possibly in a different Java Virtual Machine.

Returns:

A handle for the EJB object.

Throws:

java.rmi.RemoteException—Thrown when the method failed due to a system-level failure.

getPrimaryKey
public java.lang.Object **getPrimaryKey**()

throws java.rmi.RemoteException

Obtain the primary key of the EJB object.
This method can be called on an entity bean. An attempt to invoke this method on a session bean will result in RemoteException.

Returns:

The EJB object's primary key.

isIdentical
public boolean **isIdentical**(EJBObject obj)

throws java.rmi.RemoteException

Test if a given EJB object is identical to the invoked EJB object.

Parameters:

obj—An object to test for identity with the invoked object.

Returns:

True if the given EJB object is identical to the invoked object, false otherwise.

Throws:

java.rmi.RemoteException—Thrown when the method failed because of a system-level failure.

remove

public void **remove**()

throws java.rmi.RemoteException, RemoveException

Remove the EJB object.

Throws:

java.rmi.RemoteException—Thrown when the method failed because of a system-level failure.

RemoveException—The enterprise Bean or the container does not allow destruction of the object.

Interface EnterpriseBean

All Known Subinterfaces:

EntityBean, SessionBean

public interface **EnterpriseBean**

extends java.io.Serializable

The EnterpriseBean interface must be implemented by every enterprise Bean class. It is a common superinterface for the SessionBean and EntityBean interfaces.

Interface EntityBean

public interface **EntityBean**

extends EnterpriseBean

The EntityBean interface is implemented by every entity enterprise Bean class. The container uses the EntityBean methods to notify the enterprise Bean instances of the instance's life cycle events.

MethodSummary

void **ejbActivate()**
A container invokes this method when the instance is taken out of the pool of available instances to become associated with a specific EJB object.

void **ejbLoad()**
A container invokes this method to instruct the instance to synchronize its state by loading it state from the underlying database.

void **ejbPassivate()**
A container invokes this method on an instance before the instance becomes disassociated with a specific EJB object.

void **ejbRemove()**
A container invokes this method before it removes the EJB object that is currently associated with the instance.

void **ejbStore()**
A container invokes this method to instruct the instance to synchronize its state by storing it to the underlying database.

void **setEntityContext(EntityContext ctx)**
Set the associated entity context.

void **unsetEntityContext()**
Unset the associated entity context.

Method Detail

ejbActivate
public void **ejbActivate**()

> throws EJBException, java.rmi.RemoteException

A container invokes this method when the instance is taken out of the pool of available instances to become associated with a specific EJB object. This method transitions the instance to the ready state. This method executes in an unspecified transaction context

Throws:

EJBException—Thrown by the method to indicate a failure caused by a system-level error.

java.rmi.RemoteException—This exception is defined in the method signature to provide backward compatibility for enterprise beans written for the EJB 1.0 specification. Enterprise beans written for the EJB 1.1 and higher specification should throw the javax.ejb.EJBException instead of this exception.

ejbLoad
public void **ejbLoad**()

> throws EJBException, java.rmi.RemoteException

A container invokes this method to instruct the instance to synchronize its state by loading it state from the underlying database. This method always executes in the transaction context determined by the value of the transaction attribute in the deployment descriptor.

Throws:

EJBException—Thrown by the method to indicate a failure caused by a system-level error.

java.rmi.RemoteException—This exception is defined in the
method signature to provide backward compatibility for
enterprise beans written for the EJB 1.0 specification. Enterprise beans written for the EJB 1.1 and higher specification
should throw the javax.ejb.EJBException instead of this
exception.

ejbPassivate
public void **ejbPassivate**()

throws EJBException, java.rmi.RemoteException

A container invokes this method on an instance before the
instance becomes disassociated with a specific EJB object.

After this method completes, the container will place the
instance into the pool of available instances.

This method executes in an unspecified transaction context.

Throws:

EJBException—Thrown by the method to indicate a failure
caused by a system-level error.

java.rmi.RemoteException—This exception is defined in the
method signature to provide backward compatibility for
enterprise beans written for the EJB 1.0 specification. Enterprise beans written for the EJB 1.1 and higher specification
should throw the javax.ejb.EJBException instead of this
exception.

ejbRemove
public void **ejbRemove**()

throws RemoveException, EJBException, java.rmi.RemoteEx-
ception

A container invokes this method before it removes the EJB
object that is currently associated with the instance. This method

is invoked when a client invokes a remove operation on the enterprise Bean's home interface or the EJB object's remote interface. This method transitions the instance from the ready state to the pool of available instances.

This method is called in the transaction context of the remove operation.

Throws:

RemoveException—The enterprise Bean does not allow destruction of the object. EJBException—Thrown by the method to indicate a failure caused by a system-level error.

java.rmi.RemoteException—This exception is defined in the method signature to provide backward compatibility for enterprise beans written for the EJB 1.0 specification. Enterprise beans written for the EJB 1.1 and higher specification should throw the javax.ejb.EJBException instead of this exception.

ejbStore
public void **ejbStore**()

throws EJBException, java.rmi.RemoteException

A container invokes this method to instruct the instance to synchronize its state by storing it to the underlying database.

This method always executes in the transaction context determined by the value of the transaction attribute in the deployment descriptor.

Throws:

EJBException—Thrown by the method to indicate a failure caused by a system-level error.

java.rmi.RemoteException—This exception is defined in the method signature to provide backward compatibility for enterprise beans written for the EJB 1.0 specification. Enterprise beans written for the EJB 1.1 and higher specification should throw the javax.ejb.EJBException instead of this exception.

setEntityContext
public void **setEntityContext**(EntityContext ctx)

throws EJBException, java.rmi.RemoteException

Set the associated entity context. The container invokes this method on an instance after the instance has been created.
This method is called in an unspecified transaction context.

Parameters:

ctx—An EntityContext interface for the instance. The instance should store the reference to the context in an instance variable.

Throws:

EJBException—Thrown by the method to indicate a failure caused by a system-level error.

java.rmi.RemoteException—This exception is defined in the method signature to provide backward compatibility for enterprise beans written for the EJB 1.0 specification. Enterprise beans written for the EJB 1.1 and higher specification should throw the javax.ejb.EJBException instead of this exception.

unsetEntityContext
public void **unsetEntityContext**()

throws EJBException, java.rmi.RemoteException

Unset the associated entity context. The container calls this method before removing the instance.
This is the last method that the container invokes on the instance. The Java garbage collector will eventually invoke the finalize() method on the instance.

This method is called in an unspecified transaction context.

Throws:

EJBException—Thrown by the method to indicate a failure caused by a system-level error.

java.rmi.RemoteException—This exception is defined in the method signature to provide backward compatibility for enterprise beans written for the EJB 1.0 specification. Enterprise beans written for the EJB 1.1 and higher specification should throw the javax.ejb.EJBException instead of this exception.

Interface EntityContext

public interface **EntityContext**

extends EJBContext

The EntityContext interface provides an instance with access to the container-provided runtime context of an entity enterprise Bean instance. The container passes the EntityContext interface to an entity enterprise Bean instance after the instance has been created.

The EntityContext interface remains associated with the instance for the lifetime of the instance. Note that the information that the instance obtains using the EntityContext interface (such as the result of the getPrimaryKey() method) may change, as the container assigns the instance to different EJB objects during the instance's life cycle.

Method Summary

EJBObject	**getEJBObject()** Obtain a reference to the EJB object that is currently associated with the instance.

java.lang.Object   **getPrimaryKey()**
Obtain the primary key of the EJB object that is currently associated
with this instance.

Method Detail

getEJBObject
public EJBObject **getEJBObject**()

throws java.lang.IllegalStateException

Obtain a reference to the EJB object that is currently associated
with the instance.

An instance of an entity enterprise Bean can call this method
only when the instance is associated with an EJB object identity,
that is, in the ejbActivate, ejbPassivate, ejbPostCreate method,
ejbRemove, ejbLoad, ejbStore, and business methods.

An instance can use this method, for example, when it wants to
pass a reference to itself in a method argument or result.

Returns:

The EJB object currently associated with the instance.

Throws:

java.lang.IllegalStateException—Thrown if the instance
   invokes this method while the instance is in a state that does
   not allow the instance to invoke this method.

getPrimaryKey
public java.lang.Object **getPrimaryKey**()

throws java.lang.IllegalStateException

Obtain the primary key of the EJB object that is currently associated with this instance.

An instance of an entity enterprise Bean can call this method
only when the instance is associated with an EJB object identity,

that is, in the ejbActivate, ejbPassivate, ejbPostCreate method, ejbRemove, ejbLoad, ejbStore, and business methods.

> **NOTE:**   *The result of this method is the same as the result of getEJBObject().getPrimaryKey().*

Returns:

The EJB object currently associated with the instance.

Throws:

java.lang.IllegalStateException—Thrown if the instance invokes this method while the instance is in a state that does not allow the instance to invoke this method.

Interface Handle

public interface **Handle**

extends Serializable

The Handle interface is implemented by all EJB object handles. A handle is an abstraction of a network reference to an EJB object, and is intended to be used as a "robust" persistent reference to an EJB object.

MethodSummary

EJBObject   **getEJBObject()**
Obtain the EJB object reference represented by this handle.

Method Detail

getEJBObject
public EJBObject **getEJBObject**()

> throws java.rmi.RemoteException

> Obtain the EJB object reference represented by this handle.

Throws:

> java.rmi.RemoteException—The EJB object could not be obtained because of a system-level failure.

Interface HomeHandle

public interface **HomeHandle**

> extends java.io.Serializable

The HomeHandle interface is implemented by all home object handles. A handle is an abstraction of a network reference to a home object, and is intended to be used as a "robust" persistent reference to a home object.

Method Summary

EJBHome   **getEJBHome**()
> Obtain the home object represented by this handle.

Method Detail

getEJBHome()
public EJBHome **getEJBHome**()

throws java.rmi.RemoteException

Obtain the home object represented by this handle.

Throws:

java.rmi.RemoteException—The home object could not be
  obtained because of a system-level failure.

Interface SessionBean

public interface **SessionBean**

  extends EnterpriseBean

The SessionBean interface is implemented by every session
enterprise Bean class. The container uses the SessionBean methods to notify the enterprise Bean instances of the instance's life-
cycle events.

Method Summary

void   **ejbActivate()**
        The activate method is called when the instance is activated from its "passive"
        state.

void   **ejbPassivate()**
        The passivate method is called before the instance enters the "passive" state.

void   **ejbRemove()**
        A container invokes this method before it ends the life of the session object.

void   **setSessionContext(SessionContext ctx)**
        Set the associated session context.

Method Detail

ejbActivate
public void **ejbActivate**()

throws EJBException, java.rmi.RemoteException

The activate method is called when the instance is activated from its "passive" state. The instance should acquire any resource that it has released earlier in the ejbPassivate() method.
This method is called with no transaction context.

Throws:

EJBException—Thrown by the method to indicate a failure caused by a system-level error.

java.rmi.RemoteException—This exception is defined in the method signature to provide backward compatibility for enterprise beans written for the EJB 1.0 specification. Enterprise beans written for the EJB 1.1 and higher specification should throw the javax.ejb.EJBException instead of this exception.

ejbPassivate
public void **ejbPassivate**()

throws EJBException, java.rmi.RemoteException

The passivate method is called before the instance enters the "passive" state. The instance should release any resources that it can reacquire later in the ejbActivate() method.
After the passivate method completes, the instance must be in a state that allows the container to use the Java Serialization protocol to externalize and store away the instance's state.
This method is called with no transaction context.

Throws:

EJBException—Thrown by the method to indicate a failure
caused by a system-level error.

java.rmi.RemoteException—This exception is defined in the
method signature to provide backward compatibility for
enterprise beans written for the EJB 1.0 specification. Enterprise beans written for the EJB 1.1 and higher specification
should throw the javax.ejb.EJBException instead of this
exception.

ejbRemove
public void **ejbRemove**()

throws EJBException, java.rmi.RemoteException

A container invokes this method before it ends the life of the session object. This happens as a result of a client's invoking a remove
operation, or when a container decides to terminate the session
object after a timeout.

This method is called with no transaction context.

Throws:

EJBException—Thrown by the method to indicate a failure
caused by a system-level error.

java.rmi.RemoteException—This exception is defined in the
method signature to provide backward compatibility for
enterprise beans written for the EJB 1.0 specification. Enterprise beans written for the EJB 1.1 and higher specification
should throw the java.ejb.EJBException instead of this
exception.

setSessionContext
public void **setSessionContext**(SessionContext ctx)

throws EJBException, java.rmi.RemoteException

Set the associated session context. The container calls this method after the instance creation.

The enterprise Bean instance should store the reference to the context object in an instance variable.

This method is called with no transaction context.

Parameters:

ctx—A SessionContext interface for the instance.

Throws:

EJBException—Thrown by the method to indicate a failure caused by a system-level error.

java.rmi.RemoteException—This exception is defined in the method signature to provide backward compatibility for applications written for the EJB 1.0 specification. Enterprise beans written for the EJB 1.1 and higher specification should throw the javax.ejb.EJBException instead of this exception.

Interface SessionContext

public interface **SessionContext**

extends EJBContext

The SessionContext interface provides access to the runtime session context that the container provides for a session enterprise Bean instance. The container passes the SessionContext interface to an instance after the instance has been created. The session context remains associated with the instance for the lifetime of the instance.

Method Summary

EJBObject   **getEJBObject()**
             Obtain a reference to the EJB object that is currently associated with the
             instance.

Method Detail

getEJBObject
public EJBObject **getEJBObject**()

   throws java.lang.IllegalStateException

   Obtain a reference to the EJB object that is currently associated
with the instance.
   An instance of a session enterprise Bean can call this method at
anytime between the ejbCreate() and ejbRemove() methods,
including from within the ejbCreate() and ejbRemove() methods.
   An instance can use this method, for example, when it wants to
pass a reference to itself in a method argument or result.

Returns:

The EJB object currently associated with the instance.

Throws:

java.lang.IllegalStateException—Thrown if the instance
   invokes this method while the instance is in a state that does
   not allow the instance to invoke this method.

Interface SessionSynchronization

public interface **SessionSynchronization**
   The SessionSynchronization interface allows a session Bean
instance to be notified by its container of transaction boundaries.

A session Bean class is not required to implement this interface. A session Bean class should implement this interface only if it wishes to synchronize its state with the transactions.

Method Summary

void   **afterBegin()**
      The afterBegin method notifies a session Bean instance that a new transaction has started, and that the subsequent business methods on the instance will be invoked in the context of the transaction.

void   **afterCompletion(boolean committed)**
      The afterCompletion method notifies a session Bean instance that a transaction commit protocol has completed, and tells the instance whether the transaction has been committed or rolled back.

void   **beforeCompletion()**
      The beforeCompletion method notifies a session Bean instance that a transaction is about to be committed.

Method Detail

afterBegin
public void **afterBegin**()

     throws EJBException, java.rmi.RemoteException

The afterBegin method notifies a session Bean instance that a new transaction has started, and that the subsequent business methods on the instance will be invoked in the context of the transaction. The instance can use this method, for example, to read data from a database and cache the data in the instance fields.

This method executes in the proper transaction context.

Throws:

EJBException—Thrown by the method to indicate a failure caused by a system-level error.

java.rmi.RemoteException—This exception is defined in the method signature to provide backward compatibility for enterprise beans written for the EJB 1.0 specification. Enterprise beans written for the EJB 1.1 and higher specification should throw the javax.ejb.EJBException instead of this exception.

afterCompletion

public void **afterCompletion**(boolean committed)

   throws EJBException, java.rmi.RemoteException

The afterCompletion method notifies a session Bean instance that a transaction commit protocol has completed, and tells the instance whether the transaction has been committed or rolled back.

This method executes with no transaction context.

Parameters:

committed—True if the transaction has been committed, false if it has been rolled back.

Throws:

EJBException—Thrown by the method to indicate a failure caused by a system-level error.

java.rmi.RemoteException—This exception is defined in the method signature to provide backward compatibility for enterprise beans written for the EJB 1.0 specification. Enterprise beans written for the EJB 1.1 and higher specification should throw the javax.ejb.EJBException instead of this exception.

beforeCompletion

public void **beforeCompletion**()

   throws EJBException, java.rmi.RemoteException

The beforeCompletion method notifies a session Bean instance that a transaction is about to be committed. The instance can use this method, for example, to write any cached data to a database. This method executes in the proper transaction context.

NOTE: *The instance may still cause the container to roll back the transaction by invoking the setRollbackOnly() method on the instance context, or by throwing an exception.*

Throws:

EJBException—Thrown by the method to indicate a failure caused by a system-level error.

java.rmi.RemoteException—This exception is defined in the method signature to provide backward compatibility for enterprise beans written for the EJB 1.0 specification. Enterprise beans written for the EJB 1.1 and higher specification should throw the javax.ejb.EJBException instead of this exception.

Exception Summary

CreateException	The CreateException exception must be included in the throws clauses of all create(...) methods defined in an enterprise Bean's remote interface.
DuplicateKeyException	The DuplicateKeyException exception is thrown if an entity EJB object cannot be created because an object with the same key already exists.
EJBException	The EJBException exception is thrown by an enterprise Bean instance to its container to report that the invoked business method or callback method could not be completed because of an unexpected error.
FinderException	The FinderException exception must be included in the throws clause of every findMETHOD(...) method of an entity Bean's home interface.
NoSuchEntityException	The NoSuchEntityException exception is thrown by an enterprise Bean instance to its container to report that

the invoked business method or callback method could not be completed because of the underlying entity was removed from the database.

ObjectNotFoundException   The ObjectNotFoundException exception is thrown by a finder method to indicate that the specified EJB object does not exist.

RemoveException   The RemoveException exception is thrown by an attempt to remove an EJB object when the enterprise Bean or the container does not allow the EJB object to be removed.

Class CreateException

public class **CreateException**

    extends java.lang.Exception

The CreateException exception must be included in the throws clauses of all create(...) methods defined in an enterprise Bean's remote interface.

The exception is used as a standard application-level exception to report a failure to create an entity EJB object.

Constructor Summary

CreateException()
Constructs a CreateException with no detail message.

CreateException(java.lang.String message)
Constructs a CreateException with the specified detail message.

Constructor Detail

CreateException
public **CreateException**()
    Constructs a CreateException with no detail message.

CreateException

public **CreateException**(java.lang.String message)

Constructs a CreateException with the specified detail message.

Class DuplicateKeyException

public class **DuplicateKeyException**

extends CreateException

The DuplicateKeyException exception is thrown if an entity EJB object cannot be created because an object with the same key already exists. This exception is thrown by the create methods defined in an enterprise Bean's home interface.

Constructor Summary

DuplicateKeyException()
Constructs a DuplicateKeyException with no detail message.

DuplicateKeyException(java.lang.String message)
Constructs a DuplicateKeyException with the specified detail message.

Constructor Detail

DuplicateKeyException
public **DuplicateKeyException**()

Constructs a DuplicateKeyException with no detail message.

DuplicateKeyException
public **DuplicateKeyException**(java.lang.String message)

Constructs a DuplicateKeyException with the specified detail message.

Class EJBException

public class **EJBException**

extends java.lang.RuntimeException

The EJBException exception is thrown by an enterprise Bean instance to its container to report that the invoked business method or callback method could not be completed because of an unexpected error (e.g., the instance failed to open a database connection).

Constructor Summary

EJBException()
Constructs an EJBException with no detail message.

EJBException(java.lang.Exception ex)
Constructs an EJBException that embeds the originally thrown exception.

EJBException(java.lang.String message)
Constructs an EJBException with the specified detailed message.

Constructor Detail

EJBException
public **EJBException**()
   Constructs an EJBException with no detail message.

EJBException
public **EJBException**(java.lang.Exception ex)
   Constructs an EJBException that embeds the originally thrown exception.

EJBException
public **EJBException**(java.lang.String message)
Constructs an EJBException with the specified detailed message.

Method Summary

java.lang.Exception   **getCausedByException**()
                       Obtain the exception that caused the EJBException being thrown.

Method Detail

getCausedByException
public java.lang.Exception **getCausedByException**()
Obtain the exception that caused the EJBException being thrown.

Returns:

The exception that caused the EJBException being thrown

Class FinderException

public class **EJBException**

extends java.lang.Exception

The FinderException exception must be included in the throws clause of every findMETHOD(...) method of an entity Bean's home interface.

The exception is used as a standard application-level exception to report a failure to find the requested EJB object(s).

Constructor Summary

FinderException()
Constructs a FinderException with no detail message.

FinderException(java.lang.String message)
Constructs a FinderException with the specified detail message.

Constructor Detail

FinderException
public **FinderException**()
> Constructs a FinderException with no detail message.

FinderException
public **FinderException**(java.lang.String message)
> Constructs a FinderException with the specified detail message.

Class NoSuchEntityException

public class **NoSuchEntityException**

extends EJBException

The NoSuchEntityException exception is thrown by an enterprise Bean instance to its container to report that the invoked business method or callback method could not be completed because the underlying entity was removed from the database.

This exception may be thrown by the bean class methods that implement the business methods defined in the bean's remote interface, and by the ejbLoad and ejbStore methods.

Constructor Summary

NoSuchEntityException()
Constructs a NoSuchEntityException with no detail message.

NoSuchEntityException(java.lang.Exception ex)
Constructs a NoSuchEntityException that embeds the originally thrown exception.

NoSuchEntityException(java.lang.String message)
Constructs a NoSuchEntityException with the specified detailed message.

Constructor Detail

NoSuchEntityException
public **NoSuchEntityException**()

Constructs a NoSuchEntityException with no detail message.

NoSuchEntityException
public **NoSuchEntityException**(java.lang.Exception ex)

Constructs a NoSuchEntityException that embeds the originally thrown exception.

NoSuchExtityException
public **NoSuchEntityException**(java.lang.String message)

Constructs a NoSuchEntityException with the specified detailed message.

Class ObjectNotFoundException

public class **ObjectNotFoundException**

extends FinderException

The ObjectNotFoundException exception is thrown by a finder method to indicate that the specified EJB object does not exist.

Only the finder methods that are declared to return a single EJB object use this exception. This exception should not be thrown by finder methods that return a collection of EJB objects (they should return a null collection instead).

Constructor Summary

ObjectNotFoundException()
Constructs an ObjectNotFoundException with no detail message.

ObjectNotFoundException(java.lang.String message)
Constructs an ObjectNotFoundException with the specified detail message.

Constructor Detail

ObjectNotFoundException
public **ObjectNotFoundException**()

Constructs an ObjectNotFoundException with no detail message.

ObjectNotFoundException
public **ObjectNotFoundException**(java.lang.String message)

Constructs an ObjectNotFoundException with the specified detail message.

Class RemoveException

public class **RemoveException**

extends java.lang.Exception

The RemoveException exception is thrown at an attempt to remove an EJB object when the enterprise Bean or the container does not allow the EJB object to be removed.

Constructor Summary

RemoveException()
Constructs a RemoveException with no detail message.

RemoveException(java.lang.String message)
Constructs a RemoveException with the specified detail message.

Constructor Detail

RemoveException
public **RemoveException**()

Constructs a RemoveException with no detail message.

RemoveException
public **RemoveException**(java.lang.String message)

Constructs a RemoveException with the specified detail message.

INDEX

ABOUT THE AUTHOR

Paul Tremblett is a Distinguished Member of the Technical Staff at Cap Gemini-Ernst and Young. He has been programming in Java since the first Java Development Kit was released. Paul is the author of *Instant JavaServer Pages,* has written articles for *Dr. Dobb's Journal,* and is a frequent presenter at technical conferences.

The Hottest Magazine
for the Hottest Developers
in the Enterprise

FREE ISSUE

If you're a professional developer programming in the hottest language in the fastest growing development market in the universe, then you need the hands-on, code-intensive, product-oriented information that comes only from *Java Pro* magazine. Harness Java's unique capabilities in YOUR enterprise with no-holds-barred editorial content.

Java™ *Pro:* get beyond the hype

Special Free Issue Offer!

Osborne & FTP are offering a special 1-year subscription to Java Pro Magazine for a never heard of price of $17.95. Just think of it, 13 information-packed issues at a bare-bones price !

- ○ Practical techniques to amplify Java performance
- ○ Independent, objective product reviews to help you find only the best products for your needs
- ○ Complete source code examples using JavaBeans, servlets and more
- ○ Tips and tricks for Java power programmers

Order online today
http://marketplace.devx.com/osborne/

Subscribe by phone 1-800-848-5523

One year is thirteen issues. Annual cover price is $77.35. Subscription begins upon receipt of payment. Please allow four-to-six weeks for delivery of first issue. International subscriptions must be paid in U.S. dollars plus postage. Canada/Mexico, add $18/year; other countries add $44/year for airmail. Canadian GST included.
Java Pro is published by Fawcette Technical Publications, Inc. Java is a trademark of Sun Microsystems, Inc.

209 Hamilton Ave.
Palo Alto, CA 94301

On the CD

The CD contains the files necessary to run all of the examples in the book. There are approximately 450 files requiring a total of approximately 1.5 MB.

The files can be installed by simply creating a directory on your hard drive and copying the entire contents of the CD to that directory.

The file *readme.txt* from the CD is listed below.

On the CD: readme.txt

```
Instant Enterprise JavaBeans

All of the code you need to run all of the examples presented in
the book are contained on this CD.

Those readers who only want to run the examples can simply load and
deploy the .ear files.

For readers who want to compile all of the examples, batch files
have been provided. These files are suitable for use under NT. If
you are using another platform, you should write files suitable for
use on the platform you are using. All of the .bat files for
compiling contain a statement that sets the environment variable
J2EE_HOME. The value used in the .bat files is c:\j2sdkee1.2.1. If
you are using a different directory, you should change the .bat
files to reflect your environment.

The code contained on the CD can also be obtained from:

http://www.paulsjavabooks.com
```

CARROLL COLLEGE LIBRARY

2 5052 00657221 0

SOFTWARE AND INFORMATION LICENSE

The software and information on this CD ROM (collectively referred to as the "Product") are the property of McGraw-Hill Companies, Inc. ("McGraw-Hill") and are protected by both United States copyright law and international copyright law and international copyright treaty provision. You must treat this Product just like a book, except that you may copy it into a computer to be used and you may make archival copies of the Products for the sole purpose of backing up our software and protecting your investment from loss.

By saying "just like a book," McGraw-Hill means, for example, that the Product may be used by any number of people and may be freely moved from one computer location to another, so long as there is no possibility of the Product (or any part of the Product) being used at one location or on one computer while it is being used at another. Just as a book cannot be read by two different people in two different places at the same time (unless, of course, McGraw-Hill's rights are being violated).

McGraw-Hill reserves the right to alter or modify the contents of the Product at any time.

This agreement is effective until terminated. The Agreement will terminate automatically without notice if you fail to comply with any provision of this Agreement. In the event of termination by reason of your breach, you will destroy or erase all copies of the Product installed on any computer system or made for backup purposes and shall expunge the Product from your data storage facilities.

LIMITED WARRANTY

McGraw-Hill warrants the physical CD ROM(s) enclosed herein to be free of defects in materials and workmanship for a period of sixty days from the purchase date. If McGraw-Hill receives written notification within the warranty period of defects in materials or workmanship, and such notification is determined by McGraw-Hill to be correct, McGraw-Hill will replace the defective CD ROM(s). Send request to:

Customer Service
McGraw-Hill
Gahanna Industrial Park
860 Taylor Station Road
Blacklick, OH 43004-9615

The entire and exclusive liability and remedy for breach of this Limited Warranty shall be limited to replacement of defective CD ROM(s) and shall not include or extend in any claim for or right to cover any other damages, including but not limited to, loss of profit, data, or use of the software, or special, incidental, or consequential damages or other similar claims, even if McGraw-Hill's liability for any damages to you or any other person exceed the lower of suggested list price or actual price paid for the license to use the Product, regardless of any form of the claim.

THE McGRAW-HILL COMPANIES, INC. SPECIFICALLY DISCLAIMS ALL OTHER WARRANTIES, EXPRESS OR IMPLIED, INCLUDING BUT NOT LIMITED TO, ANY IMPLIED WARRANTY OR MERCHANTABILITY OR FITNESS FOR A PARTICULAR PURPOSE. Specifically, McGraw-Hill makes no representation or warranty that the Product is fit for any particular purpose and any implied warranty of merchantability is limited to the sixty day duration of the Limited Warranty covering the physical CD ROM(s) only (and not the software or information) and is otherwise expressly and specifically disclaimed.

This Limited Warranty gives you specific legal rights, you may have others which may vary from state to state. Some states do not allow the exclusion of incidental or consequential damages, or the limitation on how long an implied warranty lasts, so some of the above may not apply to you.

This Agreement constitutes the entire agreement between the parties related to use of the Product. The terms of any purchase order shall have no effect on the terms of this Agreement. Failure of McGraw-Hill to insist at any time on strict compliance with this Agreement shall not constitute a waiver of any rights under this Agreement. This Agreement shall be construed and governed in accordance with the laws of New York. If any provision of this Agreement is held to be contrary to law, that provision will be enforced to the maximum extent permissible and the remaining provisions will remain in force and effect.

WITHDRAWN
CARROLL UNIVERSITY LIBRARY